THE NEW
MONEY DYNAMICS

THE NEW MONEY DYNAMICS

Venita VanCaspel

President, VanCaspel & Co., Inc.
1540 Post Oak Tower
Houston, Texas 77056
713-621-9733

Reston Publishing Company, Inc., A Prentice-Hall Company
Reston, Virginia

Library of Congress Cataloging in Publication Data

VanCaspel, Venita
  The new money dynamics.

  Includes index.
  1. Investments. 2. Finance, Personal.
I. Title.
HG4521.V18   332'.024   77-17447
ISBN 0-87909-518-0

© 1978 by
Reston Publishing Company, Inc.
A Prentice-Hall Company
Reston, Virginia 22090

Drawings by Jan Smulcer.

10   9   8   7   6   5   4   3   2

Printed in the United States of America.

*To my delightful husband, Jack, who is
secure enough within himself to allow
me the freedom to share with you
how to become financially secure*

Acknowledgments

So many have touched my life and helped me toward my goals that this page could not possibly cover them all. I would like to express my special thanks to Helen Fourmy, my long, faithful, and excellent associate; to Jolieta Davis, whose talent smooths the ripples of my personal and business life; to June Owen, who brings order and daily inspiration to me; to Sandi Parkinson, for her delightful efficiency, to Donah Griffin, our beautifully talented comic; to Jan Smulcer, our charmer, who did the fun drawings in this book; to John Weatherston, who brings us the wise maturity that comes from experience, and to Walt Burton, Tom Stephens, and other members of our most talented financial planning team.

Contents

Preface

We live in a country with the highest per capita income ever known to mankind; yet of every 100 of our citizens who reach the age of 65, 95 are flat broke! Of every 100 who reach their "golden years," only 2 are financially independent, 23 must continue to work, and 75 are dependent on friends, relatives, or charity.

They lost the money game. The money game is not like any other game. You cannot choose whether you'll play. You cannot choose to sit out a hand or move to another game. For this game—the money game—is the only game in town.

Since you have no choice but to play, then the only intelligent thing to do is to learn the rules and play to win! Losing means spending 20 to 30 years of your life in angry frustration in a state of financial insecurity.

If you have no choice but to play the money game, and if it is so essential to win, why weren't you taught how to play it successfully in school?

I really don't know. There is an educational void in our country. We are spending millions of dollars teaching both our youth and our adults to earn dollars; yet we are not teaching them what to do with these dollars once they are earned. I find that they are making some tragic mistakes.

Somewhere, somehow, back in the dark pages of history, a false idea germinated and grew. This sinister concept was that "money is the root of all evil." This is not true. Money is not "the root of all evil." It is the misuse of money that brings corruption and human suffering. The right use of money provides the necessary food for your family; it helps build hospitals to aid them in regaining their health when they are ill; it helps build churches in which they may worship; it provides wood and bricks to be used in constructing a roof over their heads; and it provides fabrics to

make the clothes that will protect their bodies from the cold winds of winter and the blistering heat of summer.

Upon you falls the responsibility to be a good steward of every dollar that comes your way.

I feel I should warn you now that applying the information contained in this book will not give you instant wealth. If I knew how to do that, as committed as I am to helping others become financially independent, do you really think I would be willing to sell that secret for so small a sum of money as the price of this book or to let you subscribe to any handy dandy investment advisory service that I might establish?

On the other hand, what are your choices? I can see only three:

1 • Try to make it fast with only a very slight hope of success. (Look around you and unemotionally calculate your odds.)
2 • Try to make it slowly, with a rather good chance for success.
3 • Don't try at all. This is the choice that is being made by the majority of your fellow citizens.

I am convinced that if you are granted a reasonable amount of time, have the ability and willingness to earn an average wage, have the discipline to save a small portion of your earnings, and have the intelligence to apply the principles taught in this book, you can become financially independent. This desirable state does not take brilliance or luck. It requires discipline and the ability and willingness to make your dollars work for you as hard as you had to work to get them.

This book is written in the first person and addressed directly to you. The only things I have to offer are the observations and experiences that have been mine during my 17 years as a stockbroker and financial planner. During this career I have conducted hundreds of public investment seminars in Houston and across the United States, have been the lead speaker for a large number of national conventions, have spoken to innumerable service and social clubs, and have appeared as a guest on numerous television and radio talk shows. For the past nine years I have been the author and moderator of a 30-minute television show called "Successful Texans," shown on a CBS affiliate station. Each week on this show I interview a Texan who has attained success under our free enterprise system. Daily, in my office, I counsel from four to five persons or couples, spending two hours with each individual appointment, endeavoring to help them map a workable financial plan to fit their objectives. My aim is to help them and all with whom I come into contact to become financially independent. I feel that this is my calling—my justification for having passed this way.

This book is written to make you knowledgeable about money matters—to inspire you, to give you hope, to motivate you to act. For unless you apply this knowledge I will have left you financially where I found you.

Financial planning must be personal. You are different from any other person. You were created as a unique individual and have developed in your own unique way. You have different financial objectives, different assets, a different tax bracket, and a different temperament from even your closest friend. Your financial program, therefore, must be designed for you and for you alone because you are special.

If you and I could sit down and plan your financial future, I would ask you many pertinent questions about you and your money. I would then endeavor to design a program that fits not only your financial needs but your emotional needs as well. To design a program for your financial needs is relatively simple, once I know all the facts, but mapping a course that fits your temperament and your prejudices and then communicating these ideas to you in such a way that you will understand and then act upon them is a continuous challenge.

Since you and I may never have this opportunity, I have designed this book to give you a step-by-step guide to be used in designing your own financial blueprint.

I have found that financial planning is like navigation. If you know where you are and where you want to go, navigation is not so difficult. It's when you don't know the two points that navigating the right course becomes difficult. To illustrate this logic, let's use a comparison. Assume that you board a large luxury oceanliner with its mighty engines running in preparation to leave port. You go into the chart room and ask the captain to show you on his charts your present location, what his next port of call will be, your destination, and the route he is planning to take, and he shrugs his shoulders and answers, "I really don't know." Would you be confident of his reaching his destination? Would you want to be a passenger on his ship?

If your answer is no, use this same intelligence in plotting your own financial course. For you are the captain of your vitally important financial ship.

Enter now your chart room to plot your financial future. Here you will learn how to determine your present position, where you want to be on a certain date, and alternate courses available for arriving at your destination.

In my years of financial planning I have never met a person who planned to fail, but I have met many who failed to plan. Unfortunately, the results have been the same.

I have dedicated a large portion of my life to helping others like you to develop and successfully execute their plan for financial independence. Through the pages of this book I have endeavored to do the same for you.

To ensure that you will have a solid foundation upon which to build, it will be necessary to begin the book with some tables and charts that may at first glance not seem as exciting as we both would like for them to be. But do persevere, devour them, and let them seep deeply into your subconscious mind. You'll find them invaluable benchmarks to the successful attainment of your predetermined worthwhile goal.

VENITA VANCASPEL

1
Dear Investor

- ### YOU ARE
  ### AN INVESTOR

My salutation to you is "Dear Investor" because you are an investor. You are investing the wealth that comes your way either in present goods and services or in future goods and services. You cannot choose whether you will invest, but you can choose how you will invest. The wisdom you bring to bear on this choice will have a greater influence on your future standard of living than the amount of money that comes your way.

Your first decision is between today and tomorrow. Do you want to consume all you earn today and hope for the best for tomorrow? As short-sighted as this may seem, it is the course being taken by the vast majority of your fellow citizens.

Why in a nation with a high per capita income and unparalleled prosperity do 98 percent of our citizens reach age 65 without having made adequate preparation to retire in financial dignity?

- ## FIVE REASONS
  ## SO MANY FAIL

There are many answers. From my years of counseling a vast number of people of all ages and incomes, I have found that there are five basic reasons: procrastination, failure to set a financial goal, ignorance of what money must do to accomplish that goal, failure to understand and apply our tax laws, and being "sold" the wrong kind of life insurance. In this chapter we shall look at procrastination and ignorance, the twins of financial failure.

- ## PROCRASTINATION

Procrastination is a deadly enemy of your obligation to be able to retire in financial dignity. Sometimes we confuse goals and obligations. A larger home, a boat, travel to foreign lands—all these can be classified as goals. But preparing to retire in financial dignity is more than a goal. It is your obligation, a debt that you owe yourself and others, such as your family, your community, and other taxpayers. With proper financial planning and sound money management, it is a debt that you can pay, making your retirement years happy instead of haphazard, comfortable instead of dependent.

I have observed that in the early years of a life, when spending habits are formed, thoughts of retirement are so far away that they have little relationship to current spending patterns. There develops the habit of spending all that is earned on current needs with no thought of future needs, and the habit becomes reinforced with the same passing of time that brings retirement closer. Then when retirement time is so near as to be of immediate concern, it is often too late to make adequate preparation.

- ## THREE
  ## FINANCIAL PERIODS

A normal lifetime can be divided into three financial periods.

The first period is the "Learning Period," when you learn the vocation that will enable you to earn the money you need to sustain and enjoy your life and the lives of those dependent upon you. This usually lasts for the first 25 years of your life. The second period is the "Earning Period", when you pursue the vocation you learned during the first period. This lasts about 40 years, from age 25 to 65. The third period is determined by the decisions you make during the second period of your life. It will either be your "Yearning Years" or your "Golden Years."

If you are a male, you will probably spend 15 to 20 years in this third period. If you are female and make it to 65, plan your finances well, for you'll probably be around for a very long time.

Let's look at each of these periods.

The Learning Period · I hope that you begin learning at birth and never cease to learn until you bid this world good-bye. However, your formal learning period will probably last for your first 25 years, depending on your choice of a vocation.

If you are considering whether a college education is a good investment for yourself, your children, or your grandchildren, the answer is Yes. It will cost between $12,000 and $45,000, depending on the choice of schools, vocation, and how many years before entering college. But the investment can yield a good return. Studies show that a college graduate earns from $250,000 to $300,000 more during his life than does a person with only a high school diploma. Time, money, and effort invested in education increase the productivity of the individual. This investment in human capital is similar to an investment in capital equipment for a plant that increases productivity, which in turn yields an increase in profits. A college education can bring more than just financial rewards. The ability to think and to plan is stimulated in college. There are fewer divorces among college graduates. It can add a greatly enlarged dimension to life.

There are many who like to believe that financial gains come to a person through luck. I personally do not believe in luck and have found that luck occurs when preparedness and opportunity get together. The more you place yourself in the path of opportunity, the "luckier" you will probably become.

There are many who remind me of the man who stood in front of a wood-burning stove and said, "Give me some heat and I'll give you some wood." That's not the nature of a wood-burning stove. The wood must come first. The same is true of preparation, so do not skimp on this important ingredient. Put adequate wood in the burner, and it will yield to you the warmth of financial security.

The Earning Period • The second period of your life is the "Earning Period."

Do you realize how much wealth will pass through your hands during the 40 years between 25 and 65? Do you just consider your income as "so much a month," and never add up the tremendous amount of money that is passing your way?

If you never earn more than $300 a month, over an eighth of a million dollars will pass your way. If you earn as much as $525, over a quarter of a million dollars will pass your way. If you earn as much as $1050, over a half of a million dollars will pass your way. That's a lot of money. So what's the problem? It's how to keep some of it from passing through your fingers, isn't it?

The Secret of Accumulation of Wealth • Let me share with you a very simple secret for the accumulation of wealth. The secret has only ten words in it and is so simple you will be tempted to discard it—but if you remember it and put it to use, it will be of great value to you for the remainder of your life. The secret is this: "A part of all I earn is mine to keep."

You are tempted to say, "Everything I earn is mine to keep." It isn't so, is it? It belongs to the baker, the butcher, the mortgage company, the church.

You must learn to pay yourself first. If not first, at least along with all the others. If you were to place in a line, in the order of their importance to you, all those whom you wanted to receive a portion of your paycheck, would you place yourself at the head of the line? Is that where you have been putting yourself? If you are like so many others, you've put yourself at the end of the line, trying to save what is left over and finding that your ability to spend up to and beyond your income is utterly amazing.

. . . . over $480,000 will pass through your

hands during your earning years . . . .

Monthly income	10 years	20 years	30 years	40 years
500	60,000	120,000	180,000	240,000
600	72,000	144,000	216,000	288,000
800	96,000	192,000	288,000	384,000
1000	120,000	240,000	360,000	480,000
1500	180,000	360,000	540,000	720,000
2000	240,000	480,000	720,000	800,000
2500	300,000	600,000	900,000	1,200,000

If you were to save one-tenth of all you earned and did this for ten years, how much money would you have? A whole year's salary at one time, of course. And that's not all, for you would put this money to work, and before long you would have much more working for you.

The Yearning or Golden Years • The third period of your life will be your retirement years. These will either be your "yearning" years or your "golden" years, depending on the financial decisions you make during your "earning" years.

Will this period of your life take care of itself? The answer is NO. The future belongs to those who prepare for it—and how tragically few are preparing! Perhaps they—and you—have been lulled into a false sense of security by the cozy sound of the words "Social Security." By the time you have discovered that it should have been called "Social Insecurity," it is far too late.

Social Security was never designed to give you or your fellow countrymen financial independence. It was created to prevent mass destitution. It was meant to give you a base upon which to build, and it is your responsibility to build on this base.

It may surprise you to learn that when you reach the age to qualify for Social Security benefits, if your income from it and other sources is insufficient for you to live in financial dignity, making it necessary for you to continue to work, you will forfeit all or most of your Social Security benefits each month until you reach age 72.

Today more than 2¼ million of our citizens over 65 are caught in this financial trap, forcing them to lose their Social Security benefits. Most of them paid into the system their hard-earned dollars all of their working years, but they are disqualified from receiving their benefits because these are not enough to keep body and soul together.

If they had made provisions outside of Social Security, they could be receiving unlimited income from capital in the form of dividends, interest, and royalties and still receive their Social Security checks.

You may live a long time; yet longevity may be a mixed blessing. You may decide how long you will work, or it may be decided for you, but the decision of how long you will live is not in your hands.

Present-day medical science is getting so good at making us live longer that for every ten years we live, they add another four years to our life expectancy. Medical science may be adding years to your life, but it is still up to you to add some life to those years. Money is a necessity. It will not of itself bring you happiness—it will only give you options. However, I have yet to meet a person who found joy in poverty.

Have you ever considered what the difference in the eyes of the world is between an "old man" and an "elderly gentleman"? It's no other than income.

• THREE SOURCES OF INCOME

If you'll stand back and objectively analyze sources of income, you will find that there are three chief sources.

The first is you at work. However, there will come a time that regardless of how badly you want to work, the world will not let you. It will retire you.

The second source is your money at work. If you have made proper preparation and turned some of your past income into capital, there will come a time when you will no longer have to work for your money, but you can change places with your money and let your money work for you. I have found that income from capital is immensely more secure than income from labor.

The third source of income is charity.

Man at work, money at work, charity—which source do you want to depend on at age 65?

Since "man at work" may not be an option open to you and "charity" has rarely brought happiness, apply your intelligence toward assuring yourself that there is sufficient "money at work" to retire in financial dignity.

• HOW MUCH WILL YOU NEED PER MONTH?

How much will you need at retirement time? I do not know. Several factors will enter into this calculation. The number of years you have before you reach retirement, what inflation will have done to the cost of living by then, what standard of living you desire at that time, and what rate of return you will be receiving on your funds—all will influence the amount that will be required.

We can try to calculate how much income you will need at retirement. Let's begin with what you would need if you were retiring today; then adjust for what you feel will be the yearly rate of inflation.

Table 1–1 shows rates of inflation from 2½ to 12 percent and years until retirement from 10 years to 35 years.

Table 1–1. Additional Income Needed (in Dollars) at Retirement, with Various Inflation Rates

Years until retirement	2½%	3%	3½%	5%	8%	10%	12%
10	1.28	1.34	1.41	1.63	2.16	2.59	3.11
11	1.31	1.38	1.46	1.71	2.33	2.85	2.48
12	1.34	1.43	1.51	1.80	2.52	3.14	3.90
13	1.38	1.47	1.56	1.89	2.72	3.45	4.36
14	1.41	1.51	1.62	1.98	2.94	3.80	4.89
15	1.45	1.56	1.68	2.08	3.17	4.18	5.47
16	1.48	1.60	1.73	2.18	3.43	4.60	6.13
17	1.52	1.65	1.79	2.29	3.70	5.05	6.87
18	1.56	1.70	1.86	2.41	4.00	5.56	7.69
19	1.60	1.75	1.92	2.53	4.32	6.12	8.61
20	1.64	1.81	1.99	2.65	4.66	6.73	9.65
21	1.68	1.86	2.06	2.79	5.03	7.40	10.80
22	1.72	1.92	2.13	2.93	5.44	8.14	12.10
23	1.76	1.97	2.21	3.07	5.87	8.95	13.55
24	1.81	2.03	2.28	3.23	6.34	9.85	15.18

Table 1–1. (*Continued*)

Years until retirement	2½%	3%	3½%	5%	8%	10%	12%
25	1.85	2.09	2.36	3.39	6.85	10.83	17.00
26	1.90	2.16	2.45	3.56	7.40	11.92	19.04
27	1.95	2.22	2.53	3.73	7.99	13.11	21.32
28	2.00	2.29	2.62	3.92	8.63	14.42	23.88
29	2.05	2.36	2.71	4.12	9.32	15.86	26.75
30	2.10	2.43	2.81	4.32	10.06	17.45	29.96
31	2.15	2.50	2.91	4.54	10.87	19.19	33.56
32	2.20	2.58	3.01	4.76	11.74	21.11	37.58
33	2.26	2.65	3.11	5.00	12.68	23.23	42.09
34	2.32	2.73	3.22	5.25	13.69	25.55	47.14
35	2.37	2.81	3.33	5.52	14.79	28.10	52.80

To calculate, subtract your age from 65 to give you the years until retirement, and read across to the rate of inflation you feel is safe to assume. This will give you how many additional dollars you will need when you retire.

For example, assume that you would need $1000 per month if you were retiring today, that you are age 45, that you plan to retire in 20 years at age 65, and that you feel the government can slow inflation to 5 percent. (Unfortunately, not many economists today would agree.) Go down the left-hand column to 20 and across four columns to 2.65, your adjustment factor. Now let's adjust: $1000 × 2.65 = $2650. This would be the amount you would need per month in 20 years to obtain the same housing, food, and clothing as you do with $1000 today.

Inflation will probably not accommodate you by stopping when you retire, so you should plan an additional amount to cover continued inflation.

• HOW MUCH CAPITAL DOES THIS REQUIRE?

What goal should you set for yourself to have a monthly income of approximately $2650 per month at age 65? Assume also that you will not receive a pension from your company. How much capital will it take to produce $2650 per month?

Shall we use a 6 percent yield? If so, we will need $530,000 of capital ($2650 × 200 = $530,000). That's a lot of capital. Before you become discouraged, remember that you have 20 years before you need it, and if you decide to use a portion of your principal each month during retirement, this amount can be reduced. There is nothing sacred about principal. The sacred thing is to make you and it come out together!

Table 1-2 shows the monthly amount you would need to save at 6 percent compounded to reach goals of $100,000 to $500,000.

Table 1–2. Monthly Savings Needed at Six Percent Interest (Compounded Annually) to Attain Predetermined Amount of Capital

Age now	Years to retirement	Months to retirement	$100,000	$200,000	$300,000	$500,000
				Desired amount		
25	40	480	$ 51	$ 102	$ 153	$ 255
30	35	420	70	140	210	350
35	30	360	99	198	297	495
40	25	300	143	286	429	715
45	20	240	213	426	639	1065
50	15	180	337	674	1011	1685
55	10	120	596	1192	3576	2980

See how time helps in accomplishing your goal? If your goal is $200,000 and you begin saving at age 25, you can reach it by saving $102 per month. At age 40 the amount increases to $286 and at age 45 to $426 per month.

• TIME, NOT INSTANT PUDDING

Time can be a great ally in accomplishing your financial goal. Use it to your advantage, rather than trying to make it fast, as tempting as that may be.

You will be tempted, for we live in an age of "instants." We drink "instant coffee," eat "instant pudding," spoon "instant soup." Do not make the mistake of trying to carry this over to your money world. It takes time to accumulate a living estate. Many have difficulty accepting this fact of life. Many of our citizens have adopted an attitude of impatience, perhaps at the cost of serenity and added physical and mental strain. On the other hand, impatience to get things done deserves much of the credit for the achievements of Americans in building the wealthiest nation in the world.

Coming to grips with time is necessary because we all have been allotted just a certain amount of it. Time is a priceless commodity. A beer commercial says, "You only go around once in life, so grab all the gusto you can, even in the beer you drink." This recognizes the value of time and points up our great impatience.

Impatience can be a stimulus to getting things done. In managing your investments it can be disastrous. The enormous profits in managing lotteries and in owning legalized gambling in Las Vegas are monuments to the impatience of many who desire to get rich quickly.

Incidentally, I find that "rich," or even "comfortable," has different meanings to different people. To some I find it means $100,000, and to others it means a million dollars.

• IGNORANCE OF WHAT MONEY MUST DO

The second reason for financial failure is the ignorance of what money must do to accomplish a financial goal.

In 1748 Benjamin Franklin wrote, "Money is of a prolific, generating nature. Money can beget money, and its offspring can beget more." His was a definition and joyous explanation of the nature of money and one that can be of great value to you. Franklin's words "Money is of a prolific, generating nature" have a biblical ring to them, as well they may, because it is in the Bible that we first become aware that we are required to be good stewards of money.

In Matthew 25: 14–29 we find this illustration:

> Again, the Kingdom of Heaven can be illustrated by the story of a man going into another country, who called together his servants and loaned them money to invest for him while he was gone. He gave $5,000 to one, $2,000 to another, and $1,000 to the last—dividing it in proportion to their abilities—and then left on his trip. The man who received the $5,000 began immediately to buy and sell with it and soon earned another $5,000. The man with $2,000 went right to work, too, and earned another $2,000.
>
> But the man who received the $1,000 dug a hole in the ground and hid the money for safekeeping. After a long time their master returned from his trip and called them to him to account for his money. The man to whom he had entrusted the $5,000 brought him $10,000.
>
> His master praised him for good work. "You have been faithful in handling this small amount," he told him, "so now I will give you many more responsibilities. Begin the joyous tasks I have assigned to you." Next came the man who had received $2,000, with the report, "Sir, you gave me $2,000 to use, and I have doubled it."

Good work, his master said. "You are a good and faithful servant. You have been faithful over this small amount, so now I will give you much more."

Then the man with the $1,000 came and said, 'Sir, I knew you were a hard man, and I was afraid you would rob me of what I earned, so I hid your money in the earth and here it is." But his master replied, "Wicked man! Lazy slave! Since you knew I would demand your profit, you should at least have put my money into the bank so I could have some interest. Take the money from this man and give it to the man with the $10,000. For the man who uses well what he is given shall be given more, and he shall have abundance. But from the man who is unfaithful, even what little responsibility he has shall be taken from him."

Let's analyze what the master considered good stewardship. He praised the two who "bought and sold" with the money entrusted to them and gave them more. He severely reprimanded the one who dug a hole and buried the money, saying, "You should at *least* have put the money into the bank so I could have some interest." Note, however, that this was not what he recommended. Had the servant lived in the United States during the periods when our banks paid 3 percent interest, in order for the money to have doubled, the master would have to have taken a 24-year trip. Even if he had earned up to 5 percent, it would have taken 14.4 years. By most standards that would be a very long trip.

Table 1–3 shows the rates paid by savings and loan associations and by banks from 1947 through 1977.

Table 1–3. Interest Rates (Percent) Paid by Savings and Loan Associations and by Banks

Year	Savings accounts in savings associations	Deposits in commercial banks
1947	2.3%	0.9%
1948	2.3	0.9
1949	2.4	0.9
1950	2.5	0.9
1951	2.6	1.1
1952	2.7	1.2
1953	2.8	1.2
1954	2.9	1.3
1955	2.9	1.4
1956	3.0	1.6
1957	3.3	2.1
1958	3.38	2.21
1959	3.53	2.36
1960	3.86	2.56
1961	3.90	2.71
1962	4.08	3.18
1963	4.17	3.31
1964	4.19	3.42
1965	4.23	3.69
1966	4.45	4.04
1967	4.67	4.24

Table 1–3. (*Continued*)

Year	Savings accounts in savings associations	Deposits in commercial banks
1968	4.68	4.48
1969	4.80	4.87
1970	5.06	4.95
1971	5.33	4.78
1972	5.40	4.65
1973	5.50	5.12
1974	5.55	5.15
1975	5.25	5.00
1976	5.25	5.00
1977	5.25	5.00

• THREE THINGS YOU CAN DO WITH A DOLLAR

There are only three things that you can do with a dollar—"spend," "lend," or "own." If your choice is to "spend," you have eliminated the other two choices. If you decide not to "spend" it now, but to spend it later for something you'd rather have at that time, then you have two choices open to you. You may "lend" it to one of the many savings institutions, placing it in what is commonly called a "guaranteed" or fixed dollar position. We'll look at all the ways this can be done in the chapter entitled "Lending Your Dollars."

The third thing you can do with your dollar is to "own." You may own shares of American industry, real estate, energy, commodities, precious metals, rare stamps, art objects, antiques, and precious gems. We shall discuss the many ways that you can "own" throughout this book.

For the present, let's take a good look at what effect time, the rate of return, and the amount of money you have to put to work will have in accomplishing your financial goal.

• FORMULA FOR FINANCIAL INDEPENDENCE

A formula that I have used over the years that has helped me and my clients is

Time + money + American free enterprise = opportunity to become financially independent.

Time—the First Ingredient • If you are young and have only a small amount of money to invest, don't despair, for you possess one of the most important ingredients for financial independence—the ingredient of TIME. It doesn't take much money to compound to a tidy sum if you have time for it to grow. A savings of $10 per month started at age 25 is equivalent to $30 a month started at age 35, $100 at age 45, and $425 at age 55 (as pictured in Fig. 1–1). Or, if we calculate the importance of time in reverse, a savings of $50 a month for 10 years at 12 percent is less than $25 a month for 15 years.

Perhaps you have now acquired a lump sum of $10,000. Let's look at the difference time makes in your results:

Years	At 5 percent
10	$16,288
20	26,532
30	43,219
40	70,399

These figures point out the importance of starting as early as you can to reach your predetermined goal.

I hope you are granted a large amount of this first ingredient, and you learn early the importance of putting each day of it to maximum use.

Money is the second ingredient—an ingredient that you have every payday or that you have acquired through previous paydays of your own or your industrious and generous forefathers.

Your next challenge is to put this money to work for yourself as hard as you no doubt had to work to get it. To become financially independent you must save and let your money grow. Unfortunately, I observe many people who save and let savings institutions grow, building magnificent skyscrapers that add impressively to our skyline.

Rate of Return • The rate of return that you receive on your funds will be determined by how skillfully you put your money to work under our free enterprise system.

You've earned your "gold stars"

You have looked at how important time is in the accomplishment of your goal; now let's introduce another important factor, the rate of return, and look at the difference an additional 5 percent can make:

$10,000 Lump Sum Invested at 5 Percent and 10 Percent

Years	At 5 percent	At 10 percent	Difference
10	$16,288	$ 25,937	$ 9,649
20	26,532	67,274	40,742
30	43,219	174,494	131,275
40	70,399	492,592	422,193

If we assume that you can invest $100 per month, your results would be:

$100 Per Month Invested at 5 Percent and 10 Percent

Years	Amount invested	At 5 percent	At 10 percent	Difference
10	$12,000	$ 15,848	$ 21,031	$ 5,183
20	24,000	41,662	75,602	33,940
30	36,000	83,713	217,131	133,418
40	48,000	152,208	584,222	432,014

Don't Fight the Battle Alone • Are you amazed at the difference an additional 5 percent can make in your results?

At 5 percent you contributed $48,000 in 40 years, and the savings institution contributed $104,208 from their profits from investing your money in American industry, real estate, and natural resources.

On the other hand, if you obtained 10 percent on your investment, you contributed $48,000 and you let American industry, real estate, and natural resources contribute $536,222 to your wealth, a difference of $432,014, or approximately 418 percent.

It is not necessary to fight the battle alone if you become knowledgeable so that American free enterprise can be of help to you.

• THE EIGHTH
WONDER

One of the best ways to obtain a graphic picture of the importance of the rate of return is to study compound interest tables. Compound interest tables are fascinating. In my opinion, the "eighth wonder of the world" is not the Astrodome, but compound interest.

You will find the following collection of tables helpful in your financial programming. Don't yield to the temptation of saying, "Oh, I probably can't understand them," and flip casually by. Take a moment to study them and you'll be surprised to find some real jewels of information. I'll help you apply the information so you won't have to go it alone.

In Table 1–4 you will find how much a $10,000 lump sum will grow

Table 1–4. $10,000 Lump Sum at Varying Rates Compounded Annually—End of Year Values

	5th Yr.	10th Yr.	15th Yr.	20th Yr.	25th Yr.	30th Yr.	35th Yr.	40th Yr.
1%	10,510	11,046	11,609	12,201	12,824	13,478	14,166	14,888
2%	11,040	12,189	13,458	14,859	16,406	18,113	19,998	22,080
3%	11,592	13,439	15,579	18,061	20,937	24,272	28,138	32,620
4%	12,166	14,802	18,009	21,911	26,658	32,433	39,460	48,010
5%	12,762	16,288	20,789	26,532	33,863	43,219	55,160	70,399
6%	13,382	17,908	23,965	32,071	42,918	57,434	76,860	102,857
7%	14,025	19,671	27,590	38,696	54,274	76,122	106,765	149,744
8%	14,693	21,589	31,721	46,609	68,484	100,626	147,853	217,245
9%	15,386	23,673	36,424	56,044	86,230	132,676	204,139	314,094
10%	16,105	25,937	41,772	67,274	108,347	174,494	281,024	492,592
11%	16,850	28,394	47,845	80,623	135,854	228,922	385,748	650,008

Table 1–4. (*Continued*)

	5th Yr.	10th Yr.	15th Yr.	20th Yr.	25th Yr.	30th Yr.	35th Yr.	40th Yr.
12%	17,623	31,058	54,735	96,462	170,000	299,599	527,996	930,509
13%	18,424	33,945	62,542	115,230	212,305	391,158	720,685	1,327,815
14%	19,254	37,072	71,379	137,434	264,619	509,501	981,001	1,888,835
15%	20,113	40,455	81,370	163,665	329,189	662,117	1,331,755	2,678,635
16%	21,003	44,114	92,655	194,607	408,742	858,498	1,803,140	3,787,211
17%	21,924	48,068	105,387	231,055	506,578	1,110,646	2,435,034	5,338,687
18%	22,877	52,338	119,737	273,930	626,686	1,433,706	3,279,972	7,503,783
19%	23,863	56,946	135,895	324,294	773,880	1,846,753	4,407,006	10,516,675
20%	24,883	61,917	154,070	383,375	953,962	2,373,763	5,906,682	14,697,715
21%	25,937	67,274	174,494	452,592	1,173,908	3,044,816	7,897,469	20,484,002
22%	27,027	73,046	197,422	533,576	1,442,101	3,897,578	10,534,018	28,470,377
23%	28,153	79,259	223,139	628,206	1,768,592	4,979,128	14,017,769	39,464,304
24%	29,316	85,944	251,956	738,641	2,165,419	6,348,199	18,610,540	54,559,126
25%	30,517	93,132	284,217	867,361	2,646,698	8,077,935	24,651,903	75,231,638

over the years at varying rates of return. If you haven't yet saved $10,000, just keep dropping zeros until you reach your category. If you are fortunate enough to have $100,000, just add a zero.

Perhaps you have not acquired a lump sum but can save $100 per month. Table 1–5 then is for you, for it gives the results of putting to work $1200 per year at various rates.

Table 1–5. $1200 Per Year at Varying Rates Compounded Annually—End of Year Values

	5th Yr.	10th Yr.	15th Yr.	20th Yr.	25th Yr.	30th Yr.	35th Yr.	40th Yr.
1%	6,182	12,680	19,509	26,686	34,231	43,359	50,492	59,250
2%	6,369	13,402	21,168	29,739	39,205	49,654	61,192	73,932
3%	6,561	14,169	22,988	33,211	45,063	58,803	74,731	93,195
4%	6,760	14,983	24,990	37,162	51,974	69,993	91,917	118,592
5%	6,962	15,848	27,188	41,662	60,135	83,713	113,803	152,208
6%	7,170	16,766	29,607	46,791	69,787	100,562	141,745	196,857
7%	7,383	17,740	32,265	52,638	81,211	121,287	177,495	256,332
8%	7,603	18,774	35,188	59,307	94,744	146,815	223,322	335,737
9%	7,827	19,872	38,403	66,918	110,788	178,290	282,150	441,950
10%	8,059	21,037	41,940	75,602	129,818	217,131	357,752	584,222
11%	8,295	22,273	45,828	85,518	152,398	265,095	454,996	774,992

Table 1–5. (*Continued*)

	5th Yr.	10th Yr.	15th Yr.	20th Yr.	25th Yr.	30th Yr.	35th Yr.	40th Yr.
12%	8,538	23,586	50,103	96,838	179,200	324,351	581,355	1,030,970
13%	8,786	24,976	54,806	112,164	211,020	397,578	741,298	1,374,583
14%	9,043	26,454	59,976	124,521	248,799	488,084	948,807	1,835,890
15%	9,304	28,018	65,660	141,372	293,654	599,948	1,216,015	2,455,144
16%	9,572	29,679	71,910	160,609	346,905	726,194	1,560,032	3,286,173
17%	9,848	31,440	78,778	182,566	410,115	909,004	2,002,792	4,400,869
18%	10,130	33,306	86,326	207,625	485,126	1,119,982	2,572,378	5,895,109
19%	10,419	35,284	94,620	236,216	574,117	1,380,464	3,304,696	7,896,595
20%	10,716	37,380	103,730	268,831	679,652	1,701,909	4,245,610	10,575,154
21%	11,019	39,601	113,736	306,021	804,759	2,098,358	5,453,622	14,156,310
22%	11,330	41,954	124,722	348,416	952,998	2,587,006	7,003,256	18,939,087
23%	11,649	44,446	136,779	396,727	1,128,558	3,188,884	8,989,333	25,319,371
24%	11,976	47,085	150,013	451,758	1,336,360	3,929,683	11,532,334	33,820,458
25%	12,310	49,879	164,530	514,417	1,582,186	4,840,641	14,666,342	45,132,982

Rev.

If you are determined to have a minimum of $100,000, how much will you need to save per year to have it grow to $100,000 at various rates? Table 1–6 will reveal that number.

Table 1–6. Approximate Annual Investment Required to Equal $100,000 at the End of a Specified Period—Varying Rates

	5 Yrs.	10 Yrs.	15 Yrs.	20 Yrs.	25 Yrs.	30 Yrs.	35 Yrs.	40 Yrs.
1%	19,380	9,464	6,151	4,497	3,506	2,768	2,378	2,026
2%	18,841	8,954	5,669	4,036	3,061	2,417	1,961	1,624
3%	18,290	8,470	5,220	3,613	2,663	2,041	1,606	1,288
4%	17,751	8,009	4,802	3,229	2,309	1,714	1,306	1,011
5%	17,236	7,572	4,414	2,880	1,966	1,433	1,054	788.39
6%	16,736	7,157	4,053	2,565	1,720	1,193	846.59	609.58
7%	16,254	6,764	3,719	2,280	1,478	989.39	676.08	468.14
8%	15,783	6,392	3,410	2,024	1,267	817.36	537.34	357.42
9%	15,332	6,039	3,125	1,793	1,083	673.06	425.31	271.52
10%	14,890	5,704	2,861	1,587	924.37	552.66	335.43	205.40
11%	14,467	5,388	2,618	1,403	787.41	452.67	263.74	154.84
12%	14,055	5,088	2,395	1,239	669.64	369.97	206.41	116.40
13%	13,658	4,805	2,190	1,070	568.67	301.83	168.00	87.29

Table 1–6. (*Continued*)

	5 Yrs.	10 Yrs.	15 Yrs.	20 Yrs.	25 Yrs.	30 Yrs.	35 Yrs.	40 Yrs.
14%	13,270	4,536	2,001	963.69	482.32	245.86	126.47	65.36
15%	12,898	4,283	1,828	848.82	408.64	200.02	98.68	48.88
16%	12,537	4,043	1,669	747.16	345.92	165.25	76.92	36.52
17%	12,185	3,817	1,523	657.30	292.60	132.02	59.92	27.27
18%	11,846	3,603	1,390	577.97	247.36	107.14	46.65	20.36
19%	11,517	3,401	1,268	508.01	209.02	86.93	36.31	15.20
20%	11,198	3,210	1,157	446.38	176.56	70.51	28.26	11.35
21%	10,802	3,030	1,056	392.13	149.11	57.19	22.00	8.48
22%	10,591	2,860	962.14	344.42	125.92	46.39	17.13	6.34
23%	10,301	2,700	877.33	302.48	106.33	37.63	13.35	4.74
24%	10,020	2,549	799.93	265.63	89.80	30.53	10.41	3.55
25%	9,749	2,406	729.35	233.27	75.84	24.79	8.18	2.66

Perhaps you would rather calculate how large a lump sum you need to invest on a monthly basis to reach $100,000. Table 1–7 will give you this information.

Table 1–7. Lump Sum Required to Equal $100,000 at the End of a Specified Period—Varying Rates

	5 Yrs	10 Yrs.	15 Yrs.	20 Yrs.	25 Yrs.	30 Yrs.	35 Yrs.	40 Yrs.
1%	95,147	90,529	86,135	81,954	77,977	74,192	70,591	67,165
2%	90,573	82,348	74,301	67,297	60,953	55,207	50,003	45,289
3%	86,261	74,409	64,186	55,367	47,761	41,199	35,538	30,656
4%	82,193	67,556	55,526	45,639	37,512	30,832	25,341	20,829
5%	78,353	61,391	48,102	37,689	29,530	23,138	18,129	14,205
6%	74,726	55,839	41,727	31,180	23,300	17,411	13,011	9,722
7%	71,299	50,835	36,245	25,842	18,425	13,137	9,367	6,678
8%	68,058	46,319	31,524	21,455	14,602	9,938	6,763	4,603
9%	64,993	42,241	27,454	17,843	11,597	7,537	4,899	3,184
10%	62,092	38,554	23,940	14,864	9,230	5,731	3,558	2,209
11%	59,345	35,218	20,900	12,403	7,361	4,368	2,592	1,538
12%	56,743	32,197	18,270	10,367	5,882	3,340	1,894	1,075
13%	54,276	29,460	15,989	8,678	4,710	2,557	1,388	753.12
14%	51,937	26,974	14,010	7,276	3,780	1,963	1,019	529.43
15%	49,718	24,718	12,289	6,110	3,040	1,510	750.89	373.32
16%	47,611	22,683	10,792	5,139	2,447	1,165	554.59	264.05

Table 1–7. (*Continued*)

	5 Yrs.	10 Yrs.	15 Yrs.	20 Yrs.	25 Yrs.	30 Yrs.	35 Yrs.	40 Yrs.
17%	45,611	20,804	9,489	4,329	1,974	900.38	410.67	187.31
18%	43,711	19,107	8,352	3,651	1,596	697.49	304.88	133.27
19%	41,905	17,560	7,359	3,084	1,292	541.49	226.91	95.10
20%	40,188	16,151	6,491	2,610	1,048	421.27	169.30	68.04
21%	38,554	14,864	5,731	2,209	851.85	328.43	126.62	48.82
22%	37,000	13,690	5,065	1,874	693.43	256.57	94.93	35.12
23%	35,520	12,617	4,482	1,592	565.42	200.84	71.34	25.34
24%	34,112	11,635	3,969	1,354	461.80	157.52	53.72	18.33
25%	32,768	10,737	3,512	1,153	377.78	123.79	40.56	13.30

• THE RULE OF 72

While I am sharing ways to program, let me give you a very simple rule that you can use without elaborate compound tables. It is the "Rule of 72." How I wish it had been taught to me at a younger age! The Rule of 72 gives the answer to the question, How long does it take $1 to become $2 at various rates of return? For example, if you obtain 1 percent on your money, it will take 72 years for $1 to become $2. If you obtain 12 percent, it will take 6 years.

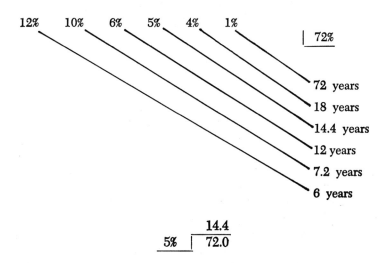

From the above you see that it takes 14.4 years for your money to double at 5 percent per year.

$$\frac{7.2}{10\% \, \overline{)\, 72.0}}$$

It takes 7.2 years for it to double at 10 percent per year.

If you have $1000 it will double or become $2000 at 5 percent in 14.4 years. But at 10 percent, $1000 would double twice, becoming $4000.

At 5 percent $1000 becomes

$2000	in 14.4 years
4000	in 28.8 years
8000	in 43.2 years

At 10 percent $1000 would become

$2000	in 7.2 years
4000	in 14.4 years
8000	in 21.6 years
16,000	in 28.8 years
32,000	in 36.0 years
64,000	in 43.2 years

As you can see, it does make a difference how well you invest your money.

A variation of the Rule of 72, though not as precise, is the Rule of 144. This rule applies to annual investments, not lump sum investments. This rule will show you when the total amount of money you have invested will approximately double, at various rates of return. Divide the interest rate into 144 to find the number of years that it takes to approximately double the total amount accumulated. For example, let us assume that you invest $1000 per year at 6 percent. Divide the interest rate into 144, and it equals 24. In 24 years you will have saved $24,000, and this should double to $48,000 in 24 years.

• THE $100,000 ESTATE

I require my clients to have as their *minimum* goal a $100,000 estate. This must be your minimum goal also—and you should adjust it upward as inflation takes its toll on your purchasing power.

Table 1–6 will reveal to you the amounts you must invest annually to reach $100,000 at various rates of return over 5- to 40-year periods.

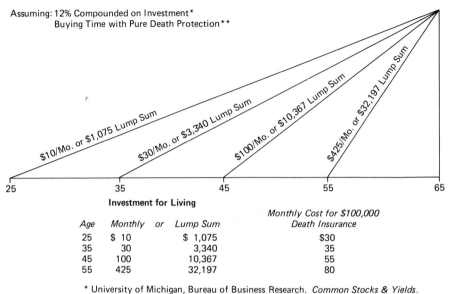

$100,000

Assuming: 12% Compounded on Investment*
Buying Time with Pure Death Protection**

$10/Mo. or $1,075 Lump Sum

$30/Mo. or $3,340 Lump Sum

$100/Mo. or $10,367 Lump Sum

$425/Mo. or $32,197 Lump Sum

25   35   45   55   65

Investment for Living

			Monthly Cost for $100,000
Age	Monthly	or Lump Sum	Death Insurance
25	$ 10	$ 1,075	$30
35	30	3,340	35
45	100	10,367	55
55	425	32,197	80

* University of Michigan, Bureau of Business Research. *Common Stocks & Yields.*
** Based on rates of a leading insurance company.

FIGURE 1–1.   Acquiring the $100,000 Estate by Age 65

After you've done some in-depth calculations to be applied to your own set of years and funds, look at Fig. 1–1. I have found that this simplified diagram helps my clients visualize the challenge and the solution.

To all my good engineering friends let me say that I am quite aware that money does not compound in a straight line, but in a curve. However, I have learned that only a few people can relate to a curve, but almost everyone can relate to a straight line—hence the straight lines. You will find a chart with the proper curves in the chapter entitled "Life Insurance—The Great National Consumer Fraud?" In that chapter I also tell you how to buy time.

To Be More Specific • Perhaps your timetable does not exactly fit into 5-year time periods, and the amounts of money you have to invest do not fit into neat blocks of $10,000 and $100 per month. There are two excellent tables that permit you to be more exact in your programming. Table 1–8, "One Dollar Principal Compounded Annually," gives you the sum to which one dollar of principal will accumulate at the indicated interest rates compounded annually for the given number of years. Table 1–9, "One Dollar Per Annum Compounded Annually," gives you

Table 1–8.   One Dollar Principal Compounded Annually

End of Year	2½%	3%	5%	6%	8%	10%	12%	15%
1	$ 1.0250	$ 1.0300	$ 1.0500	$ 1.0600	$ 1.0800	$ 1.1000	$ 1.1200	$ 1.1500
2	1.0506	1.0609	1.1025	1.1236	1.1664	1.2100	1.2544	1.3225
3	1.0769	1.0927	1.1576	1.1910	1.2597	1.3310	1.4049	1.5209
4	1.1038	1.1255	1.2155	1.2625	1.3605	1.4641	1.5735	1.7490
5	1.1314	1.1593	1.2763	1.3382	1.4693	1.6105	1.7623	2.0114
6	1.1597	1.1941	1.3401	1.4185	1.5869	1.7716	1.9738	2.3131
7	1.1887	1.2299	1.4071	1.5036	1.7138	1.9487	2.2107	2.6600
8	1.2184	1.2668	1.4775	1.5938	1.8509	2.1436	2.4760	3.0590
9	1.2489	1.3048	1.5513	1.6895	1.9990	2.3579	2.7731	3.5179
10	1.2801	1.3439	1.6289	1.7908	2.1589	2.5937	3.1058	4.0456
11	1.3121	1.3842	1.7103	1.8983	2.3316	2.8531	3.4785	4.6524
12	1.3449	1.4258	1.7959	2.0122	2.5182	3.1384	3.8960	5.3503
13	1.3785	1.4685	1.8856	2.1329	2.7196	3.4523	4.3635	6.1528
14	1.4130	1.5126	1.9799	2.2609	2.9372	3.7975	4.8871	7.0757
15	1.4483	1.5580	2.0789	2.3966	3.1722	4.1772	5.4736	8.1371
16	1.4845	1.6047	2.1829	2.5404	3.4259	4.5950	6.1304	9.3576
17	1.5216	1.6528	2.2920	2.6928	3.7000	5.0545	6.8660	10.7613
18	1.5597	1.7024	2.4066	2.8543	3.9960	5.5599	7.6900	12.3755
19	1.5987	1.7535	2.5270	3.0256	4.3157	6.1159	8.6128	14.2318
20	1.6386	1.8061	2.6533	3.2071	4.6610	6.7275	9.6463	16.3665
21	1.6796	1.8603	2.7860	3.3996	5.0338	7.4002	10.8038	18.8215
22	1.7216	1.9161	2.9253	3.6035	5.4365	8.1403	12.1003	21.6447
23	1.7646	1.9736	3.0715	3.8197	5.8715	8.9543	13.5523	24.8915
24	1.8087	2.0328	3.2251	4.0489	6.3412	9.8497	15.1786	28.6252
25	1.8539	2.0938	3.3864	4.2919	6.8485	10.8347	17.0001	32.9190

Table 1-8. (*Continued*)

End of Year	2½%	3%	5%	6%	8%	10%	12%	15%
26	$ 1.9003	$ 2.1566	$ 3.5557	$ 4.5494	$ 7.3964	$ 11.9182	$ 19.0401	$ 37.8568
27	1.9478	2.2213	3.7335	4.8223	7.9881	13.1100	21.3249	43.5353
28	1.9965	2.2879	3.9201	5.1117	8.6271	14.4210	23.8839	50.0656
29	2.0464	2.3566	4.1161	5.4184	9.3173	15.8631	26.7499	57.5755
30	2.0976	2.4273	4.3219	5.7435	10.0627	17.4494	29.9599	66.2218
31	2.1500	2.5001	4.5380	6.0881	10.8677	19.1943	33.5551	76.1435
32	2.2038	2.5751	4.7649	6.4534	11.7371	21.1138	37.5817	87.5651
33	2.2589	2.6523	5.0032	6.8406	12.6760	23.2252	42.0915	100.6998
34	2.3153	2.7319	5.2533	7.2510	13.6901	25.5477	47.1425	115.8048
35	2.3732	2.8139	5.5160	7.6861	14.7853	28.1024	52.7996	133.1755
36	2.4325	2.8983	5.7918	8.1473	15.9682	30.9127	59.1356	153.1519
37	2.4933	2.9852	6.0814	8.6361	17.2456	34.0039	66.2318	176.1246
38	2.5557	3.0748	6.3855	9.1543	18.6253	37.4043	74.1797	202.5433
39	2.6196	3.1670	6.7048	9.7035	20.1153	41.1448	83.0812	232.9248
40	2.6851	3.2620	7.0400	10.2857	21.7245	45.2593	93.0510	267.8635
41	2.7522	3.3599	7.3920	10.9029	23.4625	49.7852	104.2171	308.0431
42	2.8210	3.4607	7.7616	11.5570	25.3395	54.7637	116.7231	354.2495
43	2.8915	3.5645	8.1497	12.2505	27.3666	60.2401	130.7299	407.3870
44	2.9638	3.6715	8.5572	12.9855	29.5560	66.2641	146.4175	468.4950
45	3.0380	3.7816	8.9850	13.7646	31.9204	72.8905	163.9876	538.7693
46	3.1139	3.8950	9.4343	14.5905	34.4741	80.1795	183.6661	619.5847
47	3.1917	4.0119	9.9060	15.4659	37.2320	88.1975	205.7061	712.5224
48	3.2715	4.1323	10.4013	16.3939	40.2106	97.0172	230.3908	819.4007
49	3.3533	4.2562	10.9213	17.3775	43.4274	106.7190	258.0377	942.3103
50	3.4371	4.3839	11.4674	18.4202	46.9016	117.3909	289.0022	1083.6574

Table 1–9. One Dollar Per Annum Compounded Annually

End of Year	3%	5%	6%	8%	10%	12%	15%
1	$ 1.0300	$ 1.0500	$ 1.0600	$ 1.0800	$ 1.1000	$ 1.1200	$ 1.1500
2	2.0909	2.1525	2.1836	2.2464	2.3100	2.3744	2.4725
3	3.1836	3.3101	3.3746	3.5061	3.6410	3.7793	3.9934
4	4.3091	4.5256	4.6371	4.8666	5.1051	5.3528	5.7424
5	5.4684	5.8019	5.9753	6.3359	6.7156	7.1152	7.7537
6	6.6625	7.1420	7.3938	7.9228	8.4872	9.0890	10.0668
7	7.8923	8.5491	8.8975	9.6366	10.4359	11.2297	12.7268
8	9.1591	10.0266	10.4913	11.4876	12.5795	13.7757	15.7858
9	10.4639	11.5779	12.1808	13.4866	14.3974	16.5487	19.3037
10	11.8078	13.2068	13.9716	15.6455	17.5312	19.6546	23.3493
11	13.1920	14.9171	15.8699	17.9771	20.3843	23.1331	28.0017
12	14.6178	16.7130	17.8821	20.4953	23.5227	27.0291	33.3519
13	16.0863	18.5986	20.0151	23.2149	26.9750	31.3926	39.5047
14	17.5989	20.5786	22.2760	26.1521	30.7725	36.2797	46.5804
15	19.1569	22.6575	24.6725	29.3243	34.9497	41.7533	54.7175
16	20.7616	24.8404	27.2129	32.7502	39.5447	47.8837	64.0751
17	22.4144	27.1324	29.9057	36.4502	44.5992	54.7497	74.8364
18	24.1169	29.5390	32.7600	40.4463	50.1591	62.4397	87.2118
19	25.8704	32.0660	35.7856	44.7620	56.2750	71.0524	101.4436
20	27.6765	34.7193	38.9927	49.4229	63.0025	80.6987	117.8101
21	29.5368	37.5052	42.3923	54.4568	70.4027	91.5026	136.6316
22	31.4529	40.4305	45.9958	59.8933	78.5430	103.6029	158.2764
23	33.4265	43.5020	49.8156	65.7648	87.4973	117.1552	183.1678
24	35.4593	46.7271	53.8645	72.1059	97.3471	132.3339	211.7930
25	37.5530	50.1135	58.1564	78.9544	108.1818	149.3339	244.7120

Table 1-9. (Continued)

End of Year	3%	5%	6%	8%	10%	12%	15%
26	$ 39.7096	$ 53.6691	$ 62.7058	$ 86.3508	$ 120.0999	$ 168.3740	$ 282.5688
27	41.9309	57.4026	67.5281	94.3388	133.2099	189.6989	326.1041
28	44.2189	61.3227	72.6398	102.9659	147.6309	213.5828	376.1697
29	46.5754	65.4388	78.0582	112.2832	163.4940	240.3327	433.7451
30	49.0027	69.7608	83.8017	122.3459	180.9434	270.2926	499.9569
31	51.5028	74.2988	89.8898	133.2135	200.1378	303.8477	576.1005
32	54.0778	79.0638	96.3432	144.9506	221.2515	341.4294	663.6655
33	56.7302	84.0670	103.1838	157.6267	244.4767	383.5210	764.3654
34	59.4621	89.3203	110.4348	171.3168	270.0244	430.6635	880.1702
35	62.2759	94.8363	118.1209	186.1021	298.1268	483.4631	1013.3757
36	65.1742	100.6281	126.2681	202.0703	329.0395	542.5987	1166.4975
37	68.1594	106.7095	134.9042	219.3158	363.0434	608.8305	1342.6222
38	71.2342	113.0950	144.0585	237.9412	400.4478	683.0102	1545.1655
39	74.4013	119.7998	153.7620	258.0565	441.5926	766.0914	1778.0903
40	77.6633	126.8398	164.0477	279.7810	486.8518	859.1424	2045.9539
41	81.0232	134.2318	174.9505	303.2435	536.6370	963.3595	2353.9969
42	84.4839	141.9933	186.5076	328.5830	591.4007	1080.0826	2708.2465
43	88.0484	150.1430	198.7580	355.9496	651.6408	1210.8125	3115.6334
44	91.7199	158.7002	211.7435	385.5056	717.9048	1357.2300	3584.1285
45	95.5015	167.6852	225.5081	417.4261	790.7953	1521.2176	4122.8977
46	99.3965	177.1194	240.0986	451.9002	870.9749	1704.8838	4742.4824
47	103.4084	187.0254	255.5645	489.1322	959.1723	1910.5898	5455.0047
48	107.5406	197.4267	271.9584	529.3427	1056.1896	2140.9806	6274.4055
49	111.7969	208.3480	289.3359	572.7702	1162.9085	2399.0182	7216.7163
50	116.1808	219.8154	307.7561	619.6718	1280.2994	2688.0204	8300.3737

the sum to which one dollar per annum, paid at the beginning of each year, will accumulate at the indicated interest rates compounded annually for the given number of years.

Assume you have 17 years before retirement, that you have $14,000 you can put to work in a lump sum, and that you can save $160 per month or $1920 per annum. I promised that you would not have to go these calculations alone, so let me give you some examples of how to use these tables. I use them often and you probably will too, once you have gotten the feel of them.

Using Table 1–8, you would go down to 17 years and across:

At 5 percent	At 10 percent
$14,000	$14,000
× 2.2920	× 5.0545
$32,088	$70,763

From Table 1–9:

At 5 percent	At 10 percent
$ 1,920	$ 1,920
× 27.1324	× 44.5992
$52,094	$85,630

In 17 years at 5 percent you would have $32,088 and $52,094, or $84,182. At 10 percent you would have $70,763 and $85,630, or $156,393 (before taxes).

• WHICH RATE IS SAFER?

In the past, has it been safer to "lend" your money to a savings institution at 4 to 6 percent or to "own" shares of American industry, real estate, and energy, with the hope of averaging 10 to 12 percent or above? We shall take an in-depth look at which way has truly been the "safest" long-term approach to money management. Suffice it to say here that if you have waited the past 18 years for $1 to become $2, you have lost the fight, because inflation has more than doubled your cost of living—to say nothing of your loss through the tax bite.

At 4 percent your exercise has been similar to the little frog who was trying to hop out of the well. Every time he hopped up one foot, he slid back two. If you ignore that insidious thing called inflation, your money exercises may prove to parallel those of the little frog in the fairy tale of the frog and the princess, but without the kiss of the princess to miraculously make you an affluent prince.

Don't Confuse Safety and Stability • I find that many with whom I counsel make the mistake of confusing words with very different meanings. They use the word "safety" when in reality they are describing "stability" in the real economic world. "Stability" is the return of the same number of dollars, plus interest at a future date in time. "Safety" is the return of the same amount of food, clothing, and shelter—in other words, the same amount of purchasing power—at a future date in time. You can be stable and not be safe, as any couple who retired on a fixed income only a few years ago can tell you today. To be safe your funds must grow at least as fast as the cost of living and the cost of taxes.

• SUMMARY

You must save for the future in order to fulfill your obligation to yourself, your family, and society. You must conscientiously avoid the twins of financial failure, procrastination and ignorance of what money must do to accomplish your predetermined worthwhile goal. You have all the requirements for reaching financial independence. It is only a matter of using the talents you already have to implement your own formula for financial independence. You will not have to fight the battle alone. A dollar has fantastic earning power if you will employ it properly. The time-use of money is what I will be sharing with you throughout the chapters of this book.

Application

Knowledge of any subject is of little use unless you apply it to your own particular set of circumstances. Therefore, at the end of each chapter there will be questions for you to answer and financial data for you to assemble.

Stop now and obtain a loose-leaf notebook. Paste on the outside these words: *My Progress Reports Toward Financial Independence.*

Write in the year.

List the following questions. Complete your answers. Do this at the same time each year. January is a good time, because it is then that we make our promises to ourselves. Affirm that you will set in action everything that is necessary to achieve financial independence.

1 · What source or sources of income do I want to depend on at age 65?

2 · How many years before I plan to retire?

3 · What monthly income would I like to have if I were retiring today?

4 · What inflation factor do I feel best applies to me? (Table 1–2)

5 · Now how much will I need per month at retirement?

6 · If I choose the guaranteed route, how much capital will be required?

7 · What rate of growth is my minimum objective?

8 · If I choose the variable route, how much capital will be required?

9 · How much can I put to work today? (a) Lump sum (b) Monthly.

2
The Anatomy of Inflation

There are four basic reasons for investing that you must learn. These are

1 · To obtain a hedge against inflation.
2 · For income.
3 · For growth of capital.
4 · For tax advantage.

In this chapter we'll take an unemotional look at inflation and the devastating path it has cut across the face of the United States, bringing havoc to many a financial plan.

Inflation is a fact of life. It is a fact that you must learn to accept and to protect yourself against, or suffer the dire consequences. It has been your constant companion since the day you were born, and, from all indications, it will continue with you for the remainder of your life. This problem does not belong to the United States alone, but has been felt worldwide. Tolstoy chronicled that every civilized nation that has ever existed has experienced the ravages of inflation.

I do not believe that history always repeats itself, but I have found that if I ignore the past, I often condemn myself to repeating the same mistakes in the future.

What has been the history of inflation in the United States?

• SINCE
1900

Let's examine the past by beginning at the turn of the century—1900. Figure 2–1 plots the purchasing power of our dollar from 1900 through 1977.

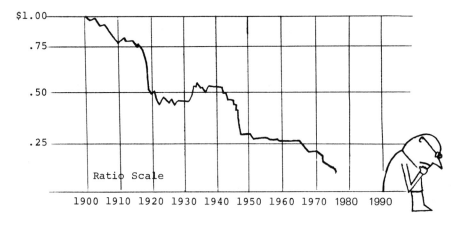

FIGURE 2–1. Purchasing Power of the Dollar

An even more graphic way of looking at the effect of inflation is to look at a dollar composed of quarters that you have held since 1900. You now go to the grocery store to make a purchase. How much do you think it will buy in the form of goods and services in comparison to what it bought in 1900?

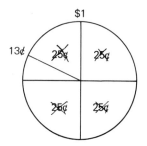

•   THE ANATOMY OF INFLATION

Your dollar has lost 87 percent of the only value it has—what it will buy. A dollar has no value in and of itself. Its only value is what you can exchange it for in the marketplace. What you want to store for the future is not so many dollars, but so many pairs of shoes, tubes of lipstick, and hamburgers.

•   THINK OF
BREAD

In 1940 you could go to your local grocery store and buy 10 loaves of bread for $1. By 1950 you could buy only six loaves. By 1960 it would buy only four, and by 1970 only three. How many will it buy today? It is the same dollar, but it has lost the major portion of its only value.

If I can do nothing else for you in this book but to help you to convert your thinking from dollars into bread, I will have done for you an immense favor. I warn you, it is an emotional transition that only a few can make. If you can make it, you will be in the minority—but remember, it's only the minority that become financially independent.

During the years between 1940 and 1977, the dollar held its own in only two years, and then by less than 1 percent. Not even a professional gambler would accept those odds. Yet, if you are holding a dollar today, you are betting against those odds. If you are a saver, placing your savings in a "guaranteed" savings account, you are a gambler, and if the past is any indication of the future, you are "guaranteed" to lose!

What if I were to say to you, "I want to recommend a stock for your serious consideration. I know that its record has not been very good, but I have faith that it will improve. It was selling for $100 in 1951; by 1956 it had dropped to $96, by 1961 to $88, by 1966 to $79, and by 1971 to $63. Today it is at $44, but, don't let that discourage you. I still have faith in this investment, and I want you to invest in it." If I were to make such a "buy" recommendation to you, what would you say to me? Before you say, "You've got to be kidding!" I want you to know that this investment is recommended by most of our state and national banks, by all of our savings and loans, by all of the nation's life insurance companies that sell cash surrender value policies, by your city, and by the federal government itself. What is this investment? It is the U.S. dollar!

"IT IS THE U.S. DOLLAR!"

- ### IT IS THE
  ### U.S. DOLLAR

"Guaranteed" dollars are recommended as a good, "safe" investment for you by all savings institutions and insurance companies that sell cash surrender value life insurance; yet they never want a "guaranteed" dollar for themselves. They want to "guarantee" your principal, "guarantee" your rate of return, and "guarantee" that your dollar will work for them—usually harder than it works for you. You will receive a "guarantee" that you can always get back each deflating dollar you have placed with them (excluding "your" savings account with the life insurance company). You are also guaranteed that you can never receive any more than that dollar, plus any compound interest you may have left with them, regardless of how much your money has earned for the institution to which you loaned it, and regardless of what the cost of living has become. (See Figure 2–2.)

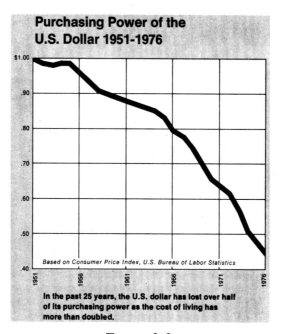

Purchasing Power of the U.S. Dollar 1951-1976

Based on Consumer Price Index, U.S. Bureau of Labor Statistics

In the past 25 years, the U.S. dollar has lost over half of its purchasing power as the cost of living has more than doubled.

FIGURE 2-2.

• VERBAL vs. EMOTIONAL ACCEPTANCE

If I were to ask you the question, "Have we had inflation in the past?" your answer would be "Why, yes!" If I now ask you, "Do you think we'll have inflation in the future?" would your answer be another resounding "Yes"? Would this be your verbal answer, but not your emotional answer?

I find it very difficult for most people to emotionally accept inflation. Inflation is such a nonvisual thing that it's hard to realize that it is happening. However, it's getting more visual every day. Next time you go grocery shopping, dig to the back of the row of canned peaches and see if you can't find a can at a lower price than the cans in front. This may help you to become the rare person who makes this transition.

Inflation continues to nibble away at the value of your dollars. The trouble with nibbles is that over a period of time, they result in deep bites. For example, if your income was $7500 in 1950, inflation and tax increases would require that you earn $15,618 by 1977 just to maintain your same purchasing power.

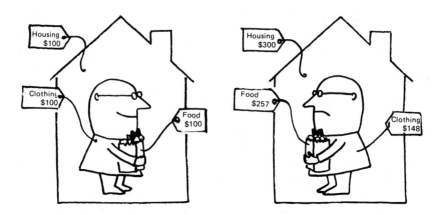

In 1939, the average family income was $1500; 30 years later, in 1969, it was $9500; 30 years from now, in 1999, it is estimated that it will have risen to $45,500.

A 5 percent inflation is equivalent to a 5 percent cut in your gross income. Any inflation even approaching this rate is a major assault on your living standard. It is also an illness with hidden, delayed symptoms. On top of the immediate increase in the price of your necessities and luxuries alike, there is the value eaten away from your fixed savings, which includes not only your bank account but also any government bonds you may own, your private pension invested in fixed securities, and, if you are banking with a life insurance company, the cash value of your life insurance policies.

It is difficult to stay ahead of rapid inflation. A married man earning $13,000 a year, for example, would need a $650-a-year raise just to keep even with the increased cost of a 5 percent inflation. Yet that amount would put him into a higher tax bracket so that he would have to pay more in federal income taxes. State, local, and Social Security taxes will take additional bites.

If you look at the record on the rate of inflation in a year such as 1974, and find it to be 11 to 13 percent, depending on the indicator used, will you a few minutes later revert to talking about your savings account being a good "guaranteed" investment at 5 percent, 6 percent, or 7½ percent? If you do, I'll know that emotionally you have not accepted the fact of inflation and the reality of a negative interest. If you are in a 25 percent tax bracket and have received the average savings institution rate of return since 1964, your net gain or loss picture looks like Figure 2–3.

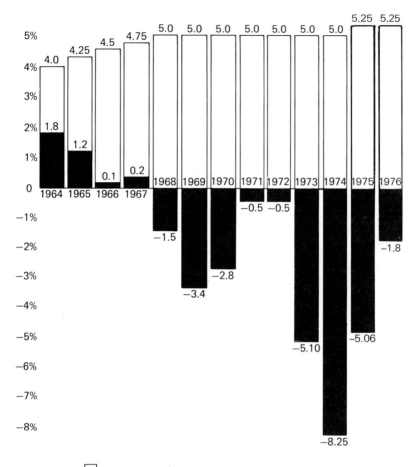

What was left after inflation and taxes (25% bracket).
Vertical bars represent savings bank interest rates.

FIGURE 2–3.   Inflation and Taxes—How They've Affected Your Savings

• WHEN WILL
INFLATION STOP?

The year after World War II, Congress passed the Full Employment Act of 1946, stating that the government would promote two economically inconsistent goals—price stability and full employment. They also legislated that from that time forward until the act is repealed, our country will have inflation. The act, for all practical purposes, makes it illegal to have a depression. When unemployment reaches a certain point, the government must intervene and take measures to accelerate the economy. This means that the natural processes of supply and demand in the labor force can no longer be a stabilizing force. In fact, when we had increased unemployment in 1971, wages actually rose.

What has happened since the passage of this bill? In the 1950s inflation was at 2 percent, in the 1960s at 2.3 percent, and in the 1970s at 6.1 percent. When you listen to the evening news on TV you will hear promises by government officials that they are going to end inflation. Don't believe them! If you do, it will spell disaster for your investment progress.

• ARE THE KNOWLEDGEABLE HURT?

Does inflation really hurt the knowledgeable investor over the long term? I believe it does not. He learns to protect himself.

Inflation brings into focus the tragic face of the hard-working, thrifty, sacrificing person who put his money into government bonds and lost—lost in purchasing power and lost the privilege of retiring in financial dignity. At least the spendthrift had the fun of spending his money until he got off the inflation train. During his working years, raises usually matched or exceeded his increases in his cost of living. But when he got off the inflation train and it went on without him, he had no chance of keeping up with the inflationary spiral.

In 1973 and 1974 our American families saw their purchasing power drop by $538 billion, pushing their financial wealth below where it was in 1965. This means that the average man worked hard for nine years with nothing to show for it.

But why should you be the "average" man? After all, inflation does not really destroy wealth. It doesn't change the number of houses that can be built, the amount of food that can be placed on the table, or the number of cars that can come off the assembly lines in Detroit.

What you must do is to accept the fact that inflation is just another economic factor that rearranges wealth. What you must learn to do is to be sure the realignment benefits you.

The Robin Hood of the 70s • Inflation is the Robin Hood of the 70s. It takes from the ignorant and gives to the well-informed. You will be either a victim or a beneficiary—you will be a loser or a winner, and it's more fun to be a winner. Your inflationary investment game plan can be exciting, profitable, and enjoyable. Don't fear inflation; learn to enjoy it. Get on the right side of it. The more volatile inflation becomes, the bigger the rewards that you can obtain. But if you yield to the temptation of burying your head in the sand and saying, "This, too, will pass," losing will be your fate.

INFLATION! THE ROBINHOOD OF THE 70'S

• POOR RICHARD'S ALMANAC HITS THE FAN

If you are sitting there stunned, asking yourself what you have done to deserve your big loser fate, the answer will make you even sadder. You'll find that all you have done is to follow the "responsible" behavior patterns that were and still are being taught in most personal finance courses. You were probably taught, as I was, the old Puritan ethic embodied in Benjamin Franklin's *Poor Richard's Almanac*: "Work hard, be thrifty, don't borrow." When prices were stable, his rules were fine, but in our current times of aggressive inflation they are the surest path to financial destruction. Poor Richard's advice may now be so engrained in your thinking that it will be hard for you to cast him off, and you'll get no help from the media. Billboards, newspapers, television, and radio urge you to buy such things as Government Series "E" bonds, stating in a loud clear voice and printed in bold captions the words, "Invest in Government Bonds to Insure Your Financial Future." I agree with the great economist Milton Friedman that a good case can be made for a suit against the federal government for false advertising. Why? Because an investment in Series E bonds has not "guaranteed your financial future" unless by "guarantee" they mean that you are guaranteed to buy less with the $25 maturity value than you could have bought with the $18.75 that you relinquished when you bought your $25 bond. Other such false encouragement comes into your and my living rooms through the living color of TV. The Savings and Loan tells you, "Your name belongs in our little black book," meaning their savings passbook. The banks advertise "growth bonds," and some insurance companies imply that you own a part of a rock "through 'your' savings account" entitled "cash surrender value."

Supposedly we all hate inflation. Our politicians contend that they do in all their political speeches. Yet government is one of the major causes of inflation. It causes it, not by giving us what we hate, but by trying to give us what we want. It causes it by trying to give us jobs, higher incomes, and big increases in government benefits. The public dislikes both inflation and unemployment. But it dislikes unemployment even more than it dislikes inflation. I do believe if our forefathers were sitting down to draft the Bill of Rights today, they would place job security right along with life, liberty, and the pursuit of happiness.

Prior to World War II this was not a commonly held belief. Consequently, prices went up, but they also went down, so on the average prices maintained some stability over the long term. Now the majority believe in the right of job security, and inflation is rampant. We have also exported this belief abroad, bringing inflation worldwide.

• ## THE NEW MATH OF THE TRANSFER OF WEALTH

To give you some examples of how Poor Richard has become obsolete in our inflationary economy, let's look at his admonition, "Don't borrow." Let's examine three situations and see which family has been the most prudent.

The Anderson family's balance sheet looks like this:

Cash	$10,000	Mortgage	$ 5,000
Home	10,000	Net worth	$15,000

Net worth is the difference between your assets and your liabilities and is a measure of how rich you are.

Now let's assume that prices double. The Andersons' balance sheet will now look like this:

Cash	$10,000	Mortgage	$ 5,000
Home	20,000	Net worth	25,000

The Andersons' net worth has now increased from $15,000 to $25,000 which at first glance appears good; however, their net worth has not doubled, as prices did; therefore, this family has fallen behind in the inflation race. Their wealth or purchasing power has been reduced by inflation.

Now let's examine the Barton family's balance sheet:

Cash	$ 5,000	Mortgage	$ 5,000
Home	10,000	Net worth	10,000

A doubling of prices has this effect on their balance sheet:

Cash	$ 5,000	Mortgage	$ 5,000
Home	20,000	Net worth	20,000

The Bartons have held their own. They have exactly kept pace with inflation.

Now let's look at the Calloway family's balance sheet:

Cash	$ 3,000	Mortgage	$10,000
Home	12,000	Net worth	5,000

When prices doubled the Calloways' net worth looked like this:

Cash	$ 3,000	Mortgage	$10,000
Home	24,000	Net worth	17,000

The Calloways' net worth increased from $5,000 to $17,000, or more than tripled, while prices only doubled. The Calloways beat inflation.

What lesson about inflation have you learned from these three families? Is it this sad commentary: "Inflation rewards those who owe money, not those who pay cash"?

You don't have to be on the verge of bankruptcy to benefit from inflation. You can and should have cash, but you will want to have a large amount of your assets invested in things—hard assets. To win the inflation game in the years ahead, you will have to be leveraged in this way. Your assets must be primarily in investments whose prices can rise as fast as the general price levels at each stage of the inflation cycle. Large amounts of cash do not fit into the inflation-benefiting category, for a dollar is still a dollar whose purchasing power shrinks with inflation. (This reminds one of the verse: "A rose is a rose is a rose.")

Though future inflation cycles may differ slightly in intensity and length, a careful study of how these cycles affect the value of your assets will give you timing guidance that should let you beat the inflation game.

Inflation will continue, but not at the same rate each year. Some years it will accelerate and other years it will decelerate, though the thrust will always be upward. These gyrations can create some tremendous investment opportunities for you if you will develop the right strategy.

Since government is the chief creator of inflation, you must watch government policy closely to determine advance warnings of the amount of inflation that government will be creating. This will come in cycles. Your understanding of these cycles is fundamental to your investment success. These gyrations up and down of the inflation rate will affect the price of everything you own or buy—stocks, bonds, mutual funds, real estate, gold, and currencies.

Government policy drives the economy and is the creator of all cycles. The government policy cycle is rooted in the inflation-unemployment tradeoff. Government policymakers can be counted on to shift between programs designed to reduce unemployment to programs designed to curb inflation and back again. But the choice they will always make when it is time to cut bait or fish will be for full employment.

You will want to design an investment portfolio that is not faddist, but one that is efficiently designed to meet your goal of beating inflation.

Once you've assembled this portfolio, you can't afford to sit comfortably and take your rest. This is a dynamic world of change in which we live. That's why this book is titled *The New Money Dynamics*. Every day is a new day. That's what I like about my role as a financial planner. It's a dynamic world of change.

• THE TOTAL PORTFOLIO

To take advantage of the transfers that inflation makes in wealth you must begin by thinking in terms of a total portfolio that you will have positioned efficiently at the proper time to beat inflation. Your portfolio must maximize your after-tax return balanced against a level of risk that provides you with peace of mind. You will want to avoid fads unless you are equipped emotionally to act rapidly. As inflation pushes up the price of your assets, faddists will start jumping in with both feet. At this point prices will begin to overdiscount inflation. The faddist will be selling as prices drop. You will want to be in a position to buy at that time.

To beat inflation, you will always want to be holding the right combination of assets. There is an investment for each season, but not an investment for all seasons. This means that nothing you have can be just put away in your safe-deposit box and forgotten. You must learn to be flexible and alert.

You should classify all the investment vehicles available to you as to their appropriateness for accelerating inflation or decelerating inflation. Then decide whether inflation is about to accelerate or decelerate. The most reliable indicator I have found is to keep my eyes on the money supply. Acceleration in the amount of the money supply leads to an acceleration in the inflation rate. Sustained deceleration has the opposite effect.

• DIVERSIFICATION

One of the first rules for successful investing is diversification—the old adage of not putting all your eggs in one basket remains true today.

If you put all your eggs in one basket and stub your toe, you may break all your eggs, but if you use several baskets and make several trips, your chances of arriving at your destination with more eggs intact are greatly increased.

How should you diversify? One of the best ways is to stand back from your money. Many times you will be too close to your hard-earned money to make rational decisions. If this is the case, a good financial planner who is not so emotionally involved can be of great help to you. A member of the International Association of Financial Planners and a Certified Financial Planner can be a good place to start. The address of the International Association is 2150 Parklake Drive, N.E., Suite 260, Atlanta, Ga. 30345, and the College for Financial Planners is 4155 E. Jewell, Suite 514, Denver, Co. 80222.

I often find that many who come to me for financial counseling have already accumulated sufficient assets, or could easily do so within a few years, to enable them to reach or work toward financial independence, if these assets were properly put to work. This is, or probably will become true with you. You may be, or will be, working extremely hard for your money, but unfortunately once it is obtained, instead of putting it to work for yourself, you have unknowingly given away its earning power.

• SUMMARY

Inflation will be a part of your life for as long as you live. You can fear it, hide your head in the sand and say that it doesn't exist or that it will go away, but you are only kidding yourself, and inviting financial disappointments. Inflation can be your valuable ally. You can use it to increase your wealth by applying your intelligence and energy to studying the inflation cycles and positioning your assets at the proper location at the proper time. You must face the reality that you will probably never own an asset that is immune to the inflation cycle.

The facing of this reality and your determination to use these forces can be a challenging and profitable undertaking.

Application

1 • Have you mentally made the necessary transition from dollars into bread?

2 • Go to the library and check out a 1940 *Life Magazine* or *Saturday Evening Post* and study the ads.

3 • Do you think the Full Employment Act of 1946 will be repealed?

4 • Are you still living under the *Poor Richard's Almanac* theory of hard work, save, and don't borrow?

5 • What steps will you now take to keep abreast of government fiscal policies?

3

Lending Your Dollars

It is your responsibility to be a good steward of every dollar that comes your way. A part of each dollar should be used to feed, clothe, house, and entertain your family and yourself. A part of your dollar you should save.

In an earlier chapter you learned that there are only three things you can do with a dollar—spend, loan, or own. You will always need to have some of your funds in a "loaned" position. How much should this be? There was a time I taught that you should keep three months expenses in cash reserves. Now I teach that you should keep as much of your funds in an idle position as it takes to give you peace of mind, for peace of mind can be a good investment. You may require a lot of what I call "patting money" to give you this peace of mind. Determine what your level should be and place those funds into a "loaned" position. However, I hope that this book will educate you so thoroughly that you will not have peace of mind if you leave too much of your funds idle, working for someone else. In this chapter we shall consider ways that you may want to "loan" your money.

A very important consideration in your plan to become financially independent is the selection of the right banker. He can play a vital role in its accomplishment. Take the time and effort to select one who is knowledgeable and creative and whose bank has sufficient assets to finance any bankable project you may want to undertake. Then open your checking accounts with him.

• CHECKING ACCOUNTS

You will always need one or more checking accounts to be used for convenience and for ease of record keeping. Keep a sufficient amount on deposit to enable you to write a check whenever you choose. Feeling "poor" is not an emotionally satisfactory feeling and does not contribute to the necessary psychology of winning.

However, do not keep your balance too large. I remember one lady who came in for counseling who had $159,000 in her checking account. I asked if she had a reason for keeping this amount there and she said, "Well, I've been thinking of taking a little trip." I suppressed the desire to ask her which planet was her desired destination.

• OTHER WAYS OF "LENDING"

When you move from a checking account to other ways of "lending" your funds, you will find a wide array of choices. These are what are commonly called fixed-income instruments. As evidence of your loan to the borrower you receive securities or instruments that represent contracts to pay back your money at a specified time and at a specified rate. These borrowers may be corporations, the federal government, or financial institutions.

Let's now examine some of the fixed-income instruments you may want to consider.

Passbook Savings Accounts • You may open a passbook savings account in any amount at either a bank or a savings and loan. Interest is earned from date of deposit to date of withdrawal or to "dividend" date. The maximum rates are fixed by the Federal Reserve System or the Federal Home Loan Bank Board. These rates (usually slightly higher at savings institutions) have ranged in recent years from $4\frac{1}{2}$ percent to $5\frac{1}{2}$ percent. Deposits and withdrawals can be made at your discretion. Deposits, in most instances, are federally insured to a maximum of $40,000.

Certificates of Deposit • This is basically a deposit account opened for a minimum amount of $1000 to $5000. Certificates of deposit are issued by both commercial banks and savings and loan associations in maturities of from 30 days to six years. Some pay interest from the date of deposit to maturity at the stated rate. Others pay from fixed dates. Interest rates are usually higher than those for regular savings accounts and have exceeded 7¾ percent for the longer maturities. However, during 1977, when the Federal Reserve Board was expanding the money supply and demands for commercial loans did not keep pace, $100,000, 30-day C.D.'s dropped to 4⅝ percent. The rate obtainable on $100,000 and up is usually negotiable, whether with a bank or a savings and loan institution. Maximum rates for C.D.'s under $100,000 are fixed by law. Savings and loan rates may be one-quarter of a percent higher than those of commercial banks. Deposits normally can be made at any time.

I personally could never feel comfortable with a long-term certificate of deposit. I feel that I would be betting against three odds, with a great likelihood of losing on one or all of them. These are: (1) I am betting that I do not need the money for 4 to 6 years. If I do need the money, my rate will revert back to passbook, and I will be penalized three months interest. (2) I am betting that long-term interest rates do not rise above 7½ to 7¾ percent for 4 to 6 years. (3) I am betting that we do not have inflation over that period of time.

Here are some examples of penalties that you could incur on a $10,000 certificate if you make an early withdrawal:

Type of account	Yield	Early withdrawal	Penalty	Effective yield
1 yr. certificate	6½%	11 months	$248.20	3.84%
2 yr. certificate	6½%	1 yr. 9 mos.	$354.00	4.53%
4 yr. certificate	7½%	3 yrs. 6 mos.	$931.50	4.91%

Commercial Paper • Corporations finance much of their short-term working capital requirements by issuing commercial paper—short-term notes with a fixed maturity of from 1 to 270 days. Paper is normally issued in a minimum amount of $25,000 or as small as $10,000 at some banks for 30 days or longer, and it can be purchased on either a discount or an interest-bearing basis. The investment return is determined by the current level of short-term interest rates and, therefore, can fluctuate significantly over relatively short periods. The returns on commercial paper historically have been about ½ percent to 1 percent below the bank prime lending rate. Paper can be purchased with or without arrangements allowing prepayment of the amount initially invested plus a return at the original investment rate. Without such arrangements, paper can be sold in the short-term market at current rates, resulting in a yield greater or less than the acquisition rate.

• **SAFETY**

When you lend your money to a bank, it is well to follow the same procedure that a bank would—check out your borrower. How can you do this? In the case of a bank, look for the gilded seal applied to the entrance door of the bank or on the window near the door. Does it contain the letters FDIC? This means that the bank is a member of the Federal Deposit Insurance Corporation and that your account is insured up to $40,000. The Federal Deposit Insurance program insures deposits in national and member state banks, both commercial and mutual savings banks. What this means to you is that if a bank gets into financial difficulties and is closed, your savings up to $40,000 will be reimbursed by the federal government. Although the process begins soon after closure, it may take some months before you receive your money.

All national banks in the United States are required to be members of the system, and state banks may become Federal Reserve System banks by meeting stringent requirements.

All FRS banks have stringent requirements with regard to the structure of their board of directors, interlocking directorates, their relationship with security and investment companies, the payment of interest on deposits, and their relationship to branch banks. They must keep reserves in cash or on deposit with their Federal Reserve bank equivalent to a certain proportion of their various types of deposits, and they are also required to subscribe to the capital of the Federal Reserve bank of their district equal to 6 percent of their capital surplus.

There are no similar requirements for savings and loan associations, although they may operate under federal regulations with guarantees. Federal regulations do not preclude bank failure. In fact, the entire nation is familiar with the failure of the Sharpstown Bank in Houston in 1971. Sharpstown was a state bank with FDIC insurance for savings accounts up to $20,000 (which was the limit at that time). However, many people had more than that amount on deposit.

The risk can be more with some savings and loan associations. It is extremely important to learn as much as you can about an association before making a deposit. However, a superficial check may not protect you. *The National Observer* publication in its December 15, 1973 issue gives an account of a widow "still in shock" who deposited $42,509 in benefits from her late husband's insurance in a Norfolk, Virginia, savings and loan corporation. She never doubted the money was safe. The 57-year-old corporation was well regarded. Its officials were among the most esteemed men in the community. There were two things she did not know: The savings and loan corporation was insolvent, and its deposits were not insured. Seven days later, Virginia banking authorities closed the institution and placed it in receivership. Her money, along with that of nearly 3500 other persons, was frozen. Unfortunately, all those people could end up with losses.

Virginia's inadequacies are not unique. In Louisville, Kentucky, savings of 22,100 persons were jeopardized when two large building and loan associations failed in 1972. Their depositors are expected to recover no more than 30 percent of their money.

If you decide to use a savings and loan association, be sure to look for the gilded seal with FSLIC on the door, for this guarantees that you will have your deposit returned someday (not always on demand) up to $40,000.

In Chicago some 14,000 savers were cut off from their funds when a large savings and loan association went under in 1964. And in Maryland an estimated 50,000 depositors lost all or part of their funds when some uninsured savings and loans passed into oblivion during the 1960s.

Such misfortunes are unusual in these times of prosperity, but nothing can entirely prevent even national bank collapses. The biggest in U.S. history was in October 1972, when a national bank located in San Diego was declared insolvent. Nearly half of the $940 million on deposit was not covered by the FDIC insurance because of the then $20,000 maximum. (All the deposits may still be protected under a government rescue plan.) The difficulties experienced by the Franklin National Bank of New York City in 1974 are also well chronicled.

In Galveston, Texas, an old, well-respected bank was closed by the Securities and Exchange Commission in September 1972. Thanks to the affluence of some of the relatives, who paid off depositors, no one lost any money.

• GOVERNMENT OBLIGATIONS

Treasury obligations are guaranteed by the U.S. government. Federal agencies, unless specifically indicated, are not technically government guaranteed but are still considered to be of very high quality.

Series E Bonds • The government obligation with which you are probably the most familiar is the Series E Bonds. These bonds are issued on a discount basis. The minimum available is $25. When held to maturity, the investment return is equivalent to 6 percent compounded semiannually. These bonds may be redeemed at any time after two months from issue at a fixed redemption value that results in a return of less than the 6 percent rate. Interest is not taxable until received.

Series H Bonds • Series H Bonds are 10-year income bonds. They are issued. at par with interest paid semiannually on a scale graduated to produce a return of 6 percent compounded semiannually when the bonds are held to maturity. The minimum amount available is $500. These bonds may be redeemed at par at the owner's option after six months from the issue date. Redemption prior to maturity results in a yield under the 6 percent rate.

If you have held Series E Bonds for some years and are now in need of income, you may want to consider exchanging them for Series H Bonds. There will be no tax liability on the accumulated interest on your Series E Bonds when the exchange is made, nor will there be any until you decide to redeem the Series H Bonds. At that time a tax liability will be incurred.

Treasury Bills • Treasury bills are normally issued in maturities of 91 days, 182 days, and 1 year, and are available in a minimum amount of $10,000 directly from any of the 12 Federal Reserve Banks or through a commercial bank or broker. Treasury bills are issued weekly on a discount basis, under competitive bidding, with the face amount payable at maturity. The investment return on bills is the difference between the cost and the face amount. Bills may be sold prior to maturity at a competitive market rate, which can result in a yield greater or smaller than the original acquisition rate. Yield on bills, like other short-term money market instruments, can fluctuate greatly, but it is generally lower than other nongovernment, short-term securities.

Treasury Notes • Notes have a fixed maturity of from 1 to 7 years and bear interest payable semiannually at fixed rates. They are available in minimum amounts of $1000. Selected notes are auctioned competitively through the Federal Reserve System on a periodic basis. Buyers can subscribe through a commercial bank or a broker. Yields on notes are determined by the acquisition price. These notes may be sold prior to maturity at the current market rate, resulting in a yield greater or smaller than the original acquisition rate. Again, yields on Treasury notes generally are lower than their corporate counterparts because of the excellent marketability and credit rating of government securities.

Treasury Bonds • Bonds have a fixed maturity of over 7 years and are the longer counterpart of Treasury notes. Yields on Treasury bonds, because they are of longer maturity, usually are higher than those of Treasury notes.

Federal Agency Obligations • Agency obligations are issued by federal authorities such as the Federal National Mortgage Association, the Federal Home Loan Bank, the Government National Mortgage Association, and others. These instruments are varied and are tailored to meet the financing needs of the individual issuing agency. Types of issues are similar to U.S. Treasury bills, notes, and bonds. You can acquire these obligations through investment banking houses. Normally, the minimum amount available is $1000 to $5000. Yields are usually one-quarter to one-half of a percent higher than U.S. Treasury obligations. These issues can be sold prior to maturity at current market rates, resulting in a return greater or smaller than the acquisition yield.

There is one group of securities that you may want to consider in this category. They were formally called "mortgage backed securities guaranteed by the Government National Mortgage Association" when they were first established. Since then they have received the friendlier nickname "Ginny Mae." Ginny Maes offer a number of special attractions, but one in particular is that they pay a fixed return that is often higher than you can get from a long-term bond.

Probably the main reason they aren't better known is that when the certificates first appeared in 1970, the minimum unit that you could buy from most brokers was $100,000. Consequently, the buyers were banks, insurance companies, pension funds, and other institutions. Soon thereafter the minimum purchase was cut back to $25,000. Since then, one brokerage firm has created a unit trust that allows individuals to start their investment in Ginny Maes for as little as $10,000.

Ginny Mae Pass-throughs were hatched during the credit crunch of 1969–70, when mortgage money was as tight as it has become from time to time since. The Government National Mortgage Association (GNMA), established by an act of Congress, said, in effect, to savings and loan associations, banks, and mortgage bankers, "When you have closed enough mortgages, collect them into a pool; then issue certificates, backed by the mortgages, to raise cash so you can loan out more mortgage money. We'll guarantee the pool, so investors will buy the certificates without worry." The packager of the mortgage pool then "passes through" the mortgage payments he receives to certificate holders.

Why should you buy a Ginny Mae Pass-through instead of a corporate bond? Well, it does give you a way of spreading a portion of your money into mortgages without any of the worries of collecting payments, defaults, or bookkeeping. Full payments, on time, are "backed by the full faith and credit of the United States Government," and no corporate bond can make that statement. Bonds can be called back by the issuer, some within 5 years of issuance date, and you would lose the high interest return you were counting on. Ginny Mae certificates usually assure you rates for 12 years.

But perhaps most important, you are buying a mortgage, and the pool sponsor sends you a monthly check. Part of the payment represents interest and part return of your principal. (The principal portion, since it is a return of your capital, is not taxed as income.) With a bond, of course, you have to wait until it matures before your principal is returned. This feature may be of special value to you if you are retired and need a monthly check. If you do not need to use the earnings for monthly expenses, you can reinvest. The effect of monthly compounding is a return higher than that of a bond that pays the same return but sends you interest checks only twice a year.

If you are receiving, for example, 7.7 percent monthly from a Ginny Mae Pass-through, this would be equivalent to a corporate bond paying 8.25 percent from a semiannual coupon payment.

A number of firms make a secondary market in Ginny Maes so there is no liquidity problem. There is the risk, however, that interest rates may go up. Therefore, since a prospective buyer can get a higher return if he buys a new pass-through instead of yours, your certificate will bring a lower figure than you paid for it. If the interest rate goes down, the reverse occurs and your pass-through can probably be sold for more than you paid for it.

Municipal Bonds • Municipal bonds (or notes) are issued by local governments (cities, states, and various districts and political subdivisions) instead of the federal government and its agencies. Municipals usually, but not always, provide lower returns or yields than government bonds, primarily because of the special feature they provide: The interest paid on municipal obligations is totally exempt from federal income tax. (I will cover them in more detail in the chapter entitled "Avoiding the One-way Trip to Washington.")

Yields on municipal issues are determined by the current level of interest rates, the credit rating of the issuer, and the tax laws.

Most municipal bonds are issued in serial form, some maturing each year for several years, with maturities as high as 30 years. Interest is normally paid semiannually. Investors tend to buy them as they are issued and hold them until maturity. However, municipals, like other bonds, can be sold prior to maturity in the secondary market at the then prevailing market rates. Such a sale may result in a return greater or less than the yield at acquisition.

• CORPORATE BONDS

Another way you may want to consider lending your money is through the purchase of corporate bonds. Corporate bonds (or notes) can be classified into a number of subcategories depending on the type of corporation issuing the bond, but from your point of view, there are essentially only two types: straight bonds and convertible bonds. Straight corporate bonds, like most government and municipal bonds, pay semi-annual interest to maturity, whereupon you receive the principal amount. Convertible bonds offer one additional feature: They can be exchanged, at any time you wish, for a fixed number of shares of the issuing company's common stock. Therefore, convertibles have dual characteristics—as fixed-income securities (like any other bonds) and as equity securities that may appreciate (or depreciate) in accordance with the stock price movement of the company's common stock. If a convertible bond trades at a price above that which it would as a straight bond for the same company, maturity, etc., it is usually thought of as an equity security rather than as a bond.

Corporate bonds are usually sold in minimum amounts of $1000, although there are some $500 bonds. The yield is subject to the current level of interest rates, the maturity, and the credit standing of the issuer. Because no corporation is considered to be as creditworthy as the federal government, corporate bonds generally pay a slightly higher return—usually ½ percent to 2 percent higher—than comparable government bonds. Obviously, even when comparing one corporation to another, some are riskier and therefore have to pay more to borrow money. There were times, such as in the mid-1970s, when low-rated bonds, commonly called "junk bonds," reached yields as high as 14 percent to 16 percent. Like other bonds, corporates can be sold prior to maturity at prevailing market rates.

Bonds are issued in registered form "interest mailed to holder" or in bearer form with coupons to be clipped and mailed to paying agent through bearer's bank connection. Many bonds permit the issuing corporation to redeem them early, usually for a price slightly higher than the maturity value. This call privilege gives the borrower an element of protection, in that he can call in his bonds and issue new ones at a lower interest rate if rates have declined since the time the original bonds were issued. Actually, only bonds trading at a premium over par (indicating that interest yields are now lower than they were at time of issue) are liable to be called.

You will want to become familiar with corporate bonds because they can be extremely useful in short-term financial planning. Bonds can be a safe short-term investment. If history repeats itself, they can become long-term speculations.

Bonds can be considered as a possible investment vehicle when stock market prices are historically high. When the market reaches a low price–earnings level and your financial objective is growth of capital, you should then consider selling them and moving into the stock market.

Let's assume the market is presently at a high level, and you desire to buy a bond. You will need to know about the issuer. The best source of this information is either Moody's or Standard and Poor's ratings. This will tell you their opinion of the company's ability to meet its principal and interest payments under adverse economic conditions. Two measures of this ability are the amount by which earnings exceed interest payments over a period of years and the amount of stock equity in a corporation in relation to borrowed funds.

If these rating services rate a bond in one of the top four categories, the bond is considered to be of investment-grade quality. To merit the very top rating, the speculative element is considered to be almost nonexistent. By the fifth rating, the speculative element has become quite significant, and by the seventh rating, the speculative element predominates.

Assume you have decided on an "A" rated bond and have selected a bond of the XYZ Corporation. Assume further that it is a 20-year bond bearing an 8½ percent interest rate. You would then receive $85 per year on your $1000 investment (if bought at par) for a period of 20 years, and at the end of the 20 years, if you still hold the bond, you would receive back your $1000 principal. If you wanted your $1000 prior to the twentieth year, you could sell your bond in the open market in much the same way that you would sell a stock. As with stocks, bonds on the open market are worth only what others will pay for them. In the bond market, buyers are usually willing to pay prices that closely coincide with the prevailing interest rate. If that rate were to remain at 8½ percent, then a bond with an income of $85 a year would continue to have a market value of $1000, and you would break even when you sold (exclusive of any commissions). But if the prevailing interest rate were to rise to 9½ percent after one year, an income of

$85 a year would no longer be worth $1000. In order to yield 9½ percent, the XYZ bond with $85 a year income would sell for about $913. And if the prevailing interest rate should decline, say, from 8½ to 7½ percent, a buyer would have to pay about $1100 for an income of $85 a year. Or you could sell your bond for about $1100. In other words, in this example (with an 8½ percent bond 19 years from maturity), an increase of one percentage point in the general interest rate would give you a loss of about $87, while a decrease of one percentage point in the general interest rate would give you a profit of about $100.

In capsule form, this is how all bonds work. Because they represent a fixed stream of income, their market value will fall when the general interest rate rises and their market value will rise when the interest falls.

Suffice it to say that although most bonds are issued at par of $1000 and may sell there or at a premium or discount on the day they are issued and will be redeemed at par on the day of maturity, their market value wanders considerably during the interim. Because the cost of money has risen so dramatically since the mid-1960s, the market values of virtually all bonds issued prior to that time have declined to well below their $1000 face values. This kind of market risk in the bond market is very real and exists regardless of the credit-worthiness of the borrower.

Bond interest rates fluctuate for a number of reasons. Probably chief among them during the past few years has been price inflation and expectations of future inflation. As inflation rates increase, consumers and businesses are willing to increase their borrowing to buy at today's lower prices, and individuals become less willing to save at existing interest rate levels. Therefore, interest rates rise to compensate the saver for the expected erosion in the purchasing power of the dollar and to wipe out the advantage to the borrower of speeding up his purchases.

Another key factor has been the policy of the Federal Reserve to control the supply of money—increasing and decreasing it in an effort to either stimulate or decelerate the economy. In the short run, an acceleration in the rate of growth of the money supply will produce lower interest rates, but over time it has promoted a higher rate of inflation that has resulted in higher interest rates.

Fluctuation of economic activity also has influenced interest rates. The demand for credit rises as economic activity picks up, and therefore interest rates tend to rise; the demand for credit falls as economic activity slows, and this pushes interest rates down.

• CORPORATE BOND
FUNDS

If you have limited funds, it will be difficult for you to buy and sell small quantities of bonds because of the spread between "bid" and "asked" prices in these small purchases. It is also difficult to diversify adequately. For this reason you may want to use professionally managed corporate bond funds. They offer a savings of the time and talent required to judge the merits of individual issues, their ratings, their maturities, coupon rates, a determination of how much to invest in each issue, the clipping of coupons (it has always sounded like fun, but it's really quite a nuisance), watching for called bonds, safekeeping securities, and year-end accounting.

The specialists managing the fund select the bonds to obtain a special combination of yield, proper diversification, marketability, suitability, and call protection. They also follow the financial progress of all the issues in the fund. You pay an initial sales charge, which is included in the offering price, plus a management fee of around one-half of 1 percent annually of the net asset value on the fund.

Current market prices are published daily, and you can redeem your shares whenever you desire.

• MUNICIPALS, MUNICIPAL BOND FUNDS,
MUNICIPAL BOND TRUSTS

You may invest in individual municipal bonds that you select or let the professionals do it for you through municipal bond funds or municipal bond trusts. Both offer diversification and professional selection. The bond fund also offers management, for a fee, after selection.

The bond trusts are the oldest form, and only after the changes made by the Tax Reform Act of 1976 did municipal bond funds come into being. Since then they have burst forth from many management groups, so a wide variety of choices is now available. Study both and see which, if either, fits your needs.

Should you invest in municipal bonds? Your answer will depend on a number of things. First of all, what do you plan to do with the money if you don't put it into municipal bonds? If you are in a tax bracket in excess of 30 percent, you may obtain more spendable income in municipals than in corporate bonds or savings accounts. Table 3–1 shows the approximate taxable bond yields that are equivalent to tax-exempt bond yields from 4 percent to 8 percent under our present federal tax laws.

Table 3–1.

Joint return [Taxable income]*	Single return*	Income tax bracket	TAX-EXEMPT YIELD Equivalent taxable yield						
			4%	5%	5½%	6%	6½%	7%	8%
$ 20– 24,000	$ 14– 16,000	31%	5.80%	7.25%	7.97%	8.70%	9.42%	10.14%	11.59%
	$ 16– 18,000	32%	5.88	7.34	8.07	8.82	9.56	10.29	11.76
	$ 18– 20,000	34%	6.06	7.58	8.34	9.09	9.85	10.61	12.12
$ 24– 28,000	$ 20– 22,000	36%	6.25	7.81	8.59	9.38	10.16	10.94	12.50
		38%	6.45	8.07	8.87	9.68	10.48	11.29	12.90
$ 28– 32,000		39%	6.56	8.20	9.02	9.84	10.66	11.48	13.11
	$ 22– 26,000	40%	6.67	8.33	9.17	10.00	10.83	11.67	13.33
$ 32– 36,000		42%	6.90	8.64	9.51	10.34	11.21	12.07	13.79
$ 36– 40,000	$ 26– 32,000	45%	7.27	9.09	10.00	10.91	11.82	12.73	14.55
$ 40– 44,000		48%	7.69	9.61	10.57	11.54	12.50	13.46	15.38
$ 44– 52,000	$ 32– 38,000	50%	8.00	10.00	11.00	12.00	13.00	14.00	16.00
$ 52– 64,000		53%	8.51	10.63	11.69	12.77	13.83	14.89	17.02
$ 64– 76,000	$ 38– 44,000	55%	8.89	11.11	12.22	13.33	14.44	15.56	17.78
$ 76– 88,000		58%	9.52	11.90	13.09	14.29	15.48	16.67	19.05
$ 88–100,000	$ 44– 50,000	60%	10.00	12.50	13.75	15.00	16.25	17.50	20.00
$100–120,000	$ 50– 60,000	62%	10.53	13.17	14.49	15.79	17.11	18.42	21.05
$120–140,000	$ 60– 70,000	64%	11.11	13.89	15.28	16.67	18.06	19.44	22.22
$140–160,000	$ 70– 80,000	66%	11.76	14.70	16.17	17.65	19.12	20.59	23.53
$160–180,000	$ 80– 90,000	68%	12.50	15.62	17.18	18.75	20.31	21.88	25.00
$180–200,000	$ 90–100,000	69%	12.90	16.12	17.73	19.35	20.97	22.58	25.81
$200,000 & over	$100,000 & over	70%	13.33	16.67	18.33	20.00	21.67	23.33	26.67

* Net amount subject to federal income tax after deductions and exemptions.

• BONDS AND INFLATION

Bonds give us one of the clearest examples of how inflation creates and destroys wealth. Let's take the example of a AAA-rated American Telephone and Telegraph bond so highly recommended for widows and orphans issued in 1946 at par ($1000) with a rate of 2⅝ percent maturing in 1986. True to their promise, AT&T has never missed paying $26.25 annually on this bond, and in 1986 will faithfully pay the owner $1000. However, if the widow needs her funds today, its market price is only $700.

What happened? Why did the AT&T bonds which were recommended as "prudent" investments by banks and trust companies for widows and orphans turn out so dismally? AT&T was not trying to take advantage of anyone. They didn't force investors to buy 2⅝ percent bonds. They themselves didn't realize what a bonanza they would reap. The real reason that the widows were hurt and AT&T was helped was that inflation greatly accelerated, bringing disastrous results to the bondholder.

American Telephone and Telegraph bonds are rated AAA, the highest-quality rating, yet they did drop tremendously in value. However, their drop was minor in comparison to bonds with lower ratings and therefore considered riskier. Two examples of these are

1 • Bonds issued by Pan American World Airways, at 4½ percent, with maturity in 1986, dropped from a par of $1000 to $515.

2 • Bonds issued by Eastern Airlines, at 5 percent, with maturity in 1992, dropped from a $1000 par to $535.

Inflation transfers wealth from the lender to the borrower. The bondholder is hurt in two ways. He is receiving less in terms of interest than he could on newly issued securities. Also, since the market value of the bond has fallen, he has suffered a decline in wealth.

Under the Poor Richard rules of yesteryears, bonds were investment vehicles that you put at the bottom of your safe-deposit box, whose coupons you clipped semiannually, and which you redeemed on redemption date. Although not exciting, these rules were fine when prices were stable.

History shows that bonds have been a bad buy even if your investment horizons are relatively short. Periods when inflation has been accelerating have lasted longer than periods in which inflation rates decelerated.

You should not plan to hold bonds to maturity. Only in a world of no inflation does a buy-and-hold posture make sense. Bonds are debt. Therefore, inflation-induced wealth transfer occurs quickly in the bond market. Bonds, if bought at all, should be bought when interest rates are at their highest—their maturities long-term.

During the 1974 market decline there developed a tremendous interest in bonds and bond funds paying around 9 percent. A large number of both were placed with investors at the investors' insistence. Let's look at the long-term effect that inflation can have on these bond yields.

Are High-yielding Investments Really the Answer to Inflation? • According to the Consumer Price Index of the Bureau of Labor and the University of Chicago Center for Research:

1 • The cost of living increased at a compound rate of 10.5 percent per year during 1973–74.

2 • Over the past 10 years the rate of inflation has been 5.2 percent.

3 • The projected average rate of inflation through the year 2000 is 6.2 percent.

The long-term effect of inflation on income from fixed-yield investments such as bonds can be devastating. Table 3–2 illustrates the loss of pur-

Table 3–2. The Effect of a 5.2% Inflation on Your Purchasing Power

Number of years	Annual dividend	Loss of purchasing power (%)	Adjusted purchasing power of dividend	Effective yield
5	$900	16%	$756	7.5%
10	900	40%	540	5.4%
15	900	53%	423	4.2%
20	900	64%	324	3.2%
25	900	72%	252	2.5%

chasing power and effective yield of a $10,000 investment in a corporate bond with a yield of 9 percent, if that yield is adjusted for an annual inflation rate of 5.2 percent, the rate of the past 10 years, and not the 6.2 percent projected.

If it were possible to have a "floating" or "self-adjusting" yield based on the annual rate of inflation, Table 3–3 illustrates the yields that you

Table 3–3. Percentage Yield Needed to Maintain Purchasing Power

Number of years	% increase in cost of living	% yield needed to maintain purchasing power
5	28%	11.5%
10	66%	14.9%
15	114%	19.3%
20	176%	24.8%
25	255%	31.9%

would need to maintain your purchasing power, based on a beginning yield of 9 percent with 5.2 percent annual inflation for 25 years.

• CREDIT UNIONS

I find many of my clients who work for corporations, the city, or our public schools use their credit union for a portion of their savings dollar. You may have a credit union available to you. It can be extremely handy for making deposits. In fact, your company may offer the service of depositing the amount you designate directly into your account. The credit union also provides a handy way to borrow.

I find, however, that many mistakenly think that they offer a less expensive way to borrow. This often is not true. Many credit unions charge 1 percent of the unpaid monthly balance, which is 12 percent per annum. Others charge three-quarters of 1 percent. This amounts to 9 percent. If you have acceptable collateral, you can usually borrow at a lower cost from your banker.

• MORTGAGES

Another way to lend money is to carry the mortgage balance on a home or other real estate you are selling. There are many who consider this quite an acceptable way to lend money. On the whole, I would not agree. The rates are frozen throughout the life of the mortgage, and the mortgage is an illiquid instrument except when sold at a considerable discount. As inflation continues its upward thrust, your wealth will be transferred to the person who bought your real estate, and you will have lost the battle with inflation.

If you are selling a piece of property and are convinced that the only way you can get the extra few thousands you desire for your property is to take a second lien for that amount, go ahead and do so. If you collect on the loan, fine. If you do not, don't worry, for you could not have sold it for the full amount you desired anyway. I have done this when selling my home on two occasions and have received payment on both second liens ahead of schedule and for the full amount.

• HISTORIC RATES
   OF RETURN

The rate of return that you will receive by "lending" your dollars through any of the above methods will vary with economic conditions. Table 3–4 shows yields on various fixed-income instruments over the past 47 years.

Table 3–4. Average Annual Yield on Selected Types of Investments, 1930–1977

Year	Savings accounts in savings associations	Time & savings deposits in commercial banks	United States government bonds	Corporate (aaa) bonds
1930	5.3%	3.9%	3.3%	4.6%
1931	5.1	3.8	3.3	4.6
1932	4.1	3.4	3.7	5.0
1933	3.4	3.4	3.3	4.5
1934	3.5	3.0	3.1	4.0
1935	3.1	2.6	2.8	3.6
1936	3.2	2.0	2.6	3.2
1937	3.5	1.8	2.7	3.3
1938	3.5	1.7	2.6	3.2
1939	3.4	1.6	2.4	3.0
1940	3.3	1.3	2.2	2.8
1941	3.1	1.3	2.0	2.8
1942	3.0	1.1	2.5	2.8
1943	2.9	0.9	2.5	2.7
1944	2.8	0.9	2.5	2.7

Table 3–4. (*Continued*)

Year	Savings accounts in savings associations	Time & savings deposits in commercial banks	United States government bonds	Corporate (aaa) bonds
1945	2.5	0.8	2.4	2.6
1946	2.2	0.8	2.2	2.5
1947	2.3	0.9	2.2	2.6
1948	2.3	0.9	2.4	2.8
1949	2.4	0.9	2.3	2.7
1950	2.5	0.9	2.3	2.6
1951	2.6	1.1	2.6	2.9
1952	2.7	1.2	2.7	3.0
1953	2.8	1.2	2.9	3.2
1954	2.9	1.3	2.6	2.9
1955	2.9	1.4	2.8	3.1
1956	3.0	1.6	3.1	3.4
1957	3.3	2.1	3.5	3.9
1958	3.38	2.21	3.43	3.79
1959	3.53	2.36	4.07	4.38
1960	3.86	2.56	4.01	4.41
1961	3.90	2.71	3.90	4.35
1962	4.08	3.18	3.95	4.33
1963	4.17	3.31	4.00	4.26
1964	4.19	3.42	4.15	4.40
1965	4.23	3.69	4.21	4.49
1966	4.45	4.04	4.66	5.13
1967	4.67	4.24	4.85	5.51
1968	4.68	4.48	5.25	6.18
1969	4.80	4.87	6.10	7.03
1970	5.06	4.95	6.59	8.04
1971	5.33	4.78	5.74	7.39
1972	5.40	4.65	5.63	7.21
1973	5.55	5.71	6.30	7.44
1974	5.98	6.93	6.99	8.57
1975	6.22	5.90	6.98	8.83
1976	5.25	5.00	6.98	8.01
1977	5.25	5.00	6.98	8.08

Sources: Federal Home Loan Bank Board; United States Savings and Loan League; National Association of Mutual Savings Banks; Federal Reserve Board; Federal Deposit Insurance Corporation; Moody's Investors Service.

Fixed-income securities may be safe short-term investments and risky long-term investments. In all of the twenty-two 10-year periods from 1945 through 1975 there was not one period when the Standard & Poor's rated composite of high-grade corporate bonds did not show a loss. These losses ranged from 2 percent to 38 percent; see Table 3–5.

What has happened to the market value of high grade corporate bonds in the past? Table 3–5 shows the long term effect of increasing interest rates on the market value of high grade corporate bonds.

Table 3–5. Standard and Poor's High-Grade Corporate Bonds 10 Year-Periods

Period	Loss
1966–75	−38%
1965–74	−41%
1964–73	−34%
1963–72	−32%
1962–71	−29%
1961–70	−32%
1960–69	−33%
1959–68	−27%
1958–67	−28%
1957–66	−19%
1956–65	−19%
1966–64	−18%
1954–63	−16%
1953–62	−15%
1952–61	−17%
1951–60	−22%
1950–59	−25%
1949–58	−17%
1948–57	−11%
1947–56	−16%
1946–55	− 8%
1945–54	− 2%

Average of 22 periods   −23%

Source: Johnson's Charts, Inc.—bond interest not included.

• CASH SURRENDER VALUE

Another way that many families lend money, probably without realizing it, is by banking with life insurance companies by buying protection that contains a savings program. Of all the ways that you can "lend" money, this is perhaps the least rewarding. The policy does indicate earnings of 2½ percent to 3½ percent on the cash reserve, but if the policyholder dies, his family receives only the face amount, not the face amount plus the savings account. I counsel with many who are under the impression that the face amount plus "their" savings account goes to their beneficiary. The estate planner, Norman F. Dacey, has published a pamphlet entitled "To the Great Northern Insurance Company I Bequeath the Cash Value of All My Life Insurance Policies." It makes provocative reading.

•   ANNUITIES

Annuities are another way some choose to save for the future. What about annuities? Should you take the beautiful full-page color ads in your weekly magazines seriously and "invest" in an annuity for your happy golden years?

The best answer to this question can be found by looking at the past advertisements of insurance companies trying to entice you to buy an annuity. Go to your local library and request that they bring to you their *Life* magazines. You might start with the February 1, 1943, issue. There you will find a half-page ad with a bold headline that reads, "$150 a Month as Long as You Live." The familiar logo at the bottom reads "_____Mutual Retirement Income Plan Guarantees Your Future." The fine print does not say how much you would need to invest to retire at 60 with $150 per month, but it does hint that the smiling couple in the picture began at age 40, 20 years previous to the time it showed them in happy retirement. Now ask the librarian for the January 16, 1950, issue of *Life*. It also carried an ad by the same company headlined "How We Retired with $200 a Month." The ad shows another mature, well-dressed couple. There are a sandy beach and waving palm trees in the background. This one also does not mention the amount of investment that they would have had to make over that period of time. The same logo appears, however: "_____Mutual Retirement Income Plan Guarantees Your Future."

Now ask for the January 15, 1951, issue of *Life*. It carried the *identical* picture as the January 16, 1950, ad, the same script, except the headline had been changed to "How We Retired with $250 a Month." Yes, it had the same guarantee at the bottom. The January 23, 1956, *Life* magazine ran another ad by the same insurance company. This headline read "How a Man of 35 Can Retire at 55 with $300 a Month." This time they did not even bother to change the picture of the smiling, delighted couple. The inflation train continues to run faster and faster, but the ad department seems to be able to keep up by increasing the ante each time.

"Retire on $150 a Month" sounded pretty good back then, so this dollar figure was commonly used in offering fixed-dollar retirement plans. But the story kept changing. The changes in these figures provide unique evidence that there is no such thing as a "guaranteed," "riskless" way to achieve financial independence.

Have you ever wondered why the annuity ads often show a man fishing? Do you think it's because he wants to eat?

• **DEFERRED
ANNUITIES**

These annuities are a different breed entirely from the old annuity contracts and can play an important part in your "guaranteed" dollar investment program.

If you feel that you must have your funds guaranteed, are in a tax bracket of 25 percent or above, and do not plan to disturb the funds for a few years, then you may went to consider a fixed deferred annuity. Rates the past few years have ranged between 7 and 8 percent, and your funds compound tax-deferred until withdrawal.

Table 3–6 gives an example of the difference tax deferral can make

Table 3–6. Hypothetical Examples of $10,000 Accounts

| No. of Years | $10,000 at 6% interest (Interest taxed as accrued) | | $10,000 Single Premium Fixed Annuity (Interest accumulates without current tax) |
	50% Tax Bracket	30% Tax Bracket	@ 7% °
5	$11,593	$12,284	$ 14,026
10	13,439	15,090	19,672
15	15,580	18,536	27,590
20	18,061	22,770	38,697
25	20,938	27,970	54,274
30	24,273	34,358	76,123
35	28,139	42,206	106,766
40	32,620	51,845	149,745

° Assumes level 7 percent interest throughout life of contract.

in your accumulation program at a fixed rate of 7 percent on your annuity and 6 percent on a taxable savings account.

Other characteristics of the single-premium fixed annuity that can be valuable to you in your long-range financial planning are

1 · The principal is guaranteed and liquid at all times.

2 · Interest is guaranteed according to the contract. Each year the current rate is stated. For example, the rate this year may be 7½ percent. The rates for future years are determined by the going rates, but you are guaranteed a minimum. Minimums could run as follows:

Years	Rate
1, 2	6¾%
3, 4, 5	6%
6, 7, 8, 9, 10	5%
after	3½%

3 · Contracts are issued in lump sums, called single-premium deferred annuities, or they may be set up to add to monthly. A typical lump sum would have a minimum of $1500 investment and a maximum of $250,000. On a monthly fixed annuity there is an excellent company that will accept as small an amount as $10 per month.

    You may also invest in variable annuities. Typically three choices are offered: (1) growth equity funds, (2) income-growth funds, or (3) bond funds. Free exchanges may be made between these.

4 · Probate with its publicity, delays, and costs can be avoided by using annuities. The proceeds are paid directly to the beneficiary.

5 · Tax benefits
    a. All income accumulates without tax during the deferred period.
    b. No income tax is payable until the withdrawals equal the full original investment.
    c. Favorable tax treatment is accorded if held to retirement and "annuitized"—meaning that the holder commences to receive regular annuity payments.
    d. Tax-free exchange can be made among the various money pools and the proceeds can also be moved to the annuity of another company without incurring a tax.

• SHOULD YOU EVER BORROW MONEY?

Should you ever consider reversing the "lending" process and being the recipient? Of course you should, if you can put the money to work so that your after-tax cost is less than the amount you will earn on the investment you made with the loan.

In fact, in these days of high taxes it is difficult to accumulate a large estate without borrowing money. The great financier Bernard Baruch, when asked how he made his fortune, replied, "O.P.M.—other people's money."

Where, when, and how should you borrow money?

If you have collateral in the form of publicly traded stocks, your least expensive source for loans in normal times will usually be your own bank. You should go to the collateral loan department (never to the consumer loan department unless you lack collateral).

Assume that you want to buy an automobile. You own 100 shares of an excellent stock for which you paid $50 a share, and it is now trading at $100 with excellent growth potential for the future. Why kill the goose that is laying the golden egg, and why realize a $5000 capital gain on which you will be required to pay federal income taxes?

Take your stock to your banker and pledge it as collateral. You will be required to leave the stock certificate with him and sign a stock power that allows him to sell the stock and keep the amount you owe to him if you do not repay or renew the loan the day it becomes due.

Collateral loans are usually made for 90 days or 180 days. You may pay on the principal in the interim, but you are not required to do so. On the date the loan becomes due you will be required to send your banker a check for the interest, and you may, if you desire, send him a letter requesting that he renew the loan. Usually this will be acceptable to your banker, for banks must lend money to earn a profit. They have already made a credit check on you and found you acceptable.

Sometimes you'll get a rookie loan officer who learned at banking school that borrowers should be reducing their principal periodically. However, after a little discussion with him as to how banks make their profit, he usually will be quite agreeable to renewing your note.

Always go boldly to borrow money—not with head bowed in an apologetic manner. If your banker had a house to rent and you were considering renting one, in what posture would go you to him? In this instance you have come to do him the "favor" of renting his money so that he can make a profit.

Your banker is always happy to rent you money if you can prove you don't need it. What is your proof that you really don't need it? Your stock certificate, of course, for you obviously could sell the stock and have the money.

Another reason for borrowing on your stock rather than cashing it in is that you are more likely to repay the bank than yourself. For example, you want to buy an automobile, but you don't have that amount in savings. Make a collateral loan to pay for the auto. Then when you finish paying the bank the loan, you will have your auto and your stock.

Build up your collateral and you'll always have the wherewithal for borrowing money that you can put to work. You may want to consider, if you have the temperament for it, putting your dollars to work 1 and 7/10 times—since 70 percent is what your banker will usually loan you on collateral.

Interest Deductible • Interest is deductible on your income tax return with certain limitations under the Tax Reform Act of 1976. Assume you borrow at 10 percent and are in the 30 percent tax bracket; your net cost after taxes will be 7 percent. If you are in the 50 percent bracket, net cost is only 5 percent. Can you invest this money so that your after-tax return will be greater than your after-tax cost? If so, rent the money. If not, your answer is obvious.

Savings Accounts as Collateral • I find that often a person with whom I'm counseling proudly tells me he has found an inexpensive source for a loan by pledging his savings account as collateral. If you need funds and you have them in a savings account, go ahead and draw them out and use them. They are probably paying you 2 percent less than they are charging you; therefore you are 2 percent in the hole by borrowing your own money.

An exception to this would be if you are very near a dividend date. For example, assume that you have a one-year $10,000 certificate of deposit with a rate of 6 percent that matures December 31. You need funds on November 1. Use your certificate of deposit for collateral. You'll pay them interest at 8 percent for two months, but they'll pay you interest at 6 percent for 12 months: $10,000 @ 6 percent for 12 months equals $600. $10,000 @ 8 percent equals $800 ÷ 12 months = $66.66 × 2 months equals $133.32. Therefore, you still salvage $466.68 of your interest and have the funds you need. This $133.32 is deductible on your income tax. (But the $600 is taxable.)

If your certificate of deposit or savings account is at a bank, you can usually borrow 100 percent. If it is in a savings and loan, they will usually loan 90 percent.

Servicing the Loan • You will need sufficient funds or income to pay your interest on your loan when due. There are some investments that have a high after-tax yield that you can use to service your loan while you are enjoying equity buildup and appreciation.

Borrowing Against Cash Value of an Insurance Policy • There are many who consider this a low-cost source of loans. In my opinion, the only time you should borrow on your cash surrender value is when your health is so poor that you cannot pass a physical for a new policy. If you can pass a physical and obtain pure protection at a lower cost, do so. When you have the new coverage, redeem the old policy. You will then have the cash you need without paying the insurance company to borrow your own money.

If your health is such that you cannot pass a physical, borrow the money each year from your policy and put it to work advantageously. Let's assume that you can borrow the cash surrender value for 5½ percent. Technically, at the same time, they claim to be paying you approximately 2½ percent on the cash reserves. This is only a 3 percent spread. In addition, the interest is deductible, thereby lowering your after-tax cost.

• MONEY MARKET
   FUNDS

You might be asking what do I consider the best way to position funds that you desire to hold as cash reserves or to have available when the right investment is available. In my opinion, one of the best ways is through the use of money market funds.

Money market funds came into existence when the Federal Reserve greatly diminished the money supply, pushing up interest rates. Those who had $100,000 or more could obtain yields of 12 percent and above from savings institutions, but those who did not were prevented from obtaining these rates by federal regulation.

Consequently, a number of the mutual fund managements offered the smaller investor a way he could obtain the rate of a million-dollar certificate of deposit by pooling his funds with others.

When you use these money pools, you receive the highest interest available on high-quality money market instruments such as large certificates of deposit of major national commercial banks and government agencies. Many of these instruments that pay higher yields are available only in such large denominations that you could not obtain them on your own.

You may use the fund as an interest-bearing checking account, and, if it is offered by a family of mutual funds, you can quickly go from a liquid position to an equity position in one of their stock or bond funds and return without a commission when the exchange is made.

There is no commission to place funds into the money market fund and no commission to take it out. You will be poised daily to receive the highest interest rates being paid for million-dollar certificates while being able to write a check on the account in the amount of $500 or more. In my opinion, money market funds eliminate the need for long-term certificates of deposit, because here you have liquidity without a penalty for early withdrawal, have check-writing privileges, and receive the going interest rate. During periods when the Federal Reserve is following an easy money policy your rate will drop as the large short-term certificates drop, but when money is tight you may obtain the same rate as a millionaire.

• SUMMARY

Should you ever put your dollars in a "loaned" position? Yes, if you need a temporary place for your investment dollars or when interest rates reach the astronomical heights they did in 1974 (12 to 13 percent on 30-day, $100,000 certificates of deposit). But you should rarely do so on a long-term basis. As you can see from Table 3–4, over the past 10 years you would have suffered a loss if you had held bonds and other fixed-dollar instruments for long periods of time. Interest rates have risen, and inflation has taken its toll. You should use fixed-income instruments when it is to your advantage to be out of equities, but do not complacently overstay.

On the other hand, should you ever do the reverse and borrow money? The answer is yes, if your return is greater than your after-tax cost and if you can sell your investment for more than you owe. Always be solvent.

Application

1 • How much "patting money" do you need for peace of mind?
2 • Is the Federal Reserve expanding or shrinking the money supply at this time?
3 • What is a good source for this information?
4 • How can you best put this knowledge to use?

5 · Where should your cash reserve be placed?

6 · What is the rate being paid by money market funds today?

7 · Can you borrow money and still have peace of mind?

8 · What collateral do you have?

9 · What steps do you plan to take to build up your collateral?

4
Stocks and Inflation

In Chapter 2 we determined that the first reason you must learn to invest is to protect your wealth against inflation. Together we accepted the reality that inflation may accelerate and decelerate but that the thrust is always upward. Now that we have accepted this fact of life, what steps can you take to protect yourself?

Over long periods of accelerated inflation we know that investments in fixed guaranteed instruments have failed to preserve your wealth. This means then that you must look to other areas, and the first that comes to mind is shares of the common stock of American industry. You and I are privileged to live in a country where we can own a part of the companies that manufacture our automobiles, provide our telephone services, and package our foods. We can, through an investment in shares of their stock, participate in their profits or lack of profits.

Have stocks been a good hedge against inflaiton? The answer is that in the long term the answer has been Yes. In the short term the answer may have been No, as demonstrated by the 1969–1974 period.

First let's look at the long term and see if stocks have offered that hedge.

72

• STOCKS—A LONG-TERM HEDGE?

One Hundred Years • In 1977 the Anchor Corporation made a comprehensive study of the stock market and its correlation to inflation covering a 105-year span. They wanted to answer three questions:

1 • Have common stocks provided an adequate hedge against rising living costs?

2 • Has income from common stocks offset rising living costs, and, if so, how adequately?

3 • How have common stock prices and dividends behaved, compared to living costs during periods of inflation?

They made no assumptions, nor do I, about any possible correlation among past experience and future common stock prices, dividends, and living costs, or any recommendations as to whether an individual should invest in stocks.

The charts in Fig. 4–1 are reprinted with their permission from *The Long View.*

How Often Have Investors Faced Inflation? • In answer to the question of how often investors have faced inflation in the past century, the Anchor Corporation found the following: Living costs rose in 63 percent of the one-year periods, 67 percent of the 10-year periods, 74 percent of the 15-year periods, 80 percent of the 20-year periods, and 95 percent of the 30-year spans. From these graphic percentages you can see that over a 20-year span, inflation has been experienced 80 percent of the time and over 30-year spans, nearly all of the time.

How Have Stocks Behaved During Inflation? • In answer to this question, survey findings indicate that stock prices rose in 67 percent of the one-year inflationary periods and in 9 out of 10 of the longer periods of rising costs. In the past century common stocks have increased in value in 96 percent of the 20-year periods and in all 30-year periods of rising costs.

Have Stock Prices Increased as Much as Living Costs? • The study revealed that increases in stock prices equaled or exceeded increases in the cost of living 71 percent of all 10-year periods, 82 percent of all 15-year periods, 91 percent of all 20-year periods, and 92 percent of all 30-year periods.

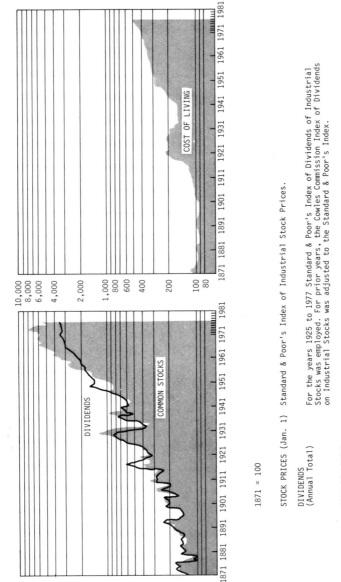

1871 = 100

STOCK PRICES (Jan. 1)   Standard & Poor's Index of Industrial Stock Prices.

DIVIDENDS   For the years 1925 to 1977 Standard & Poor's Index of Dividends of Industrial
(Annual Total)   Stocks was employed. For prior years, the Cowles Commission Index of Dividends
                        on Industrial Stocks was adjusted to the Standard & Poor's Index.

COST OF LIVING   The U.S. Bureau of Labor Statistics Index of Living Costs (annual average)
(Annual Average)   is used continuosly throughout the study.

© Anchor Corporation, March, 1977

FIGURE 4-1.   Common Stock Prices and Dividends vs. the Cost of Living

How Have Common Stock Prices Behaved During Times of Deflation?
• In 54 percent of the one-year periods of deflation, stock prices also declined in value. But they declined in only 34 percent of the 10-year periods and 13 percent of the 15-year periods.

Over long spans of deflation, the investor has been more likely to profit from common stock investments than to suffer loss. Over 20-year periods of declining living costs, the investor has experienced rising stock values more than eight times out of ten. Since 1871, common stock prices increased during both of the 30-year spans of deflation.

Moreover, when stock prices have declined during periods of deflation, the decline has generally been less than that in the cost of living.

How Have Dividends Behaved During Inflation? • Dividends increased in 74 percent of the one-year periods, 95 percent of the 10-year periods, 90 percent of the 15-year periods, and 100 percent of the 20- and 30-year periods.

How Have Dividends Behaved During Deflation? • Dividends rose in 46 percent of the one-year periods of deflation, decreased in 42 percent, and remained unchanged in 12 percent. Dividends rose in 66 percent of the 10-year periods of deflation, 61 percent of the 15-year periods, and 81 percent of the 20-year spans. Since 1871, dividends increased in both 30-year periods of deflation.

University of Chicago Study • According to a comprehensive study done by the Center For Research and Security Prices at the University of Chicago, an investment in a random cross section of stocks on the New York Stock Exchange over a forty-year period would have given you an average rate of return (before taxes) of approximately 9.3 percent a year compounded annually. To translate, an investment of $1000 compound annually at 9.3 percent would have grown to $35,000 in the forty years.

Inflation and Stock Prices—Short Term, Long Term • As you can readily determine from a quick look at the foregoing data, on a day-to-day, or even on a year-to-year, basis, common stock prices do not go hand in hand, month by month, with inflation. As a matter of fact, in the short term, they often go in opposite directions. The market likes certainties. As I mentioned, the market can live with good news and can live with bad news, but it has difficulty living without knowing what the news is. Runaway inflation causes excesses and uncertainty that can adversely affect short-term market conditions. However, over the long term, in the past, a good cross section of quality stocks has given your capital, and the income it produces, a chance to grow to offset the inroads of inflation.

• STOCKS—A SHORT-TERM HEDGE?

In the 1950s and the 1960s, if you had asked any knowledgeable financial planner how to hedge your wealth against inflation, he would have given you one primary bit of advice—buy common stocks. During that period of time, he would have been right, for stocks were super investments and on the whole, outperformed anything else in which you could have conveniently invested. This was the period in which, for the first time, American Telephone and Telegraph invested their pension money in common stocks and were joined by the American public who were setting aside dollars for retirement.

Everything went smoothly, prices were relatively stable, and the money supply was gradually increased in a fairly consistent and orderly manner.

Then Viet Nam reared its ugly head and the administration tried to become all things to all people, launching a program of warfare and welfare—guns and butter—without being able to face the need for an increase in taxes. To meet the increased costs of a wartime budget, the money supply was allowed to expand. There was no increase in taxes to leaven the number of dollars chasing the same amount of consumer goods. Result: inflation!

Inflation fouled up corporate earnings. Inflation increased interest rates and, even worse, made financing unavailable. When rates are increased, corporate officers must decide if they can pay those rates and still make a profit. When they are told that no money is available, which is what happened during the "money crunch," the conversation is abruptly ended.

Inflation made real profits hard to come by and hard to trust. Corporate taxes were paid on the basis of a sales price based on replacement cost, with no tax credit being allowed for the increased cost of replacing inventory—therefore, after taxes, real wealth was diminished. From 1966 through 1970 corporations were on the wrong side of the inflation-induced income transfers. Wages, services, and construction and borrowing costs inflated, making the cost of staying in business go up and profits go down. Consequently, during those brief years instead of stocks' being a hedge against inflation, stocks bore the brunt of inflation. In the contest of who gets what out of American industry, wages rose and profits declined.

By 1970 wages had caught up with inflation, and inflation began decelerating and brought interest down with it. Corporate profits started up, bringing stock prices with them, and again stocks were a good hedge against inflation.

But 1973 and 1974 brought two-digit inflation, and this time profits were affected. Commodity prices and wholesale prices rose. Again, inflation confused the stock market. This time profits were there, but no one trusted the numbers.

Rising prices create problems for profit reporting. The companies make big gains on products that they already have on hand at the time inflation accelerates. These gains must be reported as profits and are taxed. But business to be ongoing must replace the stock inventory. The profits generated by inventories can't be used otherwise.

Depreciation raises another problem. The cost of replacing equipment is part of the cost of doing business. Inflation causes the depreciation charges to be inadequate to replace equipment, causing profits to be overstated. The crowning blow is that these overstated profits again are taxed.

Inflation also escalates interest rates, making other areas of asset placement seem attractive.

In 1973–74 inflation increased uncertainty and brought fear of recession, fear of financial collapse, fear of worldwide inflation, and a flight from the market.

• TIMING— YOUR KEY

Timing in the market will be a tool you will want to develop. You will want to be invested in stocks when, in your best judgment, the future rate of inflation is less than the rate of inflation that the general public expects. Unless inflation is decelerating or about to decelerate, you will want to be out of the stock market and into short-term money instruments, such as money market funds. One clue is when short-term rates are above long-term rates. Also, the general news and talk on the street will be pessimistic, and there will be more bearish news (downward predictions) about stocks than bullish recommendations (upward predictions).

(If you have trouble with the bulls and bears stock market jargon, remember the bear bears down on his victim. The bull throws his in the air.)

If you have the absolutely necessary temperament for it, you should consider some of the more volatile stocks. Before you buy, do some comprehensive study of the industry you are considering so as to determine the impact that inflation will have. Inflation distorts income statements and balance sheets. Opportunities for profits can be found in interest-rate sensitive stocks when inflation begins to decelerate. You will usually find that most stocks tend to move in the opposite direction from interest rates.

Stocks can help you beat inflation if you will remember that they do best when inflation is decelerating and often do poorly when it is accelerating. Like bonds, stocks should never be put in your safe-deposit box and forgotten. You must be nimble to beat inflation.

In order to be a nimble investor, you will need to know some basic terms of the investment world and the market place. Let's take a look at how and where stocks are traded.

• THE LANGUAGE OF INVESTING

The first information you will need to know is the different kinds of securities. There are basically three with which you'll be concerned. These are

1 • Common stock, which we've just been discussing.

2 • Preferred stock.

3 • Bonds or debentures, which we considered in Chapter 3.

Common Stock • All corporations have common stock. If you organized a corporation for the purpose of buying a popcorn stand at the corner of Main Street and First, and sold one share of common stock to nine persons at $100 per share and one share to yourself at $100, the corporation would have capital of $1000 and ten stockholders. In buying one of these shares you became a shareholder of the corporation. You took an equity position and will participate in the future gains or lack of gains of the corporation for as long as you hold your share.

Preferred Stock • Preferred stock is a stock on which a fixed dividend must be paid before the common shareholder is entitled to a dividend each year. The dividend is usually higher, and if it is a cumulative preferred stock, any past dividends that have been omitted must be paid before the common shareholder is entitled to a dividend. If the preferred is also convertible, it will have a conversion ratio into the common.

There is much confusion about preferred stock. I'm amazed at how the uninitiated seem to feel that "preferred" means "better." This is rarely true. Unless it's convertible, it has neither the growth potential of a common stock nor the safety of a bond. I personally believe there are better ways for an individual to invest.

Bonds or Debentures • The third type of security is the bonds or debentures that we discussed previously. A corporate bond may be a mortgage bond. For example, if you were to invest in a particular railroad bond, you would hold a mortgage on specific freight cars.

A much larger area of the bond market is debentures. Your security for this type of bond is the general credit rating of the issuing corporation. For example, you may buy an American Telephone and Telegraph debenture, at 8.70 percent, due in 2002. In this instance you do not acquire a mortgage on specific telephones, but instead your security is based on the tremendous assets and credit of AT&T.

Characteristics of common stocks and bonds can be oversimplified by stating them in this manner:

Stocks

1 • Not guaranteed as to principal.

2 • Not guaranteed as to rate of return.

3 • Guaranteed to participate in the future destiny of the company.

Bonds

1 • "Guaranteed" as to principal if assets are available.

2 • "Guaranteed" as to rate of return if funds are available.

3 • Not guaranteed to grow, regardless of any increase in the profits of the corporation.

Convertibles • There are those who feel that convertible bonds give the best of two worlds—offering you the third characteristic under stocks, and the first two under bonds; however, they frequently fall short on both scores.

A convertible bond is a bond that usually carries a lower interest rate than a regular corporate bond, but is convertible into common at a specified ratio. For example, if a convertible is bought at par, which in a bond is usually $1000, and is convertible into 100 shares of common at the holder's option and the common is selling at $10, there would be no incentive to exchange, for the bond will usually carry a higher yield than the common. However, if the market price of the common should increase to $15, you would now have a bond with a value of $1500. If, on the other hand, the common goes below $10, you still have your bond with its higher yield acting as a cushion under the bond.

How have they performed? Not well enough for any gold stars. The size and quality of the convertible market has left much to be desired. In severe market declines they have suffered along with their common neighbors.

Our emphasis in this book will be on common stocks, since they offer you the greatest potential for gain (or loss). There is a vast array of stocks, so which ones will be best for you? To shed some light on this subject you will need to know the relationships among earnings, dividends, and yields and what they mean to you.

• "PLAYING THE MARKET"

I often have people come up to me at our seminars or at social occasions and say almost smugly, "I play the market," as if the market were a game. They seem to think I should be pleased and give them a loving pat on the head. Investing is not a game. It is a very exacting art and science that requires skill, training, knowledge, and discipline. Even with these qualifications you will not always be right. This is a very dynamic and fast-moving world we live in, and it changes every minute of every day.

Successful investing is a skill that you must learn yourself or hire the professionals to do it for you. You have no choice. You must save for the future. As you have seen, if you place your money in a fixed, "guaranteed" position, present inflation and the tax bite "guarantee" that you will have

less purchasing power at the end of the year than at the beginning. You'll become like our proverbial little frog without the magic kiss.

To be successful in the stock market, you will need to know how to use the mass network of facilities available to you for trading securities.

Stocks that are publicly held are classified as either listed or unlisted (commonly referred to as over-the-counter). "Listed" means that a stock is listed on a national or regional exchange. Listed stocks represent, in dollar assets, the largest segment of the American economy. There is no asset you own that you can so readily turn into cash as a stock listed on a national exchange. It offers almost instant liquidity.

Our four largest exchanges are the New York Stock Exchange, the American Stock Exchange, the Pacific Stock Exchange, and the Mid-West Stock Exchange.

• THE BIG
BOARD

The New York Stock Exchange is the oldest and largest. It began very informally near the time of the birth of our nation. Our first Secretary of the Treasury needed to set up a monetary system. To have a monetary system in this new nation, he needed to establish banks. To establish banks, he needed stockholders who were willing to invest capital. However, no one was willing to invest capital in bank stocks if there was no way to sell their shares. To make a market for these bank stocks and other issues, a group of 11 men used to meet under a buttonwood tree at the foot of a street called Wall, and trade among themselves and as agents for their clients. They eventually moved inside, and from this humble beginning grew the mighty New York Stock Exchange.

• HOW WALL STREET
GOT ITS NAME

It might interest you to know how Wall Street got its name. The Dutch, who first settled Manhattan Island, were very fond of pork, so they brought hogs from the Netherlands. To confine the hogs they built a wall to make a pig pen—hence the street got its name Wall Street. It's fun to note that some of our stock market history goes back to pigs and hogs. Unfortunately, we still have a few investors who get piggish. It is always good to remember an old saying, "In Wall Street, the bulls sometimes make it and the bears sometimes make it, but the hogs never do." *

* Evan, Esar, *Twenty Thousand Quips and Quotes*. New York: Doubleday, 1968.

• THE OVER-THE-COUNTER
MARKET

Another vast area of the stock market is the "unlisted" market, called the over-the-counter (OTC) market, that has no "counter" or meeting place. Once, I had a lady become confused and ask me for an "under-the-counter" stock. After she told me which stock she had in mind, I decided she had accidentally hit on a good description.

The over-the-counter market is a vast negotiated market. For many years there was no central marketplace for these stocks. Various brokerage houses would "make a market" in a particular stock. This means that they would inventory the stock they bought and sold. There are now over 50,000 stocks traded in the over-the-counter market, through a network of telephone and teletype wires linking the various brokerage houses. There is a daily "pink sheet" giving "bid" and "asked" quotations of the market makers from the previous day reporting to the National Quotation Bureau. ("Bid" means what someone is willing to pay for the stock. "Asked" is the amount for which someone is willing to sell, subject to confirmation or change in price). When you see a market report on a listed stock in the paper, you know that a trade actually took place at that price. In the over-the-counter market, you could have a quote with no trade taking place.

There is a wide range of quality in the stocks traded in the over-the-counter market. Traditionally, bank and insurance company stocks have been traded there, even though they have substantial assets. On the opposite end are "penny stocks" (those that sell for a nominal amount per share), which also trade there.

Often a stock is traded over-the-counter for years, and as it grows in assets and popularity, it may apply for listing on a national exchange and be accepted.

In the past, I have warned that if you are new to the market, you probably should avoid the over-the-counter market until you become more knowledgeable, but with the establishment of NASDAQ, the whole complexion of this market has changed.

• NASDAQ

In February, 1971, the National Association of Security Dealers Advanced Quotations appeared on the scene. Various market makers of OTC stocks feed in the changes in their markets to Bunker-Ramo Central Control, which updates the "bid" and "asked" quotes on each issue every five minutes, showing the best "bid" and "asked" offers available.

NASDAQ has had a profound effect on the OTC market, making current markets available to all parts of the country at the same time and enabling dealers to give prompt and accurate service.

• YOUR BROKERAGE ACCOUNT

How do you use this mass network of facilities? How do you open an account with a stockbroker? It's just as easy as opening a charge account. As a matter of fact, your prospective broker will probably ask fewer questions than the department store where you applied for your last charge account. He will need to know your address, home and office telephone numbers, occupation and company for whom you work, if you are over 21, spouse's name (if married), social security number, if you are a U.S. citizen, bank reference, and how you want your stocks registered.

A good financial planner will ask other information about your assets, your age, your tax bracket, your financial objective, and try to determine your temperament. (A financial planner is a stockbroker but a stockbroker is not necessarily a financial planner—unless—he or she is trained to treat your complete financial planning needs. If in doubt, you may want to choose one that has earned the Certified Financial Planner designation.)

When you make a purchase or sale, it is a firm commitment, regardless of whether the stock goes up or down. A confirmation is mailed to you showing the number of shares of stock purchased or sold, price, commission and fees, net amount due, and settlement date. Within five business days from the trade date you must pay for stocks you have bought. If you have sold a stock, you must deliver your stock certificate within the same period of time to receive payment.

How Your Order Is Executed • After your account has been opened you may place your orders by telephone with your broker and ask him to buy or sell securities for you. For example, let's assume that you place an order to buy 100 shares of General Widgets "at the market." Your broker then gives the order to his company's trader. The trader immediately contacts their floor broker on the floor of the exchange, who quickly walks (it's against the rules to run) to the post where General Widgets is traded. Since you want to buy, the floor broker tries to buy at the lowest price.

At the same time, there may be a farmer in Vermont who must have funds to pay for his son's college tuition. He contacts his broker, his broker contacts his floor broker, and the two of them meet at the General Widgets post. The exchange is an auction market, and bids and offers are made by outcry. That's why the floor of the exchange is so noisy and may look and sound like a madhouse. Your company's floor broker will be trying to buy for you at, say, $50 per share. The farmer's broker will be trying to sell at $50¼. Your broker finally decides he can't buy for you at $50, so $50⅛ is agreed upon. Millions of dollars worth of stock changes hands daily. However, no contracts are signed, and there is no shaking of hands. In this business your word is your bond; and when it isn't, you're no longer in this business. A record of the trade is written on a slip of paper and handed to a runner, who places the slip in a pneumatic tube that carries it to the tape operator. Within approximately three minutes, if you are sitting in front of a tape in a brokerage office, you will see your trade coming across the screen: GWI 50⅛. This is for 100 shares. If the trade had been for 200 shares, it would have shown GWI 2s 50⅛. If the trade was for 1000 shares, it would appear GWI 1000s 50⅛.

Round Lot, Odd Lot • All transactions shown on the tape and reported in the financial section of your newspaper are for round lots (100-share trades or multiples of 100). This does not mean, however, that if you want to own some shares of General Widgets, you have to have $5,012.50 plus commission. For instance, if you want to buy 10 shares, you certainly may. You would give your 10-share order to the broker, who would contact the odd-lot broker. The odd-lot broker buys in round lots on the exchange and divides it into odd lots. You pay an odd-lot differential for his service. In this example, it would be an additional ⅛ of a point, or $.125 per share. This is not a commission. It is an odd-lot differential. Your commission would be in addition to the differential. On the Pacific Stock Exchange, no odd-lot differential is charged if the odd lot is attached to a round-lot order. On the Pacific, New York, and American Stock Exchanges, the odd-lot differential is charged on all orders after the opening sale. No charges are made on orders entered before the market opens. As you can see, it's not enough difference to discourage you from buying in odd lots.

If you buy an odd lot on a round lot—for example, 125 shares— you pay an odd-lot differential on the 25 shares if you trade on the New York Stock Exchange. If the stock is traded on the Pacific Stock Exchange, it trades with the round lot without the odd-lot differential.

The amount you pay per share for your odd-lot purchase is determined by the price of the next round-lot trade after your order is received. For example, if the next round-lot trade is $50⅛, you would pay $50¼.

Commissions Are Low • Stocks carry one of the lowest commission rates for the exchange of property in the United States. Remember the commission you paid when you sold your last house? Was it 6 percent to the Realtor, plus all the closing costs, making your total between 10 percent and 12 percent? You can sell 100 shares of a $40 listed stock for a commission of around 1¾ percent, and this rate will probably go lower. Quite a difference, isn't it?

• BE AN INFORMED INVESTOR

The adage of "investigate before you invest" should be heeded. There is a wealth of information available to you on all listed stocks and a large number of over-the-counter securities.

Standard and Poor Reports are excellent sources of general information. Study these. Learn to analyze financial statements. An excellent booklet, entitled "Understanding a Financial Statement," which should be of help to you can be obtained by writing to the New York Stock Exchange.

The Wall Street Journal, Barrons, Business Week, and *Financial Trends* can supply you with information. As you study and invest, you will begin to get a feel for the market and, it is to be hoped, develop some "gut" feelings that will enable you to profit from owning your share of American industry.

• SUMMARY

If you have held a well diversified portfolio of quality common stocks over the long term, you have protected your wealth against the inroads of inflation. This is not always true in the short term when inflation becomes so accelerated as to approach two digits. Refuge then should be sought in money market funds or temporarily in fixed-income instruments. Timing is important if you are a short-term investor, so watch closely the money policies of the Federal Reserve Board.

Application

1 • Request that your name be placed on the mailing list of the St. Louis Federal Reserve Board, P.O. Box 442, St. Louis, Mo. 63166, and begin to chart the growth and decline in the money supply.

2 · Subscribe to *The Wall Street Journal* or *Barrons,* and *Business Week* or *Financial Trends.*

3 · Order the booklet, "Understanding a Financial Statement," from the New York Stock Exchange, 11 Wall Street, New York, N.Y. 10005.

4 · If timing is important to you, subscribe to the *Lowry Reports,* 350 Royal Palm Way, Palm Beach, Fla. 33480.

5 · Go to the library and read the Standard and Poor's Corp. stock recommendations.

5

How To Select Stocks for Income

The second reason we have determined that you must learn to invest is for income. Inflation means higher prices; therefore, one of your hopes of combatting inflation is to increase your income faster than prices. The ultimate hedge against inflation is a constantly increasing income.

Fixed-income instruments have never been a long-term hedge against inflation regardless of the current level of yield. To hedge against long-term inflation, it is necessary to have an increasing stream of income. Have common stocks been a good source of increasing dividend income?

If you had placed $10,000 in an investment composed of the thirty stocks in the Dow Jones Industrial Average in 1935, how much would your dividends have been? Let's look at your dividends at 10-year intervals:

Year	Dividends
1935	437
1945	643
1955	2074
1965	2750
1975	3601
1976	3979

I have seen a projection for 1985 of $5788. This was based on the growth rate of dividends during the most recent ten years. I do not know how accurate this will prove to be. However, note that dividends for 1976 increased to $3979.

From the years 1935 through 1976 dividends increased 810 percent and earnings, which must occur before dividends can be paid, increased 1363 percent.

To assist you in determining which income stock you should choose or if you should be investing in growth stocks instead, let's get acquainted with some basic terms that you'll need to know. First we will consider ratios.

• KNOWING THE RATIOS

Let's assume that we are studying two well-managed companies, X and Y. They both manufacture an excellent product for which there has been an increasing demand. For ease of comparison, assume that the stock of both companies sells for $10 per share and that both earn $1 per share.

Stocks X pays a 50¢ dividend, and stock Y pays a 10¢ dividend. What is the yield of each and what is the price-earnings ratio?

Stock	Market price	Earnings per share	Dividend	Yield	Price–earnings ratio
X	$10	$1	50¢	5%	10:1
Y	$10	$1	10¢	1%	10:1

Yield is the relationship of the dividend to the market price. Therefore, a 50¢ yield on a $10 stock would be 5 percent per annum. A 10¢ dividend would then be a 1 percent yield.

The price–earnings ratio, often referred to as the P/E, is the relationship of the market price to the earnings. It indicates how much the investing public is willing to pay for $1 of earnings. In both stocks the amount is $10, making the P/E ratio 10:1.

Which Stock is Best? • Which stock is best for you, X or Y? When I ask this question in the seminars, the majority choose stock X. The savings institutions' advertising campaigns have made them very income conscious.

Did you answer X or Y? The correct answer for you depends on your financial objective. Do you need income now, or do you need income later? If you need it now, you should choose stock X; if you need it later, you should choose stock Y. If the company pays out 50¢ to you and you are in a 30 percent tax bracket, you lose 15¢ to Washington. If you are in a 50 percent bracket, you lose 25¢. If your need is for income later, then you very well may come out better if the company plows back the 90¢ into enlarged plants and facilities, with the hope that some day stock Y will grow in value to perhaps $15 per share. Sometimes it's better to get your eyes off the extra 4 percent income and on to the 50 percent potential in capital gains.

There is often another factor to be considered, and that is your temperament. There is a triangle in finance as there may be in romance. Let's look at the financial triangle and see where you should place yourself for your mental comfort and for the best correlation with your financial objectives.

Triangle of Finance • At the top of the triangle I have placed "Growth," at the left "Income," and at the right "Stability." (I used to call this corner "Safety," but with our present rate of inflation, you may be "stable" without being "safe," so I have changed it to "Stability.") By stability, I mean a guarantee of the same number of dollars at a future date, not the return of the same purchasing power.

As you can see, the farther you move toward Growth, the farther you move from Stability and Income. You may be young enough to invest for Growth, but when you move in that direction, you could have increased volatility. This may disturb your peace of mind, and we have already decided that peace of mind is a good investment, too. If you were my client, I would try to determine your peace of mind level, because regardless of how well the investment fits your financial objective,

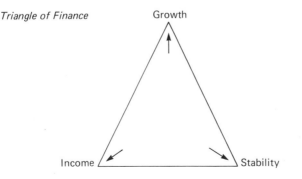

Triangle of Finance Growth

Income Stability

if you are uncomfortable with it, it's not right for you and you may abandon it before it has had time to achieve the desired goal.

Let's examine first the chief characteristics you should look for if your desire is for income.

• HOW TO SELECT
INCOME STOCKS

Income stocks are relatively easy to select as compared to growth stocks. However, there are some important points you'll want to consider before you give your broker the buy order.

Good Dividends That Keep Increasing • You want stocks that not only pay good dividends but also have a record of increasing their dividends rather consistently. If you are dependent on your dividends for your groceries, and the price of food continues to rise, you must either increase your income or reduce your intake. Most of us would probably be a lot healthier if we did the latter, but we have a tendency to reject this alternative.

Dividends That Are Earned • You should carefully determine if the corporation is earning the dividend. A few years ago many of the bank trust departments were putting shares of Sinclair Oil in trust accounts that they managed for widows who needed income. Sinclair was paying a liberal dividend. Unfortunately, the trust officers did not look to see if the company was earning the amount they were paying. They were not. The day of reckoning came, as it usually does, the dividend was cut, and many a widow's account suffered capital losses.

Do not reach too far for yield and jeopardize your capital.

Often I have calls from someone who is going through a *Standard and Poor's Stock Guide* and spots a stock paying a 12 percent to 14 percent yield. They'll excitedly call to buy it, assuming that no one else has been so observant as to have spotted this bonanza. Usually, the reason for the high yield is the poor evaluation that the market has given to the future prospects of the company.

Resistance to Business Cycles • A characteristic of all good income stocks should be that they have a good measure of resistance against cyclical waves in the economy. The consumer demand for the products produced by these companies should continue through all phases of the economic cycle.

Long Dividend Record • In selecting stocks for dependable income, it is obvious that you will want to choose quality issues, since younger, less tested companies have not been around long enough to establish an extended dividend payment record.

Income stocks usually pay out between 65 percent to 75 percent of their net earnings in cash dividends. Once a regular dividend rate has been established, it is unlikely that it will be reduced because of poor earnings in a single year.

During times of market corrections I often have calls from less sophisticated holders of income stocks who are worried that their dividend will be cut because the market price is down. If all is well with their company, I try to calm them with the explanation that short-term market prices often have no relationship to earnings. (In the long term they usually do.) 1973–1974 were banner years for corporate profits, but it was not reflected in the market prices, for no one trusted the numbers—and rightly so.

Who Decides the Amount of the Dividend? • The amount remaining after the expenses and taxes have been paid by a company is the amount available for dividends. The decision as to whether a dividend should be paid and how much it should be is made by the board of directors. The amount of the earnings, the need for retained earnings, and the past dividend record all influence the directors' decision.

Yield on Original Purchase Price • As you've learned above, the yield on a stock is the relationship of the dividend to the market price. Every shareholder is entitled to the same dividend per share. However, the market price paid by one shareholder may be different from that paid by another. If you paid $50 for a share of stock and the dividend is $2, your yield on your original investment is 4 percent ($2 divided by $50). If you paid $35, the $2 represents a return, or yield, on your original investment of slightly more than 5.7 percent.

Most yields, however, are calculated on current market price. If the price per share is now $60, still with a $2 dividend, the yield would be slightly over 3.3 percent.

Looking Ahead • If you do not need income now, consider companies with slightly lower yields. Often these companies are plowing back a larger portion of their earnings into expanded facilities that should in time yield higher earnings that would allow them to pay out higher dividends. Over a 10- to 15-year period many growth stocks have actually had a larger cash pay-out than income stock. One percent on $10,000 is only $100. But let's assume the growth stock continues to grow and reaches a value of $100,000. (One percent on $100,000 is $1000, or 10 percent on your original investment.)

A booklet that you may find of help if you are interested in selecting stocks for income is one published by the New York Stock Exchange entitled, "Investment Facts—Cash Dividends Every Three Months From 25 to 100 Years." The booklet points out that the widespread ownership of stocks listed on the New York Stock Exchange is due in large part to a growing awareness that surplus dollars can be put to work in investments that will reflect the ever-changing economic conditions of our country.

The ability of common stocks to mirror these developments constitutes their greatest attribute. Of course, it is also their greatest risk. On the plus side is the fact that over the years, good common stocks often have helped their owners keep in step with living costs. There is no such phenomenon as a "sure thing," and history carries no guarantee of the future. But the facts that history has recorded may serve as a clue to the future. If so, it may be of help to look at the long-time dividend payers listed in this booklet.

The booklet lists recent prices of the stock, the dividend record, and its yield. Of these common stocks, 466 have paid a cash dividend every single quarter for 25 years, and 100 have paid a dividend for every quarter for 50 to over 100 years.

Preferred Stocks • Preferred stocks are equities senior to the common, but junior to indebtedness of the issuer. Preferred stock dividend income is 85 percent tax-exempt for corporations, which often makes them attractive corporate investments. This fact tends to raise the price of the preferred in the market place, which will generally make them less attractive to you for your individual investment program. You will normally recieve a higher rate of return from a high-quality corporate bond than from a preferred stock.

Blue Chips, Red Chips, White Chips? • The stocks that I have described above would generally be called blue chips. What is a "blue chip" stock? First, the name can be traced to the game of poker, in which there are three colors of chips: blue for the highest value, red for next in rank, and white for the lowest value.

Sometimes people will come up to me after a seminar or a television appearance and say, "I only invest in blue chip stocks and throw them in the drawer and forget about them." They stand there seemingly anticipating my approval. I consider this approach a risky one. I would prefer to see them invest in more volatile stocks and watch them carefully than to have them plant their garden and not tend it.

However, there are some characteristics of the so-called blue chips that are worthy of your consideration. These are

1 • A long history of cash dividend payments in bad times and good.
2 • A long history of good earnings in both booms and recessions.
3 • They are leaders in an established industry.
4 • Good prospects for continued good earnings growth and dividends should pay off in the years ahead.

• INCOME vs. GROWTH

The equities market provides a wide spectrum of alternatives with respect to rates of return. When investing in growth companies, you must pay a premium in terms of P/E relationship and, therefore, receive less in the way of current income. Growth companies have an opportunity to reinvest their earnings at higher rates than are available to you as a stockholder if the earnings were paid out to you and you had only the after-tax amount to invest. Therefore, growth companies have very low pay-out ratios.

It is too simplistic, but there is some truth in the fact that the highest-yielding common stocks have lower expectations of future growth and, therefore, lower P/Es.

If you do not expect growth of the company, you should ask yourself why the price is so low, making the yield so high. Is the company in serious financial straits? Is the company likely to cut its dividends? Is the regulatory environment likely to be adverse so that the company may have to reduce its dividend to conserve its cash for working capital needs? What is the outlook for the industry, etc.?

It is clear that investing for income is not without risk. If you had bought steel company or copper company issues a few years ago for income, you would have had your dividends reduced and in some instances eliminated. Not only did the income go down, but the principal loss was substantial—more than 50 percent in some cases. It is also clear, however, that investing for high income can have its rewards. In the merger craze of the late 1960s, finance companies and cash-rich insurance companies, considered "income common stocks," became the targets of acquiring companies. Some of those acquired had spectacular rises in their prices, and if you sold your shares at the proper time, you could have realized substantial capital gains.

In summary, if your desire is for income:

1 • Look for companies that have a long unbroken dividend record.

2 • Don't reach too far for yield and jeopardize principal.

3 • Too high a yield can be dangerous and misleading.

4 • Favor companies producing consumer goods and services.

5 • Select sound companies that continue to increase their dividends.

During the mid-1970s the validity of investing in income stocks was praised by many and discouraged by others. Those who suggested their purchase pointed out that stocks paying good dividends held up better in market declines. Those who discouraged buying income stocks pointed out other vehicles that became available in good supply that paid a higher income with less risk in the short term. Good corporate bonds and bond funds offered 9 percent yields, and certificates of deposit in amounts over $100,000 reached the 12 percent level for short periods of time.

Many top investment advisory services will not accept accounts with an "income" objective, limiting themselves to "growth" and "aggressive growth."

Income stocks are not too difficult to select after you've conscientiously done your homework. However, selecting growth stocks can be one of the greatest challenges you have ever undertaken. In Chapter 6 we will embark on this challenge.

Application

1 • Order the booklets "Investment Facts—Cash Dividends Every Three Months From 25 to 100 Years," "The Language of Investing," and "How to Get Help When You Invest" from the New York Stock Exchange, 11 Wall Street, New York, N.Y. 10005.

2 • Sit down and draw the financial triangle. Place yourself on the triangle. Are you emphasizing income when your real objective is growth of capital?

6
Growth Stocks—
The Royal Road to Riches?

During the surging sixties the magic word on Wall Street, Main Street, Podunk Street or almost any street you happened to be traveling at the time, was "Growth"! Investing in "growth" stocks was the royal highway to riches. So greatly did some "investors" become enamored of that magic word that they were willing to pay fantastic prices for new and relatively untested electronic and scientific issues. So unrealistic did they become that they actually paid as high as 70 times earnings. In some instances there were no earnings at all.

• GROWTH STOCKS—
WHAT ARE THEY?

What are growth stocks, and why should you consider investing in them?

A growth company is usually one that is increasing its sales and earnings at a faster rate than the growth of the national population and business in general. The long-term annual growth rate of our population has been about 3 percent. In recent years large families have become taboo, and we are beginning to move toward zero population growth;

however, we shall probably not reach ZPG until around the year 2000. The annual growth in gross national product has been around 6.6 percent in recent years. A growth company, as a rule of thumb, should be increasing its sales and net earnings at least as fast as the combination of the two, and preferably much faster.

Growth companies are usually producing goods and/or services in dynamic and new industries. The 1940s saw the surge of oil stocks, television shares, and pharmaceutical companies. The 1950s continued the drug stocks' popularity, with flurries in uranium, cameras, electronics, missiles, and automation.

The 1960s saw leisure-time industries, baby products, electronics continued, with computer-oriented stocks keeping pace, technology-related industries, life insurance companies, drugs, retail, convenience goods, soft drinks, and, most especially, the surge of the conglomerates trying to leverage their balance sheets, many times using what became known as "funny money." Ling-Tempco-Vought, Gulf and Western, Textron, and International Telephone and Telegraph all brought visions of investor "sugar plums" during their heydays of mergers and acquisitions. There was a short period of time when there were jokes in the investment community of investment decisions becoming a matter of which one of the few conglomerates to choose. The tinsel began to tarnish, the craze passed, and we returned to sound investment evaluation based on realities rather than the new math of Wall Street, which seemed to say that 2 plus 2 equals 5.

• THE MID-SEVENTIES

During the first part of the 1970s the market suffered a major correction. This correction was much more extensive than the widely followed Dow Jones Industrial Average revealed. The decline of the Dow, though sizable, was not bad enough to explain the awful sense of despair that gripped Wall Street during the latter part of 1973 and on through 1974 and 1975. It did not tell how hard the overall stock market was hit. The only averages that showed declines approaching the true magnitude were the superbroad unweighted ones, such as the *Value Line Composite* and the *Indicator Digest* average.

The bull market of the 1960s was in the supergrowth stocks—the franchises, the computer leasers, and the like—not the staid, less volatile Dow 30. The Dow went up during those years, but the broader averages went up more rapidly and also went down more rapidly when the high flyers fell out of favor.

Why was the market plunge so severe in 1973 and 1974? There are many reasons, all interrelated and interacting. Let's look at a few of them.

Many market declines are in direct relationship to the junk some stockbrokers "peddle" on the way up. Being a broker is a volatile vocation, but it is made more so by the short memories of a large portion of its personnel. It was another case of too much sizzle and not enough steak.

The Federal Reserve Board instituted extremely restrictive money policies in an effort to slow down runaway inflation. The results of its actions could be compared to taking a man who has been accustomed to three gourmet meals a day and throwing him into solitary confinement, giving him only bread and water and then beating him with a stick. The market must have a steady flow of money to function properly. Historical studies show a direct relation between the supply of money in the economy and stock market prices.

The ugliness of Watergate disillusioned the American public as nothing else had in many a decade. Their faith in their leaders was badly shaken. A sense of uneasiness and gloom settled over our nation. When people feel bad inside, they sell their stocks. When they feel good, they buy. Gut-level feelings have no correlations with earnings. Human emotion took over, and they sold and sold.

It is at times such as those that we need to read these words: ". . . even in the general moment of gloom in which this . . . is written, when many begin to wonder if declines will never halt, the appropriate abracadabra may be: 'They always did.'" *

• HOW TO SPOT GROWTH STOCKS

To become good at selecting stocks for growth you must be aware of current events—current trends, current psychology, current money markets. In fact, you must be truly current. You live in a dynamic world that changes daily. One of the most stimulating characteristics of being a financial planner is that every day is a new day in the market. Nothing remains static. There is no way you can be a truly top-notch investor by buying blue chips and throwing them in a drawer and forgetting them. This only increases your risk and lowers your opportunity for gain.

* Bernard M. Baruch, October 1932.

Be in the Right Industry • If I were to choose the most important consideration for selecting growth stocks, I would have to say that it is to be in the right industry at the right time. There is always an industry moving up, regardless of the general overall trend of the market. During the drastic declines of 1974, the oil equipment, sugar, and gold stocks steadily gained. You should endeavor to predict a trend before it happens and to move out before the trend runs out. You should try to be aware of technological changes and opinions of the buying public. It will not pay you to be right if nobody cares. Sitting with money in a stagnant "correct" situation while other stocks are moving up just doesn't take the place of making money.

Fantasy Stocks • Do not buy what I call fantasy stocks—stocks based on an idea yet to come. The idea may be great—even correct and true—but how do you know there will be adequate financing, good and honest management, marketing ability, and public acceptance of the product? (What people want and what they need are different things.) You might say, "But look at Haloid that later became Xerox." There is no way that those who bought Haloid could have known it would become one of the best-managed sales organizations that the country had seen for many a year. Too, you could have bought Xerox many times since its beginning and made just as much money with proper timing on buys and sells. If you will wait until some of the results are in, it may save you some heartaches. (Of course, you will also need to be astute enough to avoid getting on at the front of the bus while the informed are getting off at the back.)

This is different from a story stock from which good results have already been realized, but even better results are expected. The best story is the "Good Earnings Story."

Management the Key • There is no substitute for energetic, intelligent, dedicated, and enthusiastic management. They should be a stock-minded management team that is interested in increasing the market price of their stock, and this can only be sustained in the long term by increased earnings.

With good management and an average product it is possible to make money. A superior product with poor management may well yield very disappointing results. The key is good management and a superior product together.

How can you obtain this information? It is not an easy task. Resource materials and publications you may find helpful are *Standard & Poor's, Fortune, Forbes, Barrons, Business Week, U.S. News and World Report, Financial Trends,* and *The Wall Street Journal.*

Self-generating Earnings • Select a company that has self-generating rising earnings and reserves with expectations for continued increases over the foreseeable future. Few companies really shine solely by acquisitions as many seemed to believe during the conglomerate era of mergers. Pretax earnings on assets of growth companies should be between 10 percent and 30 percent. Companies that have enjoyed such gains are Tampax, Avon, Merk, Coca Cola, Eastman Kodak, Minnesota Mining, Proctor and Gamble, IBM, Xerox, and Hewlett-Packard.

Technological Research and Development Are a Must • A growth company must retain a large portion of its earnings for research and development that will produce a saleable product that offers excellence in quality, design, or performance, and preferably all three.

Flair for Salesmanship • A growth company must have a dynamic, aggressive sales department. A good example of salesmanship is Revlon. They are masters at selling "hope in a jar." Their ads are so compelling that it takes restraint to read their brilliant magazine ads and not dash to the nearest cosmetic counter.

Consistently Superior Growth of Earnings • A growth stock is not just a stock that has gone up in price. You want stocks that have shown a consistent, year-after-year, superior growth in earnings even in the face of business reverses and that have a consistent year-in, year-out market for their products or services.

Leaders in a Fast-growing Field • You will want to search for the companies that dominate their markets or are leaders in fast-growing fields. These can be companies in emerging fields or companies that have developed new ideas in established fields.

Offer a High Return on Equity • A high return on equity means that the company's net profit related to the equity of the stockholders is high in comparison to that earned by other firms in the same industry. The average on all stocks today is about 11¢ per dollar committed. Your growth stocks should exceed this.

In entering the market for trading purposes, timing is all-important. This must be finely tuned.

Cyclical Stocks • Most short-term speculators use the so-called "cyclical" stocks. These shares are found in those industries most sensitive to swings in the business cycle. They include the heavily capitalized industries such as steel and heavy machinery. These areas are traditionally strongest in periods of prosperity and at a low ebb in times of recession. The trick is to buy cyclical stocks in the early stages of a business upturn and sell them as closely as possible to the crest. This is not easy.

Popular Favorites • Another trading technique is to move along with the popular stocks of the moment. You can make as much money, short term, on what others think a stock is worth, as on what it is really worth. In the long term we have always returned to basics.

Following the fashions in finance is hazardous. However, if, by using good logic, you are convinced that a new industry is about to boom, then cautious selections of a stock in that industry may prove rewarding. The trick to to buy early and then, when everyone is clamoring for shares in that industry, sell! Almost invariably the stock market darlings, at the height of their popularity, will sell above sensible valuations.

Special Situations • Another area of speculation is the area of special situations. This can cover a great many areas—mergers, sudden increase in the price of a valuable asset, a new mineral find, a new venture, and so on. Your success will greatly depend on your getting accurate information ahead of the pack. Is the product or service in the mainstream of a rapidly growing demand? Is the demand likely to last? If it is a new venture, determine if it is well capitalized. At least half of all new ventures fold because they run out of capital before they can get into full-fledged operation.

Who will be managing the company? Innovators may have a highly functional idea or patent, but they'll fail because they do not know how to run a business. Creative design people often are very poor at manufacturing techniques, cost control, merchandising, financing, and record keeping. Check to see if those who will run the business are personally solvent and have adequate practical or technical background. The key man may be a fantastic salesman and a poor production man, or vice versa. He may know sales promotion but have no idea about cost controls.

The third thing to consider in a new company is superiority of product or service. New products should be advanced, unusual, and ahead of the field.

Finally, can you afford to lose everything you put into the new company and not miss the money?

On the record, the chances of a new company's growing from zero to great substance are very slim. But if this kind of speculation adds zest to your life and you can afford it, happy hunting!

• INVESTOR OR SPECULATOR

We have covered some of the basic characteristics that you must consider in becoming an investor for growth. Should you ever speculate in the stock market? Are there categories between being an investor and being a rank speculator?

The Trader • In even the most valid growth stock selection there is a time to buy and a time to sell. However, there is another area of the stock market that I would classify between the growth stock investor and the rank gambler. He is the trader. I must admit that the line of demarcation does get hazy at times.

There appear to be at least three classes of people who fit this category. If you do not have ample capital, I hope you will resist the temptation to join their ranks, as most out-and-out traders die broke. These three classes are

1 • The constitutional speculators; not necessarily gamblers, but people willing to "take a chance"—to take big risks in hope of great gain.

2 • Those who truly think they can supplement their income by modest trading in and out of the market.

3 • People with large amounts of income to whom fully taxable income is unattractive, but to whom long-term capital gains, usually taxed at a lower rate, are most alluring.

• RIGHT STOCK ACTION

Don't Be Greedy • One characteristic that I have observed about the timing of all good traders is that they never try to squeeze out the last point in a stock. When the great financier Bernard Baruch was questioned on how he made so much money in the stock market, he answered, "I always sold too soon." He always tried to leave a little in it for the next buyer.

Cut Losses Quickly • In trading it is absolutely necessary to cut your losses quickly. If you've made an error in judgment, don't wait around to find out just how wrong you really were. You can't afford an ego trip. If a 10 percent drop occurs, seriously consider getting out.

Some of my clients act as if the stock knew they owned it or what they paid for it. The stock doesn't even know that your cousin, once removed, works for the company.

Don't think about an impending dividend, or that you have a loss in the stock, or that you just bought it. Also, don't hesitate to buy it back, even at a higher price, if you made a mistake in selling. Above all, don't fall in love with a stock—don't marry it. Be objective. Be flexible. Don't be guilty of prejudices in stock. We all have them occasionally, but the sooner you recognize them and shed stocks that hinder your investment judgment, the better investor you'll become.

Tax considerations should be the furthest from your mind. You are only trying to use $1 to make $2, not trying to do tax planning while in front of a stock board watching the "horses" run.

Don't Cry • Two other cardinal rules are "Don't cry" and "Don't look back." Lick your wounds and charge forward.

• SHOULD YOU BUY ON MARGIN?

From years of observing margin account investors my answer to you is No. Leave this area to the large, sophisticated—whatever that means—investors who are active in the market and who understand the risks as well as the rewards of this type of account. I find that it is usually best if you discipline yourself to the use of only your investable funds. To lose some of your savings in the market is one thing. To lose also your future savings is another. Yes, I know if it goes the other way your potential for gain is greatly enhanced. It's not that I don't believe in leverage. I very much do in real estate and other areas and in using stock as collateral for funds to purchase capital items.

If after these warnings you still want to open a margin account, here is how it works. First, the Federal Reserve Board sets the margin requirements. These requirements have ranged from 50 to 100 percent in the post-World War II period. For example, if the margin rate is 70 percent it means that if you want to buy $10,000 worth of stock you would need to put up $7000 in order to make the purchase. You would deposit the required cash or securities with your broker within five business days after the purchase.

You will pay interest for the amount you have borrowed. This has ranged from $6\frac{1}{2}$ to 13 percent. The amount of interest will be posted monthly on your statement.

To open the account you deposit $2000, or whatever minimum your brokerage firm requires, and sign a margin agreement and a securities loan consent form. This agreement gives your broker the power to pledge or lend your securities. Your securities will be held in what is called "street name," meaning that they are registered in the name of the brokerage house and you do not receive delivery of the certificates. Your broker will, however, credit you with all the dividends received, send you all the reports, and vote your stock in the manner that you direct. You must also abide by the margin maintenance requirements. This usually requires that your margin equity be at least 25 percent. For example, if you bought $10,000 worth of stock with an initial margin requirement of 70 percent, you put up $7000 and received credit of $3000. Let's assume the stock drops to the point where it is worth $4,000. Since you owe your broker $3000, your equity in the securities is only $1,000 and you are right at the 25 percent limit. At this point you will receive a margin call and you'll be asked to put up more cash or securities. If you cannot meet the call, he will sell your securities, retain the $3000 you owe him and credit you with the balance.

• SHOULD YOU BUY OR SELL OPTIONS?

The use of options has increased greatly in the past 10 years. You may have attended a seminar, read newspaper ads, or received a call from an aggressive broker extolling them as the way to lock in additional income if you are on the selling side and to make a large return on a small investment if you are on the buying side.

It's not all that easy, but in order for you to not feel left out when the conversation turns to "puts" and "calls," let's take a brief look at the world of options.

A "call" option is a contract that gives you the right to buy 100 shares of a given stock at a fixed price for a fixed period of time. The period of time usually runs nine months and ten days (for tax reasons), but can run 30, 90, 120 days or other lengths of time. The premium that you pay for the option usually runs about 10 to 15 percent of the value of the stock.

A "put" option is the reverse of a "call" option. You now have the privilege of selling 100 shares of the stock at a fixed price within the option period. These usually cost a few percentage points less than call options and are not as popular.

Why would you ever buy an option? The main reason is that it gives you a chance to make a sizable profit on the move of a stock while limiting the amount of possible loss. For example, you think that General Widgets Company stock selling at $40 may surge to $80. It would cost you $4000 to buy the shares, and you may not want to risk $4000 or you may not have $4,000 to invest. Still, you would like to take the chance that General Widgets will jump and as a result you'd make a large profit. In this case you might go the option route, buying an option for $400. Let's assume your anticipations are correct and the stock hits $70 within the option period. You exercise your option, buy the 100 shares at $40 and then turn around and sell the shares for $70. You have received $7000 from the sale of the shares. From this you would subtract the $4000 you paid for them, the $400 premium for the option, and about $110 for the brokerage commissions and you wind up with a profit of $2490.

Now let's assume that your expectations did not materialize and General Widgets goes to $30. What do you do? You do nothing. You simply let your option expire. You are out $400. Your loss is limited to the cost of your option and you are thankful that you didn't buy 100 shares at $4000 and watch your investment shrink.

"Put" options work the same but in reverse. (There are also some very fancy devices called "straddles"—a combination of a put and a call—"strips," which are composed of two puts and one call, and "straps," which are one put and two calls.)

Now let's return to portfolio basics.

• A PROFITABLE PORTFOLIO

There are three important areas in choosing and maintaining a profitable portfolio of stocks. They are diversification, proper selection, and constant supervision. Let's examine the first, diversification. Diversification means spreading the risk. The old adage of not putting all your eggs in one basket has considerable merit in assembling a good investment portfolio.

Diversification • Don't put all your faith in only one company, for it may disappoint you. You may be well informed on sales figures, competitive situations, or whatever, but always be prepared for a disaster. Going for broke on a winner could make you rich, but no one knows which stock will be the big winner. If you buy a diversified group of fundamentally sound stocks with good earnings, the chances are that in a good market you will catch at least some of the big winners. Most big money in a diversified portfolio comes from one or two big winners.

Don't be deceived into thinking that 10 oil stocks is diversification; it is not. You should have a portfolio covering a wider range of industries. For example, you may have some stocks in the soft drink industry, the retail area, drugs, home furnishings, electrical equipment, brewing, agricultural machinery, gold mining, and others.

When managing your own portfolio, you may find it extremely helpful to limit yourself to 10 stocks, regardless of the amount of money you have to invest. I'm surprised to find that investors think they can only own 100 shares of each company's stock. If the capital you have available for investing is sufficiently large, perhaps you should consider owning 1000 shares of each stock.

Moving to Strength • Don't overdiversify. You cannot be truly current on more than 10 stocks at a time. If you limit your holdings to 10 stocks and a stock comes to your attention that you feel you should buy, what will this force you to do? To eliminate one. So you go down through your list and sell the one that is doing the poorest job for you. Now, won't you? I wish this were true of all my clients. Many go through and pick out their winner to sell and smugly say, "You'll never go broke taking a profit." They are keeping their losers and selling their winners. That's not the way to upgrade a portfolio. Sell the poorest performer. This allows you the possibility of continuously moving to a position of strength.

Timing Is the Key • There is a time to buy and a time to sell. The old adage about buying low and selling high is easy to say and very hard to do. Often you never know what the high or low is until it's too late for maximum advantage.

But how do you determine when to buy and when to sell? Let's look at buying first.

When To Buy • Buying is easier to time than selling. There are times I am almost convinced that any time is a good time to buy good stocks at a reasonable price/earnings ratio.

Let me give you an example. I was counseling a young couple, and we had selected the stock that fit their financial requirements. It was selling at $23 and was not overpriced based on past earnings and anticipated growth of earnings. The husband asked if I thought it might be possible to buy the stock at $22 by waiting a while. The market did look as if it could make a slight correction so I agreed to call them when it reached $22. It reached their price in about a month, and I called them to let them know it was time to purchase. Their response was, "Oh, I'm sorry, but we've already spent the money." A good rule for them very well might have been "Any time is a good time to buy good stocks." There is also a good time to sell good stocks.

When To Sell • I have a very simple rule for judging when to sell a stock I own. It's so simple you'll probably dismiss the whole idea. However, I've found over the years that it has helped me cut through the tinsel and fog and to reach good decisions as to when to sell.

I do not look at what price I paid for a stock unless selling it would cause me to incur a large capital gains tax liability. I simply ask myself, "If I had the money this stock would bring in my hands at this moment, would I buy this stock at this price?" If my answer is Yes, I hold. If it is No, I sell. The only difference between my owning this stock and having the money is a small amount of commission which I should not let affect my judgment.

You may have great difficulty selling. Most people do. If you have a gain, you may not be able to bear the thought of selling and paying the capital gains tax. When you analyze the situation, there are only two ways to avoid eventually paying it—neither of which you are going to like. You can hold it until it goes back to what you paid for it, or hold it until your death, and let your heirs worry about the tax when they sell it.

On the other hand, if you have a loss, you may say, "I won't sell for I just can't afford to take a loss." You already have the loss. You only have two questions now that you should ask yourself. Can you deduct the loss advantageously on your income tax, and where are you most likely to make up your losses—where you are or in another stock?

Lay your hand over the cost basis of your stocks and judge them individually on their potential over the next six months.

Don't Average Down • I am not in agreement with a large number of stockbrokers who advise their clients to average down. What is meant by averaging down?

Let's assume that you bought 100 shares of a stock at $30 per share, and it has dropped in price to $20. There are those who recommend that you buy another 100 shares at $20. This would give you an average cost per share of $25 on the 200 shares.

I feel you can average yourself right into the basement of the poorhouse. I never mind paying a higher price than my original purchase price if there is earnings justification. It just means the market has confirmed my own good judgment.

No One Rings a Bell • Are you bearish or bullish for the next 2 months? How about the next 8 months? What about the next 18 months? (That's long term for the dynamic market we have. As a matter of fact, I find that most people consider twelve months and one day long term.)

Are you bearish for the short term and bullish for the long term? If so, you probably have lots of company. The only problem is that no one rings a bell when the bottom (or the top) of the market has been reached, and those who wait often continue to wait until the market has climbed to new highs. They then panic on the upside and say, "What a fool I was not to have bought back when the market was low. I've already waited too long, but there must be plenty of good buys left." And they hop in with both feet.

With the continuously growing appetite and importance of the institutional investor, it is well to consider if the individual investor can successfully compete.

•   THE INSTITUTIONAL INVESTOR

The institutional investor is one who usually buys in large blocks at advantageously lower negotiated commissions. He is the large life insurance company, the large bank, the large pension fund manager, the large college endowment fund manager, the large mutual fund.

There is considerable evidence that their demand for stock will be a strong force in the market place. Projections show that in the 1980s nonprofit institutions will have in their portfolios $4 billion worth of stocks, life insurance companies $5.5 billion, private pension funds $13.3 billion, open-end investment trusts $90 billion, and state and local government retirement plans $1.5 billion (even under our new pension laws).

There are just not this many new quality issues coming into the market to fill the demand. As we learned in basic economics, if demand is greater than supply, the price will rise.

Logic would seem to indicate that with this much money in the hands of trained, informed, unemotional money managers, this would lend a high degree of stability to the market. I'm sorry to say that I don't think this is what will be happening. Their equipment for becoming better informed has reached a high degree of electronic sophistication. Unfortunately, they all seem to be availing themselves of the same tools. They are all reading the same computer printouts from their very advanced monitoring equipment. This shows all of them the same buy and sell signals at the same time, causing simultaneous buying and selling that results in sudden and often preciptitous price changes.

An example might be found in the stock of Wrigley. Their commercials may have been a bit staid—"Double your pleasure, double your fun"—but you always knew Wrigley was there. Then suddenly at 1 P.M. on that fateful day in October, trading was halted by the New York Stock Exchange. When it reopened around 2:30, there was no pleasure and no fun. Wrigley was off 27 points, almost a 20 percent drop. Just like that. By year's end it had shed another 15 points. (I'm happy to report that it has now come back.)

Had the bottom suddenly fallen out of the chewing gum market? No, as a matter of fact, third-quarter earnings were well above the previous year's earnings, but they were not what Wall Street expected. Wall Street becomes nervous when its expectations are not met, and 20,000 shares were dumped. That is what is called "bombing" a stock.

• YOU CAN COMPETE

Can you as an individual investor compete with so many institutional buyers in the market?

Yes, you can probably beat all but the well-managed mutual funds if you will conscientiously do your homework and keep reasonably calm. One of your greatest assets is flexibility. There will be times when you will be skittish about the economy and believe it wise to convert all or a portion of your assets into cash.

It may be more difficult for the professional money manager to unload a block of 200,000 shares of the kinds of stocks institutions hold without depressing the market in that stock.

For example, suppose you decide that IBM's multiple (the stock's price relative to its earnings per share) is too high, and you'd like to sell your 50 shares. Fine. No problem. But could Morgan Guaranty, which may hold over $2 billion in IBM stock, do the same? They are locked in, unless they want to see their last shares sold at prices much lower than their first.

Very often, the way to make big money in the market is to find small, well-managed, rapidly growing companies. Most institutions are too big to be able to take advantage of that strategy. You can buy meaningful positions in smaller companies that the "big boys" cannot touch. (An investment company trust cannot, by regulation, own more than 10 percent of the shares outstanding of any one company.) You would hope, however, that as the company grew, the institutions would be able to move in, which in turn should help move up the price of the stock you "discovered."

• KEEP YOUR
PERSPECTIVE

When news seems at its worst, remember that good news has always followed bad news. Things do move in cycles and waves. (I know you feel some of them may engulf you.) Interest rates do adjust downward as well as upward. The crisis shortages are solved. A nation that can go to the moon can also produce energy, good food, and unpolluted air and water. Inflation is something you must learn to live with. It may slow slightly, but you must accept it as a continuing fact of life.

It's important to be in the stock market for it offers you opportunities for gains, favorable tax treatment on these gains, and liquidity. Yes, there are risks. But all of life is a risk. Investing will always be a delicate balance between risk and reward.

• WHICH STOCKS
FOR THE DECADE AHEAD?

Don't I wish I knew. And don't you wish I knew and would pass on the secret to you?

From all indications, the decade ahead can be a very good one, but emphasis will be in different areas than before. It will probably be an economy of shortages of natural resources with higher capital investment requirements than in the 1970s. While the 1970s were consumer-oriented, the 1980s will probably be investment-oriented. We will have greater emphasis on how to manufacture products more cheaply and to conserve our natural resources such as oil and gas, lumber, iron ore, and copper. Greater emphasis will be on technology—of building smaller cars that consume less fuel; of constructing homes that are smaller and better insulated and probably located nearer to places of employment; of producing heating and air conditioning units that are designed to consume less electricity. "Recycling," "recovery," and "reuse" will be words that we'll use often in our day-to-day conversations.

In the 1980s we should move away from planned obsolescence and build things to last. Eating habits may change. As the prices of animal feeds increase, we may see more meat substitutes. There will be a rash of changes. But is this bad?

The decade ahead will offer you a dynamic challenge—a challenge that you cannot afford to turn down. It is a challenge you must accept. Do so with intelligence, knowledge, vigor, and enthusiasm! You may find that the world of stocks is your oyster.

Application

1 • A good way to become knowledgeable about growth industries is to be alert to current trends. In which areas should you be attuned as you read the daily newspaper?

2 • How will you become informed about the management of the corporations in the industries that you feel offer the most growth potential?

3 • How do you determine the right time to invest?

4 • How will you time your sales?

7

The Stock Market
Is Like a Yo-Yo

- ## IGNORANCE AND FEAR,
  ## DETERRENTS TO INVESTING

If stocks over the long term have been a good investment, why do so many of our citizens miss the opportunity to own their share of American industry and the growth of income and capital that has occurred through ownership?

Ignorance and fear!

As I mentioned earlier, our school system seems to have allowed an educational void in this particular field. Millions of dollars are spent yearly to teach our youth how to equip themselves for a vocation so that they can earn the money necessary to provide a living. Yet they are not taught what to do with this money once it is earned.

Every day I'm appalled at the basic ignorance of money management that exists. Yet I'm exposed to only a small portion of the total. Most of those with whom I counsel have at least recognized that they have a problem and have attended a financial planning seminar to try to correct it. Recognition that you have a problem is a giant step toward its solution.

The vast majority of people are ignorant of what money must do to attain their financial objective. Even if they have calculated the rate of return their money must yield, they are ignorant as to how to attain that rate. This kind of ignorance yields two unfavorable results:

1 • A lack of financial independence at 65 and, therefore, dependence on friends, relatives, and charity.
2 • A lack of interest in preserving the free enterprise system, since they do not participate in its ownership.

I find that those who become owners of individual stocks or mutual funds look at American industry in a different way. They are more interested in their productivity and the productivity of their fellow workers, for they feel they have a stake in the results. They feel they are robbing themselves if they goof off on the jobs for which they are being paid. One of the major cures for inflation is worker productivity.

A second major reason our citizens do not own shares of the very same companies they literally "vote for" every time they go to the grocery store is fear—fear that if they invest, they will not be returned the same number of dollars they put into the stocks.

• INTRINSIC
VALUE

People fear anything they do not understand. What they do not understand is that the market is made up of two basic ingredients. The first, and only ingredient of long-term importance, is intrinsic value. Intrinsic value is the true worth of a company's stock. This is dependent upon the company's assets, its ability to produce a product or service that is wanted or needed by a sufficient number of people, and its ability to market that product or service at a profit. One of the best measuring sticks of our country's total overall productivity is the gross national product. The gross national product is the total value of the goods and services produced in our nation within a year. It also comprises the total expenditures by consumers and government, plus gross private investment. In other words, it is everything we as a country produce in a one-year period. It is all that you produce, that your neighbors produce, that your co-workers produce. Also included are the government's production and expenditures. If you hire a maid and pay her a salary, this salary is included in the gross national product. If you do your own housework, this productivity is not included.

Let's go back to the depths of the depression—1933. At that black period in the nation's history, economic conditions were so depressed that we have a tendency to believe that nothing was being produced. However, this country produced $56 billion in gross national product in 1933. This amount has steadily increased until, in 1971, the GNP of the United States crossed the $1 trillion mark (1.055), and 1976 brought a GNP of $1.743 trillion.

It took our nation 195 years to reach the first trillion. Do you know when economists predict we will reach the second trillion? In 1980!

Can you visualize the magnitude of just $1 trillion? If you ever get discouraged about the U.S. economy, get out a sheet of paper and pencil and start writing. First you write "1"; then start adding zeros. When you write the twelfth zero, you've reached a trillion. By then, perhaps you, too, will have become optimistic about our economy.

Our increase in GNP in just one year is greater than the total GNP of a nation the size of Canada.

A simple illustration would look something like Fig. 7–1.

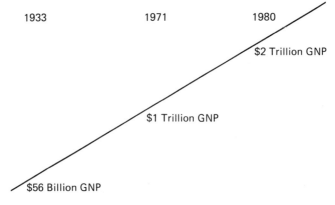

FIGURE 7–1

Here are the actual GNP figures for 1933 through 1976. Start reading GNP figures in your daily newspaper. They are truly exciting if you'll take the time to relate to just what this productivity means.

In the chart below, I've added two other factors to help you identify with the events around the figures!

Year	Events since 1933	Cost of living 1933 = 100	Gross national product in billions
1933	Depression, bank holiday, FDR begins first term, NIRA	100.0	$ 56.0
1934	Millions on relief, dollar revaluated, Hitler becomes Fuehrer	103.4	65.0
1935	Italy attacks Ethiopia, P.W.A., Public Utility Holding Co. Act	106.1	72.5
1936	Civil war in Spain, Germany reoccupies Rhineland	107.2	82.7
1937	Business "recession," stock market break	111.0	90.8
1938	Munich, Austria invaded, Czechoslovakia partitioned	109.0	85.2
1939	War begins, U.S. neutral, $552 million for defense	107.4	91.1
1940	Nazi "blitzkrieg," France falls, U.S. Selective Serv. Act	108.3	100.6
1941	Atlantic Charter, Pearl Harbor, U.S. enters war	113.7	125.8
1942	African campaign, Guadalcanal, stock market reaches low	126.0	159.1
1943	Casablanca, Quebec, U.S. advance in Pacific, withholding tax	133.8	192.5
1944	D-Day in Europe, Guam recaptured, Philippines invaded	136.0	211.4
1945	Yalta, Potsdam, FDR dies, atom bomb, war ends, U.N.	139.1	213.6
1946	Nationwide strikes, inflation, market decline	150.8	210.7
1947	Marshall Plan, Taft-Hartley Act	172.7	234.3
1948	Israel formed, Berlin blockade, Truman elected	185.9	259.4
1949	NATO, Red China formed, Russia explodes atom bomb	184.1	258.1
1950	India independent, war in Korea	185.9	284.6

Year	Events since 1933	Cost of living 1933 = 100	Gross national product in billions
1951	Excess profits tax, wage–price freeze, transcontinental TV	200.7	329.0
1952	Living cost at new high, U.S. H-bomb, Eisenhower elected	205.2	347.0
1953	Korean armistice, U.S.S.R. hydrogen bomb, mild recession	206.9	365.4
1954	First atomic submarine, taxes reduced	207.6	363.1
1955	Israeli–Egyptian clashes, Eisenhower's heart attack	207.1	397.5
1956	Nasser seizes Suez Canal, Eisenhower reelected	210.1	419.2
1957	Sputnik, business declines, European Common Market formed	217.4	442.8
1958	Middle East troubles, business recovery, first U.S. satellite	223.3	444.5
1959	Castro wins, Russian moon shots, longest steel strike	225.3	482.7
1960	African turmoil, Polaris launched underwater, JFK elected	228.8	503.8
1961	Berlin and Congo crises, business activity at new peaks	231.1	520.1
1962	Manned space orbits, stock market break, Cuba quarantined	233.7	560.3
1963	Stock market and earnings up, Kennedy assassinated	236.6	590.5
1964	Business expansion continues, tax cut, LBJ elected	239.7	632.4
1965	Vietnam crisis, Gemini 6 and 7	243.7	684.9
1966	Stock market break, Vietnam War	250.8	749.9
1967	Israeli–Arab war, devaluation of British pound	257.9	793.9
1968	Apollo crew circles moon, Nixon elected	268.7	864.2
1969	Moon explorations, stock market break	283.1	930.3
1970	Deescalation of Vietnam, stock market dips lower and starts recovery	299.8	977.1

Year	Events since 1933	Cost of living 1933 = 100	Gross national product in billions
1971	Wage–price freeze, stock market recovery continues	312.9	1054.9
1972	Phase III of wage–price freeze, Nixon reelected	323.1	1155.0
1973	Dollar devaluation, Watergate, Phase IV, energy crisis	343.2	1306.6
1974	Year of Watergate	380.9	1413.2
1975	New York City fiscal problems	415.7	1516.3
1976	Carter elected	439.7	1692.4
1977	Uncertainties of new administration		

As you will note, in only three of the 43 years did the GNP fail to increase over the previous year. These years were 1946, 1949, and 1954. In 40 of those 43 years it increased. (It's also shattering to see that the cost of living went up in 40 of the 43 years.)

• HUMAN EMOTION

If we can agree that our GNP is an indication of the true long-term intrinsic value of stocks, and this figure has increased almost each year, then why does the stock market fluctuate? Because the market includes another ingredient—human emotion. We become overly optimistic and overly depressed. Our confidence factor reflects this picture and goes back and forth across the intrinsic value line. This can be illustrated in this way:

Intrinsic Value GNP

Human Emotion

The market to date, with the exception of the recent period, has been like a man with a yo-yo walking up the stairs. If you could get your eyes off the yo-yo, you had the opportunity to climb a high flight of stairs. If you could not, you may have condemned yourself to staying

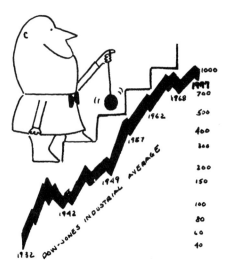

in the financial basement. The market is very much like the human body
—it runs and rests, runs and rests.

In the 1970s the Federal Reserve instituted a program of money
supply management that was superimposed on top of the two basic
components of intrinsic value and human emotion. Their goal was to
try to slow inflation by controlling the availability of credit. Inflation did
moderate, though perhaps only temporarily, but one of the most visual
effects of money supply management was the fact that it certainly made
the yo-yo drop precipitously and stay there a long enough time to frighten
the populace.

•   OPPORTUNITY OR
   DISASTER

When the market dips, do you say, "Oh, what a disaster"? Or do
you say, "Oh, what an opportunity"? Your response to this question may
very well determine where you will be financially 10 years from now.
If you say, "What a disaster!" the financial basement may be yours. If
you say, "What an opportunity!" you may have the opportunity to climb
the financial stairs.

What difference does it really make in attaining your long-
term financial objective if the market fluctuates? For example, if you
have 10 years before you plan to retire, and your funds are invested in a
well-selected portfolio of quality stocks, the fact that their market value
fluctuates during the period shouldn't be your major concern. What is
important is "What will the market value of my securities be when I
need to use them?"

• THE EMOTION
   CURVE

Your emotions may be preventing you from being a good investor. The reason that you have not invested is fear of loss, which may be a much stronger motivator than your desire for gain. So you stay out of the stock market because of fear and ignorance. You never really trust or are "for" anything you do not know and understand.

However, as time goes on, you hear bits of scuttlebutt and glorious claims made by others on the cocktail circuit about big gains in the market. At that point your interest begins to become more intense, and hope begins to replace your fear. As the headlines get bigger and the TV commentator nightly reports, "The market soared again today," greed begins to rear its head. That's when you may be tempted to jump in with a mighty splash and shout, "Buy!" Then when there occurs a correction in the market, hope begins to wane. "But surely," you say, "my stocks will recover shortly. I just could not have made a mistake. After all, the market must know I've just bought or that my cousin twice removed works for the company." As the market continues its decline, fear seizes you and you cry, "Sell!"

These stages on your emotion curve can be illustrated in this way:

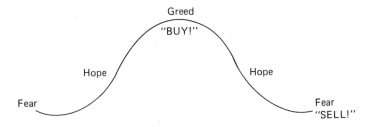

If you follow this example, you have assured yourself of the most infallible way I know to lose money in the market—buy high, sell low!

• HOW NOW,
   MR. DOW?

When clients call to ask "How's the market?" what they are really asking is the level of the Dow Jones Industrial Average. To answer this question, I punch the appropriate symbol, IDJN, on my Bunker-Ramo stock quotation machine that is connected directly to the stock exchange and give them the current average. Actually, the level of the Dow probably makes little or no difference if they are invested in individual stocks. What does make a difference is how their particular stocks are doing.

The Dow Jones Average is not the best indicator, but we've used it for so long that it will probably be with us for a long time.

There are really four Dow Jones Averages—the Industrial, the Composite, the Utility, and the Rails. However, the best known is the Industrial Average, which has 29 industrials and 1 utility—American Telephone and Telegraph.

Charles S. Dow published his first Dow Jones Average on July 3, 1884. It first appeared in his financial news bulletin called the *Customer's Afternoon Letter* (a forerunner of *The Wall Street Journal.*) It was distributed to brokers and bankers from an office behind a soda fountain in the basement of 15 Wall Street. In 1896, *The Wall Street Journal* began publication of the first Industrial Stock Average of 12 stocks. It has had a long climb. It took 60 years to reach the first 500 points, 16 more to go to 1000 and retreat. Table 7–1 shows some Dow Jones milestones and how it has climbed over the years.

Table 7–1

First close over

100	Jan. 12, 1906	100.25
200	Dec. 19, 1927	200.93
300	Dec. 31, 1928	300.00
400	Dec. 29, 1954	401.97
500	Mar. 12, 1956	500.24
600	Feb. 20, 1959	602.21
700	May 17, 1961.	705.52
800	Feb. 28, 1964	800.14
900	Jan. 28, 1965	900.25
1000	Nov. 14, 1972	1003.16

The Dow Jones Industrial Average is not an average anymore. When it first began, the average was computed by adding the price of the stocks in the Average and dividing by the number of issues. The divisor has been changed over the years to adjust whenever a component stock was split or declared a stock dividend. Also, 18 stocks have been added.

The Stocks in the Dow • Here are the 30 stocks in our present Dow Jones Industrial Average. They are

Allied Chemical
Aluminum Companies of
  America
American Brands
American Can
American Telephone &
  Telegraph
Bethlehem Steel
Chrysler
du Pont
Eastman Kodak
Esmark
Exxon
General Electric
General Foods
General Motors
Goodyear Tire and Rubber

International Harvester
INCO
International Paper
Johns-Manville
Minnesota Mining &
  Manufacturing
Owens-Illinois
Procter and Gamble
Sears, Roebuck
Standard Oil of California
Texaco
Union Carbide
United Technologies
United States Steel
Westinghouse Electric
Woolworth (F.W.)

"That valve controls the Dow Jones Average"

The size of the company has no bearing on its weight in the Dow
Average. AT&T, with $94,167,000,000 in assets, has the same weight as

Esmark, Inc. (Swift & Co.) with slightly less than $1,083,100,000 in assets.

Only two stocks remain that were in the original average. They are American Tobacco, now American Brands, and General Electric. IBM was once in the average, but "Who is interested in office equipment?" our forefathers reasoned, so it was dropped. Just think where the Dow would be now if IBM had been left in!

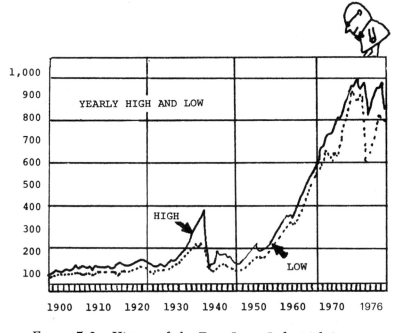

FIGURE 7–2.   History of the Dow Jones Industrial Average

Seventy Years with Mr. Dow •   Figure 7–2 illustrates the Dow Jones Average in graph form, showing both highs and lows.

Where Will the Dow Be by 1980? •   I do not know! But let's see if we can make a sensible estimate. If you have an opinion about the future course of the American economy, it's also a stock market prediction.

Before deciding where we're going, let's consider where we've been. From 1959 to 1969, the gross national product rose from $484 billion to $932 billion—a 6.6 percent compound annual growth rate. A shade over one-third of this gain represented price increases, but two-thirds was real growth. Thus, price inflation averaged 2.3 percent per year, and real growth was 4.3 percent per year.

Several government agencies and outside forecasters are predicting greater real growth for the future.

But you be the predictor. Do you think we will have a lower rate of growth, the same, or higher? If you feel a lower rate, choose "A" below; if the same, choose "B"; if higher, choose "C."

A • Lower rate (5.5 percent a year).
B • Same rate (6.6 percent a year).
C • Higher rate (7.5 percent a year).

Based on the growth rate you selected, you can now calculate your estimate of the 1980 GNP.

A • 5.5 percent compound annual growth rate will produce $1.678 trillion.
B • 6.6 percent compound annual growth rate will produce $1.883 trillion.
C • 7.5 percent compound annual growth rate will produce $2.069 trillion.

In the past, our experience has been that the DJIA earnings averaged about 6¢ per billion of GNP. If this ratio continues, our forecast then would be

Forecast	1980 GNP will be	DJIA earnings
A	$1.678 trillion	$100.70
B	$1.883 trillion	$113.00
C	$2.069 trillion	$124.15

During the postwar period the DJIA has sold at an average of around 15 times earnings. It has ranged from a low of under 6 times to a high of just over 20 times. Based on your estimate of the price–earnings ratio, the 1980 DJIA becomes:

		Price–earnings ratio		
Earnings estimate	10×	15×	17×	20×
A $100.70	1007.00	1510.00	1711.00	2014.00
B $113.00	1130.00	1695.00	1921.00	2260.00
C $124.15	1241.00	1862.00	2110.00	2482.00

If you chose the middle course, your estimate of the DJIA is 1695. The future Dow price–earning ratios may go higher or lower than any of these. The relationship between GNP and the Dow earnings may be

Table 7-2. Relationship of Price to Earnings

Possibilities for the Dow-Jones Industrial Average in 1980

Dow-Jones Earnings per Share	9	10	11	12	13	14	15	16	17	18	19	20	21	22	23	24	25
$130	1170	1300	1430	1560	1690	1820	1950	2080	2210	2340	2470	2600	2730	2860	2990	3120	3250
125	1125	1250	1375	1500	1625	1750	1875	2000	2125	2250	2375	2500	2625	2750	2875	3000	3125
120	1080	1200	1320	1440	1560	1680	1800	1920	2040	2160	2280	2400	2520	2640	2760	2880	3000
115	1035	1150	1265	1380	1495	1610	1725	1840	1955	2070	2185	2300	2415	2530	2645	2760	2875
110	990	1100	1210	1320	1430	1540	1650	1760	1870	1980	2090	2200	2310	2420	2530	2640	2750
105	945	1050	1155	1260	1365	1470	1575	1680	1785	1890	1995	2100	2205	2310	2415	2520	2625
100	900	1000	1100	1200	1300	1400	1500	1600	1700	1800	1900	2000	2100	2200	2300	2400	2500
95	855	950	1045	1140	1235	1330	1425	1520	1615	1710	1805	1900	1995	2090	2185	2280	2375
90	810	900	990	1080	1170	1260	1350	1440	1530	1620	1710	1800	1890	1980	2070	2160	2250
85	765	850	935	1020	1105	1190	1275	1360	1445	1530	1615	1700	1785	1870	1955	2040	2125
80	720	800	880	960	1040	1120	1200	1280	1360	1440	1520	1600	1680	1760	1840	1920	2000
75	675	750	825	900	975	1050	1125	1200	1275	1350	1425	1500	1575	1650	1725	1800	1875
Price Earnings Ratio	9	10	11	12	13	14	15	16	17	18	19	20	21	22	23	24	25

subjected to wide fluctuations. Inflation may be more or less than estimated.

Your earnings predictions may differ from any of the ones we have used. You may feel that the P/E ratios will be higher or lower than they have been in the past. Table 7–2 will help you pick the combination you believe the future may hold.

Despite the many areas of possible fluctuation, this exercise in forecasting vividly demonstrates that it is difficult to be pessimistic about long-term stock prices if you are at all optimistic about the economy!

• SUMMARY

Weighing possible risks and rewards, I think the future of common stock investing appears bright—provided that the investor holds a diversified list of selected common stocks, either directly or through a professionally managed common stock mutual fund.

If ignorance and fear have kept you from being a shareholder of American industry, conscientiously work to change both of these by becoming well-informed. The annual report of the gross national product can be an exciting statistic if you relate it to the intrinsic value of stocks. Remember that the market does fluctuate but always in the past it has returned to intrinsic value.

Application

1 • What is the gross national product today?

2 • What is your prediction of what the GNP will be in 10 years?

3 • Prepare a graph of the GNP similar to Fig. 7–2. Plot your 10-year projection on the graph.

4 • What is your prediction of the price–earnings ratio of the stocks on the Dow in 10 years?

5 • What action will you take to apply your predictions to benefit your own financial future?

    a.

    b.

    c.

8
Mutual Funds: Pro and Con

By now you've taken a good hard look at some of the requirements necessary to become a successful investor in individual stocks. But you may be protesting that you do not have that kind of time and expertise. You are a topnotch professional in your chosen vocation, and the reason you are is that you devote almost every waking hour at being good at it, which doesn't leave time for studying the market. Yet you realize that you must have your money working for you so that your children can go to college, and so that you can some day retire in financial dignity. What should you do? If you do not have what I call the 3 "T"s and an "M," I recommend that you put professional money managers to work for you.

• TIME

The first "T" is for Time. Do you have the time to truly study the market trends? I don't mean, do you have a moment before you settle down to watch the next murder mystery, police or hospital drama on TV to take a quick glance at the evening newspaper to learn whether your stocks went up or down during the day?

Do you really have the time to spend studying balance sheets, profit and loss statements, market trends, economic indicators, changes in monetary policies, increases in government expenditures, decreases in other areas of government expenditures, shortages, surpluses, consumer buying trends, international competition due to lower labor costs, access to raw materials, and so forth?

If you can answer that you do have this time and feel that it would be more rewarding financially and emotionally to spend this time being a professional in the market than spending it pursuing a hobby or engaging in recreational activities, then you have the first "T."

• TRAINING

The second "T" is for Training. What is your educational background—accounting, statistical analysis, money and banking, marketing, economics, finance, human psychology? Even if you have the first "T" of Time, can you properly translate this knowledge into action? If you can and if you are thoroughly schooled in these areas and have developed some reasonable expertise in them, you qualify for the second "T."

• TEMPERAMENT

The third "T" is for Temperament. Are you temperamentally suited for successful investing in the stock market? Did you work very hard for your money? Were you a child of the Depression? Does your memory of hard times make you squeeze every nickel until it screams loudly?

I was raised in the hard times of the dust bowl of Oklahoma. That trying experience made an indelible impression on me. In my counseling I have observed many others from a similar background. In most of them I have found that it has caused their emotional decisions about money to be more black and white than they should be. Money decisions must often be based on various shades of gray. I find that if a person has experienced bad times, he either clutches a dollar very tightly to his bosom for fear of losing it, or determines that once he gets a dollar, he is going to put it to work aggressively to see if he can turn that dollar into an additional dollar. My reaction to my dust bowl experience was and still is the latter. It's not that I enjoy hoarding money or even spending it. My challenge has been to take one dollar and make two, and then take the two and make four, and so on.

Analyze your own personality. This is not an easy thing to do. Some basic books on psychology may be of help to you. One I have enjoyed is Dr. Muriel James' book on transactional analysis entitled *Born to Win*. I also recommend Dr. Maxwell Maltz's book, *Psycho-Cybernetics*. The whole field of psychology can be fascinating, and through it you may discover why you and others react to certain stimuli and conditions the way you do. In the world of finance this knowledge can pay handsome dividends.

Can you act when you have reasonable facts before you? You'll never know all the facts. If you wait until you are 100 percent sure, your decision will invariably be too late. I find that most investment decisions are made far too late rather than too soon. Don't ever deceive yourself into thinking that if you don't make a decision, you haven't made a decision. You have. You have decided that where your money is right now is the best place for it to be.

I've found the difference between mediocre and superb performance in the market is the ability to evaluate and then take the appropriate action.

I observe many who plant good fruit trees in the form of good stocks, and refuse to harvest the fruit, letting it rot on the trees.

Don't become enamored with a stock because it has made you an unrealized capital gain (meaning it went up). Don't be afraid of taking a profit if it appears that the stock has topped out and will probably be flat for six months to a year. Don't back off from taking a profit just because you'll have a capital gains tax to pay.

There is a time to buy and a time to sell—regardless of which stocks you own. Can you unemotionally move when it's time to do so? If so, you have the third "T," Temperament.

• MONEY

You have analyzed your three "T"s. Now let's look at how you fit the "M." "M" represents Money. Do you have enough money to diversify your holdings? Diversification is one of the first rules of successful investing. Do you have sufficient funds to enable you not to put all your eggs in one basket, but to have at least 10 baskets—one basket for office equipment, another for natural resources, still another for beverages, another for retail stores, another for automobile stocks, etc.?

You may feel the need to subscribe to an advisory service. You should calculate this cost in money and in the time needed to digest the contents.

If you have the 3 "T"s and an "M," you will find being your own pro fun and rewarding. Therefore, you should plan to devote considerable time and energy to this important facet of your financial future. If not, let the pros do it for you.

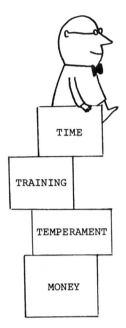

• LETTING THE
PROS DO IT

You may find letting the professionals do your investing for you very hard to do. It is especially hard for some professionals. You would think it would be otherwise, since they are so aware of how much time, training, and experience it took to bring them to their present level of proficiency. The admission that someone can do something better than they can do it often is just too hard an admission for some persons to make. The same doctor who would be aghast if I should suggest diagnosing my own pains will hop into the stock market arena without any more preparation.

Even when the professional becomes a pro in the market, I usually find that the good full-time pros outperform the part-time pros.

Let's assume that you are willing to let the professionals help you. What choices are available to you?

Private Professional Management • There are two ways to obtain professional management. If you have a large amount of funds to invest, you may qualify for private professional management through an investment advisory service. There are some that will accept as small an account as $50,000 for a fee of 1 percent of the net assets per annum.

Most of the top services will not accept an account of less than $300,000. Some services will not accept a private account of less than $20 million. On this size account one-half of 1 percent of the net asset value is the usual management charge.

Let's assume that you have sufficient funds to qualify for private professional management. What should you do?

First, do an in-depth study of the professional teams available. Become acquainted with their personnel, and take a good hard look at their past performance. After all, you are buying brains. You might as well get the best "brains" you can for the money you are paying.

Second, you will sign an agreement giving the management service discretionary power to buy and sell for your account. This can be cancelled or amended at your discretion. In the agreement you should designate the stockbroker of your choice.

Third, you will need to transfer the agreed amount of money or stocks to the bank or broker that is to act as the custodian of the assets in the account. They will then make the proper delivery of stocks and money at the directions of the advisors.

After these necessary steps have been taken, you will begin to receive confirmations from your broker on each buy and sell. Your service will also make a monthly or quarterly report to you, giving you a resumé of all transactions, a report on gains and losses, and often a comparison of your portfolio's performance against that of the popular averages.

You may withdraw the account at any time.

Public Professional Management • If the amount you have for investment is less than $100,000, you should consider using public professional management, through the investment medium of the investment company trusts, commonly called mutual funds.

I would prefer calling them by another name. Not that the term "mutual fund" does not give an indication of their nature, but I find that so many confuse them with mutual savings and loan or mutual insurance companies, and worry that they can be assessed, which of course is not true.

The Feeling Is Mutual • "Mutual" means you may mutually benefit from pooling your resources with others. For example, let's say you have $1000. Alone you could not obtain diversification or professional management. But let's assume there are 999 others who each have $1000 and have the same financial objective that you do. If all of you pooled your funds, you would have a million dollars. With a million dollars you would have sufficient money to spread your risk among a number of different industries. You would also have enough money to hire some top professional money managers to select and constantly supervise your holdings. A mutual fund, then, should do for you what you would do for yourself if you had sufficient Time, the proper Training, the right Temperament, and sufficient Money to diversify. It offers the same advantages to the small investor that the wealthy have always had. The wealthy have enough money to diversify and enough money to hire the pros.

In a previous chapter we concluded that there were three basic requirements for successful investing: diversification, proper selection, and constant supervision. Let's examine these three to see if a quality mutual fund with excellent management will fulfill these requirements. (There is a wide range of expertise in managements. Spend considerable time and study choosing the one or ones you will use.)

• THE SEMINAR
FUND

For the past 16 years I have conducted financial planning seminars in Houston, Texas. Fourteen of these years I have conducted six to eight 3-session seminars a year in one of Foley's seven department stores. Foley's (a part of Federated Stores) is superbly managed by the extremely talented Chairman of the Board, Milton Berman, and their extraordinarily gifted President, Stewart Orton. Foley's is very customer-oriented and offers these seminars as a public service.

At the second session of each seminar I discuss mutual funds and how they work. As an example I always use the same mutual fund. It is middle of the road in its financial objectives, has a good 43-year record and has averaged approximately 12.2 percent compounded over its lifetime with all distributions reinvested. It's not the top performer but its record is good.

Incidentally, I remember using this fund one night at a seminar when a lady, evidently impressed with the possibilities of what the fund could offer, came up to me and blurted out, "Whatever will the savings and loans do?" When I asked her what she meant, she said she feared that everybody would now take their money out of them, and they would not have sufficient money to lend for home mortgages. I calmed her fears by assuring her that much of the money would remain there so she need not be so concerned.

I always use a fund that has averaged 12 percent over the long term, for I'm convinced that that's the minimum long-term performance you should accept on your money. With our present rate of inflation and progressive tax bite, you have to obtain that performance to make any reasonable progress.

In this book I'll call this fund The Seminar Fund. That's not its real name. If I were to use its real name I would have to hand you a prospectus before I could tell you about it, and send you a new one each year. I do encourage you to go to your broker and get the prospectus of a real fund. Most prospecti are pretty much the same. They may differ as to financial objective, fees, commissions, performance, and incentive fees, and each family of funds will have its chosen investment advisers. The performance and the quality of management can vary vastly, yet I have found each prospectus very similar.

In our chapter on selecting stocks we agreed that one of the first requirements of successful investing was diversification—spreading your risk. Mutual funds uniquely fulfill this requirement.

Diversification • The Investment Company Act of 1940 provides that a mutual fund may not have more than 5 percent of its assets in any one company, nor own more than 10 percent of the outstanding shares of any one company. By this regulation you know that you should always have at least 20 stocks in your mutual funds portfolio, and also that any one of the 20 will not represent more than 10 percent of the outstanding shares of that company. This in itself insures a fair degree of diversification.

You will find as you explore the large number of funds available that most of them have from 100 to 150 different stocks in their portfolio, and will cover a wide spectrum of industry groups.

For example, Table 8–1 shows the way $10,000 would have been spread if you had invested in The Seminar on December 31, 1976.

Table 8–1.

Largest individual holdings			Other portfolio securities		
Philip Morris	$	364	Abbott Laboratories	$	67
Connecticut General Insurance		346	Alcan Aluminum		73
RCA		340	Alco Standard		57
International Business			Allis-Chalmers		57
Machines		335	Aluminum Company of		
Ford Motor		312	America		143
Federal National Mortgage			American Airlines		81
Association		262	Amfac		50
American Telephone and			Anheuser-Busch		28
Telegraph		244	Armco Steel		45
MCA		235	BankAmerica		73
Cities Service		224	Bethlehem Steel		104
Union Oil of California		205	Boeing		146

Table 8-1. (*Continued*)

Other portfolio securities		Other portfolio securities	
Braniff International	41	McDonald's	38
Bristol-Myers	75	McDonnell Douglas	41
Burlington Industries	128	Middle South Utilities	18
Burroughs	51	Miles Laboratories	14
Capital Cities Communications	126	Missouri Pacific	112
Caterpillar Tractor	12	Mohasco	35
Champion International	9	Monroe Auto Equipment	20
Chessie System	28	NCR	93
Clark Equipment	55	National Semiconductor	34
Colt Industries	101	Norfolk and Western Railway	65
Communications Satellite	39	Northwest Airlines	153
Control Data	56	Northwestern National Life	
Crown Zellerbach	68	Insurance	22
Deere	16	Norton Simon	52
Delta Air Lines	100	Outboard Marine	27
DeSoto	14	Overnite Transportation	22
Diamond Shamrock	113	Pacific Gas and Electric	98
Fairchild Camera & Instrument	68	Panhandle Eastern Pipe Line	66
Firestone	68	PepsiCo	38
First Charter Financial	42	Polaroid	109
First Chicago	60	Public Service of Colorado	20
Florida Power	77	Revlon	64
General Dynamics	155	Reynolds Industries (R. J.)	42
General Motors	32	Reynolds Metals	19
General Telephone &		Royal Dutch Petroleum	47
Electronics	52	SAFECO	102
Goodyear Tire	41	St. Regis Paper	46
Government Employees		Scott Paper	158
Insurance	75	Shell Oil	97
Great Northern Nekoosa	139	SmithKline	79
Great Western Financial	77	Southern California Edison	36
Hart Schaffner & Marx	23	Sperry Rand	154
Heinz (H. J.)	69	Standard Oil of California	112
Host International	16	Stevens (J. P.)	38
Houdaille Industries	31	Superior Oil	113
Ideal Basic Industries	39	TRW	120
Imperial Corporation of		Tenneco	146
America	49	Texaco	200
Interco	136	Tidewater Marine Service	23
International Telephone &		Transway International	32
Telegraph	100	UAL	61
Jonathan Logan	27	Union Carbide	40
Kaiser Aluminum & Chemical	134	United Technologies	11
Kaiser Cement & Gypsum	17	Wells Fargo	46
Knight Ridder Newspapers	65	Westvaco	46
Leaseway Transportation	72	Other Stocks	58
Louisiana Land & Exploration	86	Total Stocks	$ 9,736
Manufacturers Hanover	54	Net Cash and Equivalent	264
Masco	63		
McDermott (J. Ray)	79	**Total**	$10,000

This array of stocks should fulfill the first requirement for successful investing—diversification.

Proper Selection and Constant Supervision • The Seminar Fund often has a picture in its guidebook of some very learned-looking men and women sitting around a large conference table with research reports in front of them. They are having one of their daily conferences to determine which stocks to add and which to take out of the portfolio, or to just be as certain as they can that the stocks they presently hold fulfill the requirements that the shareholders designated when they chose this particular fund.

A staff of analysts, each a specialist in his own field, constantly reports to the investment committee. There will be specialists in the oils, the chemicals, the automotives, and so forth. Not only do they read, analyze, and project figures on each company in their industry specialty, but they also make on-the-spot studies and conduct fact-finding interviews with the top officers of these companies.

I remember an officer of an oil company calling me to invest in a particular fund after one of the fund's analysts had called on him. He was very impressed with the analyst's thorough knowledge of the oil industry and especially of his company.

The thoroughness and training of these specialists fulfill the two other requirements of successful investing—proper selection and constant supervision.

In addition to these three requirements of successful investing, the properly selected mutual fund can provide 12 other valuable characteristics.

Convenience, an Essential Ingredient • The first is convenience. We all do what is convenient for us. Mutual funds can offer this convenience with a plan that will fit almost any pocketbook. You may start an investment program in a mutual fund with a relatively small amount of money; in fact, some funds have no minimum initial investment. Others will accept as small an amount as $100. You may then add in many funds any amount or as small an amount as $25. In addition, you have the privilege of automatically reinvesting both your dividends and your capital gains, usually without commission. Some funds charge to reinvest dividends. None charge to reinvest capital gains. If you were to receive these same dividends from individual stocks in your private portfolio and you realized capital gains from your buys and sells and wanted to reinvest, you would be charged a commission. With a mutual fund you can have immediate reinvestment of small or large amounts of money, giving you an opportunity to speed up your compounding potential.

Dollar-Cost-Averaging as You Earn • The second item in the list of
12 additional advantages that a mutual fund may offer is that you can
truly dollar-cost average. This means putting the same amount of money
into the same security at the same interval. One certainty of the stock
market is that it will fluctuate. So put this characteristic to work for you
instead of worrying so much about it. Choose an amount you can comfortably invest each month (not too comfortably or you may not save
anything) and invest that amount on the same day each month.

Many funds provide a bank draft authorization so that the bank
can automatically draft your account each month. I find this to be an
extremely satisfactory arrangement for my clients. Banks never forget!
I find my clients often do.

The mutual funds will carry your share purchase out to the third
decimal point, which allows you to truly dollar-cost-average. This makes
this investment medium a good one to use for this purpose.

The chapter entitled, "Is There an Infallible Way to Invest?" covers
this point in more detail.

Record Keeping Made Easy • Another characteristic of the mutual
fund is that you have professionals doing your record keeping. You will
have five choices when you open an account. Regardless of which
choice you make, the fund will provide you a historical record of your
account.

1 • Reinvest all distributions.

2 • Reinvest all distributions, and you may add amounts systematically or when you desire.

3 • Receive dividends in cash and reinvest capital gains.

4 • Receive dividends and capital gains in cash.

5 • Receive a check a month. (Discussed later.)

All you need to do is keep the last confirmation you receive that
year, and you will have a complete record of your account. The mutual
fund also will send you (and IRS) a Form 1099 showing the dividends
and capital gains paid to you for the year. This you will want to keep
and attach to your federal income tax return.

Where Do You Fit on the Triangle? • Do you remember our triangle
of finance that we used when we were discussing individual stocks? It is
applicable here, too. A fund must state in its prospectus its financial
objective. This objective cannot be changed without the consent of the

shareholders. The fund rarely changes its objective. If it is presently an income fund and management also desires to manage a growth fund, they will establish a new fund and add it to their family of funds. They may also add a middle-of-the-road fund, a corporate bond fund, or a convertible bond fund. The financial triangle would look something like this:

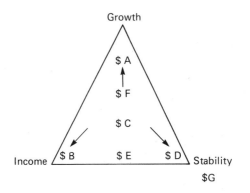

As you can see, you can't be a Paul Revere who hops on his horse and rides off in all directions. You must decide in which direction you want to go. When you maximize "Income," you move farther from "Growth." The same is true if you select "Stability" as your primary concern.

A fund management group may have a family of funds, attempting to provide a fund for each place on the triangle, or it may have only one or two.

There are approximately nine kinds of mutual funds: growth (aggressive and moderate), income, corporate bond, balanced, convertible bond, specialty funds, option, municipal bond, and money market funds.

Growth Funds • Under the growth designation you could have four subheadings: "go-go," very aggressive growth, quality growth, and growth with income funds.

The go-go funds are discussed in the next chapter.

If you invest in a quality growth fund you would be placing your dollar nearer to the top of the triangle at A, because its objective is long-term growth. Intermittent volatility should not be of great concern. You should not be interested in dividends when you invest in a growth fund. As a matter of fact, if it were possible for the fund managers to select stocks that paid no dividends and just grew in value, with no need to buy and sell and realize capital gains, this would be ideal for you. What you really want is for $1 to grow to $3 at least in 10 years. You would prefer not having any tax liability in the meantime if such were possible.

When I've asked a prospective client his financial objective and he has answered that it is growth, I may recommend a particular quality growth fund to him. When he asks me, "How much does it pay?" meaning what the dividend is, I know I have not communicated properly what a growth fund is designed to do.

Income Funds • There is a good selection of quality income funds. Their portfolio managers choose stocks that have paid good dividends in the past, have a record of increasing dividends, and have a reasonable expectation of continuing good dividends and market stability of their shares. If your need is for income now rather than later, this is the type of fund you should consider. Your location on the triangle would be *B*.

Bond Funds • When you invest in a bond fund, you are placing your dollar in the lower right-hand side of the triangle (*D*). Bond funds have been around for many years; however, during the growth craze of the 1960s they attracted very little attention. With the agonizing reappraisals of the early 1970s they became increasingly popular. The magic word was no longer "growth," but "income."

Bond funds invest most of their funds in debt-type securities. These are corporate bonds and debentures, perhaps a few convertible bonds, treasuries, commercial paper, etc. Instead of taking an equity position in the market, you become a lender of money.

When you invest in a bond fund, do not think that the price of the shares will remain fixed. It will not. It does have some fluctuation, though usually not as great as in other security investments.

If your fund is composed of bonds with an average yield of 8 percent and the going interest rate is 9 percent, then the fund will not be able to sell the bond at par; therefore, the price of your shares could decline. On the other hand, if the going rate drops to 7 percent, they probably can sell the bonds at a premium (above par) and the price of your shares would increase. If they purchased a bond at par (usually $1000) that carries a rate of 8 percent, which matures January 1, 2000, this does not mean that they must hold the bond until the year 2000 to turn it into cash. It means that on January 1, 2000, the person holding the bond is guaranteed $1000. Between now and that date, the value will usually fluctuate with the country's going interest rate.

Balanced Funds • In position *C* on the triangle you will find balanced funds. These are funds that invest approximately 60 percent of their funds in high-quality bonds and the remainder in high-quality, income-producing "blue chip" stocks. In periods of market decline they offer a safer haven than the growth funds. Conversely, in a rising market they usually lag behind.

Convertible Bond Funds • In an effort to obtain the best of two worlds, some management groups have established convertible bond funds. These funds were designed to have a relatively good yield—around 5 to 6 percent—and have the potential of growth. They listed the characteristics of their fund by showing the advantages and disadvantages of bonds and stocks, and proposed that they would combine the best from both. Your dollar with them would be placed around E on the triangle.

As discussed earlier, its characteristics are supposed to be the best of two worlds: the guarantee of principal and rate of return of a bond, and the potential for growth of common stock.

The theory runs that even though you may be placing a bit of a damper on maximum growth potential, there is down-side protection, for the convertible bond should only drop in price to a level where it will take on the characteristics of a bond yielding the current interest level.

The theory sounds good, but its performance has not been outstanding. The number of quality convertible bonds available in the marketplace has been limited. This tends to make a thin market (not enough traders to make it competitive). Also, many of the firms offering convertible bonds are not the blue-chip companies. They had to offer convertibles to "sweeten the kitty" to sell their bonds to the investing public. So the convertible bonds were tied to less stable securities, causing more volatility than some shareholders were willing to accept.

Specialty Funds • Personally, I would rarely select a specialty fund. In my opinion, they destroy one of the main reasons you chose to invest in investment company shares, and that reason was diversification. I have not placed it on the triangle, for it has maverick characteristics. I would most often place it at the top of the triangle along with "go-go" funds. Specialty funds have specialized mostly in either insurance stocks, bank stocks, or gold stocks. They have for that reason been rather cyclical in their performance.

Common Stock Funds • The middle-of-the-road fund that seeks a balance among income, growth, and stability is the stronghold of the mutual fund industry. It would fit in the middle of your triangle and is the place where most investors feel the greatest amount of comfort.

When deciding where you should be on the triangle, you should remember that your temperament is important in your investment program. I find in my counseling that once I have sufficient information about a client's time schedule, assets, and tax bracket, it is not difficult to choose the investment I feel would fulfill his needs financially, but it may not fit his temperament. Regardless of how much I think he should invest for maximum growth, if I detect that volatility would disturb his peace of mind, then the best investment for him will probably be in the middle. Peace of mind is a good investment, too.

Our Seminar Fund fits in the middle, and it is letter *F* on the triangle. Let's say that *F* stands for "just fine" for most investors. Trying to make it too fast is what causes most failures. Remember, those who make it to their goal of financial independence have usually done it slowly. If you select your fund well from this category, you should be able to obtain your 12 percent compounded over a 20-year period. The Seminar Fund has in the past averaged 12 percent or better in fifteen of the nineteen 20-year periods.

Municipal Bond Funds • These are covered in Chapter 2. They provide tax-free income, permit additions in smaller amounts, and provide reinvestment privileges.

Money Market Funds • During the extremely high interest rates of the mid-1970s a new kind of fund appeared called the Money Market or Reserve Funds. Its purpose was to offer its investors a haven for their money until the storms of the stock market subsided. It placed funds in relatively risk-free, fixed-income instruments such as bank commercial paper, certificates of deposit, Treasury bills, and federal agency paper. Most of these had no sales charge and a relatively low management fee. It is represented by the letter *G* and is outside the triangle, since it would be out of the market. *G* here could represent "Good" if money is tight and is attracting interest rates of 10 to 12 percent.

The Exchange Privilege • Another characteristic of most mutual funds is that they have an exchange privilege. If you select a fund that is a member of a family of funds, you have the privilege of exchanging that fund for another of their funds for only a $5 exchange fee that goes to the custodian bank to compensate it for setting up a new account and canceling your old certificates and issuing you new ones. Some funds charge no fee.

You may consider doing this if your financial objective has changed. For instance, if you have been interested in growth but are now retiring, you may now be more interested in income. You have the privilege of changing from one fund to the other without a sales charge. You should be aware, however, that if you realize a gain on your shares, the IRS considers this a sale, and you'll have to pay a capital gains tax on your profit. A better way may be for you to just begin your check-a-month from your growth fund, hoping that appreciation will replace the value of the shares redeemed.

You may also establish a loss for tax purposes using the exchange privilege. Let's assume that the market has dropped below your cost. You are still confident of the investment ability of the management team and believe that temporary market conditions have adversely affected anticipated performance. You are nearing the end of the year and have some capital gains already established for the year. You may want to exchange the fund that you own for one of their other funds, thereby establishing a loss for your tax purposes. You would need to wait at least 31 days before moving back to your original fund, or the IRS would disallow the deduction, calling it a "wash sale." Again, there is no commission to exchange it back to your original position.

•   TIMING

The greatest advantage to the exchange privilege is that it gives you the opportunity to move in and out of the market without a commission. If the Federal Reserve is severely tightening the money supply which chokes the market, and your fund is part of a family of funds that has a money market fund, you just move over to a safer harbor, ride out the storm and draw a tidy interest in the meantime.

You may be wondering why the fund managers do not take this action for you. They do move into as defensive a position as they can under the regulations by which they must abide. However, to qualify as a regulated investment company, which is important to you in terms of your taxes, less than 30 percent of their gross income in any fiscal year can be derived from holding securities less than three months. This regulation may inhibit moving from stock to cash on a short-term basis, which for your purposes may be the most prudent action to take. The exchange privilege gives you the opportunity to take advantage of the strengths of top professional management while avoiding the weakness caused by these regulations. This can make it possible for you to exploit their offensive ability by holding their funds during rising markets and avoiding what may be short-term weakness by moving out of the funds entirely during down markets.

Now let's take a look at the long-term performance of The Seminar Fund. (Remember, this is what has happened in the past, with no future guarantees! But what is guaranteed?) By using Timing you may have increased your performance.

Figure 8–1 is a bar chart covering the Seminar Fund over its life. It covers years when the market went up and years when it went down. The general trend, as you can see, has been upward. You must decide for yourself what you feel will be the trend in the future.

Take time, right now, to really study this chart. If you are a speed reader, don't zip past this. It deserves your conscientious study.

• THE YO-YO
AND THE STAIRS

Now that you've studied the chart, what are your reactions? Remember, it covers a long period of time. As a matter of fact, it covers a 43-year period from 1934 through 1976. Do you agree that this is a fairly graphic picture of a man with a yo-yo going up the stairs? What difference did it make to him how many times the yo-yo yo-yoed during the life of the fund? The stairs he climbed reached quite a height. If you had invested $10,000 on January 1, 1934, reinvested all your capital gains distribution (classified as a part of capital by regulation), and on December 31, 1976 decided to cash in your shares at that lower spot in the market, you would have received $383,767 net to you after all costs had been taken out, with the exception of your federal and state income tax responsibility. In addition, during that period you would have received cash dividends of $168,918. If you had reinvested both the capital gains and dividends, your $10,000 would have grown to $1,428,770. (Just think how many life insurance policies, by contrast, have been sold to men age 22 with the idea that the $10,000 placed in the cash value would be growing for their retirement incomes.) We, of course, do not know what the next 43 years will bring, but if our economy is no better or no worse than the past 43 years, surely this performance can be one of the possibilities you should consider.

Now, if you just can't get your eyes off that yo-yo and absolutely must have your dollars "guaranteed," take out your pencil and draw a straight line from left to right on the illustration of the Seminar Fund and connect the $10,000 marks on each side. (That's the first square at the bottom.) This is your basement position from which you can look up the flight of stairs (remember, in this example, we are spending the income from either source). This means that in the savings institution, you were guaranteed that you could always go back and get your $10,000. It also means that that is all you could get, regardless of what

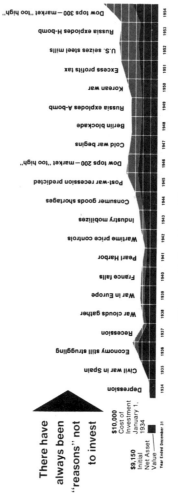

FIGURE 8-1. Bar Chart

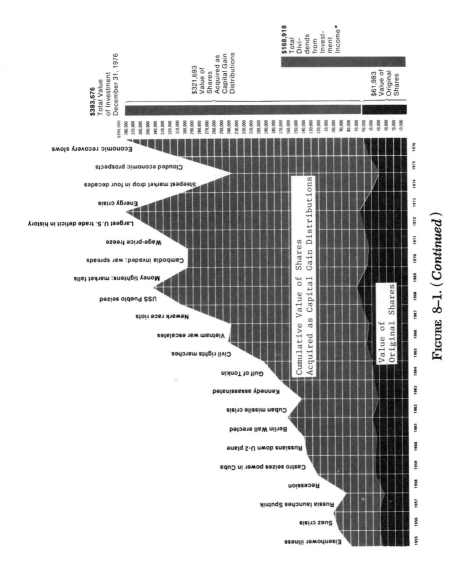

FIGURE 8-1. (*Continued*)

143

inflation had done to the purchasing power of your money, and regardless of how much the savings institution had made investing your money for themselves. You can't be critical of them, however, because you, of your own free will, loaned them your money. In return, they "guaranteed" the return of the same number of dollars plus a fixed rate of return.

• IS THE "GUARANTEE" PREMIUM TOO HIGH?

If I came to you and told you I wanted to sell you an insurance policy that would guarantee you that you could always have your $10,000 back regardless of what that money would buy at that time and regardless of how much I had made on your $10,000, and all I wanted to charge you was $724.18 per month, every month for 516 months, or $8,690.16 per year, would you buy the policy? That is what it would have cost you to have had your $10,000 guaranteed over that period of time. (The diagram does not show reinvestment of dividends.)

What do the letters F.D.I.C. stand for on a bank door or bank billboard? Federal Deposit Insurance Corporation. Have you ever obtained an insurance policy for which you did not pay an insurance premium?

• DIRECT OR INDIRECT INVESTING?

All money is invested in American industry either directly or indirectly. The direct method can be accomplished by putting your money to work in an investment similar to the Seminar Fund. An indirect method would be to lend your funds to a savings institution and let it invest in American industry. When you choose the latter method, you in effect place a filter along that $10,000 line in our example. The screen in that filter has in the past been equipped with a very fine mesh, and very little has filtered through to you.

Remember, to become financially independent you must save and let your money grow. Many save and let savings institutions grow.

To participate in the profits of American industry, you must get your eyes off the yo-yo and on the stairs.

• ALL ASSETS FLUCTUATE IN VALUE

Why should you let daily fluctuations bother you? Everything you own fluctuates in value. The market value of any asset you own is only what someone is willing to pay you for it.

Your home fluctuates in value every day, but the newspaper doesn't carry a market page quoting its value. What if it did? You come home on Monday, pick up the newspaper, and find that the market value of your house is quoted at $25,000. On Thursday evening you come home, pick up the paper, and find that it is quoted at $22,000. Would you panic and begin crying? Would you be alarmed and begin to weep over your $3000 loss? The loss is just as real if you need to sell. Fortunately for your peace of mind, the values of your home and other assets are not published every day; therefore, you are unaware of their fluctuation in value, and you are saved the agony of existing in a state of panic as some do when they own securities.

Don't succumb to the yo-yo panic! If you do, you may find it very costly.

• THE BRADLEYS AND THE KICKERILLOS

Another way to examine the cost of the guarantee is to take the hypothetical case of Sue and Tom Bradley and Vanessa and John Kickerillo. Both inherited $30,000 on January 1, 1950.

The Bradleys placed theirs in a guaranteed position where they could obtain a 6 percent return with the principal guaranteed. (This was no small feat, since the rate being paid by savings and loans in the U.S. in 1950 was 2.5 percent.) The first year and every year thereafter they earned $1800. Eighteen hundred dollars in 1950 bought the Bradley's the top line that Chevrolet had to offer.

The Kickerillos, on the other hand, invested their $30,000 in shares of the Seminar Fund. That first year in 1950 they received only $1366 in dividends. Since their automobile purchase had to come from the income from their investment, they had to accept the middle line of the Chevrolet that year.

For the next four years the Bradleys received more income than the Kickerillos. But in 1955 the Kickerillos began receiving more income than the Bradleys, and they continued to do so from that point on. The value of the Kickerillos' shares in the fund fluctuated, but this did not adversely affect their constantly increasing flow of income. By 1976, the market had gone through one of its worst periods in around forty years, yet the market value of their shares had grown to $283,708. And their income for 1976 was $9124. This bought them a 1977 Cadillac. What kind of an automobile could the Bradleys afford in 1976? Eighteen hundred dollars would buy them only a 1974 Plymouth.

I daresay the next 26 years will not be the same as the past 26 years, but perhaps there is something to be learned from the Bradleys and the Kickerillos. If you are tempted to say to me, "But Venita, I can now get 9 percent interest on my money on an A-rated corporate bond," then let's play this scenario again using 9 percent and see how the Bradleys would have fared. At 9 percent their interest on $30,000 would now be $2700. So let's go shopping with the Bradleys again for an auto. Still mighty discouraging, isn't it? To say nothing of the fact that the Bradleys $30,000 is still $30,000, while the Kickerillos' mutual fund is worth $283,708.

Is the Guaranteed Dollar a Guaranteed Loss? • In the past it has been. If you are tempted to say, "Well, the last 20 years were really pretty good; let's look at those depression years." The Seminar Fund was born during those bleak years, so let's look at all the 20-year periods during the life of the fund. Table 8–2 shows you how you would have done if you had invested $10,000 in any of the twenty-four 20-year periods in the history of the fund. To help you I've circled the best period, the median period, and the worst period.

Going back to the depression years, you will note that during the 20-year period 1934–1953 your $10,000 would have grown to $98,601 with all distributions reinvested. If you'll look back at the compound interest tables in Chapter 1, you will find that during this period your fund grew in excess of 12 percent compounded ($10,000 at 12 percent = $96,462). A bank in 1953 was paying 1.2 percent, a savings and loan 2.8 percent, the U.S. Government bonds 2.6 percent, and AAA corporate bonds 2.9 percent. The median period of the fund was 1952–1971 when your $10,000 grew to $107,693, again in excess of 12 percent. In the worst 20-year period that ended in 1974, when our country was being subjected to a severe money crunch, your $10,000 would have grown to $48,421. However, this was in excess of 8 percent compounded.

Table 8–2. Summaries of Assumed
$10,000 Investments in "The Seminar Fund"

	Jan. 1–Dec. 31	Income dividends reinvested	Total investment cost	Ending value of shares
	1934–1953	$31,721	$41,721	$ 98,601
	1935–1954	28,557	38,557	122,847
	1936–1955	17,754	27,754	84,107
	1937–1956	13,707	23,707	64,003
. . . here's how you	1938–1957	24,729	34,729	91,656
would have done	1939–1958	21,717	31,717	103,898
if you had in-	1940–1959	23,914	33,914	117,702
vested $10,000	1941–1960	27,247	37,247	126,187
in any of the	1942–1961	32,260	42,260	167,492
twenty-four 20-year	1943–1962	30,369	40,369	124,448
periods in the	1944–1963	25,112	35,112	115,269
Fund's history:	1945–1964	22,339	32,339	108,530
	1946–1965	18,019	28,019	100,686
BEST	1947–1966	20,658	30,658	104,248
PERIOD	1948–1967	22,946	32,946	133,016
	1949–1968	26,017	36,017	155,206
MEDIAN	1950–1969	27,007	37,007	126,635
PERIOD	1951–1970	25,427	35,427	108,472
	1952–1971	24,123	34,123	107,693
WORST	1953–1972	23,894	33,894	111,243
PERIOD	1954–1973	26,405	36,405	92,048
	1955–1974	19,692	29,692	48,421
	1956–1975	17,741	27,741	52,228
	1957–1976	17,710	27,710	61,116

The average of the 20-year periods, not that you'll hit an average period, and this should be used as academic information is $105,239, considerably in excess of 12 percent.

As you can see, over the long term, investing in a professionally selected, diversified portfolio of common stocks has in the past been a satisfactory hedge against the inroads of inflation and has definitely earned the right to be considered as one of the hedges you should care-fully examine in your battle to protect your future purchasing power.

I personally believe that the next 20 years hold great promise because by the end of 1974, at the end of the worst 20-year period, 65 percent of the common stocks listed on the New York Stock Exchange were selling at no more than seven times their earnings. About one out of three stocks was selling at no more than five times earnings.

To put this into perspective, if you could buy all of the outstanding stock of a company that's selling at five times earnings, you'd be getting a 20 percent return on your investment. Even if you were to assume a decline of 25 percent, this would still mean a price-earnings ratio of only 6.7 or an earnings return of 15 percent.

• UNDERLYING VALUE
IS THE KEY

Companies create wealth, and, in the past, successful investing in common stocks has resulted from becoming one of the owners of the companies creating this wealth. Stock prices in the long term are determined by the earnings and assets of these companies.

Do not make the mistake so many investors do of taking the short-term view of the stock market when providing for your long-term goals. I find that so many predict the future by making straight-line extrapolations of the latest three- or five-year periods. When the market has gone down over a period of several years, instead of welcoming it as a buying opportunity, they sit on their hands. When the market has been going up for a period of years, they assume the opposite and eagerly jump in with the full anticipation that this happy condition will continue for the next three to five years.

Watch for times in the market when good solid values are available, and have the courage to buy at bargain prices.

Table 8–2 showed what happened in the past if you had a lump sum of $10,000 to invest. Perhaps you do have a lump sum and can add $100 per month, or you may not have $10,000 but can invest $100 per month. Table 8–3 gives a record of past performance for each 20-year period if you started with $250 and added $100 per month over twenty-four 20-year periods.

• SUMMARY

Do you possess the necessary three "T"s and an "M?" If you do, that's great. I hope you actively manage your account and bring joy to yourself and to your broker. A trading account is almost always a greater source of revenue to a broker than a mutual fund account.

If you have chosen well, you probably will stay contentedly in that position with your funds working for you for many years, but they will

Table 8–3. Summary of Assumed Investment of $250 and Adding $100 Per Month in "The Seminar Fund"

Jan. 1– Dec. 31	Income dividends reinvested	Total cost (including dividends reinvested)	Capital gain distributions taken in shares	Ending value of shares
1934–1953	$20,861	$45,011	$22,048	$ 75,835
1935–1954	20,019	44,169	22,850	102,663
1936–1955	19,664	43,814	26,779	112,505
1937–1956	20,560	44,710	32,292	115,159
1938–1957	22,031	46,181	35,861	95,907
1939–1958	21,844	45,994	35,423	123,818
1940–1959	21,756	45,906	39,423	127,013
1941–1960	21,527	45,677	40,550	118,075
1942–1961	20,736	44,886	41,190	127,313
1943–1962	19,263	43,413	38,132	94,127
1944–1963	18,352	42,502	36,422	101,188
1945–1964	17,697	41,847	36,987	103,764
1946–1965	17,438	41,588	39,150	117,860
1947–1966	17,893	42,043	42,903	108,313
1948–1967	17,972	42,122	42,894	123,883
1949–1968	18,144	42,294	41,296	127,574
1950–1969	17,732	41,882	40,827	97,863
1951–1970	17,190	41,340	37,485	86,544
1952–1971	16,693	40,843	32,931	88,179
1953–1972	15,988	40,138	29,876	88,579
1954–1973	15,077	39,227	25,885	63,228
1955–1974	15,103	39,253	20,915	44,983
1956–1975	15,309	39,459	17,905	54,826
1957–1976	15,288	39,438	16,167	64,472

not be working for your broker. Most individual trading accounts have several trades a year—some have daily trades—and with a commission to buy and a commission to sell and also to reinvest dividends and capital gains made from trading.

If you don't have the three "T"s and an "M," do put excellent professional money managers to work for you. Choose well. They all charge about the same management fees, but there is often a vast difference in quality. You are buying brains, so get the best brains available.

Application

Applications will be given at the end of the next chapter.

9
How the Professionals Invest

In this chapter let's continue our study of how the professionals invest.

- ## "WILL SOME BRAINS"

I have a client who has been an excellent stock trader for years. . We have made very good profits together. He has thoroughly enjoyed the challenge of predicting trends before they happened, buying the leading stocks in those industries, moving out of them before the trend ran out, and moving into the next trend ahead of the other traders. A few years ago he said that he wanted to invest in a particular mutual fund. Since he had never shown any interest in mutual funds over the years he had been my client, and since he obviously was very good at selecting his own portfolio, I asked him why he had now decided to avail himself of outside professional management.

He described to me his wife and daughter. He obviously loved them very much and was proud of their accomplishments. Then he added, "They know nothing about money management. It's probably my own fault. Stock analysis and projections have been my avocation for many years, but I've never attempted to share this information with them. On the other hand, I don't really think it's their cup of tea. They are both creative, artistic, very social people who have taken delight in the luxuries my talent has provided for them, but I don't think they have ever given much thought to the source of the funds that provide these luxuries. I'm getting up in years now and want to will some brains to my wife and daughter so that they may continue to have professional management of their money in the event that I'm not here to provide it for them."

The selection he made was good, and his reasoning was sound. He selected a management team with a 43-year record of consistent, prudent, and good performance.

You may find that another advantage of a well-managed quality mutual fund may be that you, too, can have professional management readily available to members of your family.

• EASE OF ESTATE
SETTLEMENT

Another reason that my client chose to place some of his funds under professional management as he grew older was the ease of estate settlement. He knew that upon his death the individual stocks in his portfolio would be frozen and could only be changed with the permission of the courts.

For example, let's say that shares of U.S. Steel had been in this portfolio at the time of steel's confrontation with the Kennedy administration, when for all practical purposes they were told they would not be allowed to make a profit. There had been earlier storm warnings on the horizon. Quick action to sell looked prudent. But if the estate had not been probated, the shares could not have been sold quickly enough to protect the estate.

Now let's assume that U.S. Steel had been in the portfolio of his fund. The fund's portfolio managers were free to sell U.S. Steel from the fund and replace it with another stock. The shares of the fund were frozen in the estate, but not the securities that made up the portfolio of the fund. Therefore, the mutual fund could have provided professional management of his assets while awaiting settlement of the estate, which can take several years.

• DIVERSIFICATION MAINTAINED
AFTER PROBATE

Another advantage that the fund makes available is the ease with which an estate can be divided with no disruption of diversification. Let's assume that there were four heirs instead of two, that he wanted them to share and share alike, and that the securities in the estate were in the form of 4000 shares of the Seminar Fund. Each heir would receive 1000 shares. There would be no disruption of diversification in each of the four portfolios. Each would still own a proportionate share of 100 to 150 stocks, all professionally selected and managed as if they belonged to one billionaire.

• BUYING BRAINS
AT A DISCOUNT

Earlier I said that mutual funds enabled the smaller investor to obtain the same advantages as the wealthier investor. The investor who has larger amounts does obtain quantity discounts on his original purchases. Table 9–1 gives some typical acquisition costs.

Table 9–1.

Amount of purchase	Total acquisition cost
Under $10,000	8.50%
$ 10,000 but less than $ 25,000	7.50%
$ 25,000 but less than $ 50,000	6.00%
$ 50,000 but less than $ 100,000	4.50%
$ 100,000 but less than $ 250,000	3.50%
$ 250,000 but less than $ 500,000	2.50%
$ 500,000 but less than $1,000,000	2.00%
$1,000,000 but less than $2,000,000	1.50%
$2,000,000 and more	1.00%

Letter of Intent • Perhaps you do not have a sufficiently large enough sum today to cross one of the discounts, but you will during the next 13 months. Then you may want to consider buying under a letter of intent. The letter of intent is not a commitment to buy, but a privilege to buy at a discount during the 13-month period. For example, let's assume that you have $10,000 to invest today, but anticipate having an additional $15,000 to invest during the coming 13 months. You would then invest under a $25,000 letter of intent. When you do that, you receive the same discount on your $10,000 purchase as if you had invested $25,000. The custodian bank then escrows some of your shares. When the additional $15,000 is added, they release your shares. If you decide you do not want to add the remaining $15,000, that is your privilege. If the 13 months pass and you have not completed your letter, you have two choices: Return the discount, which you would not have received anyway without the letter, or the custodian bank will sell enough of your escrowed shares to return to the fund the second discount you received and will send you the remaining shares. Your discount would be adjusted back to the $10,000 level. Therefore, the letter of intent never cost you more and can save you money. You are not required to return the dividends and capital gains on the extra shares you received during the period they were in escrow.

• THE LARGE
INVESTOR

As you reached the $500,000 level in Table 9–1, you may have said, "Big deal. Who has that kind of money?" Contrary to what many people think, many large investors buy mutual funds. Many financial planners report that their clients' average mutual fund purchase is over $27,000. The Seminar Fund's average appears to have been around $9300 for 1977. If you are investing $100,000, your sales charge to buy in would be 3.5 percent; that for $500,000 would be 2 percent. There is no charge to sell or exchange, regardless of the growth of your shares. Your dividends and capital gains would also be reinvested, if you chose, without charge.

Adding More at a Discount • Under what is called "rights of accumulation," you may also qualify for additional discounts. Let's assume that you own shares that have a value of $20,000 and that you have $5000 you would like to add to your account. You may do so under the "rights of accumulation" at the $25,000 discount level. As your account grows, you may continue to add at progressively smaller opportunity fees as you cross each discount. One of the reasons pension and profit-sharing plans use mutual fund shares is their lower cost of acquisition, diversification, ease of record keeping, and to meet the "prudent man" rule and fiduciary requirements.

Let's assume that the fund in which you have invested $100,000 has 100 stocks in its portfolio. Have you calculated your commission, in and out, if you were obtaining the same diversification through a portfolio of individually selected stocks? In the fund this can be obtained at $3\frac{1}{2}$ percent in and no cost out, or, if compared to individual stock transactions, an average of $1\frac{3}{4}$ percent in and $1\frac{3}{4}$ percent out, with no odd-lot differentials. Or let's say you have only $10,000 to invest. Your opportunity fee would be $7\frac{1}{2}$ percent in and zero out, regardless of the value of your shares at the time. Have you tried getting comparable diversification with $10,000 in and out—or for that matter just going in, with the present minimum sales charge per ticket and the odd-lot differential when you are trading odd lots?

A study conducted by the National Association of Security Dealers indicated that an investment of $5000 in 16 individual issues, which is what they deem is necessary for adequate diversification, would cost 7 percent in commissions, assuming an "in and out" transaction in listed securities. If you conclude that dividend reinvestment at asset value is worth 1 percent to the average investor, and that rights of accumulation are worth 0.5 percent, and that the exchange privilege is worth 0.4 percent, the total opportunity cost of individual stocks would be 8.9 percent. They also found that the average sales charge on fund sales is only 4.4 percent because of the discounts obtained on purchases of over $10,000 and cumulative discounts.

• WHAT DOES
IT PAY?

I find that many people get hung up on what something costs them. I hope you do not. I never worry about what something "costs" me, but I am vitally concerned about what it "pays" me. It makes no difference what it "costs."

Let's assume that you turn over $1 to me to manage for you. I charge you no sales charge to do this. I will charge you, however, one-half of 1 percent yearly management fee. At the end of 10 years I return to you $2 net after all costs are taken out.

Now let's assume that you turn over another $1 to me, and on the $1 I charge you 8½ pennies. Again I charge you one-half of 1 percent yearly management fee and at the end of 10 years I return to you $3. Which was the best investment for you? Which really cost you the most? Did your efforts to save 8½ pennies "cost" you $1?

• DISTILLING THE
WISDOM OF THE AGES

If I were to distill all the wisdom that I have acquired reading and observing, I could put it all in just nine words: "There is no such thing as a free lunch."

For example, you had $10,000 twenty years ago. A savings institution would not have charged you to open a savings account with them. As a matter of fact, they may have given you a handy Teflon skillet or a fuzzy wuzzy blanket for doing so. But how much did it cost? If you had averaged 5 percent, which you could not have done at most savings institutions, your $10,000 would have grown to $26,532 in 20 years.

Had you taken the same $10,000 and placed it in our Seminar Fund during the worst 20-year period in its history, it would have grown to $48,421; in its median 20-year period, to $107,693; in its best 20-year period, to $167,492.

• "OPPORTUNITY FEE"

I call the mutual fund sales charge an opportunity fee. My reason for doing so is this:

Lets assume that you want to travel from Houston to Dallas. You find that the only way to get there is by bus. You go to the bus station; the clerk writes out your ticket and says, "That will be $14.65, please." You answer, "I'm just not going to pay that." If you don't, you're just not going to Dallas.

It's not what something costs you, but what it pays you that should be your chief concern.

There are, however, a few well-managed funds that do not make a sales charge. Carefully examine their performance, too. Remember, though, you will not have the help of a financial planner in selecting stocks and in timing their purchase or exchange, and lack of cash flow may affect their performance. You will be buying them very much as you would a suit of clothes from a mail order catalogue or Sunday supplement of your newspaper.

• HOW TO RECEIVE A CHECK A MONTH

You've been working for your money, saving a portion, and putting it to work. Now it's retirement time. Time for you to change places with your money and let your money work for you.

A plan that I have found that has worked very well for my clients for retirement income has been to establish a withdrawal plan called a Check-A-Month, using a high-quality mutual fund.

This plan has made it possible for the fund to send them a check each month for a specified amount. They can increase, decrease, or discontinue their check any month by notifying the fund. The source of the money for their checks has come from one or a combination of the following:

1 • Dividends.

2 • Realized capital gains.

3 • Unrealized capital gains.

4 • Original investment.

If you were to set up a check-a-month plan from your fund and the check is for more than the dividends the fund is earning, the second source of funds would be the realized capital gains—the profits the fund has made buying and selling stocks. If your withdrawal is more than these two, they will use some of your unrealized gains. When the fund has bought a stock and it has increased in value, but the fund has not yet sold it, the gain is unrealized. If the amount per month you request is greater than these three, you will be using a portion of your original investment. Don't be too concerned about doing so. You have saved it for this purpose.

The check-a-month can be an excellent way to use your accumulation in an orderly fashion while keeping the remainder at work in a diversified, continuously managed portfolio of common stocks.

As hard as it may be for you to believe, it was not until the mid-1960s that mutual funds were allowed to show a check-a-month withdrawal record.

They can be tabulated now in the manner shown in Tables 9–2 and 9–3.

First, let's look at $10,000 and then at $100,000 (our minimum goal). The figures in these illustrations are based on the assumption that withdrawals were made first from dividend income reinvested that year, and then from principal, as represented by reinvested capital gains and unrealized capital gains, and from the original shares acquired.

Common stock prices fluctuated, as you can see. Every month when you receive a check, your share balance will be shown on your confirmation, so you can easily calculate the value of the shares in your account. If you experience a period of severe market decline, you may want to reduce or discontinue your withdrawal. Don't panic at fluctuations, but do be aware of the rate at which capital is being used. During the period in Tables 9–2 and 9–3, it was somewhat like dollar-cost-averaging in reverse.

The Kettle of Nutritious Broth • You might picture this as a kettle filled with nutritious broth. This broth represents housing, clothing, food, etc., for your retirement years.

Let's assume that you've paid yourself first for the last 20 years and that you now have $100,000 at retirement. Let's further assume that

Table 9-2. If You Had Invested $10,000 (Initial Net Asset Value: $9150) and Taken Monthly Withdrawals of $50 . . .

Year ended Dec. 31	Amount withdrawn *				Value of remaining shares *		
	From investment income dividends	From principal	Annual total	Cumulative total	Value of remaining original shares	+ Value of shares acquired through capital gain distributions †	= Total value of shares held at year end
1967	$ 275	$ 325	$ 600	$ 600	$11,435	$ 505	$11,940
1968	311	289	600	1,200	13,383	1,317	14,700
1969	339	261	600	1,800	10,279	1,561	11,840
1970	365	235	600	2,400	9,137	2,164	11,301
1971	370	230	600	3,000	9,586	2,600	12,186
1972	382	218	600	3,600	10,066	3,345	13,411
1973	400	200	600	4,200	8,784	3,584	12,368
1974	443	157	600	4,800	6,388	3,135	9,523
1975	470	130	600	5,400	8,247	4,331	12,578
1976	520	80	600	6,000	10,620	5,916	16,536
	$3,875	$2,125	$6,000				

Results if plan had commenced January 1, 1976

1976	$ 375	$ 225	$ 600	$ 600	$11,633	$ 212	$11,845

† The dollar amounts of capital gain distributions accepted in shares were 1967—$482, 1968—$715, 1969—$585, 1970—$759, 1971—$271, 1972—$529, 1973—$620, 1974—$623, 1975—$172, 1976—$246, Total—$5002. For the one-year period—$179.

* The figures in these illustrations are based on the assumption that withdrawals were made first from income for the year, then from principal. Withdrawals from principal representing the sale of shares were assumed to have been in the order shares were acquired. No adjustments have been made for any income taxes payable by shareholders on investment income dividends and capital gain distributions or on any net capital gains realized on the liquidation of shares in connection with periodic withdrawals.

Table 9–3. If You Had Invested $100,000 (Initial Net Asset Value: $96,500), and Taken Monthly Withdrawals of $500 . . .

Year ended Dec. 31	Amount withdrawn *				Value of remaining shares *		
	From investment income dividends	From principal	Annual total	Cumulative total	Value of remaining original shares +	Value of shares acquired through capital gain distributions † =	Total value of shares held at year end
1967	$ 2,902	$ 3,098	$ 6,000	$ 6,000	$120,946	$ 5,342	$126,288
1968	3,293	2,707	6,000	12,000	141,935	13,943	155,878
1969	3,599	2,401	6,000	18,000	109,342	16,542	125,884
1970	3,893	2,107	6,000	24,000	97,603	22,962	120,565
1971	3,954	2,046	6,000	30,000	102,816	27,610	130,426
1972	4,098	1,902	6,000	36,000	108,421	35,566	143,987
1973	4,299	1,701	6,000	42,000	95,050	38,180	133,230
1974	4,784	1,216	6,000	48,000	69,543	33,448	102,991
1975	5,099	901	6,000	54,000	90,312	46,253	136,565
1976	5,657	343	6,000	60,000	116,893	63,224	180,117
	$41,578	$18,422	$60,000				
Results if plan had commenced January 1, 1976							
1976	$ 3,964	$ 2,036	$ 6,000	$ 6,000	$123,015	$ 2,232	$125,247

† The dollar amounts of capital gain distributions accepted in shares were 1967–$5099, 1968–$7580, 1969–$6214, 1970–$8073, 1971–$2896, 1972–$5668, 1973–$6661, 1974–$6712, 1975–$1865, 1976–$2675, Total–$53,443. For the one-year period–$1887.

you begin a 6 percent withdrawal plan. We would place the $100,000 in the kettle, and then we would put a faucet or gauge at the bottom of the kettle and set it at 6 percent per annum on a monthly basis, based on the value of the shares at the time the withdrawal plan was started. Actually, the beginning net asset value used here is $96,500, for it has been adjusted for the commission. If you have been accumulating shares over the 20-year period and if you have $100,000 in share value, there would be no reduction at the beginning.

Your kettle would look like this:

$100,000

6% Spigot
$500 Per Month
$6,000 Per Year

You begin a 6 percent withdrawal based on a beginning value of $100,000 on January 1, 1967. That would amount to $500 per month. (A convenient way to determine what 6 percent would be is to know that 6 percent is $5 per month on each $1000.) Our illustration shows you beginning your $500 check the very first month. (I usually recommend waiting for a few months with the hopes that the fund will increase in value before the withdrawal is begun.)

As described above, as the fund needs dollars to send you your check each month, they will redeem shares. When the fund distributes dividends or capital gains, these are reinvested in additional shares. Therefore, the number of shares you own will change with any activity in your account. This is the reason you deposit your shares with the custodian bank when you begin your withdrawal program.

Your concern should not be with the number of total shares in your account but with the net asset value of the shares in the account.

In the above you will note that by the end of 1976, you share value was $180,117. As you can see, the value fluctuated from year to year. This should not cause you undue alarm. Remember, we have learned that the market has always fluctuated.

Now let's take a look at your 10-year record. You started with $100,000. You withdrew a total of $60,000. Your remaining shares would have been worth $180,117 on December 31, 1976. (Remember, this is the past. Remember all the hedge clauses throughout this book.)

Instead of using up your broth, the amount has increased. While you were taking out at the bottom, American industry was ladling the broth in at the top. It's often not necessary to fight the battle alone if you will let American free enterprise help you.

How Long Will Capital Last? • Let's assume that instead of the level of the kettle increasing, it decreased. There is nothing sacred about principal. There is nothing that says you are obligated to leave an estate to your heirs. The "sacred" thing is to make you and it come out together.

If you used capital at 7 percent while it was only earning 6 percent, do you know how long your capital would last? Thirty-three years! If you begin your withdrawal at 65, in 33 years you'll be 98 years of age!

Figure 9–1 is a handy chart to use in programming how long capital will last:

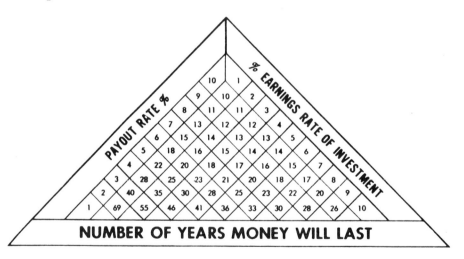

FIGURE 9–1

Another way to visualize how long capital will last is to use Table 9–4.

Suppose you have $100,000 that is growing at the rate of 7 percent a year, and you withdraw at an annual rate of 8 percent—$8000 a year or $666.67 per month. Look at the box where these two percentage figures intersect, and you will see that principal will last 30 years.

Table 9–4. How Long Will Your Money Last?

Total return per annum on balance of principal

Percentage of original principal withdrawn per annum	3%	4%	5%	6%	7%	8%	9%
				Principal will last . . .			
4%	46 yr						
5	30	41 yr					
6	23	28	36 yr				
7	18	21	25	33 yr			
8	15	17	20	23	30 yr		
9	13	14	16	18	22	28 yr	
10	12	13	14	15	17	20	26 yr

• YOU'RE NOT SPENDING BUT REPOSITIONING

I find that often a prospective client feels that he is spending his money when he makes an investment.

If you make an investment by withdrawing funds from a savings account, you are not spending your money but repositioning it, so that it will work for you rather than for the savings institution.

If you should desire to redeem your shares, you may do so on any business day. You may cash in all or part of your shares. When you sell your shares back to the fund, you will receive an amount representing your share of the value of all the securities and other assets of the fund at the time. It could be more or less than your cost. The amount you receive will depend on the investment performance of the fund.

If your need for money is temporary or if it is not a favorable time in the market, you may want to consider using your shares as collateral at your bank. You can usually rent time in this way with the hope that the value will increase at a later date.

Even if the market is progressing nicely, you may decide to borrow against the value of the stocks instead of disturbing the goose that you feel is producing satisfactory eggs.

The rent (interest) is deductible on your federal income tax return.

• WHO INVESTS IN MUTUAL FUNDS?

A recent New York Stock Exchange study compared 22 million investors who owned only common stocks with 9 million investors who owned mutual funds. (Five million owned both mutual funds and common stocks; four million owned funds only.) It contrasted the "stock only" investors with the fund investors and found:

1 • Fund investors are the better-educated clients; 65 percent are college graduates vs. 50 percent of the "stock only" clients.

2 • Fund investors are the wealthiest clients, with the largest assets; 23 percent have portfolios of more than $25,000 vs. 15 percent of the other clients.

3 • Fund investors are the highest-income clients. Nearly one-half have incomes of $15,000 vs. only one-third of the other clients.

4 • And finally, to put away the idea that mutual fund investors lock up their money forever, fund investors are the most active clients, with one-fourth making more than six transactions per year vs. only one-tenth of other clients.

We are indebted to *Wiesenberger Financial Services Marketer* (an excellent publication) for this breakdown on mutual fund clients.

•   IF IT'S A "BETTER MOUSETRAP"

If quality mutual funds have performed in the way I've enumerated in my examples, why haven't investors embraced them with great enthusiasm and in massive numbers?

The chief reason is that state securities boards, the Securities and Exchange Commission, and the National Association of Securities Dealers have prohibited them from telling their story. About all they have allowed those recommending mutual funds as a valid way to invest to do legally is to warn you that you might lose your money. That's not the best way to spread the good word, I'm sure you will agree. It has been said that it is easier to get an ad for pornographic literature approved than it is an ad for a mutual fund.

A mutual fund prospectus giving full disclosure of all pertinent facts was rejected by one of the states because it showed a loaf of bread in color. Even though it had in bold print on the front of the prospectus these words:

THESE SECURITIES HAVE NOT BEEN APPROVED OR DIS-APPROVED BY THE SECURITIES AND EXCHANGE COMMIS-SION, NOR HAS THE COMMISSION PASSED UPON THE ACCURACY OR ADEQUACY OF THIS PROSPECTUS. ANY REP-RESENTATION TO THE CONTRARY IS A CRIMINAL OFFENSE.

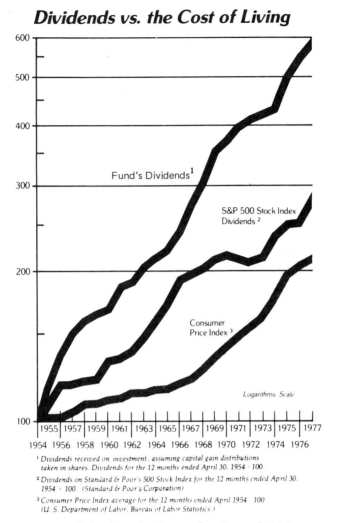

Dividends vs. the Cost of Living

Fund's Dividends[1]

S&P 500 Stock Index Dividends[2]

Consumer Price Index[3]

Logarithmic Scale

1954 1955 1956 1957 1958 1959 1960 1961 1962 1963 1964 1965 1966 1967 1968 1969 1970 1971 1972 1973 1974 1975 1976 1977

[1] *Dividends received on investment, assuming capital gain distributions taken in shares. Dividends for the 12 months ended April 30, 1954 = 100.*

[2] *Dividends on Standard & Poor's 500 Stock Index for the 12 months ended April 30, 1954 = 100. (Standard & Poor's Corporation)*

[3] *Consumer Price Index average for the 12 months ended April 1954 = 100. (U. S. Department of Labor, Bureau of Labor Statistics.)*

FIGURE 9–2.   Dividends vs. the Cost of Living

I've had many clients call panic-stricken when they reread the packet of material after they had made an investment. One in particular was a lady for whom I had made an investment in a fund that contains shares only of companies that are on the Registry of Wills of the District of Columbia. It is a fund that qualifies under "the prudent man rule" and is often used by attorneys who are in a fiduciary capacity. After reading this caption again she called and was incensed that I would have the audacity to recommend an investment that was not "approved by the Securities and Exchange Commission." No amount of explaining ever convinced her that the SEC neither approved or disapproved, so we cancelled the trade. What she missed in income is pictured in Fig. 9–2.

The mutual fund record.
What other investment program
do you know that can match it?

Year	Initial Investment* $10,000	% Change	Gain	Loss	Compared with 5% interest compounded annually $10,000
1950	$11,089	+10.89	$1,089		$10,500
1951	12,734	+14.84	1,645		11,025
1952	14,166	+11.24	1,432		11,576
1953	14,150	− .11		$16	12,155
1954	20,233	+42.99	6,083		12,763
1955	23,805	+17.65	3,572		13,401
1956	25,604	+ 7.56	1,799		14,071
1957	23,023	−10.08		2,581	14,775
1958	32,088	+39.37	9,065		15,514
1959	36,198	+12.81	4,110		16,290
1960	37,403	+ 3.33	1,205		17,105
1961	46,911	+25.42	9,508		17,960
1962	41,484	−11.57		5,427	18,858
1963	48,519	+16.96	7,035		19,801
1964	54,866	+13.08	6,347		20,791
1965	66,256	+20.76	11,390		21,831
1966	62,785	− 5.24		3,471	22,923
1967	84,294	+34.26	21,509		24,069
1968	99,138	+17.61	14,844		25,272
1969	85,100	−14.16		14,038	26,536
1970	78,616	− 7.62		6,484	27,863
1971	94,008	+19.58	15,392		29,256
1972	103,898	+10.52	9,890		30,719

*Figures in this table are based on annual performance averages of funds listed in the Management Results section of Wiesenberger's *Investment Companies*, except for the categories of bond and preferred stock funds, tax-free exchange funds and international funds. Annual average performance was derived by adding each fund's performance and dividing by the number of funds. New funds were added as they appeared in the Wiesenberger volumes which were used. In 1950, 1961 and 1970, for example, the number of funds was 40, 145 and 307, respectively. Investment results assume initial investment of $9,150 following deduction of sales charge of 8½ percent and subsequent reinvestment of dividends and capital gains. 1972 numbers are preliminary.

I pride myself on having informed investors, but a prospectus may be a deterrent to intelligent investing.

The regulatory agencies also have not allowed sales literature that pictures people who showed any signs of reasonable solvency. I remember one brochure that was rejected because the man had cuff links in the cuffs of his shirt. They were not diamond-studded but looked more like the dime store variety.

As the table on the opposite page demonstrates, mutual funds, on the average, have piled up a pretty impressive record over the years.

$10,000 to $103,898

It shows how an investment of $10,000 in 1950, measured by the average performance of mutual funds, would have grown to $103,898 by the beginning of 1973.

That's a net gain of $93,898—after paying management fees and any sales charges.

In contrast, $10,000 at 5% interest compounded annually would have produced a guaranteed net gain of $20,719 over the same period.

(Note: Naturally, you don't have to invest $10,000. You can buy mutual fund shares with virtually any amount from $100 up. Or as little as $25 a month after a modest initial payment.)

Past performance, of course, is no guarantee of the future, and the record of any individual fund varies with its investment objectives.

Giving your dollars a chance to multiply

For people with long-range financial goals, such as retirement or a child's education, mutual funds can be particularly suitable.

Perhaps their greatest attraction is that, unlike savings accounts and other fixed-return investments, mutual funds are designed to grow with the economy.

The investment performance of mutual funds generally reflects long-term stock market trends as well as the overall conditions of the economy. However, mutual funds are based solidly on the premise that over the long haul, the U.S. economy will continue to expand and flourish. As it has, by and large, ever since 1776.

So they give your dollars a chance to multiply.

A chance to stay ahead of inflation.

What is a mutual fund?

Basically, it's a group of people with the same financial goals who invest their money together under the direction of professional money managers.

When you buy shares in a mutual fund, your money is combined with that of the other investors in a diversified group of securities, usually stocks. The securities are selected, and constantly reviewed, by the fund's managers on the basis of the fund's stated objectives.

There are several kinds of funds. One kind may specialize in securities the managers believe will increase in value (growth funds). Another may look for those with good income as well as prospects for growth (income plus growth funds).

Although there's some degree of risk in any investment, full-time professional management, plus diversification helps reduce the risks for mutual fund shareholders.

In 1971, for the first time in history, the Investment Company Institute was allowed, under very specific "don't rules," to publish the mutual fund performance record.

• THE RECORD

"The Record" was published first in 1971, and then an updated record was published for 1972. Above is "The Record" printed in its entirety as it appeared in our national magazines. (Permission to print their Record for later years has now been withdrawn—hence the use of the 1972 Record.)

What "The Record" Reveals • First of all, during the 22-year period, 1950 to 1972, you could not have averaged 5 percent on your "guaranteed" savings account. An earlier chapter shows the percentage that you would have actually received with various savings institutions.

Now let me be sure to point out that if you had experienced this exact performance of "The Record" shown above, you would have had a "loss" in 1953, 1957, 1962, 1966, 1969, and 1970, a total of six years. The fear of loss I find to be a much stronger motivator than the hope for gain. Many will stop looking at "The Record" right after this discovery and fail to notice that there were gains in 16 of the 22 years.

Remember our example of the yo-yo and the stairs. If you can't get your eyes off the yo-yo and on the stairs, you may be condemned to stay in the savings institutions basement, where your $10,000 over a 22-year period, before income taxes (remember this yield was interest and fully taxable), grew to only $30,719, or a gain of $20,719.

If you had done no better than the average above (if you didn't, were you really working at it?), your $10,000 grew to $103,898, or a gain of $93,848—a difference of over 4.6 to 1.

Perspective on Performance • With respect to performance, I find it difficult to see how the mutual fund industry's long-term record could be very much better, even when we add into the industry total the dismal record of the go-go funds.

The I.C.I. advertisement shows that $10,000 invested in the average mutual fund 23 years ago, with income compounded, would have grown to about $104,000 at the end of 1972. It may surprise you to learn that the performance figures are in fact unfairly negative, for the industry's average was heavily weighted by conservative funds in the early years, when it paid handsomely to speculate, and by aggressive funds in 1969–1970, when it paid to be conservative. Despite its statistical limitations, the advertisement understates the industry's record. If the table had been limited to equity funds in business throughout the entire period, the final value would have been approximately $120,000. The overall annual return of 10.7 percent reflected in the advertisement is not only wholly creditable but also wholly credible.

• COMPARED
TO WHAT?

Beginning in 1971, it became fashionable among financial writers to give a sharp jab to the stomach of the mutual fund industry. There are at least two reasons for this: First, I think the writers just got tired of reporting the same old news each day, which in substance said the market went down again. Second, the mutual fund industry had been a knight in shining armor. When spots of tarnish began to show, it was much more fun to kick the knight than to polish away the tarnish to let the shining metal beneath show through.

The incongruous part of this development was that these same financial writers were the ones who had placed the crown of victory on the heads of some of the "go-go" fund managers with such headlines as "_____ Fund up 113 percent for the Year!" (Regulations require that I omit the name of the fund.)

Headlines such as these and interviews quoting the "bright" young men who were managing a very small number of "hot" funds brought on a performance race like we've never seen before and, it is to be hoped, will never see again. The older, well-managed funds, with seasoned money managers at the helm and with true dedication to sound investment principles, did not engage in these wild excesses as did the few gunslingers who had their field day in the speculative heat of 1967.

I'm convinced, as I've mentioned, that many of the agonizing reappraisals we have had in the stock market (that's stockbroker jargon for saying that the market went to pot) are in direct proportion to the amount of junk peddled by stockbrokers during speculative periods.

As a financial planner dedicated to faithfully helping my clients accomplish their long-range plans, I have had one whale of a time trying to justify why I recommended a fund that only increased 39 percent in 1967, after they have read a headline that year stating "_____ Fund up 113 Percent." My warning about "letter stock" (stock that could not be sold until a certain time had elapsed) fell on deaf ears. I had to either sell the fund to the client or know that he would buy it from some other broker. With us, we could at least warn him when we saw the storm warnings.

A large number of funds were sold to life insurance companies during this period. The more sophisticated investors were beginning to see the error of placing their savings in cash surrender value of life insurance policies. This caused the insurance companies that had built their vast empires on high-cost, low-protection, cash surrender value policies to become extremely nervous. They were beginning to lose the "savings" dollar. They began to look for equity products, with possible hedges against inflation, that their agents could sell. They hoped to keep their agents and to train them to add this new product to their line of wares. They found, however, that it was very hard to undo all the indoctrination they had subjected their agents to when they had taught them to sell "guarantees."

• THE GUNSLINGERS
OF THE GO-GO ERA

There were excesses in 1967. The young gunslingers who were the "portfolio managers" of a minority of "go-go" funds, as these performance-crazed funds were called, were too young to remember a severe market decline. They thought the only direction the market could go was up.

Even the more temperate managers were tempted to chase rainbows. Fortunately, the majority did not succumb to the temptation. When the plug was pulled in 1969–1970, the go-go era went down the drain. Along with it went its idols and much of the capital of those who idolized them. While only a small percentage of industry assets was engulfed in the go-go era, regrettably this portion was very visible. The press had a field day.

Don't be too sure that you would have avoided these excesses if you had been in the thick of the 1967 frenzy.

When I have someone say to me, "Mutual funds are not doing so well," again, I ask, "Compared to what?" Compared to what the average speculator did on his own—even as badly as these few funds did—they still fared better than he did, due mostly to the funds' diversification. So again I ask, "Compared to what?" Compared to the man who bought Ling-Tempco-Vought (LTV Corp.) at 169½ and later sold for 8¾?

We'll skip such "delicacies" as Four Seasons Nursing Home and National Student Marketing and look at some others:

Stock	Highs	Later lows
Wyly Corporation (formerly University Computer)	$187	$1⅛
Kalvar Corp.	176½	1½
Tex-Sym (formerly Westec)	67⅞	⅜
Levitz Furniture	60½	1¼
Winnebago Industries	48¼	1

• DID YOU KNOW THE DOW JONES AVERAGE IS NOT FOR SALE?

In some financial publications, find mutual fund performances lumped together and actually compared to the Standard and Poor's 500 Stock Index, as if the Index were for sale. It's not for sale. Neither is the Dow Jones Industrial Average.

Your problem may be not what the Dow has done performance-wise, but how you can intelligently put to work $10,000.

The most common comparison I've seen in the press matches Standard and Poor's 500 Stock Index and the Lipper Average of 530 mutual funds. All the comparisons I've seen wholly ignore the critical fact that the S&P index is weighted by the value of each company's common stock. Twenty-five giant "blue chips" account for about one-half of the weight of the Index, with the 475 remaining securities accounting for the other half.

• COMPARING INDEX APPLES AND LIPPER ORANGES

In the fund figures, the situation is reversed. While 52 percent of industry assets are represented by the 25 largest funds, they have a weighting of only 2 percent in the Lipper Average. Conversely, 209 small growth funds, generally highly volatile, account for 40 percent of the weight of the average, but only 2½ percent of industry assets.

Does it matter? Of course it does. For while it purports to compare "the market" with "the fund industry," it is really, to use a trite phrase, comparing "apples and oranges." Thus, in a year such as 1972, when large companies were the best market performers and small funds were the worst industry performers, we had a comparison showing a 15½ percent gain for "the market" (the Standard and Poor's 500) and only 9½ percent for "the industry" (the Lipper 530). And on the basis of that comparison, despite its obvious unfairness, a theory gained credence in the press that might be described as the "idiot theory of performance" —if fund managers fall that far short of the market, they must be idiots.

But if market "apples" can be compared with fund "oranges," so can market "oranges" be compared with fund "apples." This would then give the "genius theory of performance." Using 1972 as a criterion, the fund managers could claim brilliance. In 1972 the average stock on the New York Stock Exchange (unweighted by inflation) rose by just one-half of 1 percent. The fund industry, taking into account all its assets and weighting each fund's performance by its assets, rose by 13 percent —a gain 26 times larger than the New York Stock Exchange Index. If we were so foolish as to rely on this comparison, the fund managers could be acclaimed as geniuses. This comparison never made any headlines.

Obviously the fund managers are not geniuses, nor are they idiots. However, most of them did outperform what the average person did on his own in the same period.

This is not to say that you are not far superior to the average investor. You very well may be if you have the 3 Ts and an M. If so, do buy and sell individual stocks. You'll love yourself and your broker will love you more, since he will earn a great deal more in commission.

I have accounts that I've been servicing for 16 years without any additional compensation for doing so. Some of these bore only a 3 percent commission at the time of purchase. Had they done a bit of trading —just once a year in and out at ½ per cent, this would have amounted to a total of 16 percent, and at 1 percent commission per trade in and out to 32 percent, even if the assets had not grown (they happened to have increased over 150 percent exclusive of dividends).

One very large brokerage house refused to sell funds for many years because they did not want to lock up funds, but wanted them in more actively traded accounts.

• CAN YOU BEAT DOW JONES?

The June 1976 issue of *Fortune* magazine features an article on the embarrassments of institutional managers (banks, insurance companies, and pension funds) when matching their performances against well-known averages. Several have, and some others are considering, setting up an index fund to duplicate the holdings of the Standard and Poor's 500 stock average. Even with identical holdings the professional is handicapped, as the averages do not have to contend with brokerage fees, tranfer taxes, and bid and offered prices.

Consider, then, the problem that you may have. When the Dow Jones Industrials with great fanfare reached the historic 1000 level, it may have been a humbling and exasperating experience to see your own stocks lag behind. Perhaps also you could not afford to buy all of the 30 holdings in round lots.

Three stocks were lower at the 1000 mark than they had been when the Dow was at 400: Allied Chemical, American Can, and Westinghouse. Anaconda was unchanged, and Chrysler was up but a point from 18 to 19.

Only Eastman Kodak rose in every single period, although Procter & Gamble came close with no change between 700 and 800.

The percentage increase in Dow Jones for the period December 29, 1954 to March 24, 1976 was 150 percent. Of the 30 stocks, 21 were below the average, and three did approximately as well: Standard Oil of California, 154 percent; Exxon, 151 percent; American Brands, 147 percent. Six stocks carried the burden: Eastman Kodak, 1350 percent; Procter & Gamble, 590 percent; Sears Roebuck, 310 percent; General Foods, 200 percent; International Paper, 188 percent; Goodyear, 175 percent. The ultimate, of course, was Eastman Kodak, but the investor had one chance in 30 of achieving it.

One in 30, or even the six in 30, are not particularly good odds. Yet the overall average was good, despite the few notable albatrosses. The answer would appear to be diversification of investment risk.

A practical solution may be a well-managed fund, particularly one that concentrates on blue chips of the Dow Jones type.

In its May 1976 report to shareholders, one large fund showed 108 common stock holdings, all of high investment quality. Eighteen holdings were in the Dow Jones 30, including the six star performers indicated above. Besides cash dividends, which have increased steadily for 43 years, the fund has made a capital gain distribution for 42 consecutive years.

• HOW DID THE SEMINAR
FUND MEASURE UP?

How did the Seminar Fund do in comparison to the average? (Remember that the averages are not for sale and that the comparisons are past history.) See Table 9–6.

• HOW DID YOUR STOCKS
MEASURE UP?

If you have owned stocks during these periods, why don't you make a tally and see how your stock selections compare? Unemotionally compare your performance with theirs. Now, don't just pick out your winners. Put all your buys and sells into the pot and then compare. If you've outperformed the Seminar Fund, you'll be very pleased with yourself. If you have not, perhaps you should put these or other professionals to work for you.

Table 9–6.

Summary	Latest 10 years (to 12/31/76)	Latest 15 years (to 12/31/76)	Latest 20 years (to 12/31/76)	Latest 30 years (to 12/31/76)	Latest 43 years (to 12/31/76)
The Seminar Fund *	+60.5%	+127.0%	+274.5%	+876.3%	+4,093.2%
Standard & Poor's 500 Stock Index	+33.8	+ 50.2	+130.3	+602.4	+ 964.0
Dow Jones Average of 30 Industrial Stocks	+27.9	+ 37.4	+101.1	+467.0	+ 905.7
New York Stock Exchange Composite Index †	+32.4	+ 50.8	+137.7	+513.1	na

* Figures reflect changes in net asset value per share adjusted for capital gain distributions.

† Prior to June 1964 this index was calculated weekly. Therefore, some of the "years" before 1964 actually represent periods of 52 or 53 weeks. (na–Index not computed for this period.)

Table 9–6. (Continued)

	The Seminar Fund	S&P 500	DJIA	NYSE		The Seminar Fund	S&P 500	DJIA	NYSE
1934	+25.4%	− 5.9%	+ 4.1%	na	1956	+ 7.9%	+ 2.6%	+ 2.3%	+ 2.7%
1935	+83.1	+41.4	+38.5	na	1957	−14.5	−14.3	−12.8	−13.3
1936	+43.2	+27.9	+24.8	na	1958	+40.8	+38.0	+34.0	+36.7
1937	−40.9	−38.6	−32.8	na	1959	+11.6	+ 8.5	+16.4	+11.4
1938	+26.5	+25.2	+28.0	na	1960	+ 1.9	− 3.0	− 9.3	− 3.8
1939	− 1.5	− 5.4	− 2.9	na	1961	+20.4	+23.1	+18.7	+24.1
1940	+ 6.1	−15.3	−12.7	−12.9%	1962	−15.5	−11.8	−10.8	−11.9
1941	−12.4	−17.9	−15.4	−18.0	1963	+20.0	+18.9	+17.0	+18.1
1942	+10.9	+12.4	+ 7.6	+12.5	1964	+13.8	+13.0	+14.6	+14.4
1943	+28.4	+19.4	+13.8	+20.4	1965	+24.3	+ 9.1	+10.9	+ 9.5
1944	+19.6	+13.8	+12.1	+14.0	1966	− 1.4	−13.1	−18.9	−12.6
1945	+33.7	+30.7	+26.6	+31.1	1967	+26.0	+20.1	+15.2	+23.1
1946	− 5.2	−11.9	− 8.1	−11.5	1968	+14.1	+ 7.7	+ 4.3	+ 9.4
1947	− 3.4	0	+ 2.2	− 2.0	1969	−13.2	−11.4	−15.2	−12.5
1948	− 4.1	− 0.6	− 2.1	− 2.8	1970	− 0.7	+ 0.1	+ 4.8	− 2.5
1949	+ 4.6	+10.3	+12.9	+10.2	1971	+13.8	+10.8	+ 6.1	+12.3
1950	+14.6	+21.8	+17.6	+21.2	1972	+12.9	+15.6	+14.6	+14.3
1951	+13.2	+16.5	+14.4	+13.2	1973	−19.5	−17.4	−16.6	−19.6
1952	+ 8.1	+11.8	+ 8.4	+ 6.5	1974	−22.8	−29.7	−27.6	−30.3
1953	− 3.6	− 6.6	− 3.8	− 6.1	1975	+29.4	+31.6	+38.3	+31.9
1954	+51.3	+45.0	+44.0	+42.6	1976	+25.4	+19.1	+17.9	+21.5
1955	+22.0	+26.4	+20.8	+22.2					

• WHEN THE PROS
FAIL YOU

Let's say that you were faithful about doing your homework and selected a fund that had a good past performance record with good management. Now let's assume that the management changes. They lose some of their top pros, or they are bought out by an industry that has more experience in managing debt instruments than equities. What do you do? If, after you have given the new management a reasonable amount of time to prove their professional management abilities, they are failing to perform, get out. Deal with reality—not with what you hoped would be or will be.

I should warn you that regulatory agencies may make it difficult for even the most dedicated and conscientious financial planner to be of maximum help to you. The regulatory personnel may not be trained in money management and look only at cost, not results, and may reprimand him for moving you from a "sacred" investment. (It may become "sacred" to them when you pay a commission.) Ask him, before you become his client, if his first allegiance is to you, or if his fear of being questioned on "suitability" will make him leave you in an investment that has changed in suitability for your purposes.

• SUMMARY

A mutual fund can do for you what you would do for yourself if you had sufficient time, training, and money to diversify, plus the temperament to stand back from your money and make rational decisions. It should make available to you what the very wealthy have had: sufficient money to diversify and sufficient money to buy some of the best brains in the country.

If you can do better than the professionals and can spare the necessary time from your full-time vocation, by all means do your own buying and selling. If not, don't let your ego keep you from hiring these professionals to work for you for $5 per thousand or less.

Mutual funds offer you some valuable characteristics that may contribute to your accomplishing financial independence. Fifteen of these are

1 • Diversification
2 • Proper selection
3 • Constant supervision
4 • Convenience

5 · Dollar-cost-averaging

6 · Financial objective to fit yours

7 · Record keeping

8 · Exchange privilege

9 · "Will brains"—professional management

10 · Ease of estate settlement

11 · Management during probate

12 · Lower cost

13 · Check a month

14 · Orderly use of capital

15 · Performance

Application

1 · How much can you invest today in a lump sum to begin your journey toward a minimum $100,000 estate?

2 · Should your goal be $200,000? $300,000?

3 · What amount can you add each month?

4 · Why is your life expectancy based on your family record?

5 · Will your present life style increase or decrease this life expectancy?

6 · Analyze your performance record on your stocks, using a record similar to the one in the appendix. What has been your percentage of gain?

	Your Record	Seminar Fund Record
Last year	_____	_____
Last 5 years	_____	_____
Last 10 years	_____	_____
Last 15 years	_____	_____
Last 20 years	_____	_____

7 · Rate yourself with regard to the 3 Ts and an M as they relate to investments:

	Excellent	Good	Poor
Time	_____	_____	_____
Training	_____	_____	_____
Temperament	_____	_____	_____
Money to diversify	_____	_____	_____

8 · Which type of fund best fits your financial objective and temperament?

Aggressive growth   _____
Growth   _____
Growth with income   _____
Income   _____
Corporate   _____
Convertible bond   _____
Balanced   _____
Specialty   _____
Municipal bond   _____
Money market   _____

10
Is There an Infallible Way to Invest?

• **DOLLAR-COST-AVERAGING**

Is there an infallible way to invest in the stock market? Perhaps not. But then what in life is infallible?

However, there is one way of investing I've found that comes closer than any other. It's called dollar-cost-averaging. This concept has been widely practiced by astute investors for years. Instead of trying to time the "highs" and "lows" for their purchases (which, as we've learned already, is a lot easier said than done, since you never seem to know what the low is until it's too late to do anything about it), they have learned the value of investing a fixed amount of money on a regular schedule and letting the principle of dollar-cost-averaging work for them.

This plan does not require brilliance or luck, but the discipline to save and invest over a long period of time. How dull—no brilliance or luck, just discipline. That doesn't make your adrenal glands surge, make bells ring in your cerebrum, or bring a sparkle to your eyes. Nor will it lend itself to sharing enticing tidbits at the "happy hour" about your marvelous astuteness in the market.

But let's assume that you are going to get your kicks in other ways and that you feel becoming financially independent does have some compensating features. Just what is dollor-cost-averaging, and why should you consider it as one method for attempting to build your estate?

When you dollar-cost-average, as you will remember, you invest the same amount of money in the same security at the same interval over a long period of time, with the assumption that the stock market will fluctuate and eventually go up. (These two things have always happened in the past.)

Let's assume that you can discipline yourself to save $100 a month, or a quarter, or at any regular interval, and that you have the earning capacity and the discipline to do this for a long period of time. Then get started immediately, because it makes little or no difference in your end results whether the market is going up, down, or sideways when you start.

If you are paralyzed into a state of inertia as to when to buy, what to buy, and when to sell, which has caused you to be in the delay–linger–wait syndrome, skip buying a particular stock and choose a mutual fund that has an excellent reputation for good management and a commendable record of past performance. A fund is especially adaptable to dollar-cost-averaging because under an accumulation plan you can buy fractional shares carried out to the third decimal point. You may also invest monthly or quarterly in a Monthly Investment Program (MIP) Plan in a stock listed on the New York Stock Exchange. However, you may find the MIP Plan in the end more costly and without sufficient diversification.

Let's assume you have $100 per quarter to invest. For the sake of simplicity, we will assume that you have chosen an investment company trust and it is selling at $10 per share. You invest $100 and receive 10 shares. Then a correction occurs in the market and the fund in which you are investing goes down to $5 per share. You still plop in your $100 for the quarter. (You're not masterminding this program, once you've made your decision regarding the investment to be used, but you are investing each quarter, regardless of what the market is doing.) At $5 per share you would receive 20 shares for you $100. Let's assume by the next quarter the market has returned to where it was when you started and is now selling at $10 per share. You will now receive 10 shares for your $100.

An overly simplified illustration would look something like this:

$100 – $10 – 10 shares $100 – $10 – 10 shares

$100 – $5 – 20 shares

Let's take an inventory:

	Regular investment	Share price	Shares acquired
	$100	$10	10
	100	5	20
	100	10	10
TOTALS	$300	$25	40

Results: Total invested $300. Total shares owned 40.

Ending market price per share $10: 40 × $10 = $400.

You have made a $100 gain with the market dropping 50 percent and only returning to where it started. Average price per share ($25/3) = $8.33. Average cost per share ($300/40) = $7.50. You bought more shares (20) at a low cost ($5) than at a high cost ($10) and received an average cost for your securities. In the past, when I have followed this program, I've always made money.

If you are investing in a mutual fund, it should have a tendency to fluctuate with the market because of its wide diversification, and if our long-term upward trend continues, you should benefit from this fluctuation.

If you are one of those who enjoys playing with numbers, here are three hypothetical examples started at different points in varying business cycles. I've simplified and somewhat exaggerated the examples to more clearly demonstrate the principles of dollar-cost-averaging. In actual application you should take into consideration the period of your overall program.

In a declining market

	Regular investment	Share price	Shares acquired
	$ 300	$25	12
	300	15	20
	300	20	15
	300	10	30
	300	5	60
TOTALS	$1500	$75	137

Average price per share ($75/5) = $15.00

Dollar-cost-average per share ($1500/137) = $10.95.

This example shows the importance of continuing your investment program throughout a declining market. When the share value dropped from $25 to $5, the greatest number of shares was acquired. So any recovery above the dollar-cost-average of $10.95 would establish a profit.

In a steady market

Regular investment	Share price	Shares acquired
$ 300	$12	25
300	15	20
300	12	25
300	15	20
300	12	25
TOTALS $1500	$66	115

Average price per share ($66/5) = $13.20

Dollar-cost-average per share ($1500/115) = $13.04

Even in a relatively steady market, dollar-cost-averaging can work to your advantage, As the above example shows, the actual per share cost is 16¢ less than the average price of $13.20 per share.

In a rising market

Regular investment	Share price	Shares acquired
$ 300	$ 5	60
300	15	20
300	10	30
300	15	20
300	25	12
TOTALS $1500	$70	142

Average price per share ($70/5) = $14.00

Dollar-cost-average per share ($1500/142) = $10.57

As the above example shows, the dollar-cost-average per share of the five regular investments is $10.57. When compared with the current $25 per share value, it does demonstrate the importance of fluctuations in prices to the success of dollar-cost-averaging.

The practice of dollar-cost-averaging does not remove the possibility of loss when the market is below the average cost, but it clearly demonstrates that the successful pursuit of the system will lessen the amount of loss in a declining market and increase the opportunity of greater profit in a rising market.

So you see, dollar-cost-averaging doesn't give you the fun of sharing your brilliance at the coffee klatch; but if it helps you to increase your assets, it could make it possible for you to enjoy a fattening, gooey Danish pastry later.

If your real reason for investing is to make money, dollar-cost-averaging is the most infallible way that I have found to approach the market.

• INVESTING
FOR GAIN?

You would be surprised how many people are in the market not to make money but for the thrill it offers!

One afternoon a dentist and his wife came to my office to open a brokerage account. They said they did not expect or want my advice. All they would require of me were good executions. They explained that his profession kept him extremely busy with little time off and "playing the market" would be their diversion. Their chief goal was not to make money but to use their brokerage account as a mini-Las Vegas. (This type of account brings joy to the heart of a broker who enjoys receiving a good income. No investment responsibilities, just the delight of taking the commission checks to the bank.)

This case history reminds me of another. One of my young CPA clients stopped me on the street one day to tell me he would be calling me in about a month to make an investment of some funds he would be receiving. A month passed—then two months passed. One afternoon our paths crossed again, and I asked, "Tommy, have you received your money yet?" A sheepish grin appeared on his face. He said, "Yes, but tax time was so busy, we just couldn't get away for our planned trip to Las Vegas, so I put the money in the commodity market and lost it."

I'm going to assume that you are reading this book because you want to become financially independent and not for the kicks gambling may give you.

• EGO,
THE DETERRENT

Let me again remind you that one of the greatest deterrents to successful investing is the three-letter word, EGO. Dollar-cost-averaging will not do a thing to bolster your ego. Ego causes investors to hold a stock long after it has gone sour because their ego will not let them admit that they could make a mistake. They harbor the hope that by some miracle it will return to what they paid for it; then, they tell me, "I'll sell." Don't say to me, "I've never had a loss," and expect me to be impressed. It means to me that you've probably never been in there trying or that your ego made you hold long past the time when you should have let go.

One of the major reasons many refuse to use professional management is that it's an admission that someone can do something better than they can do it. Again, EGO.

Let's assume that your masculine or feminine prowess is not threatened by the admission that someone can do something better than you, and that you've decided to let the professionals managing the Seminar Fund do your investing for you.

• JOHN WORKED FOR THE TELEPHONE CO.

I've been using a lot of figures, and sometimes they can seem very impersonal. Does your mind clap shut when a row of figures or a chart rears its ugly head? I hope not and that you are still with me.

To help you relate to the figures in Table 10–1 below, let me give them the identities of John, Martha, and Julia.

John worked for the telephone company and he reached the historic day when he became 50. His wife, Martha, gave a big birthday party for him, and loads of friends came to help him celebrate. They had a great time that evening.

However, the next day, John began to have some somber thoughts. "I'm 50. I'll retire from the company in 15 years. We haven't saved much toward retirement. I wonder what my pension will be?" John went to the personnel office the next day to inquire about his pension and found it would be only $250 per month.

That night, as they sat at the kitchen table, John told Martha of his unhappy findings and said, "Martha, even with Social Security our pension will not be enough to allow us to retire in dignity."

The children were all out on their own by then, and, after scrutinizing their budget, they decided that they could save $100 a month. So each month after that John sent the custodian bank of The Seminar Fund a check for $100 and requested that they invest it for him in shares of the Fund.

John and Martha did this for 15 years. Then came John's happy retirement day, and on that day he sat down at the same kitchen table and wrote a letter to the same bank, saying, "I've been sending you a

check for $100 a month, but I'm retiring now and won't be able to send you any more money. Would you be so kind as to now send me a check for my dividends each quarter and to also send to me any capital gains you make each year."

This the bank did. John lived 20 more years, and when he was 85 he departed this life.

A few weeks later Martha's friend Julia also lost her husband. She came to Martha saying, "I've received these life insurance proceeds, and I have such a strong sense of stewardship about their use that I'm endeavoring to invest these funds as prudently as I can. I've been considering a particular mutual fund and remembered that you and John owned it. I need to know, if you have been happy with the results?" Martha said, "Oh yes, and I still own the fund." Julia answered, "I know it's a personal matter, but would you tell me how well you have done?"

Martha began walking toward a drawer in the kitchen saying, "I don't mind sharing this information with you at all. John kept excellent records, so let's take a look."

When they looked at John's records, this is what they found. John and Martha had received $46,604 in dividends and $71,789 in capital gains distribution during the 20 years of John's retirement. Martha said, "I especially remember these capital gains distributions because John liked them the best. He kept reminding me that they were "half tax-free." Then she added, "Would you believe that I still have all the shares we had at the time John retired? We often looked up their net asset value in the paper together, so I know how to calculate their value."

When Martha and Julia multiplied the number of shares times the net asset value per share, they found they had a value of $98,929.

All John and Martha had ever done was save $100 a month from age 50 to 65!

Table 10–1 gives the record of The Seminar Fund, showing a beginning investment of $250 and adding $100 per month for 15 years for

Table 10–1. 15-Year Share Accumulation Illustrations

Total Investments: $18,150
Initial Investment $250, adding $100 per month

Jan. 1– Dec. 31	Dividends reinvested	Total cost (including dividends reinvested)	Capital gain distributions taken in shares †	Ending value of shares
1934–1948	$ 8,820	$26,970	$10,867	$39,366
1935–1949	8,634	26,784	9,909	37,398
1936–1950	8,604	26,754	9,041	39,338
1937–1951	9,164	27,314	9,685	43,197
1938–1952	9,932	28,082	10,860	46,250
1939–1953	9,972	28,122	10,272	41,669
1940–1954	10,002	28,152	11,491	58,790
1941–1955	10,042	28,192	14,229	65,553
1942–1956	9,844	27,994	16,408	(63,506)
1943–1957	9,262	27,412	16,079	47,503
1944–1958	8,934	27,084	15,351	60,126
1945–1959	8,669	26,819	16,714	60,404
1946–1960	8,650	26,800	17,216	56,513
1947–1961	8,730	26,880	18,286	63,320
1948–1962	8,506	26,656	17,656	48,866
1949–1963	8,163	26,313	16,966	53,007
1950–1964	7,592	25,742	16,705	52,864
1951–1965	7,087	25,237	16,877	57,534

20-Year Use of Investment

$63,506—Net asset value of shares accumulated as of December 31, 1956 *

Year ended Dec. 31	Cash from income dividends	Cash from capital gain distributions	Ending value of shares
1957	$ 1,751	$ 3,367	$ 51,047
1958	1,684	2,492	69,163
1959	1,684	5,051	71,991
1960	1,751	3,973	69,163
1961	1,684	4,310	78,861
1962	1,684	3,031	63,910
1963	1,684	3,165	73,406
1964	1,751	4,781	78,659
1965	1,818	5,859	91,656
1966	2,088	6,869	83,777
1967	2,290	4,984	100,344
1968	2,559	4,243	109,300
1969	2,626	6,600	88,962
1970	2,626	3,906	84,383
1971	2,626	1,751	94,215
1972	2,626	3,165	103,105
1973	2,761	2,222	80,746
1974	4,041	—	62,361

Table 10–1. (Continued)

Jan. 1–Dec. 31	Dividends reinvested	Total cost (including dividends reinvested)	Capital gain distributions taken in shares†	Ending value of shares
1952–1966	6,880	25,030	17,522	50,383
1953–1967	6,703	24,853	16,799	55,983
1954–1968	6,510	24,660	15,240	55,597
1955–1969	6,318	24,468	14,785	42,388
1956–1970	6,389	24,539	13,864	38,918
1957–1971	6,469	24,619	12,357	41,109
1958–1972	6,421	24,571	11,484	42,657
1959–1973	6,212	24,362	10,000	31,286
1960–1974	6,677	24,827	8,269	23,543
1961–1975	6,850	25,000	6,881	29,073
1962–1976	6,879	25,029	6,119	34,508

Year ended Dec. 31	Cash from income dividends	Cash from capital gain distributions	Ending value of shares
1975	3,637	471	80,207
1976	3,233	1,549	98,929
Totals:	$46,604	$71,789	

† The value of the shares acquired with these capital gain distributions is reflected in "Ending Value of Shares."

* If all the shares had been purchased at offering price (which includes the sales commission as described in the prospectus) on December 31, 1956, instead of accumulated in the shareholder account, the cost would have been $69,405.

a total investment of $18,150, and then taking in cash the dividends and capital gains for the next 20 years.

Perhaps you are five years older than John and have only ten years before you reach retirement age. Let's assume that you can begin with $250 and can faithfully add $100 a month, rain or shine, market going up, market going down, Elliot Janeway's predictions of bust, or Kiplinger's *Changing Times* headline of "Boom Ahead!" For 119 additional months, you faithfully send in your money to the custodian bank or service corporation. How will you come out? I don't know. I can show you (Table 10–2) how you would have done during each of the thirty-

Table 10–2. Performance of the "Seminar Fund" All 10-year Periods, Initial Investment $250, Adding $100 per Month

Jan. 1– Dec. 31	Dividends reinvested	Total cost (including dividends reinvested)	Capital gain distributions taken in shares *	Ending value of shares
1934–1943	$2,875	$15,025	$2,087	$19,821
1935–1944	2,756	14,906	2,064	21,018
1936–1945	2,548	14,698	3,029	24,892
1937–1946	2,789	14,939	3,923	22,571
1938–1947	3,352	15,502	4,521	21,975
1939–1948	3,558	15,708	4,287	19,745
1940–1949	3,667	15,817	4,232	19,739
1941–1950	3,755	15,905	4,056	21,279
1942–1951	3,711	15,861	4,119	22,063
1943–1952	3,428	15,578	3,933	21,032
1944–1953	3,329	15,479	3,471	18,646
1945–1954	3,239	15,389	3,797	25,869
1946–1955	3,309	15,459	4,961	29,052
1947–1956	3,455	15,605	6,249	29,362
1948–1957	3,450	15,600	6,507	22,976
1949–1958	3,367	15,517	6,265	29,365
1950–1959	3,129	15,279	6,676	28,486
1951–1960	2,928	15,078	6,455	25,362
1952–1961	2,750	14,900	6,360	26,862
1953–1962	2,554	14,704	5,712	20,103
1954–1963	2,292	14,442	5,016	20,973
1955–1964	2,066	14,216	4,746	20,727
1956–1965	2,010	14,160	5,023	23,408
1957–1966	2,067	14,217	5,528	21,276
1958–1967	2,125	14,275	5,497	24,388

Table 10–2. (Continued)

Jan. 1– Dec. 31	Dividends reinvested	Total cost (including dividends reinvested)	Capital gain distributions taken in shares *	Ending value of shares
1959–1968	2,150	14,300	5,013	24,696
1960–1969	2,264	14,414	5,241	19,811
1961–1970	2,316	14,466	4,862	18,365
1962–1971	2,361	14,510	4,191	19,511
1963–1972	2,302	14,452	3,762	20,077
1964–1973	2,210	14,360	3,120	14,834
1965–1974	2,384	14,534	2,262	11,231
1966–1975	2,466	14,616	1,665	14,139
1967–1976	2,479	14,629	1,430	17,043

four 10-year periods between 1934 and 1976 using the Seminar Fund. The last column on the right shows the results.

• DOES LIFE BEGIN AT FORTY?

Perhaps you are only a tender 40. Does "life begin at 40"? I don't know that it does, but I do know that if you come to me at that age and do not plan to retire until 65, I have 25 years to be of help to you.

In 43 years there have been nineteen 25-year periods, and Table 10–3 shows what happened during those years. Again, the right-hand column tells the results.

Table 10–3. Performance of "The Seminar Fund" in 25-year Periods. Initial Investment $250, Adding $100 per Month

Jan. 1– Dec. 31	Dividends reinvested	Total cost (including dividends reinvested)	Capital gain distributions taken in shares *	Ending value of shares
1934–1958	$42,035	$72,185	$66,896	$218,338
1935–1959	40,202	70,352	70,791	215,782
1936–1960	39,053	69,203	71,193	197,266
1937–1961	39,951	70,101	76,353	224,126

Table 10–3. (*Continued*)

Jan. 1– Dec. 31	Dividends reinvested	Total cost (including dividends reinvested)	Capital gain distributions taken in shares *	Ending value of shares
1938–1962	41,791	71,941	79,437	183,451
1939–1963	40,828	70,978	77,965	200,956
1940–1964	40,312	70,462	81,069	209,991
1941–1965	39,466	69,616	85,233	237,080
1942–1966	38,731	66,881	89,425	209,990
1943–1967	37,093	67,243	85,638	230,718
1944–1968	37,001	67,151	81,972	235,832
1945–1969	37,165	67,315	83,416	185,728
1946–1970	37,658	67,808	80,557	170,727
1947–1971	38,480	68,630	75,390	181,873
1948–1972	37,979	68,129	71,213	187,288
1949–1973	37,209	67,359	65,122	137,638
1950–1974	37,259	67,409	54,580	97,670
1951–1975	36,275	66,425	46,207	114,491
1952–1976	34,890	65,040	40,840	129,777

• ARE YOU A TENDER 22?

Let's assume that you are a mere 22 years of age. Table 10–4 is the total record that was attained by dollar-cost-averaging over a 43-year period. The total results from January 1, 1934 to December 31, 1976, after all costs were taken out, with the exception of federal income taxes, was $1,192,463. Over a million dollars dollar-cost-averaging with $100 per month.

Again, the now-familiar disclaimer for these and all other tables shown:

"This table covers the period from January 1, 1934 through December 31, 1976. While this period, on the whole, was one of generally rising common stock prices, it also included some interim periods of substantial market decline. Results shown should not be considered as a representation of the dividend income or capital gain or loss that may be realized from an investment made in the Fund today. A program of the type illustrated does not ensure or protect against depreciation in declining markets."

Table 10–4. Performance of "Seminar Fund," 1934 to 1976, Initial Investment $250, Adding $100 per Month

Year ended Dec. 31	Cost of shares				Value of shares acquired					Capital gain distributions taken in shares *
	Total periodic investments (cumulative)	Dividends reinvested Annually	Cumulative	Total cost (including dividends reinvested)	Through periodic investments	As capital gain distributions (cumulative)	Sub-total	Through reinvestment of dividends (cumulative)	Total value	
1934	$1,350	—	—	$1,350	$1,416	—	$1,416	—	$1,416	—
1935	2,550	—	—	2,550	4,380	—	4,380	—	4,380	—
1936	3,750	$101	$101	3,851	6,501	$1,200	7,701	$132	7,833	$962
1937	4,950	278	379	5,329	4,493	742	5,235	293	5,528	69
1938	6,150	54	433	6,583	6,759	1,278	8,037	419	8,456	328
1939	7,350	211	644	7,994	7,624	1,499	9,123	614	9,737	236
1940	8,550	379	1,023	9,573	8,157	1,540	9,697	961	10,658	152
1941	9,750	597	1,620	11,370	8,147	1,374	9,521	1,412	10,933	29
1942	10,950	627	2,247	13,197	10,162	1,629	11,791	2,234	14,025	106
1943	12,150	628	2,875	15,025	14,075	2,278	16,353	3,468	19,821	205
1944	13,350	737	3,612	16,962	17,388	3,539	20,927	4,755	25,682	890
1945	14,550	715	4,327	18,877	22,834	6,939	29,773	6,685	36,458	2,505
1946	15,750	1,108	5,435	21,185	21,172	8,503	29,675	6,961	36,636	2,413
1947	16,950	1,591	7,026	23,976	20,576	9,574	30,150	7,983	38,133	1,755
1948	18,150	1,794	8,820	26,970	20,133	10,108	30,241	9,125	39,366	1,217
1949	19,350	1,830	10,650	30,000	21,460	11,733	33,193	11,110	44,303	1,528
1950	20,550	2,221	12,871	33,421	25,014	14,656	39,670	14,665	54,335	1,596
1951	21,750	2,436	15,307	37,057	28,184	18,685	46,869	18,336	65,205	2,788
1952	22,950	2,580	17,887	40,837	30,228	22,582	52,810	21,551	74,361	3,253
1953	24,150	2,974	20,861	45,011	29,449	23,185	52,634	23,201	75,835	2,016
1954	25,350	3,149	24,010	49,360	43,770	39,027	82,797	37,021	119,818	5,509

189

Table 10–4. (Continued)

Year ended Dec. 31	Total periodic investments (cumulative)	Dividends reinvested Annually	Cumulative	Total cost (including dividends reinvested)	Through periodic investments	As capital gain distributions (cumulative)	Sub-total	Through reinvestment of dividends (cumulative)	Total value	Capital gain distributions taken in shares°
						Cost of shares		Value of shares acquired		
1955	26,550	3,887	27,897	54,447	50,651	54,982	105,633	45,865	151,498	10,455
1956	27,750	4,284	32,181	59,931	51,767	67,084	118,851	50,100	168,951	12,118
1957	28,950	4,789	36,970	65,920	42,539	62,778	105,317	44,549	149,866	9,235
1958	30,150	5,065	42,035	72,185	58,955	93,229	152,184	66,154	218,338	7,531
1959	31,350	5,454	47,489	78,839	62,469	113,682	176,151	74,342	250,493	16,427
1960	32,550	6,359	53,848	86,398	61,147	123,933	185,080	77,952	263,032	14,130
1961	33,750	6,576	60,424	94,174	70,867	158,424	229,291	95,655	324,946	16,820
1962	34,950	7,184	67,608	102,558	58,500	139,687	198,187	84,839	283,026	12,660
1963	36,150	7,606	75,214	111,364	68,352	175,266	243,618	105,389	349,007	14,369
1964	37,350	8,491	83,705	121,055	74,334	211,270	285,604	121,310	406,914	23,290
1965	38,550	9,630	93,335	131,885	87,805	278,293	366,098	151,703	517,801	31,109
1966	39,750	12,361	105,696	145,446	81,317	291,906	373,223	150,785	524,008	39,745
1967	40,950	14,656	120,352	161,302	98,550	382,540	481,090	195,522	676,612	31,929
1968	42,150	18,097	138,449	180,599	108,549	451,792	560,341	232,303	792,644	28,616
1969	43,350	20,278	158,727	202,077	89,357	410,838	500,195	208,823	709,018	47,878
1970	44,550	21,900	180,627	225,177	85,951	421,184	507,135	221,697	728,832	31,143
1971	45,750	22,946	203,573	249,323	97,113	485,977	583,090	271,047	854,137	15,458
1972	46,950	24,063	227,636	274,586	107,419	561,679	669,098	321,620	990,718	29,283
1973	48,150	26,861	254,497	302,647	85,106	462,475	547,581	277,566	825,147	21,844
1974	49,350	42,094	296,591	345,941	66,671	357,175	423,846	254,224	678,070	—
1975	50,550	40,222	336,813	387,363	86,896	464,681	551,577	367,623	919,200	5,265
1976	51,750	37,546	374,359	426,109	108,347	591,854	700,201	492,262	1,192,463	18,225

The total cost column represents the initial investment of $250, plus the cumulative total monthly investments of $100, plus the cumulative amount of income dividends reinvested. As described in the prospectus, a sales commission of 8⅝% was included in the price of the shares purchased through initial and monthly investments. There was no sales charge, however, on shares acquired through reinvestment of dividends and capital gain distributions.

° Capital gain distributions taken in shares totaled $465,087. The value of the shares acquired with these distributions is reflected in "Total Value."

• LUMP SUM
INVESTING

You can also use dollar-cost-averaging for larger lump sum investments. For example, you have $25,000 for investment, but you are uncertain whether this is the right time to commit so large a portion of your assets to the market.

You may select the fund or list of stocks that fits your financial objective. If you are using a fund, you may file a letter of intent with the fund as discussed in the chapter on mutual funds. This gives you the privilege of investing at two discounts over the full offering price. There is usually a discount at $10,000 and a second one at $25,000. You have 13 months to cross one of these discounts.

The lump-sum method is also helpful when you do not have the $25,000 now but will have it within the 13-month period. You may be selling some of your assets at a capital gains or cashing in some government bonds with a large amount of accrued interest. If you space their disposition over two tax years, you may be able to save some tax dollars.

Realize that dollar-cost-averaging takes time because it means placing your investment dollars in your chosen securities month after month, year after year, sweating out recessions, confidence crises, and so forth. Compared to the horse races or a turn at the crap table, it's disgustingly dull. If the thought of retiring in financial dignity and enjoying the Golden Years brings you joy, perhaps dollar-cost-averaging is for you.

Our formula still remains:

Time + Money + American Free Enterprise =
Opportunity To Retire in Financial Dignity

• SUMMARY

You will find as you go through life that there are very few things that you can consistently count on to be true over long periods of time. But I am convinced that if you have the ability to earn a reasonable income, have the discipline to systematically save and invest the same amount of that income each month, have the intelligence to select a fund as good or better than The Seminar Fund, are granted a sufficient number of years, and if our economy is no better or no worse than it has been in the past, you should become financially independent. Substitute DCA (dollar-cost-averaging) for EGO and do it NOW. Again I repeat: The secret of financial independence is not brilliance or luck, but discipline!

Application

1 · How many years do you have before retirement?

2 · How much can you save each month for this purpose?

3 · Which day of the month is most convenient for you to make your investment?

4 · Should you send in your check each month or let the bank draft your account automatically?

5 · If you decide to use mutual funds, which fund best fits your objectives?

6 · What other method have you found to attain financial independence that has a greater likelihood for success?

7 · What is the secret of financial independence?

11

Investing in Real Estate

There are three major areas you should consider when determining how best to employ your investment dollars. These are, first, shares of American industry. You have looked at the criteria you must learn and follow to realize success in this area. The second major area is real estate, which we will examine in this chapter. The third is natural resources, with which you will become more familiar in a later chapter.

In times of uncertainties, such as occurred in the early 1970s, investors tend to "return to the earth." This exhibits itself in revived interest in investments closely allied with the land—either under, in, or attached to the land.

Let's first consider which, if any, of these areas offers a valid investment medium for you.

• RAW LAND—
THE GLAMOUR INVESTMENT

Often a young couple who has attended one of my seminars will come to my office for counseling, as each person who attends a seminar is entitled to do. They will be very starry eyed about their future and

say, "We want to invest in land. They're not making any more of it, you know."

Yes, I know they're not making any more of it—with perhaps the exception of the Dutch reclamation from the sea. That does not mean, however, that land is a valid investment consideration for them. To begin with, young couples usually have no more than $5000 in liquid assets, they frequently have two or more children, and they have a very small equity in their home. It will be very difficult for them to take a meaningful position in raw land. Larger tracts—which they do not have the resources to secure—offer the best profit potential. Taxes must be paid while they wait for the land to "mature"—meaning waiting for the ultimate commercial user. Also, if they borrow money to finance the purchase, interest payments must be paid. In their lower tax bracket Uncle Sam can not give them much help. They must also forgo liquidity while waiting. Investing in "land" becomes more of a wistful dream than a valid investment possibility for this couple.

Your financial situation may be quite different. You may possess liquid assets and have a high cash flow from other income sources to service the interest on the loan and to pay taxes while you wait. This makes raw land investing a valid possibility for you. Your next consideration should be whether to invest on an individual basis or to join others in a land syndication.

Historical Perspective • Although America has built most of her cities, building is still going on at a rapid pace. Far more vacant land remains

available than you might think. Not counting reserves of government
property or the Alaskan wilderness, there are over five acres of land
per person in the United States. Much of this land is usable and accessible.

Our present land boom began after World War II and appears to
have years to run. Most of the war babies who made such a demand on
school facilities in the 1950s and the colleges in the 1960s are now having
babies of their own and are entering the market for shelter. This will
cause a great demand for places to live and for the land upon which to
build the places to live. It is estimated that the demand for housing will
increase steadily in the next decade. Housing construction brings other
real estate activities. Shopping centers, office buildings, and industry follow new centers of population into expanding suburbs.

There are many indications that land and its development hold
greater profit potential than at any time since the building boom of the
1950s.

Land has always been the glamour growth area of real estate. It
comes unfettered with buildings to manage and tenants to satisfy. However, you must also realize that an investment in empty land is the most
speculative kind of real estate venture.

Principles To Follow • If you decide that investing in raw land is for
you, there are six basic principles you should remember. The first principle is: Don't follow the population. Get out in front of it. Put your
dollars in advance of a population or business trend. The second is to
realize that timing of land purchases is all-important. The third is to
be prepared financially to service your holdings. The cost of property
taxes, liability insurance, and interest on financing makes it necessary to
have around a 10 percent a year increase in the price of the land just to
cover expenses.

It is important that you fully comprehend the nature of the ultimate
land use, which will determine what a developer can afford to pay for
your property. It is also necessary for you to understand the timing of
the return of your invested capital. For a property to double in value
may seem to be good; however, if the property should take 20 years to
double, it will not be quite so attractive. Successful real estate investment requires a forward-looking investigation and an understanding of
the nature and character of the property being considered.

Fourth, keep your down payment low—paying down as little cash
as possible. Sellers are often willing to accept 29 percent or less down
and to finance the remainder to spread out tax payments on capital gains.

If you want to take the risk of maximum leverage, you should endeavor to negotiate the smallest down payment you can get—perhaps as low as 10 percent. If you take this course, you will need to obtain around a 20 percent annual appreciation. In other words, you would be counting on the price of the land's doubling in a little over four years.

Fifth, be prepared to wait. The price of raw land seldom climbs steadily over a long period. Instead, values tend to remain fairly level for years.

When prices are rising, it may be easy to sell land, but if the price doesn't rise, money invested in land may be tied up for years while the expenses of ownership roll on. Even if a buyer can be found, financing may be difficult. Many banks will not carry mortgages on undeveloped land. You, the seller, may have to finance the buyer over a period of years. This may very well make land the least liquid of investments.

Some of the saddest plights I have seen have been widows who could not find a buyer for their raw land and had to sacrifice essentials to pay the taxes and interest payments on the land.

Sixth, if you make a land purchase and incur a large indebtedness, be sure to buy adequate term life insurance to cover the indebtedness to avoid a possible hardship on your heirs. Even if you own the land outright, without any indebtedness, land is not liquid. Insurance proceeds will allow your heirs to have enough ready cash to pay inheritance taxes and avoid a forced sale at the wrong time.

If you have already accumulated a substantial net worth with some liquidity, raw land may be a viable investment consideration for your investment dollars. If not, as glamorous as owning raw land may appear, you should probably pass up the temptation.

Raw Land Syndications • In recent years raw land syndications have enjoyed considerable popularity. Should you consider owning a small interest in a syndication? It all depends. Here are some criteria you should carefully examine:

1 • Who is the general partner or syndicator? What is his track record? Is it excellent or just fair? Syndications can be good or very poor depending on the know-how of the syndicator to buy right and to find a satisfactory buyer when it's time to sell.

2 • Who are the other investors? Can they meet their portion of the payments on principal, interest, and taxes when they are due?

3 • Ask yourself, "Is it a good investment?" If the answer is yes, then look at the tax savings potential. Too many syndications are structured to save taxes and have slim chances of earning

you a good return on your invested dollar. Too many syndications have been put together on the "greater fool theory"—
meaning, "I'll find a greater fool than I am and sell it to him."
Raw land can become an alligator—an alligator that eats
money. Avoid alligators.

4 • Examine what your after-tax cost will be on the investment,
and then calculate what you feel your yearly return will be
on your cost basis.

Recreational Lots • Should you buy recreational lots at the seashore,
on the lakes, in the desert, in the mountains? Probably not. Some work
out well, but the majority have been marked up so much before being
offered to the investor that the opportunity to sell at a profit is minimal.
Liquidity is a definite problem after all the lots have been sold and the
aggressive sales force has moved on to other developments.

• INVESTING IN COMMERCIAL INCOME-PRODUCING REAL ESTATE

Indirect Investing • It has been an interesting psychological study to
me during my many years as a financial planner to find that many who
make deposits in savings and loan institutions are convinced that the
officers of those institutions are rigidly standing there, guarding their
little nest egg to guarantee its safety. It never seems to occur to them
that while they are depositing their hard-earned money at the teller's
window, the loan officer at a desk a few steps away is lending out the
same money to be invested directly into real estate.

If you are a depositor in a savings and loan association, you are an
indirect investor in real estate. You are "guaranteed" your sliver of the
interest the borrower pays plus your original deposit, and the institution
is entitled to what very well may be the larger portion of the pie. Let's
say, for example, that you have $100,000 and you place it in a savings
and loan and are willing to leave it there for one year in a certificate
of deposit. Also, let's assume that you are in a 40 percent tax bracket.
Your mathematics at the end of the year could look something like this:

$100,000	Deposit
6,000	Interest for one year
$106,000	Total at the end of the year

2,400	Taxes due @ 40%
$103,600	Net after taxes
3.6%	After-tax return

And what was the rate of inflation last year? It was 5.2 percent for the last ten years and is projected by the University of Chicago to be 6.2 percent over the next 25 years.

By the year's end you just didn't make it. You were like the little frog that hopped up one step and slid back two; you just didn't make it out of the financial well.

Direct Investing in a Nonmortgaged Building • Let's say instead that you became a direct investor by taking the same $100,000 and buying and paying cash for a building. You then leased that building for $10,000 or 10 percent per year under an arrangement that is called a triple-net-lease. In a triple-net-lease you would be a nonoperating owner, and the lease holder would be the operator and pay all variable costs such as taxes, insurance, and maintenance, as well as a lease rental each month.

The leasing company may like this arrangement, for it may enable them to obtain their lease at a lower rate, while at the same time freeing their funds for investing in inventory that they hope to turn several times during the year to generate larger profits, or in other facets of their business. You, as the owner, on the other hand, may like the arrangement because you have no variable costs to surprise you and you should have a predictable income stream from the lease for the next 20 to 25 years.

As a direct investor not only do you place yourself in a position to obtain the full earning power of your money, but you introduce the vital ingredient of tax shelter on all or a portion of your cash flow due to allowable depreciation.

Depreciation • Depreciation assumes that the building is wearing out or decreasing in value with use. This may be true. Often the contrary is true. In fact, it may actually be increasing in value as replacement costs escalate. Depreciation is a bookkeeping entry. No checks are sent, and it does not reduce the actual cash flow.

There are varying kinds of depreciation schedules, but for now let's assume that we are using what is called a simple straight line of depreciation, meaning that it is depreciated in equal amounts over its expected life. Let's see how allowable depreciation affects the taxation of your cash flow.

Your mathematics might run something like this if you had purchased land and building for $100,000, leased it for $10,000, or 10 percent, and your accountant had set a value of $60,000 on the building and determined that it had a 30-year life. He allocated $40,000 as the cost of the land. The example below is grossly oversimplified, but should introduce to you the basic effects of depreciation on your taxable cash flow:

Hypothetical Example of a $100,000 Non-Leveraged Building, Triple-Net-Leased

$100,000 @ 10%, cash flow	$10,000
Building $60,000—depreciation	2,000
Taxable cash flow	8,000
Taxes @ 40%	3,200
Cash flow	$10,000
Minus taxes	3,200
Net after taxes	$ 6,800 or 6.8%

At 6.8 percent after tax return you've improved your situation, but considering our present rate of inflation, you may feel you are just holding on with your bare knuckles.

Direct Investing in a Mortgaged Building • Again let's buy a building for $100,000, but this time let's only put down $25,000 of your money and borrow the remaining $75,000 from a life insurance company at 10 percent interest per annum. You have now introduced another deductible item—interest expense.

Your savings from this deduction will be determined by your tax bracket. In our example you are in a 40 percent bracket, so Uncle Sam picks up 40 percent and you the remaining 60 percent. In other words, you have been able to shift a portion of the burden of carrying the mortgage. Shifting the burden back to the government is a vital lesson that you must learn in order to survive financially.

In addition to being able to deduct interest payments, you are also allowed to deduct depreciation on the entire $100,000 price of the building, not just on that portion represented by your $25,000 down payment.

Let's look at some possible mathematics that illustrates the possible effects of depreciation and interest deductions. (This is intentionally oversimplified with amortization of the loan and salvage value omitted.)

Hypothetical Example of a $100,000
Leveraged Building, Triple-Net-Leased

$100,000 @ 10%—cash flow	$10,000
$25,000 down payment	
$75,000 mortgage @ 10% interest	7,500
Net cash flow after interest	$ 2,500
Minus depreciation	2,000
Taxable income	500
40% tax bracket	200
Net cash flow	$ 2,500
Minus taxes	200
Net after-tax cash flow	$2,300

$2,300 on $25,000 equals 9.2%.

At 9.2 percent after-tax cash flow you may now be making progress.

After studying the above mathematics you may have been inspired to go look for a building to buy and then lease. After long searching you may have come away bewildered, finding that you lack the expertise to select the building and/or sufficient funds to make an economically viable investment in a commercially leasable building. If this has occurred, don't give up the idea of investing in triple-net-leased buildings, because the shortage of capital for business expansion that is a current condition in our economy today makes this type of investing one that you should consider.

Let me now introduce you to a method of investing that may offer you one of the best approaches to investing today under our present tax laws. This method is called the limited partnership.

• LIMITED
PARTNERSHIP

A limited partnership is composed of one or more general partners who have professional expertise and who are willing to assume unlimited liability and several or a large number of limited partners, usually without expertise, but with some investable funds, who do not want liability beyond the extent of their investment. The limited partners are treated, from the standpoint of taxes and income, as individuals, with all the benefits flowing directly through to them, if certain IRS criteria are met. This is called the *conduit principle.*

A limited partnership may be diagramed in this manner.

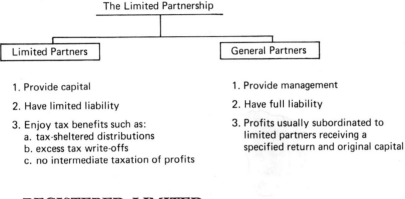

The Limited Partnership

Limited Partners

1. Provide capital

2. Have limited liability

3. Enjoy tax benefits such as:
   a. tax-sheltered distributions
   b. excess tax write-offs
   c. no intermediate taxation of profits

General Partners

1. Provide management

2. Have full liability

3. Profits usually subordinated to limited partners receiving a specified return and original capital

• REGISTERED LIMITED PARTNERSHIPS

A limited partnership offering made on a national public basis must be registered with the Securities and Exchange Commission and with the Securities Commission of any state where it is offered.

The Securities and Exchange Commission neither approves nor disapproves the offering. They do not rule on its investment merits, but attempt to see that those making the offering make "full disclosure" of all material facts relative to the offering in the prospectus, which may be interpreted by the particular SEC examiner as full disclosure of all the possible negatives that could possibly occur. (In Chapter 18, "How to Read a Prospectus," you may become painfully aware of the difficulty you may have in obtaining a clear understanding of just what is being offered.) You will rarely become aware of any of the positive attributes of the offering from reading the prospectus, especially if you do not read to the end of a usually very long document. After reading it you may be completely stunned and wonder how your financial planner ever had the audacity to recommend such a "risky" investment. Don't stop there. Continue to investigate and study, and find out if there are merits to the investment that may outweigh the negatives.

Some states, in addition to determining if there has been full disclosure, will attempt to judge the merits of the offering and also determine suitability guidelines for the residents of their state. They may, in fact, decide "what is good for you," or what is "fair, just, and equitable," what is the minimum you can invest, and what assets you must own for it to be "suitable" for you.

It may appear ironical to you that the proverbial little old lady in tennis shoes can open a trading account with a swinging brokerage firm, can trade in such commodities as pork bellies and cocoa futures, can trade options—naked or covered—and can speculate in computer and uranium stocks, with or without any hopes of future earnings. When, however, the same little old lady wants to invest in a limited partnership that invests in a diversified portfolio of professionally selected triple-net-leased buildings from corporations that have assets in excess of $50 million dollars, and are publicly traded, such as General Motors, Sears, and Safeway, she must in most states have $20,000 in income and $20,000 in net worth, exclusive of home and furnishings. In other states she may be required to have assets in excess of $100,000 for it to be "suitable" for her to make an investment of as small an amount as $2500.

You should carefully consider the limited partnership as an investment medium. Under the expert management of the *right* general partners, in the *right* investment area, at the *right* time, you may find that it offers excellent potential for tax-sheltered cash flow, excess deductions to shelter other income, equity buildup, and appreciation. This is not to say that all limited partnerships are without risk. Everything that has to do with investing or not investing money has risk. Doing nothing with your funds during periods of accelerated inflation has great risks, too.

You should look into publicly registered income-producing limited partnerships:

1 • If you are willing to give your investment a bit of time to mature.

2 • If you do not demand instant liquidity on all your assets.

3 • If you do not have an emotional need to tally up your net worth daily by looking up quotations in the daily newspaper.

4 • If you are in a tax bracket above 25 to 28 percent.

5 • If you are willing to forego ego and admit that there might be those who, through economy of scale and expertise, can do your real estate investing for you better than you can do it for yourself.

These real estate limited partnerships usually can be divided into two broad classifications—nonoperating and operating. Each offers different types of properties, different potential benefits, and different exposures to risk. Let's first look at the nonoperating partnerships.

• NONOPERATING PARTNERSHIPS

Let's look at the nonoperating partnerships. In the early nineteen seventies the Federal Reserve Board began a bold attempt to slow down inflation by adopting a very restrictive money supply policy. This brought about such a shortage of capital that only corporations with the assets of a company like General Motors could go into the market and successfully float a bond issue, and then only at very high interest rates. This left many large, very credit-worthy corporations with expansion plans already on the drawing boards with no or limited access to capital needed for these plans. In order to continue their pattern of growth, these corporations began selling their buildings and then leasing them back under a triple-net-lease arrangement. This freed their capital to continue their expansion and inventory as they had originally planned.

• TRIPLE-NET LEASES

The mechanics of the triple-net lease work something like this: Let's say that the J. C. Penney Company builds a building for $3 million, pays a million dollars down and obtains a two-million-dollar mortgage. Penney's then sells its building to a limited partnership and leases it back under the triple-net-lease arrangement, whereby they agree to pay the partnership a monthly lease payment and also agree to pay all the variable costs, such as taxes, upkeep, and insurance (hence the "triple-net" designation). Sears, Safeway, Federated Department Stores, and others might do the same. If many companies take this approach, a demand is created for large pools of capital, and this is just the economic condition that occurred in the period described above. To fill this great need, an organization of real estate experts whom I highly respect registered with the SEC for national distribution units of a large limited partnership to invest in the triple-net leases of these major U.S. corporations. For their buildings to be eligible for purchase by this partnership, each corporation had to have a minimum of $50 million in assets, be credit worthy, and be publicly traded. Thirty to 35 of these buildings were then placed in each partnership. The partnership was divided into $500 units, and investors were allowed to purchase as few as five units ($2500). They have now been doing this for seven years.

Each offering is usually for $30 million of capital, which allows the general partners, with three to one leverage, to invest approximately $90 million in triple-net-leased buildings each year.

Actually, the investments are made as the money comes in from the offering. If you make an investment in this type of partnership, you may not know which buildings will be purchased. The general partners will notify you as purchases are made. This procedure is known as investing in nonspecified properties, or a "blind pool."

In every prospectus I have ever read for an offering where the properties were nonspecified and where long-term mortgages were to be used as a part of the financing, there has always been in bold frightening print HIGH RISK on the front page. (I have often wondered if money market instruments such as U.S. government bonds and certificates of deposit of large commercial banks and savings institutions were to be the investment, but at the time the investor made the investment he did not know which instruments, and if any leverage was going to be used, if the caption HIGH RISK would be required on the front of the prospectus.)

I do not consider this type of investment high risk. I would personally rather own, for example, J. C. Penney's buildings than own its bonds. Any court in the land will throw out a tenant for nonpayment of the rent. Of course, recourse is also available to a bondholder if the interest is not paid when due, but this is a much slower process, and there is less potential for full recovery. Also, there is not a specific building that can be rented to another tenant in the meantime.

The potential benefits of an investment in a nonoperating real estate limited partnership are:

1 · Potential cash distributions paid quarterly or monthly.

2 · Equity buildup (mortgage paydown).

3 · Current tax shelter of a portion of your cash flow.

Let's look at some oversimplified mathematics that could occur if the partnership that I've been using for my clients continues to meet its financial objectives. It has in the past, but it may not in the future. Let's assume that after careful study you feel this investment meets your financial objectives and fits your temperament. Let's further assume the following: You make a $10,000 investment; the partnership, on the average, pays you a 9 percent cash distribution each year, with 75 percent of it tax sheltered; the properties are held for 10 years, and they appreciate 1 percent per year.

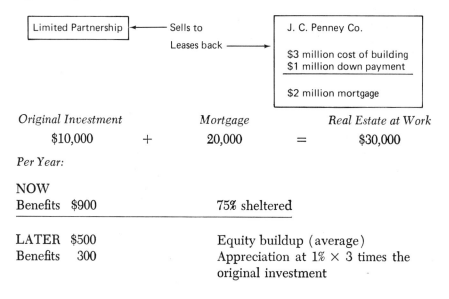

Original Investment		*Mortgage*		*Real Estate at Work*
$10,000	+	20,000	=	$30,000

Per Year:

NOW
Benefits $900   75% sheltered

LATER $500   Equity buildup (average)
Benefits   300   Appreciation at 1% × 3 times the
                                              original investment

Or, if we use percentages, here's another way of picturing their objectives for you:

	Quarterly Cash Distributions	*Excess Deductions*
NOW Benefits	9% (cumulative average) (75% tax sheltered)	0

	Equity Buildup	*Appreciation*
LATER Benefits	5–6%	3–9% (1% to 3% × 3 times of leverage)

In this oversimplified example, to your $10,000 investment the mortgages the partnership assumed would add an additional $20,000, for a total of $30,000 in real estate working for you.

Let's further assume that you are in the 30 percent tax bracket. If your cash distributions are $900 per year and 75 percent is tax sheltered, the remaining $225 will be taxed. At 30 percent you would lose $67.50 to Washington, leaving you with $832.50, or a 8.32 percent after-tax cash flow. This would be your NOW benefit.

• **LATER
  BENEFITS**

Equity Buildup • Every month when the lessees pay the rent, the general partner in turn pays a portion of the amount received to you and a portion to the mortgage company. This builds up your equity.

Equity buildup through the reduction of mortgage balances is one of the primary sources of your potential gain in this type of partnership. This is the reason that the partnerships usually hold properties long enough to provide a meaningful reduction of the mortgage balances. You do not, of course, receive this equity buildup until the building is sold for a profit or for at least the original purchase price. However, a big plus for you is the fact that any buildup that occurs does so from funds paid by the lessee and without current taxation to you.

Let's look at the mathematics if the partnership in which you may have invested sells all the buildings in its portfolio in 10 years and was able to sell them for just their original purchase price:

Hypothetical Example of Possible Results

	Investment		Mortgage		Real Estate
	$10,000	+	20,000	=	$30,000
NOW					
Benefits	9,000	Cash distributions ($900 × 10 years)			
LATER					
Benefits	5,000	Equity buildup ($500 × 10 years)			
Total					
Benefits	$24,000	Total cash distributions, equity buildup and original capital before capital gains taxes			

Over the ten years you would have received a total of $9000 cash distributions paid out on a quarterly basis, and would now cash in on your equity buildup of $5000. This plus your original investment of $10,000 would total $24,000. Therefore, your benefits would have been 9 percent NOW and 5 percent LATER, or a total of 14 percent per year before taxes. (Remember, at 5.2 percent inflation rate, a 9 percent corporate bond would have to float up to an interest rate of 14.9 percent to keep you even.) Perhaps this type of investment might keep you even or nearly so.

Appreciation • Let's now hope that some appreciation occurs because of escalating replacement costs and the increased cost of strategically located commercial land. If the buildings appreciate one percent a year and you are leveraged three to one, (meaning you invested $10,000 and the general partner borrowed $20,000 on your behalf) this would provide you with another $300 per year for a total of $3000 appreciation in 10 years. This added to the $24,000 would bring your total to $27,000. If a 2 percent appreciation occurs, this would add $6000 for a total of $30,000. Capital gains taxes would then be due based on the amount that your sales price exceeds your adjusted cost basis. Adjusted cost basis is arrived at by taking your original investment, which was $10,000, and subtracting all the cash distributions on which you did not pay taxes. The government never forgives a tax but it will allow you to defer it and oftentimes it can be turned into the more favorable capital gains.

Possible Disadvantages • You should be aware that the long-term triple-net leases that contribute so much to the dependability of your cash distributions can have an adverse effect on appreciation potential. The partnership may not be in a position to raise rentals, and current cash flow is the most important item in determining the sales price of your property when it is sold. (However, today more and more leases contain escalation clauses.)

This type of partnership usually also must use a more conservative depreciation schedule; therefore, the distributions may be only partially sheltered and will not provide excess deductions that can save taxes on income from other sources.

Investing in triple-net-leased properties is not without risk. While the management need not be concerned with fluctuations in occupancy rates and operating expenses, nor with variation in rent schedules, it does need to be concerned with the credit-worthiness of its corporate tenants. Great expertise is necessary to evaluate the properties as well as the financial strength of the corporate tenant.

If you are a conservative, income-seeking investor, and you want some tax shelter and some opportunity for appreciation to hedge against inflation, you may want to consider committing some of your investment dollars to this type of partnership.

We've been appraising here the characteristics of partnerships that are nonoperating. Let's now turn our attention to those partnerships where the general partners actually operate the properties purchased.

Operating Limited Partnerships • An operating partnership usually invests in multiple-tenanted properties, such as apartment buildings, office buildings, and shopping centers, and operates the properties. In this type of real estate investment, leases are generally of short duration, which can be a major advantage. Rents can be raised each year as the leases are renewed. This provides appreciation potential. However, it can also be a major disadvantage if your buildings do not stay fully rented. If the vacancy factor goes up, the cash flow goes down and can go down to the point where there is no income. This usually occurs when 20 percent or more of the units are vacant and there are mortgage payments to be met.

Multiple Family Housing • If I keep in mind the law of supply and demand, my thoughts today must turn to the area of multiple-family housing. An unprecedented shortage appears to be on the horizon. A conservative estimate of the need for new housing in the United States for the next ten years is 2.5 million units per year. In 1977 only an estimated 1,800,000 units were built. If we subtract from this figure the

600,000 to 800,000 units lost each year to fire, condemnation, and obsolescence, we begin to understand the magnitude of the problem.

In addition, because of the dramatic increase in construction costs, 85 percent of the heads of households can no longer afford the basic American home. The average American family income today is $13,800; the average home costs in excess of $53,800 (in many areas such as San Francisco, it is $62,000 and higher). Even if these families were to be offered interest-free mortgages, they could not qualify. This leaves them only two choices: to live in mobile homes or in garden-type apartments. If these families want to live in the more desirable areas of their city, want access to such facilities as swimming pools and tennis courts, they have no other option but to live in garden-type apartments. They may be frustrated potential homeowners, but home ownership is not one of the options open to them.

Also, there usually is a 12 to 18 months lag between demand and the appearance of new construction, with severe shortages in the interim.

Rents are currently increasing approximately 5.6 percent per year, while at the same time building costs have been increasing at the rate of over 10 percent. Rent today is one of the consumer's best buys. Historically, rents have run 36 to 40 months behind inflation. Also, the Tax Reform Act of 1976, which required capitalization of interim financing, will eliminate many potential apartment builders, and apartments will now be built on the basis of dire need and profitability rather than on the amount of money savings institutions have available to loan.

Now that you have been apprised of this situation, how can you best turn this knowledge into a profit? Should you go out and buy some apartments? Probably not, unless you have a large amount of money to invest, because economy of scale is often necessary for maximum profitability. Probably not, unless you are either very talented at repair and upkeep, or have the ability to supervise others, and truly want to be bothered about repairing a renter's commode. You very well may enjoy a larger return on your money by investing, along with a large number of others, in very selected limited partnerships that invest in garden-type apartments, selected shopping centers, and office buildings across the growth areas of the United States, with chief emphasis on the Sun Belt. In this way you can invest as small an amount as $5000 or in multiples of $500 above that amount, and can have the potential for quarterly distribution, tax sheltered. You also may have excess deductions to save taxes on other income, equity buildup, and possible appreciation with no effort on your part but to deposit the hoped-for quarterly distributions into your bank account and to enter the proper amounts for distributions and excess deductions in the proper place on your income tax return each year.

Management the Key • For many years I have recommended to my clients a registered offering by a general partner whose expertise I greatly respect and with whom my clients and I are very comfortable. The partnership is now making its thirty-seventh offering; it makes one each year. Each current offering should allow it to obtain $90 to $130 million of property. Its past performance has been excellent. It has an integrated real estate company that has had the ability to buy excellent properties at the right price and location, and has been able to manage these properties with outstanding expertise and to sell them profitably at the right time for maximum profits. This may or may not continue, but the quality and depth of its personnel, its very conservative approach to financing and its stringent reserve requirements encourage me to think that the trend will go on.

You As An Investor • Let's assume that you are in the 30 percent tax bracket. (You may come out with greater current keepable cash flow investing in the triple-net-lease partnership discussed above if you are below 28 percent.) Let's further assume that you have $20,000 you do not need to grab back over the next five to seven years (minimum investment is $5000), and that you are investing in a limited partnership that has leverage of around three to one and has as its objective a 5 to 7 percent cash flow. In this type of investment your cash flow may vary. You are investing in an operating business, and like other business operations, cash flow can fluctuate. Some months, for example, a carport may need to be added to enhance a property or other improvements may need to be made. It's not like the partnership investing in triple-net leases, where all the costs are paid by the lessees. Here they are paid by the partnership. Let's further assume that not only will the cash flow be sheltered from current taxation, but that there will be excess deductions of 10 to 12 percent that you can use to save taxes on other income. This is produced because the apartments may be on a 125 percent depreciation schedule (200 percent if they were new, which they usually are not; 125 percent if they are not). But the key ingredient is the depreciation allowed on component parts—drapes, carpets, refrigerators, etc., which can be depreciated over very short periods of time.

These quarterly distributions and excess deductions can provide you with your NOW benefits. Your LATER benefits can come from equity buildup (mortgage paydown) and appreciation. Equity buildup in these partnerships will probably be smaller per year than in the triple-net-lease partnerships, because the properties are usually held for shorter periods of time. If you've ever looked at the amortization table on your own home, you will have discovered that equity buildup occurs in a

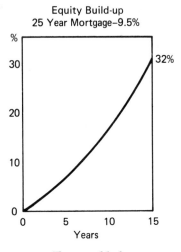

FIGURE 11–1.

curve. It is small at the beginning, with most of your payment going to interest, and larger as you get further into the schedule. Figure 11–1 gives you a picture of how equity buildup escalates the longer the property is held.

The equity buildup may be only around 3.5 percent if the apartments are held for only brief periods of time and more if they are held longer.

This type of partnership offers greater appreciation potential than the triple-net leases. Sears, Safeway, General Motors, etc. have tremendous bargaining power when it comes to negotiating lease terms. Apartment renters, in sharp contrast, have no bargaining power at all when there is a shortage of housing. Consequently, the apartment owners should be able to raise the rents to keep up or ahead of inflation. This in turn should increase the cash flow, which in turn usually increases the sales price.

• MULTIPLE-TENANT MATHEMATICS

If we assume a 5 percent cash flow, a 10 percent excess deduction, a 3½ percent equity buildup, a conservative 3 percent inflation, your tax bracket at 30 percent, $10,000 investment and three-to-one leverage, your mathematics could look something like this each year while investing in this type of partnership:

Hypothetical Example of $10,000 Invested in a
ted Partnership Investing in Multiple-Tenant Real Estate

	Original Investment	Mortgage	Real Estate
	$10,000	+ 30,000 =	$40,000
NOW	500	Tax sheltered, paid quarterly	
Benefits	300	10% excess deduction ($1000 × 30%)	
	$ 800	Current after-tax benefit (or 8%)	
LATER	350	Equity buildup	
Benefits	1200	Appreciation ($300 × 4 of leverage)	

Using percentages, a way that might give you a better visual picture of what the partnership hopes to accomplish would be the following:

Hypothetical Example of the Above Using Percentages

	Quarterly Cash Distributions Tax Sheltered	Excess Deductions
NOW BENEFITS	5–7%	8–12%

	Equity Buildup	Appreciation
LATER BENEFITS	2.5–3.5%	10–20%

Now Benefits • Your $500 cash distribution, tax sheltered, plus your excess deductions would make up your NOW benefits. In a 30 percent tax bracket you would keep $500 plus another $300 if depreciation, interest expense, etc. brought you a total of a 10 percent excess deduction. This would provide you with a total benefit of $800. (The $500 they paid to you plus the $300 you did not have to send to Washington.) How much would you have to earn on $10,000 to have $800 left after taxes? You would have to earn $1142 taxable income, or 11.42 percent per annum, to obtain an equivalent to your current keepable income here. In a 40 percent bracket you would have to earn $1500, or 15 percent; in a 50 percent bracket, $2000, or 20 percent; and in a 60 percent bracket, $2750, or 27 percent. These would be your NOW benefits, and they can be most attractive. However, your chief reason for investing should be your LATER benefits when the apartments are sold and you hope to cash in on the equity buildup and appreciation.

Later Benefits • When the properties are sold for as much or more than the original purchase price, and only then, do you reap any later benefits. Various payout arrangements can be used, so you should study each carefully and see which ones appear to give you the fairest return. A typical arrangement may be that when you have received back your original investment plus 12 percent per year, the general partner then receives 10 percent of the capital gains, and you and the other limited partners receive the other 90 percent. Other programs may provide that this split or others occur once you've received your original investment plus 10 percent. Your net results may be as great in one as the other. It all depends on the sale price.

On receiving your proportionate part of the sales proceeds, you will owe a capital gains tax on any gain above your adjusted cost basis unless you take steps to shelter it again. Remember all those distributions that you have been receiving without current taxation and the excess deductions that have saved you taxes on your other income? Now the IRS wants its due. Taxes are rarely forgiven, but they can be postponed with good tax planning. In the interim you have the earning power of the money. Also, it gives you time to plan with the hopes of converting ordinary income into capital gains, lowering your tax bite, and giving you time to figure out how to postpone paying the tax until even a further point in the future.

Tax avoidance or postponement must be a vital part of your program for economic survival.

• PERFORMANCE
PAST AND PROJECTED

Past performance of the partnerships my clients have used have been most gratifying. I do not know the future. However, I do know that this performance was obtained under circumstances not as favorable as I view them today. This performance was obtained when our country was experiencing 2 to 4 percent inflation, devaluations of the dollar, overbuilding of apartments and office buildings, and periods of rent control. Now we have inflation at 6 to 10 percent, our dollar is sometimes undervalued, we have underbuilding, and we have no rent control. The partnerships are still able to buy properties on the basis of current cash flow rather than replacement costs, and these are rapidly escalating. Rent is still one of America's best buys, and I feel it must increase before sufficient new building will occur. This should allow the partnerships to continue to make substantial rent increases while maintaining high occupancies. You should consider investing some of your "hard" after-tax dollars in large, well-managed, limited partnerships investing in multiple-family housing:

1 · If you thoroughly understand that investing in commercial income-producing real estate entails giving up some liquidity, and that the past is no guarantee of the future.

2 · If you are in a 30 percent tax bracket or above.

3 · If you want your funds invested where demand is greater than supply.

You may want to use this type of partnership or the triple-net lease, or you may use both, as many of my clients choose to do. The triple-net lease is the more conservative of the two and should pay out higher current cash distributions. The latter should pay out distributions completely tax sheltered with excess deductions to save taxes on other income. If growth of capital is your primary objective, multiple-family housing and multiple-tenant properties should offer you greater potential.

• PRIVATE
PLACEMENTS

If you are in the 50 percent tax bracket or above, have assets in excess of $200,000, excluding home and furnishings, and your temperament does not require greater safety of diversification, you may want to consider investing in a private placement if it is offered by a general partner with high integrity, a very large net worth, and a long and excellent performance record. Never, never invest in one that does not meet these criteria. A private placement is offered under SEC Rule 146 and can, under certain provisions, qualify for exemption from registration. However, these private placement documents, called the *prospectus*, must disclose all pertinent information as they would if they were registered. They may contain even more.

A SEC regulator will not have scrutinized the offering memorandum, but our laws are such that all the negatives and disaster possibilities that they can possibly think of will be in the offering memorandum, and it will be a very long and weighty document with pages and pages of dire warnings.

The maximum number of investors can be only 35, and they must be "sophisticated and wealthy" or have a "sophisticated offeree's representative and be wealthy."

A private placement usually contains only one property. One in which I have invested required that I make investments over a three-year period. The first year I invested $13,062.50, writing off 55.4 percent of the investment. The second year I invested $13,433.33, writing off 99.7 percent, and the third year $14,473.33, writing off 64.5 percent. This made my average investment approximately $13,670 per year over the three-year period. I will not be required to make further investments, but I anticipate receiving write-offs for an additional six years, with a total anticipated write-off of 122 percent of the amount I have invested. My cash flow the second year was 3.2 percent tax sheltered (in reality it was over 5 percent, since this was 3.2 percent on the total three-year investment and I did not make the third-year investment until the third year and was actually earning on the funds in another position) with equity buildup at 4.2 percent. By the fourth year tax-sheltered cash flow moved up to 8 percent, and the equity buildup was 4.9 percent that year.

By the end of the third year I calculated that my benefits in a 50 percent tax bracket had been:

	Year	Cash Distribution Tax Sheltered	Tax Savings From Excess Deductions
	1st	Minimal	3,636
NOW	2nd	1,262	6,480
	3rd	2,614	4,190
		3,876	14,307

		Equity Buildup	Appreciation
	1st	$ 48	
LATER	2nd	155	?
	3rd	169	

My first three years:

$ 3,876   Cash distributions received
14,307   Tax savings from write-offs
372   Equity buildup
$18,555 ÷ 3 years = $6,185 average benefits per year.

The average benefits per year, $6185, divided by $13,670, the

average investment per year, gave me 45 percent average *after-tax* benefit per year. To obtain the same current equivalent net after-tax benefit
on a taxable cash flow, I would have had to earn 90 percent annually
on a certificate of deposit. In addition, I anticipate six more years of
tax write-offs without any additional investment, and I anticipate receiving tax-sheltered cash distributions of 8 percent or more from the fourth
year on, plus capital appreciation.

I've only pointed out the plus side of what I hope for from this
investment, but let's also look at the possible negatives. The chief one
is lack of diversification. I do not have 10 to 15 properties, as I would
have had in a good diversified public offering. If, for example, the area
should suffer a sharp decline in employment, such as happened in Se-
attle a few years ago, I could suffer a negative cash flow. For that reason
I must be sure I have staying power—meaning other funds to carry me
through if this should happen.

Perhaps you already know how "write-offs" or deductions occur;
but nevertheless, let's look at the two most important sources for my
deductions in the above investments:

1 • Depreciation. I was allowed my proportionate part of the
depreciation of the apartment complex's total purchase price,
even though the mortgage company provided approximately
four times as much capital as I did. The buildings can be depreciated in an accelerated manner or what is called "straight-
line," meaning in equal amounts each year over the life of the
building. However, the apartments amenities can be set apart
for tax purposes and "component part" depreciation can be
used. This means such items as drapes and carpets can be
depreciated over much shorter periods of time.

2 • Interest expense. Interest paid on the mortgage (subject to
some restrictions) are also allowable deductions.

Because of borrowed funds, I could eventually deduct more than
I had invested.

If you are financially able to assume greater risks, private placements by the right general partners are something you should consider.
They can be structured for greater tax benefits so that you can invest
some "soft" before-tax dollars, and the burdensome expense of registration can be reduced.

Let's now turn to another form of real estate that can be income
producing—farmlands.

•   FARMLANDS

Farmlands have had an excellent record of price appreciation. An average dollar invested in farmlands in 1944 would be worth approximately $7.50 today. Even if you deflate the value of today's dollar to its 1944 level, the value is still nearly $1.90, or $.90 higher than the 1944 dollar (see Fig. 11–2).

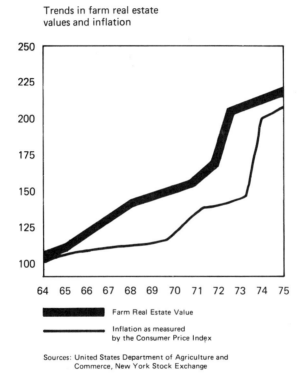

Trends in farm real estate values and inflation

 Farm Real Estate Value

———————— Inflation as measured by the Consumer Price Index

Sources: United States Department of Agriculture and Commerce, New York Stock Exchange

FIGURE 11–2.

There has been an almost uninterrupted appreciation of 6.9 percent each year since 1935. During the past 10 years farmlands have increased in price about 10 percent per year. The price has more than doubled in the past five years. Last year's increase averaged 17 percent. In the Midwest this figure was 33 percent.

In addition to inflation there are other factors that may contribute to the increase in farmland values. These are

1 • The increasing demand for and the ability to pay for food.

2 • The scarcity of good crop-growing land.

3 • The export of U.S. food items and commodities.

4 • Urbanization, or the conversion of farm property to nonfarm use.

Let's look at these:

Population Growth • Present indications are that the world population will increase by two percent a year compounded. If this occurs, there will be approximately eight billion people on the face of the earth around the year 2010. Even if growth should be slowed to a rate of as low as one-half of one percent a year, the population would grow to over six billion (see Fig. 11–3).

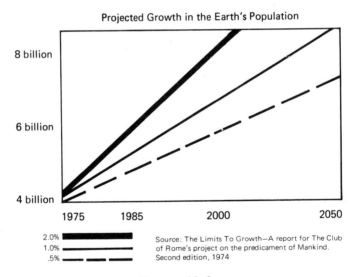

Projected Growth in the Earth's Population

Source: The Limits To Growth—A report for The Club of Rome's project on the predicament of Mankind. Second edition, 1974

FIGURE 11–3.

It seems highly likely that the world's population is going to continue to increase and possibly double in the next years. This in turn will double the demand for food.

The world's population growth and food problem is not equally distributed. If you look at Fig. 11–4, you will see that there is a band, 30 degrees north and 30 degrees south of the equator. Within this area lives 65 percent of the world's population and 60 percent of the world's animals, but it produces only about 20 percent of the world's food.

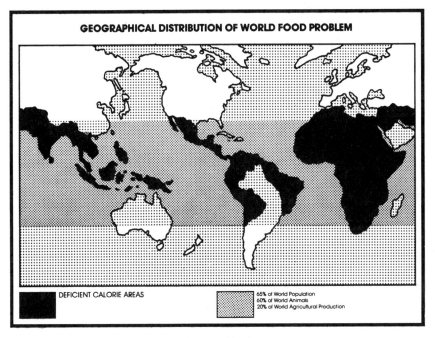

GEOGRAPHICAL DISTRIBUTION OF WORLD FOOD PROBLEM

DEFICIENT CALORIE AREAS

65% of World Population
60% of World Animals
20% of World Agricultural Production

FIGURE 11–4.

Added to this problem is the fact that approximately 72 percent of the world's population growth occurs in this same area. The second area shown is where the population has a calorie-deficient diet. This means everything from starvation to not having enough food to sustain reasonable longevity. At present there are only five nations that produce more food than they consume. These are the United States, Canada, Australia, New Zealand, and, in normal years, the USSR.

Nearly all other parts of the world, including western Europe and Japan, must rely on food imports. For some nations of the world, like the U.S., this means a market for excess food production. For other nations it means that food shortages will increase and imports will continue to grow. What the Arab world is to oil, the U.S. is to food.

It has been suggested that the solution to feeding the growing population is to double the amount of acres being farmed. Is this possible?

According to a study done by the University of California, the amount of land available for production during the period of 1950 to 1970 changed very little. Projections through 1985 also indicate that there will be little change in spite of the greatly increased demand. Only an eight to ten percent increase in the amount of arable lands throughout the world is expected in the next 10 years. Most of the food required since 1972 to feed the hungry world has come from the United States. The balance of U.S. agricultural trade from 1972 through 1977 shows major increases in exports. In 1975, 1976, and 1977 the U.S. exported approximately 75 percent of all world food exports. This is 25 percent of all U.S. farm output and up to 50 percent of some of its crops. A good portion of the food that will be required in the next decade must come from the United States, because there are very few countries that can produce in excess of their own needs.

Urbanization • In addition to inflation, population growth, scarcity of farmland, and export demands for U.S. food items, there is another important reason for the escalation of the price of farmlands. That is urbanization, or the conversion of farm property to nonfarm use. Each year about five million acres of land are removed from potential or existing agricultural uses. The remaining land must produce an ever-increasing amount of food to feed the growing population. The net results should be that land which remains available for agricultural production should increase in value.

Should you consider investing monies in farmland as an inflationary hedge and to produce an income stream? If so, what investment strategy should you use?

If you are knowledgeable in farming and have sufficient time and the desire, you may want to consider buying some farmland and putting it into production. This takes great expertise, usually fairly large amounts of money, and may not offer you the amount of diversification needed to reduce risks.

Limited Partnerships in Producing Croplands • A program you may want to consider is a limited partnership in producing croplands in which you can invest as small an amount as $5000, and which has as its financial objective the following:

1 • The prediction of the demand for specific food items and the availability of land for their production.

2 • The minimization of production variations and fluctuation of market prices by crop diversification.

3 • The purchase of only improved and income-producing farmland to avoid negative cash flow.

4 • The control of labor costs by mechanization.

5 • The professional selection of the land best suited for the crops to be grown.

6 • A management team that has had success in growing all of the crops they plan to grow.

A limited partnership, where you can pool your funds with other investors, may be able to offer you the potential of profitable farmland investing that only a few wealthy investors could afford in the past.

If you do decide to invest in this type of partnership, what should you anticipate? I don't know, for this type of partnership is a new one that has no performance history, and there is no guarantee that they can accomplish their objectives. I can only state what they hope to do.

First, they hope to be able to give you 40 to 50 percent write-off on your original investment. This comes from reimbursing the former owner that year for his growing crop, fertilizer, and seed consumed, depreciation of vines, trees and irrigation equipment, and cultivation, spraying, and weeding the crops. If you are in a 50 percent tax bracket you would receive approximately a $5000 deduction on a $10,000 investment. Beginning the second year, they hope to be able to pay out to you a minimum of 8 percent or $800, on a $10,000 investment with approximately half of the distribution tax sheltered. In addition, they hope to build your equity each year by 2 to 4 percent through amortizing the mortgage used in purchasing the land. They also hope to provide you with capital appreciation of at least the average amount of increase in farm values that has occurred over the last 35 years. This has been around 7 percent per year. If they leverage 2 to 1, then 7 percent doubled should give you approximately 14 percent appreciation.

If all of these possibilities seem feasible to you, then you may want to consider investing in limited partnerships that invest in producing croplands in this manner. This could offer you the potential of participating in the production and growth in the value of croplands.

The minimum investment in these limited partnerships is usually $5000, and suitability requirements for this type of investment may require $25,000 of income and $25,000 in assets exclusive of home and furnishings.

• REAL ESTATE
INVESTMENT TRUSTS

All of the types of participation in commercial income-producing real estate we have discussed so far may appeal to you, but at this point in your financial life you may not meet all the suitability requirements, or do not choose to invest this amount of money in a less liquid limited partnership. Are there ways you can participate with smaller amounts of money? Yes, you can, through what are known as real estate investment trusts. This type of real estate investment was developed in response to the needs of those who wanted to invest small amounts of money in the profit potentials that real estate investing had to offer, but wanted at the same time to maintain the liquidity of a stock. To fulfill this desire the modern equity trust was created to acquire and hold income properties of all types, yet have the shares publicly traded.

The REIT industry expanded dramatically in the late nineteen sixties and early nineteen seventies, when many financial institutions, with the encouragement of Wall Street, established affiliated mortgage trusts in order to provide additional sources of capital. Though a few trusts used little leverage, many aggressively sought higher yields by lending to builders for construction. Their yields, together with their price per share, escalated and they became the darlings of the brokerage industry and of our largest national banks. Some of these REITs bore the prestigious names of such banking institutions as Chase Manhattan Bank and Bank of America. The nation's largest brokerage firms brought forth underwritings in REITs and held many public seminars extolling their virtues. Unfortunately, neither they nor others ever anticipated the drastic steps that would be taken by the Federal Reserve Board shortly thereafter to restrict the nation's money supply, causing a disastrous money crunch and sending interest rates reeling skyward. Many of the mortgage REITs had loaned funds for longer terms while borrowing for short terms and making a tidy sum on the spread between the two. But suddenly their cost to borrow money escalated beyond the rates at which they had made their loans. This spelled immediate and devastating trouble. Also, rapid inflation caused construction costs to mushroom and made many projects uneconomical to complete. Many builders were forced out of business, leaving numerous REITs with unfinished or unsold projects, nonearning loans, and overinflated assets. These disasters had great repercussions in the banking industry and on Wall Street, both of whom were partly responsible for the creation of the problem in the first place. The difficulties of the REITs were widely publicized in the newspapers and trade journals, with the result that still today the very mention of the word sends shudders down the spines of many potential investors.

Even in less perilous times REITs may have a rough time. A REIT, for example, may have made an excellent purchase of property, but it may be what is known as a "turn-around situation." During the period when needed improvements are being made, the REIT's earnings may be lower. A drop in earnings of a stock frightens traders and often causes them to virtually bomb a stock, driving down its price and causing general chaos and disappointment to the investor.

I'm convinced that my beloved Wall Street has never really understood real estate investing and that, properly structured, REITs can offer a valid investment opportunity for those who want to participate in commercial income real estate while being able at the same time to maintain liquidity.

Open-end REITS • There are some new *equity* REITs that have come forth in recent years that are struggling to overcome the notoriety of their namesake. The new equity trusts (as opposed to mortgage REITs, which loan funds and do not own the property) are designed to be offered and available on as continuous a basis as is permitted by law. Their open-endedness, their low price per share, their small minimum investment requirements, and no suitability standards extend the possible benefits of real estate investing to many who could not otherwise be able to participate. Some of these REITs have distribution reinvestment privileges and monthly automatic check plans, making them a good flexible accumulation vehicle. They are also providing special packaging arrangements that qualify these trusts for use in Keogh and IRA plans.

REITs may fit your needs. Their shares can be freely transferable, in contrast to limited partnership interests. The trust must by regulation be a passive entity and must employ outside agents to perform required services. So long as it meets certain asset and income tests and distributes at least 90 percent of its net taxable income each year, it will not be separately taxed. However, distributions may be partially or wholly tax sheltered, but net operating losses cannot be passed through to you as an investor to be used to shelter income from other sources as can occur with the limited partnership arrangement.

You may find the operation of a REIT very much like that of a limited partnership with the exceptions that more emphasis will be placed on cash flow and equity buildup because of their inability to pass through excess tax losses. However, the increased liquidity of their shares and the restrictions on resale of their properties may encourage them to periodically refinance their properties, which in turn could allow current realization of some of the equity buildup.

Presently a number of changes in our tax laws governing REITs have been proposed and are pending. If these are obtained, they should allow greater flexibility in REIT operations and make the REIT a valuable financial planning tool in the future.

•   REAL ESTATE vs. EQUITIES

I believe in the long-term economic viability of investing in stocks. However, I am equally convinced that carefully selected income-producing real estate can be a suitable and prudent investment for you, no matter how conservative your investment philosophy may be.

The Federal Reserve Board's control of the money supply in recent years has brought sluggish growth and disquieting volatility to the stock market and has made us painfully aware that all, or even a large portion, of our assets can no longer be in only one area of investing.

An excellent article written by Dennis G. Kedleher was published in the Summer 1976 *Real Estate Review* entitled, "How Real Estate Stacks Up To The S & P 500." It's a scholarly work that makes some interesting comparisons of return on monies invested. The contention of the article is that regardless of the time period selected, multiple-tenant real estate yields have been historically more stable than common stocks, and consistently exceeded returns from the S & P 500. In fact, in the 1967–1973 period of the study, annual real estate returns for real estate properties were almost double those from the S & P. Table 11–1 gives the interesting comparisons done by Mr. Kedleher.

Table 11–1.   Comparison of Annual Returns for S & P 500 Stocks and Real Estate Properties

| | Standard & Poor's 500 Stocks | | Multiple-Tenant Real Estate | |
	Price Index on December 31	Annual Dividend as Percent of Price	Net Operating Income Index	Annual Yield— Income as Percent of Price
1960	58.11	3.35	77.6	8.9
1961	71.55	2.86	84.9	8.8
1962	63.10	3.38	81.0	8.6
1963	75.02	3.11	82.0	8.4
1964	84.75	3.03	93.4	8.4
1965	92.43	3.04	96.7	8.5
1966	80.44	3.64	97.8	8.4
1967	96.47	3.06	100.0	8.6
1968	103.86	2.99	103.3	9.0
1969	92.06	3.48	111.1	9.6
1970	92.15	3.36	121.3	10.8
1971	102.10	2.99	121.5	10.0
1972	118.10	2.71	132.1	9.6
1973	97.55	3.64	140.1	9.5

In this study Mr. Kedleher designed a system based upon the internal rate of return to assist clients in evaluating and comparing real estate with other investment possibilities. He believes that every real estate investment can be separated into three elements—price, dividend, and time—and that these can be extracted by the use of this performance measure. This rate converts the irregular cash flows of any investment project into the percentage equivalent of an investment that you leave to compound at a fixed rate of interest and should allow you to compare those "apples and oranges," common stocks and real estate.

In order for you properly to understand these comparisons, it may be necessary to define some commonly used real estate terms.

Net Operating Income • First is "net operating income." This figure is derived from annual rent collections minus all operating expenses and real estate taxes. Mortgage payments are not included in costs, because in order to compare real estate with common stocks, the properties must be viewed as free and clear of mortgage debt. Net operating income is, then, the annual cash return from a real estate project, and it may be compared with the dividend income received from common stocks. When the level of net operating income is expressed as a percentage, it may be called "annual return."

Capitalization Rate • Another important term is "capitalization rate." The "cap rate" is the ratio of current net operating income to price. It is the reciprocal of the price-earnings ratio for common stocks. For example, if an investment of $1 million yields a net operating income of $90,000 annually, we derive the following:

Capitalization rate: $\dfrac{\$90,000}{\$1,000,000} = 0.09 = 9$ percent

Price-earnings ratio: $\dfrac{\$1,000,000}{\$90,000} = 11.11$ (the reciprocal of 9 percent)

To avoid the misunderstanding that the cap rate represents the return only on equity interest, the term "overall capitalization rate" is used.

Table 11–2 gives examples of five types of typical real estate investment results that Mr. Kedleher presented that should enable you to better understand internal rates of return. In each example the holding period is assumed to be seven years.

Mr. Kedleher came to the conclusions in Table 11–3 regarding

Table 11–2. Cash Flows from Various Investments and Resulting Internal Rates of Return

CASH FLOWS FROM VARIOUS INVESTMENTS
AND RESULTING INTERNAL RATES OF RETURN

Investment Model 1:
Stable Income and Stable Sale Price

This pattern of behavior is unusual for any type of investment, although some investment experience with bonds or net-leased real estate may be similar. The purpose of this example is simply to illustrate the internal rate of return measurement.

Acquisition price:	$1,000	
Sale price:	$1,000	
Annual return:	Year 1	$100
	2	$100
	3	$100
	4	$100
	5	$100
	6	$100
	7	$100
Internal rate of return:	10.00 percent	

Investment Model 2:
Increasing Income and Stable Sale Price

Some income property investments may show this pattern. ·If cap rates increase because of an inflationary climate, an investor might receive increased annual income during the holding period but realize no appreciation in value upon selling the project. This pattern also is found when an owner "milks" real estate by deferring substantial maintenance expenditures. It is then a means of trading off capital gain for current income.

Acquisition price:	$1,000	
Sale price:	$1,000	
Annual return:	Year 1	$100
	2	$105
	3	$110
	4	$115
	5	$120
	6	$125
	7	$130
Internal rate of return:	11.26 percent	

Investment Model 3:
Increasing Income and Increasing Price

Most higher quality income property with multiple tenancy follows this pattern. Of course, the degrees of income increase and the amount of appreciation in price vary widely among specific projects.

Acquisition price:	$1,000
Sale price:	$1,300

Annual return:	Year 1	$100
	2	$105
	3	$110
	4	$115
	5	$120
	6	$125
	7	$130
Internal rate of return:	13.85 percent	

Investment Model 4:
Stable Income and Increasing Sale Price

An example of an income property with this pattern is one that may have a few years remaining under terms of a flat net lease. Upon expiration of the existing lease, the annual net income (and hence value) may increase substantially, or the land may be improved with a more intensive use.

Acquisition price:	$1,000	
Sale price:	$1,300	
Annual return:	Year 1	$100
	2	$100
	3	$100
	4	$100
	5	$100
	6	$100
	7	$100
Internal rate of return:	12.73 percent	

Investment Model 5: Land Investment Pattern
(No Annual Income and Increasing Price)

This example illustrates an income pattern for a speculative land investment. In order to hedge against the carrying costs of land (annual real estate taxes, municipal assessments, etc.), land lease arrangements are sometimes made. And to hedge against a lack of price appreciation, the investor in land may seek a "buy back" arrangement. In recent years particularly, land investment hedges such as leases and "buybacks" have failed because the typical security for such contracts is the seller's credit and the seller is often an illiquid, or even insolvent, entrepreneur.

Acquisition price:	$1,000	
Sale price:	$1,950 ($1,000 compounded at 10 percent annually)	
Annual return: (amount is negative because of holding costs)	Year 1	($30)
	2	($30)
	3	($30)
	4	($30)
	5	($30)
	6	($30)
	7	($30)
Internal rate of return:	7.46 percent	

Table 11–3.   Internal Rates of Return for S & P 500
Stocks and Multiple-Tenant Real Estate

Time period for which investment is held	S & P 500 stocks	Multiple-tenant real estate
1960 through 1966	Assume single investment on January 1, 1960	
Jan. 1960–Dec. 1960	0.3	11.4
Jan. 1960–Dec. 1961	12.5	15.6
Jan. 1960–Dec. 1962	5.1	12.6
Jan. 1960–Dec. 1963	9.0	12.5
Jan. 1960–Dec. 1964	10.4	14.3
Jan. 1960–Dec. 1965	10.7	13.9
Jan. 1960–Dec. 1966	7.8	13.5
1967 through 1973	Assume single investment on January 1, 1960	
Jan. 1967–Dec. 1967	23.6	8.5
Jan. 1967–Dec. 1968	17.2	8.0
Jan. 1967–Dec. 1969	8.3	8.8
Jan. 1967–Dec. 1970	7.1	8.5
Jan. 1967–Dec. 1971	8.4	10.2
Jan. 1967–Dec. 1972	9.9	11.9
Jan. 1967–Dec. 1973	6.4	12.5
Summary	Assume single investment on January 1, 1960	
Jan. 1960–Dec. 1973	7.2	13.2

internal rates of return for the S & P 500 stocks as compared to investing in multiple-tenant real estate:

A study of these results appears to give strong indications that commercial income-producing real estate should be one of your investment considerations.

Possible Disadvantages • What are some of the risks and disadvantages of investing in registered limited partnerships that invest in income-producing commercial real estate?

First, there can be delays between the time you make your investment and the time the money is actually invested in properties. During the interim you will receive interest, but you will not be receiving tax-sheltered cash flow from real estate.

Second, if the partnership has not obtained a prior IRS ruling that it is a limited partnership, it could be treated taxwise as an association and taxed as a corporation. If this should occur, the depreciation and interest deductions would be reflected only on the partnership's tax return and not passed through to you.

Third, any accelerated depreciation, if such a schedule is used, leaves smaller amounts to be deducted in later years, and can also be classified as a "preference item" under the Tax Reform Act of 1976.

Fourth, partnership units can only be transferred with the consent of the general partner. (In the past this has not been unreasonably withheld.) Therefore, there will usually be no public market for the units.

Fifth, borrowing money permits the acquisition of more properties than you have cash, but it also requires that you pay on that mortgage regardless of whether you are netting that amount each month after expenses. This then increases your exposure to loss.

• THE IDEAL INVESTMENT?

I have never found an ideal investment. If you do, please let me know. However, I have found that the right kind of commercial income-producing real estate limited partnerships under the guidance and management of the right general partners has in the past contained some of the characteristics of an ideal investment. These are

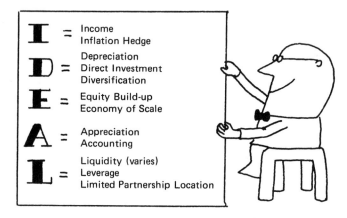

I	=	Income Inflation Hedge
D	=	Depreciation Direct Investment Diversification
E	=	Equity Build-up Economy of Scale
A	=	Appreciation Accounting
L	=	Liquidity (varies) Leverage Limited Partnership Location

Let's consider each in summary:

Income With Tax Shelter • The only money you'll ever spend at the grocery store is what the IRS lets you keep. Income-producing real estate limited partnerships investing in triple-net leases have in the past paid out cash flow quarterly with the major portion sheltered. This has come about because they are allowed to pass through to the limited partners the depreciation and interest expense on the properties. Those investing in multiple-tenant properties have been able not only to shelter the cash distributions paid quarterly but to provide excess deductions to save taxes on income from other sources.

Inflation Hedge • If you have received no other message from this book, I do hope the one you have not missed is the absolute reality that inflation came thundering in with our government's dedication to full employment and will never go away until this philosophy is changed. My advice to you is to quit worrying about inflation and get on the right side of it. Inflation can make you a lot of money if you intelligently place your funds in those areas where demand is greater than supply.

Depreciation • The limited partnership form of investing permits the pass-through of the depreciation expense deduction allowed by the IRS. Another important characteristic of real estate is that depreciation is allowed on the total cost of the building—not just on your investment. You may have only put in $10,000 and the mortgage company $30,000, but your depreciation is based on the total $40,000. You are allowed a deduction for depreciation even when your asset is actually growing in value.

Direct Investing • All money placed in a savings and loan association is invested in real estate. If you are a depositor, you are an indirect investor in real estate, and you will receive a portion of the return on the real estate investment. If you invest in a limited partnership, the partnership may borrow the mortgage money from the savings and loan, but you have a direct investment and are in a position to receive your money's full earning power (but you also give up the fixed dollar guarantees.) In my opinion, your only hope of staying even after inflation and taxes is to be a direct investor.

Diversification • One of the first rules of successful investing is diversification. Never put all your eggs in the proverbial one basket. Spread your precious eggs out in several baskets of various kinds of real estate and in various locations. Ten properties located in ten locations should offer more safety than one property in one location.

Equity Buildup • If you own a home on which you have a mortgage, you are already familiar with equity buildup (mortgage paydown). The difference between the equity buildup in your home and the equity buildup in the commercial properties of the limited partnerships is that you had to build up the equity in your home by your monthly mortgage payments, but in the limited partnerships the renters build up your equity by their monthly rent payments. Equity buildup is also occurring without current taxation.

Economy of Scale • I can't emphasize enough how important economy of scale can be in the purchase, management, and sale of commercial real estate. The truly significant profits are more often made on the very large real estate properties. As a limited partner, you have the opportunity to participate in a proportionate part of larger properties than you may be able to do on an individual basis.

Appreciation • "Capital gains" has always been and still remains the golden word of the investment world. No federal income taxes are paid on the appreciation of real estate until the properties are sold. The properties can just sit there and grow in value without taxes. (They can go down in value, too.) Appreciation is realized when and if the properties are sold for a larger amount than was paid for their purchase. If the properties have been held for over a year, the profit on the sale is considered a capital gain and usually half of it is not taxable, except under certain circumstances under the new tax law.

    As inflation pushes up replacement costs, appreciation in real estate has a good likelihood of occurring.

Accounting • My clients especially enjoy the accounting done for them by the general partners for their real estate investments. They are sent a completed Schedule K-1 (schedule used for limited partnership), as well as a blank one to complete and attach to their income tax returns, plus a guide with red lines and arrows stating, "Put this figure on this line." By following their detailed instructions the clients can complete their own returns if they desire. (I find that a truly creative C.P.A. is worth more than he will cost.)

Leverage • Remember Bernard Baruch and his answer to the question of how he made so much money. He said, "O.P.M.—Other People's Money." Let other people's money work for you. Inflation rewards those who owe money, not those who pay cash. Here I am talking about long-term real estate mortgages, not revolving charge accounts. When and if appreciation occurs, the total value of the building appreciates, including the borrowed portion. Leverage can work for you if properly used. It can spell disaster if it is abused or if the economy of the area turns against you.

Liquidity • Real estate investment trusts provide you with liquidity. Many of the other forms of investing in real estate curtail liquidity. Do not place funds into real estate that you want to be free to grab back on very short notice.

Location • The three most important rules in selecting the right piece of real estate are location, location, location. Your objective should be to be a proportionate owner of a diversified portfolio of properties selected and managed by top professionals who have established a long record of success, and who have large pools of money for investing. This enables them to purchase properties that have the necessary characteristics of good location.

• CONCLUSION

If you are willing to give up instant liquidity, are in a 25 percent tax bracket or above, and can forego the pleasure of looking up the market value of your properties in the paper each day, you may find that the limited partnership is a good way to prevent double taxation and to allow you to participate in investment that, if made individually, would require large amounts of capital.

Investing in real estate should be considered in any program designed to build toward financial independence. In my opinion, the opportunity for relatively high leverage with relatively low risk makes it a viable inflation hedge. Unusual tax benefits also can enhance its attractiveness, but they should not be your principal motivation.

Current tax-sheltered cash distributions can also be attractive. If your income stream needs to be steady, then be prepared to sacrifice some of the growth potential. If current income is not your chief objective, then look at the operating partnerships where income may fluctuate but where the potential for appreciation is greater.

Our formula for financial independence should now add real estate and might read this way:

Time + money + real estate = opportunity for financial independence.

Application

1 · Which areas of real estate investing best fit your tax bracket and your temperament?

2 · What steps will you take to become better informed of investment alternatives?

3 · Make a list of all your alternative investment possibilities. Calculate your expected rate of return, your loss to taxes, your keepable funds after taxes, your potential to hedge against inflation, and your potential for equity buildup and growth of capital.

Your Worksheet for Comparing Real Estate Investing with Other Types

$ _____ investment, ____% tax bracket.

Indirect Investing

	Income	Taxes	Keepable	Inflation Hedge	Equity Buildup	Appreci- ation
Savings & loan						
Corporate bonds						
Municipal bonds						
Single-premium deferred annuity						
Direct Investing						
Triple-net leases						
Multiple tenant						

4 · List here the areas of our economy where you feel demand will be greater than supply over the next three years:

a.

b.

c.

d.

5 · List here the course of action you plan to take to profit from these shortages:

a.

b.

c.

d.

12

The Roof Over Your Head

There is one kind of real estate about which you have no option—you must have a place to live during every period of your life. You do, however, have a number of choices about how you allocate your funds to meet this and other needs.

Food, clothing, shelter—the three essentials of life! Thats what you learned in grade school, and as an adult you probably do not question these necessities. Since shelter is a necessity, but only one of your necessities, it behooves you to approach its provision as coolly and economically as possible, for you will want to have funds left over for a few of the other goodies that put a bit of frosting on the cake of life.

There is much fuzzy thinking about how to best provide shelter. Many couples, particularly young ones, hate to rent even for a short period of time. They are convinced that rent receipts are pure waste, not realizing that rent money is no more wasted than the money spent for food or medicine. Many view house payments as almost pure "savings" and rent money in terms of a leaky faucet.

You may be one of those who are deliberately closing their minds to economic realities in order to own their own homes.

• SINGLE-FAMILY DWELLING— HOBBY OR INVESTMENT?

To put this matter of renting vs. owning into proper perspective, let's look at the landlord–tenant relationship. A landlord renting a one-family dwelling would probably earn a net of 6 percent on his equity—the market value of the home less the mortgage. This could happen only if he kept the home rented most of the time and the renter paid the rent promptly. (He may, however, be enjoying considerable tax shelter by way of depreciation.)

If the landlord has a $5000 equity in a $25,000 home, he might hope to earn about 6 percent net on his $5000 each year or $300, or $25 per month. Or put in another way, if you had that much equity in your own $25,000 home, you'd be saving $25 per month by not renting the house from the landlord. However, you may not save that much because you can't claim as many deductions as the landlord.

Real estate ads often cite the fact that homeowners can deduct interest on their house loan and real estate taxes from their income taxes. The ads are true but do not give the whole story. The landlord also can deduct these items, plus many more that the IRS will not allow the home-owner to take. These cover insurance, repairs, painting, the green shrubbery, depreciation, and so on.

Every house has a potential rental value—the sum that could be realized by renting to a tenant, As a rule of thumb, the rental value is about 10 percent per year of the market value. A $25,000 home then has an approximate annual rental value of 2500, or a little over $200 per month. If you live in a $25,000 home, the real cost to you each year is about $2500.

A single-family dwelling may not be a good investment, in the real sense of the word, for either the landlords or the homeowners who are in the lower income tax brackets (with the exception of during the mid-1970s, when high interest rates and high replacement costs greatly escalated home values). Homes often are more of a hobby than an investment unless you have chosen a home in what later becomes a growth area where land values rapidly accelerate. This could then be an excellent investment. However, don't go overboard; inflation or a shift in location desirability may not bail you out of a costly real estate purchase. While you're waiting for the property to inflate in value, taxes and interest may put a very bad dent in your family budget.

- ## TAX
  ## SAVINGS?

Let's go back to the fact that taxes and interest are deductible on your income tax. When you are considering buying a home, you may reason that Uncle Sam is helping you make the monthly payments, and you should not miss this help. This may well be true if you are in a high enough tax bracket. In the lower brackets the relief it brings may be only an illusion.

If your income is $10,000 per year, you may not get much of a tax break from the extra deductions. Even if you are in the middle income bracket, you will probably save no more than 15 percent of the net cost of your interest and property taxes by deducting them from gross income.

The IRS allows each family a 16 percent flat standard deduction anyway (not to exceed $3200), and unless you have enough deductions to itemize, including interest and property taxes, these last two costs become pure expenses.

If you have ever had a really aggressive real estate agent pull out his form entitled "Analysis of Home Ownership Costs," he may endeavor to persuade you that owning your own house will cost practically nothing, since the monthly charges consist almost entirely of tax-deductible interest and property taxes, and the remainder is your contribution to your equity, which will, of course, increase. He will then proceed to tell you that all you need is a down payment, which will be the best investment you have ever made. He will attempt to persuade you that you should be a wise house hunter and buy, and not a foolish house hunter and rent, with nothing to show for it but rent receipts.

But this arithmetic omits two crucial elements. One of these is the loss of income that the down payment might produce if invested elsewhere. Another is the transfer costs—the expense of buying and selling a house, which can amount to over 8 percent of its value. When these costs are put into your analysis, they can turn the calculations around in favor of renting.

However, our whole U.S. housing system encourages buying, not renting. Spouses, children, pets, neighbors, politicians, and bankers all argue for home ownership. It has become one of those fundamentals we look to as securing the nation. Our tax laws favor ownership. The Brookings Institution estimates that homeowners get $7 billion worth of federal tax breaks annually.

The IRS also exempts an owner of capital gains tax when he sells a house as long as he buys another house that is as expensive within a year, or builds another within 18 months. This all encourages home ownership to become a habit.

The 1970 census established that 62.9 percent of U.S. families live in houses that they own. This still leaves a substantial minority who rent.

You may need to have an income above $20,000 to approach any meaningful break on your tax return through home ownership.

There are many legitimate reasons for buying a home. You may feel that it is a better place to raise your children. It may give you a sense of security, of belonging, or of status. A lovely home can be a true joy and a prestige symbol that adds to your self-confidence.

However, don't plunge into home ownership only because others are doing it—a kind of follow-the-follower pattern of thinking—without truly weighing the pros and cons. Even though there are a number of valid reasons for home ownership, I find that most of them are sociologic and very few are based on genuine economic facts.

If you truly feel that owning your own home will bring you a greater enjoyment of life, will make you a more responsible citizen, and will offer you that additional privacy that may be important to you, then consider buying a home. But if your reasons are to boast about all the money you are saving, be careful not to boast to an economist.

• THE HYBRID HOMEOWNER

If you want the advantages of owning your home and the advantages of an apartment, perhaps you should consider owning your own apartment.

This can be done either in a co-operative apartment or townhouse, or a condominium. What's the difference?

In a co-op, you buy "shares" in the building and facilities, including recreational facilities. When shares are sold in co-ops, it must be by vote of the majority of the shareholders. You become both landlord and tenant, which means that you take your share of both economic and managerial responsibilities.

Co-op ownership does give the tax advantages of home ownership together with recreational facilities and maintenance at a lower cost than an individual family dwelling.

In a condominium you own your own apartment and a pro rata share of the facilities rather than stock in the building. This means that you have the same responsibility for common areas, but you may sell your apartment to whomever you wish. The tax and facilities cost advantages are identical to the co-op.

The methods of financing for both are similar to financing a one-family home.

What are some of the problems with these forms of home owner-ship? First, in co-op apartments, owners have occasionally had problems with the co-owners vetoing the sale of their shares, which means, effec-tively, they could not sell their home. More important, poor maintenance of an apartment complex seriously lowers the value and salability of your apartment, so it is imperative to buy in a well-located, well-maintained building, just as you should buy a home in a well-located and well-maintained neighborhood.

• AVOID THE APPLES
AND ORANGES COMPARISON

The rather unemotional approach I've given home ownership should do one thing for you, and that is to make you aware that the monthly payments have little to do with the real cost of owning a home.

How do you go about comparing the cost of renting an apartment with the cost of buying a home? One way is to compare the annual rental for an apartment with 10 percent of the value of the home whose purchase you are considering. If you foolishly compare the monthly payments on the house with the monthly payments on the apartment, you are, in effect, comparing apples and oranges. There is no comparative relation-ship. Mortgage payments have nothing to do with the cost of home ownership. Mortgage payments only relate to debt reduction.

The Real Cost • The real cost of home ownership includes upkeep and repair, fire and homeowner insurance, property taxes, equity investment, and depreciation (value loss). These expenses are just as real if you are a homeowner as if you are a landlord. The big difference often lies in the fact that a landlord recognizes them and includes them in the price he charges for the use of his property, whereas you may be tempted as a homeowner to pretend that these expenses do not exist.

The landlord knows that he must get at least 10 percent per year in rent on his property to cover his expenses and net him a profit. You, as a potential or present homeowner, would be wise to think as he does.

If you have been living in an apartment, feeling you just must buy your own home and save all that rent money, do slow down and take heart. The drain on your solvency may not be as bad as you have been thinking.

Mobility—The American Way • Another fact to recommend renting is that we are a very mobile society. Renting allows you to move more easily without the worry and delay of selling a home and the expense of sales commissions and horrendous closing costs.

At this point you may be thinking that if you owned a home, you would have built an equity in return for your payments as the years go by, whereas now you have nothing but rent receipts.

But, remember, I've been comparing the cost of renting with the cost of owning. You can save money and acquire net worth in other ways than by paying on a mortgage. You could open a savings account or start a monthly investment program with the difference.

The Case of Mrs. Bailey • An elderly widow client of mine lives in a house that is debt free and has a market value of $25,000. She asked if she should sell her house and rent an apartment. I told her that if she would bring me a list of her expenditures for the past year, I would be happy to advise her from a financial point of view. She gave me a list of her utilities, yard work expenses, house repairs, insurance, and taxes. I then added the 6 percent "guaranteed" return she could obtain on the $25,000 that would be available for investment after the sale of the house. When we added all of these together, we found that she could live in a $250 per month apartment more cheaply than she could live in her own home. In addition, she did not have to worry about watering her yard or possible vandalism during trips out of town.

I advised her, however, not to rush into selling her home. Answering a question on a financial basis is one thing; answering it on an emotional basis is quite another matter. Sometimes we need to consider that some expenditures are an investment in living.

- ## WHAT PRICE HOME
  ## CAN YOU AFFORD?

If you decide to purchase a home, it may be the largest single investment that you will make in your whole lifetime; therefore, invest carefully and within your budget.

There is no magic rule as to what percentage of your income should be spent for a roof over your head; however, I have found that usually this expenditure should not exceed 25 percent of your income. We've already concluded that there are other things in life as important as housing. You may desire good clothing, nutritional and tasty food, excellent medical care, a sporty or at least an adequate automobile, and an annual vacation. This makes it necessary to apportion your income.

To determine what price home you can afford, compute one-fourth of your annual income and multiply that figure by 10. Let's assume that you earn $20,000 per year. One-fourth of $20,000 is $5000 which, multiplied by 10, comes to $50,000. That figure is probably what you can afford to pay for your home.

There is nothing sacred about the 25 percent rule. Home financing agencies will approach your housing percentage figures a little differently, though the figures will probably come out in the same general category. Most of them will use as their general rule 2½ times your annual salary. In my opinion, you may want to be a little more conservative and use only 2 times annual salary in your calculations so that you will have funds for other household improvements. Property taxes are going up yearly; interest costs have increased greatly; you probably now view a built-in dishwasher, garbage disposal, built-in conventional and maybe a micro-wave oven, and perhaps even a trash masher, as essentials, to say nothing of central heating and air conditioning. These conveniences will often cause you to have high maintenance and utility bills. Also, the taxes, insurance, and interest are usually in proportion to the cost of the home.

Toward the end of 1977, lending agencies began using the guideline that one week's income must equal the monthly house payment on the mortgage for an applicant to qualify for a loan. Prior to the 1974 housing law, lending institutions excluded the salary of the wife during child-bearing years. Now they must include all of the wife's paycheck when they calculate how much a working couple can borrow to finance a home.

Monthly Payments • You may be asking, "Don't the monthly payments really determine how much home I can buy?" Yes, they do determine how much you can buy, but they don't measure your ability to keep the house insured, heated and cooled, and in good repair, and the taxes paid.

In the higher income ranges other factors should be considered. You may not need, or want, to spend the full 25 percent of your income for housing; 20 percent may be sufficient. On the other hand, you may have a large number of children. If so, you may need to buy a less expensive house with more bedrooms. If you are childless, you may want to buy a one- or two-bedroom elegant home and stretch your budget beyond the 25 percent.

Location • I once interviewed the head of the real estate department for Prudential Life Insurance Company. When I asked him what the most important considerations in choosing real estate were, he drew himself up to his quite considerable height and said that there are three requirements you must never forget. They are "Location, location, location!"

The same is true in selecting your home. The three requirements you should never forget are neighborhood, neighborhood, neighborhood! The homes and people around you not only affect the resale value of your home but also your enjoyment of it.

The Least Expensive in the Neighborhood • Resist the temptation to buy the most expensive home in the neighborhood. It is much wiser to own a modest home in an expensive neighborhood. Your modest home may gain in value by being surrounded by more expensive homes, but an expensive home in a less expensive neighborhood will probably suffer.

Distance from Work • Distance from work should also be seriously considered. Before you yield to the temptation to move far out from town to escape high land and tax costs, consider the cost of driving long distances to work. This cost can easily wipe out any savings.

Saving $4500 in the price of a home 30 miles from work could be used up in a few years if it were necessary to drive an extra 1500 miles a year.

The time required to drive the extra distance should also be of prime consideration. Time is money. Extra time spent in driving may subtract from your earning power and sap your energy.

If you find, after considering all of these factors, that you still want to live farther out, may I suggest that you utilize your commuting time by installing a tape cassette in your automobile. There are excellent tapes available on a wide variety of educational and professional subjects. I never get into my automobile without turning on my cassette player. I especially enjoy the Earl Nightingale series. His voice is motivating, and his ideas, if applied daily, can revolutionize your thinking and attitude. I have found his advice "You become what you think about" very true.*

• SHOP
FOR TERMS

Money is a commodity. It is a commodity like peanuts, warehouses, and even houses. Never be emotional about money. If you do, you won't make rational decisions about it. Put it in its proper commodity status. Therefore, go in a businesslike manner to secure your mortgage.

If you have a contact at a lending institution, be sure to avail yourself of any help this person can give you; it does make a difference whom you know. Do not accept the first loan offered to you. Shop for rates and terms. Each institution's circumstances vary from time to time, so their lending conditions and rates will vary accordingly.

Rates are important; but, as I will discuss later, the down payment and length of payment period far outweigh a slight differential in rates.

There was a time when the very word "mortgage" was tainted, and melodramas such as "Damsels in Distress" were presented from theater stages across the land portraying the villain as the man who held the mortgage. (There is still a delightful rendition of this melodrama presented nightly on a riverboat moored on the banks of the Mississippi River in St. Louis. It's fun to hiss the villain and cheer the hero and heroine.)

Today, instead of evoking visions of "The Perils of Pauline," mortgages are an acceptable and honorable way of American life; so go ahead and rent money, but do shop for the best terms available.

• TIMING
YOUR PURCHASE

No doubt, some years are better than others for buying a home. If you buy your home when money is abundant, your interest costs will be lower, which will result in lower monthly payments for you. The quan-

---

* You can obtain a list of his tapes by writing or calling Nightingale-Conant Corp., 6677 North Lincoln Ave., Chicago, Ill. 60645, Telephone (312) 478-0050. Another motivating person and a true "possibilitarian" is Dr. Robert Schuler, Pastor of the Garden Grove Community Church and television pastor of the Hour of Power. He has a series of tapes that you can obtain by writing his office in Garden Grove, Ca.

tity of money, which influences the cost, is regulated by action of the Federal Reserve Board, which in turn is based on consumer borrowing demands and whether the current objective is to try to slow inflation or to increase employment. If the main thrust is to slow inflation, money will be tighter and interest rates higher. If the latter, credit will be more available and will cost less.

But what if you decide that you've reached that period in your family's life when you should buy a home, and it turns out that this is the time the Federal Reserve Board's money policies are restrictive and have driven money rates to a high level? Should you postpone your purchase?

The answer is probably No. Such Federal Reserve Board action is usually taken only to slow down inflation. This means that you are looking for a house during a period of constantly rising building costs. During these times costs are probably rising faster than the carpenter can drive a tenpenny nail. If you wait until interest rates are lower, the price of the house will by then have inflated; and your monthly payments will be just as great or greater. Since the part that is interest is tax deductible and the part that is principal is not, you may be better off with the combination of lower price and slightly higher interest.

So if you feel you must buy a home, go ahead regardless of present interest rates.

• DOWN PAYMENT— LARGE OR SMALL?

If you have decided, after looking at all the facts, that a home of your own is best for you economically and/or emotionally, then you must decide on the amount of down payment that you should make. To help you decide, let's look at two couples of similar circumstances. Study their attitudes and their realities, and determine which couple most closely fits your temperament.

Both couples have found a new home that fulfills their housing requirements. The cost of each home is $30,000. Each couple has $30,000 in savings in the bank, an income of $20,000 per year, and two healthy children of approximately the same ages.

The Allens • The Allens were reared by parents who programmed them with such admonitions as "Always pay cash," "Never owe money," "You might come upon hard times, so have your house paid for so you'll have a roof over your head."

When it was time to close on their home, the Allens felt that the most prudent way was to pay cash, which they did. They then complimented themselves on saving "all that interest" and not having to make house payments each month.

The Bakers   •   The Bakers were reared by parents who were business oriented and held the earning power of a dollar in high respect. They had taught their children to use or rent each dollar they could and to put it to work at its maximum potential. So when it came time. to close on their home, they felt that the prudent course for their family was to move in with the minimum down payment and to obtain the best mortgage available.

Then they began shopping terms and rates. First, they went to a life insurance company—choosing the kind that has enticed their policyholders to do their "banking" with them in the form of cash surrender value. These companies, consequently, have large sums to lend. In fact, they are the largest single underwriters of real estate mortgage money in America today.

The Bakers also shopped the savings and loan associations, which also have vast sums of lendable funds. These funds have been placed on deposit with them by those who wanted a "guarantee" of only a portion of the earning power of their money. These depositors were willing to settle for indirect investing in real estate by investing in the mortgage of the Bakers' home. The Bakers found that the rates and terms varied from one savings association to the other, depending on the amount of lendable money each had at that particular time and the value judgment of each of their loan officers as to the Bakers' ability to pay.

They also shopped mortgage companies and found that the rates varied by the same criteria as did those of the savings and loans.

The Bakers decided on a financing plan that would allow them to make a $5000 down payment, with a $25,000 mortgage for 30 years at 8½ percent from a life insurance company, with monthly payments of $207.61, principal and interest. (Their taxes were estimated to be around $50 per month and the insurance around $20. This makes a total of $277.61 per month.)

Assuming a Mortgage   •   Since the homes were new, it was necessary for the Allens and Bakers to either buy with cash or obtain a new mortgage. Had the homes been "used," a third option might have been available and desirable. This is to "assume" a mortgage—that is, to take over responsibility for the mortgage that the seller has on the house. Frequently an older mortgage has a lower interest rate than a new mortgage, and the closing costs are considerably less if the home is in a community in which banks charge "points" for a loan (a "point" is 1 percent of the amount of the loan). The purchaser pays the seller for his "equity" (the difference between the sale price and the mortgage) and then assumes the monthly payments. Ultimate legal responsibility for the mortgage, however, lies with the original buyer, so it is important for the seller to check the buyer carefully. If the owner's equity is high, it will usually be advisable to obtain a new loan commitment in order to avoid a high down payment.

Which Couple Made the Right Decision? • Let's look at the Allens. They will not have a monthly house payment, and they will not have to pay interest on $25,000. They reasoned that over the 30-year period they will "save" $49,739 in interest on the $25,000 loan. They felt smugly proud of their decision.

The Bakers, on the other hand, felt that they had made the right decision.

Which do you think made the right choice? Measure your value system against each of theirs and see where you feel you will be the most comfortable. This will help you to decide which course would be best for you.

Looking at the two cases from the point of view of a financial planner, I would choose the course taken by the Bakers for the following reasons.

Inflation rewards those who owe money, not those who pay cash. I realize that this is a sad commentary on life, but it is fact you must learn to accept. You must learn to be a realist. Look at life the way it truly is, rather than the way you wish it were.

If the government is successful in slowing the rate of inflation to 4 percent (and there is great doubt among most of our economists that this can be accomplished), you would be paying off your "loaned" dollars in 10 years with 60¢ dollars, in 15 years with 40¢ dollars, and in 20 years with 20¢ dollars.

Think how long your Dad had to work for a dollar 30 years ago, and then compare it with the minutes of work you have to do today. Any time you can postpone paying back a dollar that you have obtained on a long-term basis at a reasonable rate, always avail yourself of the opportunity. You must, of course, invest the money you have not paid down on the house in such a way as to earn more than the after-tax cost of renting it.

Making the House Payments • The Allens do not have to concern themselves with paying monthly house payments. The Bakers do. The Bakers also have the responsibility of investing $25,000. How should the Bakers invest these funds to provide the extra $200 needed monthly for house payments?

There are various investment possibilities that they should consider. One approach that our clients have used quite successfully has been to make a $25,000 investment in a middle-of-the-road quality mutual fund, similar to the Seminar Fund, and then take a check-a-month withdrawal. If $200 per month is withdrawn, that would be a 9.6 percent withdrawal. These withdrawals may come from four possible sources: (1) dividends, (2) realized capital gains, (3) unrealized capital gains, and, if these are insufficient, (4) the original investment. You cannot know what the future will bring. For example, if your fund grows at 12 percent and you take out 9.6 percent, or $200 per month, your original investment will grow. If it does not grow at 9.6 percent, you will use a portion of your original investment and, in time, perhaps all of it. If all of it is consumed, you obviously would have to look to other sources for your monthly house payment.

Had the Bakers placed their $25,000 in the Seminar Fund on December 31, 1946, it would have purchased 4091.653 shares. Had the fund sent the mortgage company a check for $200 each month for the next 30 years, the fund would have paid the mortgage company $72,000, and there would have been 3114 shares left in the account, which would have had a value of $45,759 on December 31, 1976. Of course, if you were to follow the example of the Bakers, you may not do so well, or you may do better.

Meeting an Emergency • The Allens paid cash for their home, remembering their parents' warnings about possible hard times. However, if the Allens have an emergency, they will not be able to redeem a few square feet of their house. If they live in a state with a homestead law, they can't even pledge it as collateral for a loan. The loan-free home may have given them joy at the time of purchase, but if they should have a real emergency, they may find that their home is a dead asset that does not offer liquidity.

The Bakers, on the other hand, could redeem a few shares of their stock or take their shares to the bank and use them for collateral to borrow any needed funds.

• AVAILING YOURSELF OF AN OPPORTUNITY

In money management, always put yourself in the driver's seat. Leave options open to yourself. Using your stock as collateral at the bank does not necessarily require an emergency. A good business opportunity may present itself. You'll have to pass it up if you don't have available funds. With collateral you can obtain these funds.

• INTEREST
   IS DEDUCTIBLE

To give you an idea of how much of the Bakers' monthly payment is interest, which is deductible, the percentage schedule for the first five years of their loan was: 99.2%, 98.4%, 97.5%, and 95.5%. For the first year, 99.2% × $207 = $2053 interest.

The IRS lets the Bakers deduct interest payments, so if they are in a 25 percent tax bracket, Uncle Sam bears 25 percent of their interest cost.

Of the 8½ percent interest they are paying, their net cost is only 6.38 percent (8.5% × 25% = 2.125%; 8.5% − 2.12% = 6.38%).

• SALABILITY

We've mentioned earlier, as one of the reasons you should consider renting, the fact that Americans are a mobile lot. Recent studies show that the average family moves every seven years. The letters IBM, in our neighborhood, stand for "I've Been Moved." If moving is necessary, you may find it easier to find a buyer with $5000 for a down payment than one with $30,000. A $5000 equity is a salable equity, whereas the $30,000 one is probably not. The Allens will have higher selling costs because seller's points on the new mortgage can amount to several hundred dollars.

There are reasons other than transfers for moving. The children may have grown and left the nest, making a large home a burden rather than a necessity. The desirability of the neighborhood may have changed, or your company offices may have moved to another section of town. The reasons for moving can make a lengthy list.

• RATE OF GAIN
   ON INVESTED CAPITAL

It is estimated that homes have appreciated an average of 6 percent per year over the past 10 years.

The Allens have $30,000 invested in their home. Six percent appreciation would increase their net worth by $1800 per year.

The Bakers' $30,000 home has also appreciated the same 6 percent or $1800, but they have only $5000 invested. An increase of $1800 is 36 percent on their invested capital, as compared to the Allen's 6 percent. (The figure for the Bakers must be adjusted for their net after-tax interest expense.)

• SUMMARY

1 • It may be less expensive to rent a multifamily dwelling than to own a single-family dwelling. Your costs are fixed, making budgeting more precise. Rental frees down payment money for other investments, and also allows you mobility to move to larger or smaller quarters or another location quickly and easily.

2 • Unemotionally calculate your true housing costs, remembering that the mortgage payment is only one of several major items in your housing costs.

3 • Monthly house payments should not exceed one week's earnings.

4 • If you anticipate moving, buy a home similar in style to that of your neighbors. This does not do much for your sense of creativity, but it may help you avoid taking a shellacking on resale. A good rule to remember when making an investment in any asset of considerable value is "Be a conformist." The more conventional you are, the better your chances are of increasing the value of your assets. Preserve some of your individuality, but don't go overboard. You may find it quite expensive if you do.

5 • Avoid paying too much for gimmicks. The builder may have spent an extra $1000 on gadgets for flashy first-impression eye appeal and be able to sell you the house for an extra $3000. As the years go by, you will want to build in your own charm, and the "gook" the builder originally added may turn out to be a hindrance rather than an enchantment.

6 • Avoid paying too much for a view. Surroundings are important, but after a year you'll probably take the view for granted and wish that this extra expenditure had been avoided.

7 • Keep your down payment as low as possible: Inflation lets you repay with cheaper dollars; resale should be easier; return on invested capital can be higher; and liquidity or pledgability can be available in times of emergency or investment opportunity.

Your home can be your castle or, under unfortunate circumstances, your prison, so use both your heart and your head in choosing how you'll provide that roof over your head.

Application

1 • Should you rent or buy?

2 • How long do you plan to live there?

3 • If you decide to buy, should it be a house, a cluster home, a condominium, or a townhouse?

4 • How much is available for a down payment?

5 • Emotionally do you identify with the Allens or the Bakers in this chapter?

6 • On the basis of our formula, what price home can you afford?

7 • What kind of neighborhood best fits your way of life?

8 • Is availability of a clubhouse with social facilities, tennis courts, and swimming pools important to you?

9 • Whom do you know, or what contacts can you make, to obtain favorable financing?

10 • Is the prime interest rate rising or dropping at this time?

11 • If you have chosen to make a low down payment, how will you employ the remaining funds?

12 • Items to include in your housing checklist:
    a. First and foremost, remember location, location, location. How is the location?
    b. Accessibility to work?
    c. Accessibility to schools?
    d. Accessibility to shopping facilities?
    e. Access to recreational facilities?
    f. Rate of price increase of homes in the neighborhood? Percent per year.
    g. Neighbors?
    h. Traffic patterns?
    i. Noise?
    j. Smells?
    k. How does the cost of the home that you are considering compare with recent sales in the neighborhood?
    l. Conditions of the maintenance fund for upkeep of the neighborhood?
    m. Determine whether or not it is located within the bounds of the 100-year flood plain as determined by the National tional Flood Insurance Program. (If it is, to obtain a loan you must buy flood insurance at a cost of $125 per year.)

n. Towns grow and values tend to increase west, north, up-hill, and away from rivers. Where is the house in relation to these?
o. How old is the home?
p. If the home is 10 years old, are you a good handyman on repairs?
q. Does the home fit your style? Yard work? Entertaining?

13

Life Insurance –
The Great National
Consumer Fraud?

**THE GREAT
MYSTERY**

The great mystery of life is the length of it. You should have a plan with the hope you will live a normal lifetime. You should have a plan in the event you should die prematurely. You do not know which will occur; therefore, you should prepare for either eventuality. It is not difficult to acquire financial independence if you apply your talents and if you have sufficient time.

How can you be sure you will have this time? You cannot. There is a way to "buy" time, however, and it is called "life insurance." This is the name given to it by life insurance companies who desire to sell it. A better term would be "protection for dependents." There is nothing that can insure your life.

• THE PURPOSE OF
LIFE INSURANCE

Life insurance is a wonderful thing. There is no substitute for it until a sufficiently large estate has been acquired to protect those dependent upon you. It can provide you with a way to guarantee that your dependents will have the financial means to continue to maintain a standard of living in the event you should die prematurely. It can be an economic extension of yourself. You should provide this protection for your dependents before you begin an investment program.

At the beginning of this book I stated that there are five main reasons why most of our citizens reach the age of 65 flat broke: (1) procrastination, (2) failure to establish a goal, (3) ignorance of what money must do to attain that goal, (4) failure to learn and apply our tax laws, and (5) being sold the wrong kind of life insurance. I say "sold" because I believe that had they been told how to obtain protection properly, they would not have made such glaring errors.

So that you will not fall victim to being sold the wrong kind of life insurance, I hope to give you a clear understanding of how policies are constructed. This should enable you to select the proper type of coverage to protect your dependents during the time you will need to acquire a living estate.

There is only one kind of life insurance, and that is pure protection based on a mortality table. All other kinds are pure protection plus a savings account that I call "banking." It is the "banking" portion that can be the culprit, so it is necessary for you to thoroughly understand this part of a vast number of policies that are in existence today and are being so aggressively sold.

As a rule of thumb, you can avoid most of the errors made in the acquisition of life insurance protection if you refuse to "bank" with any insurance company under conditions that you would not bank with your own bank.

The purpose of insurance is to protect those dependent upon you in the event you should die before accumulating a living estate. After you have accumulated a living estate, your need to protect their livelihood has already been accomplished. You should plan to be self-insured by age 65. Life insurance is to protect an economic potential. You have either made it financially by 65, or you'll probably never make it.

After you have "made it" you have fulfilled your obligation to your dependents and yourself. However, at that point you may have another desire. You may want to pass on your estate intact or at least partially so, to your heirs. I've never read anything that said you had this obligation, but if it is your desire, it is easy to calculate how much insurance will be needed to pay inheritance taxes.

• NAMES GIVEN TO LIFE INSURANCE POLICIES

There are four major names given to life insurance policies sold in the United States today. They are *term, ordinary* or *whole life, limited payment life,* and *endowment.* Each can be participating or nonparticipating. In addition, there are "special" policies that provide combinations of the above.

You will need a clear understanding of how each kind is constructed so that you can avoid being sold the wrong kind. Regardless of what kind of life insurance policy you purchase or what it is called, the true cost of insurance goes up each year. Rates are based on likelihood of death, and each year you become older you are more apt to die. All life insurance is pure insurance, called term, or term plus a savings program.

There are three basic kinds of pure protection plus some special kinds that contain the basic characteristics.

Annual Renewable Term • Let's first look at annual renewable term. If you have this type of policy, the face amount of your insurance remains the same and the rate per thousand increases each year. You can obtain annual renewable term in most states to age 100. This amount of time should adequately take care of any needs you may have to protect your dependents. However, some states allow you to renew as annual renewable term only to age 75. At that time, if you have purchased the policy properly, so that it is renewable and convertible without evidence of insurability, you can convert it into a number of other types of policies.

Decreasing Term • Another type of term insurance you may want to consider is decreasing term. In decreasing term, your rate remains the same and the amount of insurance decreases. This type may fit your family's needs if your family is young and their need for coverage is great. As the children mature and become more self-sufficient and your living assets increase, your need for "outside protection" will probably decrease. Decreasing term insurance can fit this picture very well.

With your decreasing term program, you will want to have an increasing investment program to replace the protection that is diminishing. You are, in effect, substituting a living estate for a death estate, which is the direction you want to go. You don't want a. death estate, but until you have had time to accumulate a living estate, buying a death estate is a necessity.

There was a time in my career as a financial planner that I recommended decreasing term joined with an investment program with the hope of increasing my clients' living assets. But suddenly the economy was hit by two-digit inflation, and the stock market suffered a precipitous drop. At that bleak period in history I felt a change in direction could be advisable. Fortunately, I had provided them with policies that were convertible at their options without evidence of insurability, so I went back to them and suggested they consider changing.

Decreasing term may serve your purpose very well, but the coverage does diminish each year. Perhaps you should place yourself in the driver's seat, so that you can decide whether or not your coverage should decline rather than have the decision automatically made for you. You can make your annual renewable term policy decreasing term by just dropping the amount of coverage your family no longer needs.

Mortgage insurance is in reality a decreasing term policy. If knowing that your family will have extra funds to pay off the mortgage on your home provides you with greater peace of mind, you can consider mortgage insurance. However, paying off the mortgage may not be the most prudent thing for them to do. They need only to continue making the monthly payments as before. If you have given them the proper investment instructions, using the information obtained from this book, they should be able to invest the funds in a more beneficial manner where these dollars have a chance to grow and at least keep pace with inflation. Why should they place a portion of their assets in a dead position earnings-wise when it is not required of them?

Level Term • Level term means that the face amount of the policy remains level for the term of time chosen. The most common periods are 5, 10, 15, 20, 25, and 30 years, and level term to 65. For example, if you chose a 10-year level term, basically what the insurance company would do is add up the annual renewable term rates for 10 years, divide the total by 10, and you would pay the same rate for 10 years. You would be overpaying in the early years and underpaying in the later years.

These three are your basic pure term policies. There are some special policies that contain similar provisions as they affect you.

Deposit Level Term • Deposit level term is a level term policy, usually of 8-, 10-, 12-, 15-, or 20-year periods, where you make a premium deposit to the company as evidence of your intent to retain your policy for the specified period of time. The one most commonly used by financial planners is ten years in duration, renewable and convertible at your option without evidence of insurability.

The deposit term concept was developed because of the high lapse (cancellation) rate on conventional policies. Reportedly, of every three new policies written today, one is lapsed within two or three years. This lapsed policy is expensive to an insurance company because of the substantial costs to place the policy in force initially. They have paid for your physical examination, paid a sales commission to the agent, and paid other numerous charges in relation to the policy.

If you drop your policy in the first few years of its life, it is an unattractive investment for the company. To protect themselves, insurance companies must "load" the premium of each policyholder in order to recapture some of these costs. Since they do not know which one will lapse the policy, they charge all three.

This is helpful in solving their expense problem, but what about your expense problem? If you are one of the "good" guys who keeps his policy, you are having to pay for the one "bad" guy who drops his.

To some insurance companies this did not seem fair. So they constructed a policy so that the "good" guy would not have to pay for the "bad" guy.

All three policyholders now make a premium deposit in the first year. The premium deposit can be set lower at younger ages and higher at older ones, or it can be some fixed amount, such as $10 per $1000 of coverage regardless of age. As a result, all three insurance purchasers get a reduced annual premium.

When the "bad" guy lapses his policy, he forfeits all or a part of his premium deposit, depending on the length of time he has kept it. However, unlike before, the "good" guys just keep paying the reduced premium and this time the "bad" guy pays for his own mistake.

What happens if you don't lapse your policy? There are two possibilities: (1) you complete the period, or (2) you die within the period. If you live to complete the period, the company will usually return your premium deposit doubled or more and tax-free.

In the event of your death, some companies will return the premium deposit to the beneficiary, while others will pay the maturity value as an additional death benefit. (The maturity value is the amount it would have grown to if you had lived to the end of the contract period.)

At the end of the term you will have various options if you still have a need to protect dependents with life insurance. You may want to renew for the same amount or for less, and for a like or different period of time. For example, let's say you have a 10-year deposit term and your beneficiaries still have need for protection for another 10 years. At that time, if you choose to renew, you would again make a premium deposit, and your new premium for the period would be based on your then attained age. All premiums for all life insurance policies are based on a mortality table, and as you grow older your rate per thousand increases.

Some companies may require you to pay an extra exchange premium for the privilege of renewing your coverage as deposit term, but their total premiums may not be any higher than those who do not require it. You will have several conversion choices that you may make at the end of the period. Usually, if you do not exercise any choices, it will automatically convert to decreasing term.

Some policies that have the same basic provision are called *modified premium whole life*. However, instead of automatically converting to some form of term, they automatically convert to whole life, if no other election is made.

This type of policy, though it doesn't affect the essential elements you want in your coverage, can be of great help to the insurance company offering it. It can often help the company in clearing the policy for sale in some states. Also, our tax laws are such that this designation may save the company considerable amounts of taxes.

Whole Life, Straight Life, Ordinary Life • Whole life, also called straight life and ordinary life, is the most commonly sold life insurance policy. If you have bought this type of policy, you own a decreasing term policy, to which has been added a low interest—and for the early years of the policy—a *no interest* "savings account." (Many experts contend that it basically is always a no interest account.) The face amount of your policy and your yearly premiums will remain level throughout your whole life, and it will endow or mature at age 100.

With this type of policy, cash surrender value accumulates from a portion of the premiums you pay. You can obtain this cash in two ways: You may cash in your policy and thereby lose your insurance protection, or you may pay 4½ to 8 percent to borrow out the cash. If death occurs while your loan is outstanding, the amount of your loan and the interest, if it has not been paid as you went along, are subtracted from the face amount of your policy.

If your death occurs with no loan outstanding against your policy, the cash value is not added to the face value of the policy and paid to your beneficiary, but only the face amount is paid, regardless of the amount in "your" savings account. Your cash value is a part of your death benefit—not in addition to it.

In the past, whole life has been the most commonly sold type of policy. But as consumers have become more knowledgeable and inflation has taken its devastating toll, it has been increasingly difficult to sell, and the number of this type of policy has greatly declined.

Limited Payment Life • Another type of life insurance policy you may encounter is one on which you pay for a limited period of time.

This type of coverage is called limited payment life. It provides lifetime coverage, with premiums payable for the specified period of time: 20 years, 30 years, or paid-up at age 65 (which would be a variable number of years depending on your age). At the end of that period it is "paid up" and no more premiums need be paid. The premiums on this type of policy are naturally higher than for a whole life policy, for you are paying premiums for only a portion of your life; hence the term "limited payment life."

A great disservice has been done to you and your family whether you live or die if you have been sold this type of policy, especially if you have several small children for whom you must provide. As a young family you are likely to have only a limited number of dollars to spend for life insurance, and this type of policy offers your family less coverage in the years when they most need the protection, so that you can pay little or no premiums when your need for protection has lessened and your ability to pay has probably increased. In addition, with our pattern of continued inflation, you have used "expensive" dollars while you were young—meaning dollars for which you had to work many hours —so that you could use less expensive ones later on—meaning dollars for which you have worked fewer hours.

Endowment • Another type of life insurance policy you may have been sold is endowment. In this kind of policy the face amount will be paid to you if you are still living on a specified date or to your beneficiary if you should die prior to that date. Some are designed to endow in 20 years, others to endow at age 65, although I am amazed at the number of policies I come across that endow at age 80. Yes, 80!

In reality, a whole life policy is really an endowment policy that endows at age 100.

In an endowment policy, as well as in other policies that accumulate cash surrender value, you may choose a lump-sum payout or an annuity of a specified amount per month for as long as you live. If you make the latter choice, the monthly payments would cease on your death. You may choose, however, to have your beneficiary continue to receive payments after your death for a set number of years. If you make this choice, your payments would be less per month. The premiums on an endowment policy, as you might expect, are very high.

Endowment policies are often sold as retirement programs or college education programs. Since these premiums are paid with after-tax dollars and the cash surrender values often compound at a very low rate, they can make an endowment policy an expensive way to invest for retirement or for college.

For example, if you are in a 30 percent tax bracket, you must earn

$6014 to have $4210 left to pay insurance premiums on a $100,000 policy at age 35. In a 40 percent bracket you would have to earn $7016, and in a 50 percent bracket you must earn the princely sum of $8420 to have $4210 left to begin its meager climb in value. Surely we can design a better retirement program for you.

The Sales Presentation • In an effort to increase your level of awareness, I feel it would be helpful at this time if I were to pretend that I am a life insurance agent who has come to sell you the life insurance policy that would best benefit me and *my* children. (Let me hasten to add this is not a blanket condemnation of life insurance agents. I firmly believe that most of the agents who sell the wrong kind of insurance do so out of ignorance and not from malicious intent.)

Okay, here I come. Are you ready?

You are a male, age 35, and I come to you and say, "I can obtain for you a $10,000 level term to 65 policy for only $100 per year." You decide the price fits your budget and begin to say, "Yes," but I interrupt you to say, "But your insurance is all gone at age 65, and you don't want that to happen, do you?"

At this point you stammer, "Why, no, I wouldn't want to be without life insurance." (Analyze that statement. "You've either made it financially by 65, or you'll probably never make it.)

So I say, "Well, now here's a policy for only $200 a year that never runs out; it's called whole life." (I don't add, "You must pay premiums your whole life and it endows at age 100.")

Just as you are about to agree to this policy, I say, "You don't want to pay premiums all your life, do you? Here is a policy for $300 on which you can quit paying premiums in 20 years. It's all paid up."

Just before you sign I say, "But let me tell you about another policy. At the end of 20 years you've only put in $9000, we will give you $10,000, you've had your insurance free for 20 years and made $1000 profit, isn't that great?"

But how great was it? Let's analyze the purpose of your life insurance. Its purpose was to protect those dependent upon you in the event that you do not live long enough to accumulate a living estate. Right?

Let's say that you really did die in 10 years. (Take a few minutes here to thoroughly study Fig. 13–1, *Four Basic Types of Level Coverage.*)

In the first policy pictured you would have spent $1000 in ten years and your beneficiaries would have received $10,000. In the second, $2000 would have been spent and they would have received $10,000. In the third, $3,000 would have been spent and they would have received

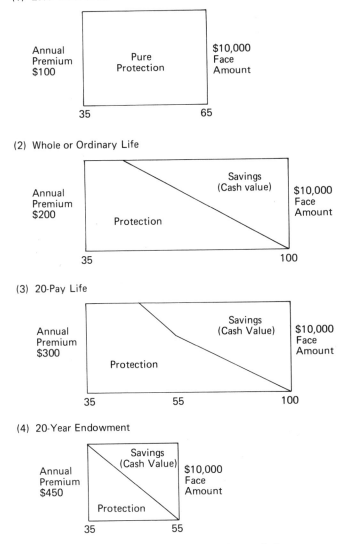

FIGURE 13-1.   Four Basic Types of Level Coverage

$10,000. In the fourth policy you had a first class demise; $4500 was spent and your beneficiaries received $10,000.

How Much For Protection? • How much of each of your premiums went to provide protection, and how much was earmarked for "your"

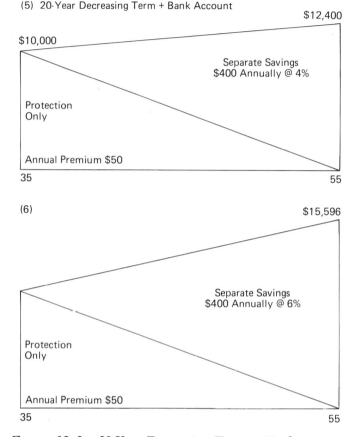

(5) 20-Year Decreasing Term + Bank Account

$12,400

$10,000

Separate Savings
$400 Annually @ 4%

Protection
Only

Annual Premium $50

35   55

(6) $15,596

Separate Savings
$400 Annually @ 6%

Protection
Only

Annual Premium $50

35   55

FIGURE 13–2.   20-Year Decreasing Term + Bank Account

savings account? Look at the two diagrams in Fig. 13–2, and you will find that the answer is around $50. You have been paying for two things: protection *and* savings. But your beneficiary receives only the face amount of the policy.

What if I had told you that for $50 you could have bought a $10,000, 20-year, decreasing-term policy and that if you did nothing more constructive than take the $400 savings in premiums each year to the bank, and your bankers would pay you only 4 percent on your savings, that in 20 years you would have $12,400 instead of just the $10,000 you would have received from the endowment policy? If you obtained 6 percent from your banker, your $400 savings per year would have grown to $15,596 instead of $10,000. Your "free insurance and $1000 profit" were indeed expensive. Tax-free municipal bonds currently pay this or more. So don't be seduced by an agent's "compounding tax-free" pitch on your cash surrender value; if you want a "guaranteed" investment without current taxation, use Series E government bonds or deferred annuities for your guarantees.

Remember, never combine two incompatible things—living and dying.

"Banking" with the insurance company, as you can see, can prove to be very costly.

A Diagram of a Whole Life Policy • Since the most commonly sold policy is whole life, let's assume that you own a $10,000 whole life policy on which you pay annual premiums of $200 and that you've had it for a sufficient period of time to have built up $4000 in cash surrender value.

A diagram of your policy might look something like Fig. 13–3.

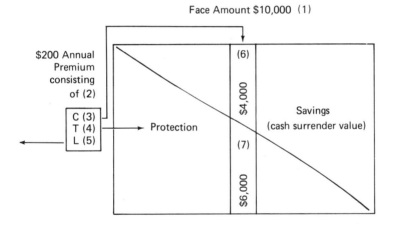

FIGURE 13–3. Diagram of a Whole Life Policy

The face amount of the policy is $10,000 and is marked (1). This is the amount that would be paid to your beneficiary if you should die, providing that you had paid your premiums and there were no out-standing loans against the policy.

The premium that you would pay would be $200, marked (2). Under (2), you will see that the premium is divided into three parts: The first is "C," marked (3). This represents "cash." This is the portion of your premium that is deposited into "your" savings account each year. The second is "T," for "term" or "true insurance" and is marked (4). This is the portion that is used to buy true protection on your life and to pay company expenses and provide the company with a profit. The third, is "L" for "Load" (5) and represents the expenses incurred by the company for sales commissions, administrative expenses, and taxes. Now look at (6). This is "your" savings account. As you can see, as you increase "your" savings account, you decrease your insurance portion, which is marked (7). If cash surrender value (6) increases and the face amount (1) remains the same, then insurance protection (7) must decrease.

Let me again repeat: My objection is not to life insurance; there is no substitute for it if you have beneficiaries to protect. My objection is to the "banking" element. I don't feel that it is good economics for you to take an after-tax dollar for which you had to earn $1.43 in a 30 percent tax bracket and $2 in a 50 percent bracket, and to substitute it for an insurance dollar that I can buy for you for a few pennies. Also, once the dollar is there, you lose its earning power. (Yes, I know it's supposed to compound at 2½ to 3½ percent on the reserves,* but if you die with it there, that's small consolation to your beneficiaries, for they receive only the $10,000.) At 6 percent on "your" $4000 savings account, you are losing earnings of $240 per year, and at 7.5 percent, the amount lost is $300. If you were calculating your cost per thousand for keeping such a policy, your costs could be as follows:

True Cost per Thousand of the Policy in Figure 13–3

Premium	$ 200
Lost earnings @ 6% on $4000 cash value	240
Total cost	$ 440
Amount of insurance left in policy	$6,000
Cost per thousand today ($440 ÷ 6)	$ 73.33

When you took out the policy, you were paying $200 per year for $10,000 of insurance, or $20 per thousand. Now it is costing you $73.33 per thousand.

To help you get a clearer picture of the true cost of insurance, let's look at Fig. 13–4. The shaded area all the way across is labeled

---

* The reason I say "supposed to" is that there are some very respected insurance analysts who contend that interest return to the policyholder is always 0 percent, unless cash values should exceed face amount. Also, you should be aware that the percentage shown in your policies are only premium discounts. For example, if you are a male age 60 on a 2½ percent American Experience table, your cash value should be $710.22 per thousand. If you were on a 3 percent table, it would be $666.74. Were you aware of this reverse arithmetic?

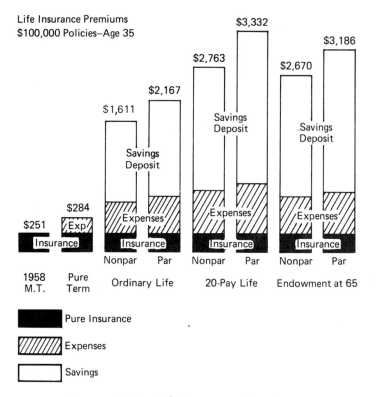

FIGURE 13–4.   Life Insurance Premiums

"Insurance." This shows that the cost of insurance in each policy is the same, regardless of the kind you buy. Differences in savings and expenses cause the premiums charged to vary.

Take a moment to study Fig. 13–4.

• WHY COST PER THOUSAND VARIES

As you can see, Fig. 13–4 illustrates a $100,000 policy at age 35. The first column shows that if you could get your coverage on the 1958 mortality table rate, you could obtain a $100,000 policy for $251 a year. But it's difficult to get a company to sell you insurance at the mortality rate. (Actually, they reinsure you with a reinsurance company to spread their risk for only $1.06 per thousand or $116 including policy fee, and the reinsurance company still makes money.) You can, however, find a company that will sell it to you on a pure term basis. This could cost you $284 a year. Now if you want to have a "participating" whole life policy, you can obtain an ordinary life policy for $2167 per year. If you decide you do not want to "participate" in the "profits" of the company, they can sell it to you at a lower premium of $1611.

Let's go on now to the 20-pay life in our illustration. Remember, that's the policy "you don't have to pay on all your life. It's paid up." Again, if you want to participate in the profits it can cost $3332 per year, but if you're willing not to participate in the profits, you can buy it for $2763.

You can obtain an endowment at age 65 nonparticipating policy for $2633 per year; the premium for a participating policy is $3186.

As you can see, the true cost for insurance protection is the same in every policy. The amount of premium you pay for this insurance is determined by how wisely you select your policy and how much forced "savings" you desire.

Endowment vs Decreasing Term • Figure 13–5 shows the difference between buying a $100,000 "endowment" at age 65 and buying "decreasing term to age 65" with premium savings invested separately at 3 percent, 4 percent, 5 percent, 6 percent, and 8.5 percent. At only 8.5 percent (and I would not give you any special awards if that's all you averaged), you would have $305,662 in savings as compared to $100,000 in the endowment policy.

As you can readily see, it does make a difference where you "bank."

To help you get a clearer picture of the reasons that you should separate living and dying, let's take a look at the difference that it could make to you if you save inside a policy or outside an insurance policy.

•   LIFE INSURANCE
   AS AN "INVESTMENT"

Have you ever been told that life insurance is a good investment? Figure 13–6 shows the investment results of compound interest versus ordinary life, with an annual investment of $1000 versus an annual insurance premium of $1000 for a $55,000 face amount policy for a male aged 35. As you will note, cash surrender value of this policy would be $28,380 at age 65 and $55,000 at age 100.

Here are the results of compounding $1000 per annum at various rates of return from age 35 to age 65 (30 years), outside the policy:

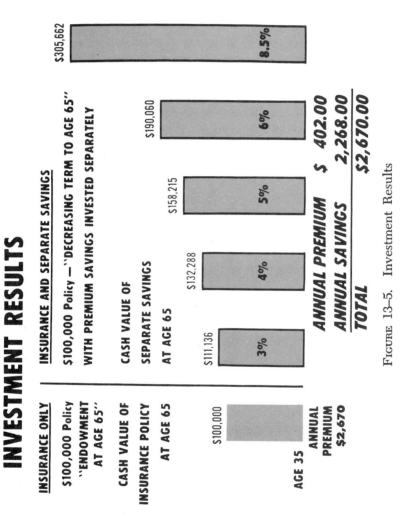

FIGURE 13–5. Investment Results

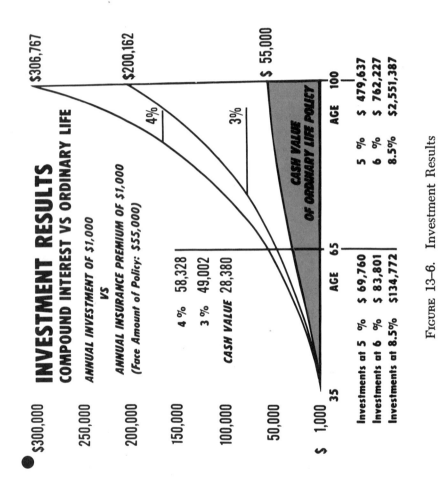

FIGURE 13–6.   Investment Results

3%	$ 49,002
4%	$ 58,328
5%	$ 69,760
6%	$ 83,801
8.5%	$134,772

Here are the results of compounding until age 100—the endowment age for the whole life policy:

3%	$ 200,162
4%	$ 306,767
5%	$ 479,637
6%	$ 762,227
8.5%	$2,551,387

• DIVIDENDS—MYTH OR REALITY

A rose is a rose is a rose. But a life insurance dividend is not a dividend, is not a dividend, is not a dividend! It is a return of an over-charge. Those policies that pay "dividends" are often called "partici-pating" policies. (On the front lower left-hand side of the policy you may read "PAR" or "NON-PAR." The words "participating" and "divi-dends" have a nice ring to them. After all, you certainly enjoy your divi-dends from your 100 shares of General Motors or Exxon, or your Seminar Fund. But what is a "dividend" from an insurance policy? I refer you to no less an authority than the United States Treasury Decision No. 1743. When the Tarill Bill of 1911 proposed an income tax on life insurance dividends, representatives of life insurance companies protested the tax. I quote from the decision arrived at after the protest:

> Reduced to final analysis the contention of the various companies are. . . .
> That dividends declared by participating companies are not divi-dends in a commercial sense of the word, but are simply refunds to the policyholder of a portion of the overcharge collected, which overcharge is merely held in trust by the company issuing the policy. Annually, or at stated periods, all, or a portion thereof, is returned to the person holding the policy. . . .
> It was vigorously contended by counsel representing certain of these companies that it was necessary in order to secure new business, to convince the prospective policyholder of the desirability of the same,

and that this commercial necessity had resulted in the companies making misrepresentations of facts as to dividends to prospective purchasers of insurance, and that names and designations, having a single specific meaning in the commercial world and which were therefore attractive to prospective policyholders, had been adopted to represent transactions which they now hold are entirely different from that their name implies and represents, and from which the policyholder himself believed he was receiving and that business necessities had caused a continuance of these misnomers. *It was represented that, in fact, there were no dividends, but merely a refund of overcharges, which, for reasons above stated, were usually referred to as dividends.*

Participation—How much does it cost? • Carefully study Table 13–1, and you will discover that your cost for "participating" depends on your age. Generally, the younger you are, the more you are overcharged. For example, if you purchased a participating policy at age 20 from one of the largest insurance companies you could have paid $13.60 per thousand. If you had purchased a nonparticipating policy from another large company using the same mortality table, you could have paid $9.04. The amount of your overcharge was $4.56 per thousand, or 50 percent. At age 35 your overcharge was 35 percent, and at age 50 it was 27 percent.

Mortality Tables • The mortality table is the base for calculating cost per thousand of a life insurance policy. Every year you live you are that more apt to die and "funny banking" will never repeal that table, regardless of how many tantalizing names the advertising industry dreams up to call the various policies. The "insurance" factor is the likelihood of death and is listed by age per thousand.

The first table used by insurance companies was the American Experience Table. It was based on statistics gathered between 1843 and 1858. During that time, of 1000 men age 35, statistically 8.95 died during that year. This is the death rate in the days of Abraham Lincoln. The second table the insurance companies were required to use was the Commissioners' 1941 Standard Ordinary Table based on death statistics between 1930 and 1940—before penicillin. During that period the death rate had dropped to 4.59 per thousand men aged 35. Later, in 1966, the insurance companies were required to go on to the Commissioners' 1958 Standard Ordinary Table based on death statistics between 1950 and 1954. Now woefully outdated, this is the last table regulatory agencies have required and is the one currently being used. On this table, the death rate has dropped to 2.51 per thousand. It is my understanding that sufficient statistics have been gathered for a later mor-

Table 13–1. Comparative Annual Whole Life Premiums
(Par and Nonpar)

Issue Age	Whole life (par)	Whole life (nonpar)	Amount of overcharge	Percentage overcharge
20	$13.60	$ 9.04	$ 4.56	50%
21	13.99	9.40	4.59	49%
22	14.40	9.81	4.59	47%
23	14.82	10.23	4.59	45%
24	15.26	10.67	5.00	47%
25	15.72	11.09	4.63	42%
26	16.20	11.49	4.71	41%
27	16.70	11.88	4.82	41%
28	17.23	12.28	4.95	40%
29	17.77	12.70	5.07	40%
30	18.35	13.16	5.19	39%
31	18.95	13.71	5.24	38%
32	19.58	14.28	5.30	37%
33	20.24	14.87	5.37	36%
34	20.93	15.48	5.45	35%
35	21.67	16.11	5.56	35%
36	22.43	16.77	5.66	38%
37	23.24	17.46	5.78	33%
38	24.10	18.18	5.92	33%
39	24.99	18.94	6.05	32%
40	25.94	19.74	6.20	31%
41	26.93	20.59	6.34	31%
42	27.97	21.48	6.49	30%
43	29.07	22.42	6.65	30%
44	30.22	23.41	6.81	29%
45	31.45	24.45	7.00	29%
46	32.74	25.53	7.21	28%
47	34.10	26.68	7.42	28%
48	35.54	27.88	7.66	27%
49	37.07	29.15	7.92	27%
50	38.69	30.50	8.19	27%
51	40.40	31.93	8.47	27%
52	42.21	33.46	8.75	26%
53	44.14	35.08	9.06	26%
54	46.18	36.80	9.38	25%
55	48.35	38.61	9.74	25%
56	50.66	40.54	10.12	25%
57	53.12	42.59	10.53	25%
58	55.74	44.77	10.97	25%
59	58.53	47.08	11.45	24%
60	61.60	49.53	12.07	24%

tality table, on which the death rate should be in the neighborhood of 1.63 per thousand, or lower, at age 35.

If you are 35 years of age and have a policy on the American Experience Table, you may be paying 356 percent more than you would need to pay on the 1958 CSO Table. If you have a policy on the 1941 CSO Table and are healthy enough to pass a physical, you may be paying 180 percent more than you need to pay.

It may surprise you to learn that insurance companies are not required to go back to old policyholders when a new mortality table becomes available. They continue year after year to charge on the old table.

Table 13–2 is a combination of all three mortality tables showing deaths per thousand at each age and life expectancy. Study it carefully.

•   WHOSE CASH VALUE?

If you presently own a policy in which there is cash surrender value, you may be under the impression that you are earning on "your" savings account. However, you do not receive any current economic benefit as income as the policy reserve in the hands of the insurance company earns interest. The policy provisions, if you'll take the time to study them, make this clear. There is no provision in the policy that says you own a part of the company reserves. The policy promises to pay benefits in certain events—usually upon death or upon living to a certain age or date. *Tax Facts*, published by the National Underwriters Co., states:

> The right to cash value upon surrender of the policy or the right to borrow against the cash value are, however, sometimes viewed as suggesting the ownership of a fund in the hands of the company upon which interest is being earned. Perhaps this misconception forms the basis of the conclusion that the policyholder is enjoying current interest income that should be taxed. It is true that in our sales talks and to some extent in our actuarial reasoning we have attributed to the cash value of a life insurance policy some of the characteristics of a savings account. But this popular notion is without legal foundation.

There is a good deal of confusion in the minds of insurance agents and the public as to the ownership of the cash values of insurance policies. This confusion has gone largely unchecked by any government agency such as the Securities and Exchange Commission, which regulates the securities industry.

In summary, it is a fact that the cash value in your insurance policy does not belong to you, as you may have supposed. It does, in fact, belong to the insurance company issuing the policy. Consequently, any

Table 13–2. Deaths per 1000 in Three Mortality Tables

Age	American experience table	Commissioners' 1941 table	Commissioners' 1958 table	Expectation of Life 1958 table in years
20	7.80	2.43	1.79	50.37
21	7.86	2.51	1.83	49.46
22	7.91	2.59	1.86	48.55
23	7.96	2.68	1.89	47.64
24	8.01	2.77	1.91	46.73
25	8.06	2.88	1.93	45.82
26	8.13	2.99	1.96	44.90
27	8.20	3.11	1.99	43.99
28	8.26	3.25	2.03	43.08
29	8.34	3.40	2.08	42.16
30	8.43	3.56	2.13	41.25
31	8.51	3.73	2.19	40.34
32	8.61	3.92	2.25	39.43
33	8.72	4.12	2.32	38.51
34	8.83	4.35	2.40	37.60
35	8.95	4.59	2.51	36.69
36	9.09	4.86	2.64	35.78
37	9.23	5.15	2.80	34.88
38	9.41	5.46	3.01	33.97
39	9.59	5.81	3.25	33.07
40	9.79	6.18	3.53	32.18
41	10.01	6.59	3.84	31.29
42	10.25	7.03	4.17	30.41
43	10.52	7.51	4.53	29.54
44	10.83	8.04	4.92	28.67
45	11.16	8.61	5.35	27.81
46	11.56	9.23	5.83	26.95
47	12.00	9.91	6.36	26.11
48	12.51	10.64	6.95	25.27
49	13.11	11.45	7.60	24.45
50	13.78	12.32	8.32	23.63
51	14.54	13.27	9.11	22.82
52	15.39	14.30	9.96	22.03
53	16.33	15.43	10.89	21.25
54	17.40	16.65	11.90	20.47
55	18.57	17.98	13.00	19.71
56	19.89	19.43	14.21	18.97
57	21.34	21.00	15.24	18.23
58	22.94	22.71	17.00	17.51
59	24.72	24.57	18.59	16.81
60	26.69	26.59	20.34	16.13

increase in the cash values of your policies, either by interest earned or by your deposits, serves only one purpose—that is, the reduction of the insurance company's risk based on actuarial assumptions.

The Six-month Wait • Did you also know that most companies have a provision in their policies allowing them the privilege of waiting six months to make a loan to you or to let you have your cash surrender value? Did you ever wonder how the six-month waiting period happened to be a part of your policy if you carry the kind that has cash surrender value? It has a very interesting history. During the Depression many people were cashing in their insurance policies, and many insurance companies were on the verge of bankruptcy. Around that time President Franklin Roosevelt declared a bank holiday, saying, in effect, "Sorry about that, but we can not return to you the funds you have deposited in your bank checking and savings accounts." With this announcement, lights began flashing in the home offices of many insurance companies, and their executives said, "Oh, my goodness! Why didn't we think of that?" They got permission to suspend paying cash value, and ever since that date this six-month waiting period has been in most insurance policies. If you should ask an agent about this provision, the agent may assure you that his company would never make you wait. If he is so confident, why is the provision in the policy?

• NET
   COST

Now let's look at another term used so frequently to confuse. It's called "net cost," a term to convince the unwary that life insurance is very inexpensive if bought the "permanent" way. The presentation will go something like this:

Total premiums paid ages 35–65 ($200/yr)	$6000.00
Minus cash value at age 65	5000.00
Net cost	$1000.00
Average cost per year	$ 33.33

Don't you believe it!

If your death occurred at 65, your net cost was the total of the premiums you had paid to date, $200 × 30 years, or $6000. Your beneficiaries did not receive the face amount plus your savings account. They received $10,000, not $15,000.

Let's go a step further, and see if the agent can prove there is a way that you can receive your insurance free and make a profit to boot. Net cost on a 20-year endowment policy:

Total premiums, ages 35–55	$9,000
Maturity value at age 55	10,000
Net profit	$1,000

Isn't this great? $10,000 of insurance for twenty years, and you get all your money back, plus $1000. The insurance company is actually giving you free protection. How can you afford to turn down this marvelous opportunity? If you truly care about your family's welfare, you had better turn it down.

As you can see, if they overcharge you enough, they can prove that not only have you had your insurance free, but you've also made a profit.

What about the earning power of your money all those years? We have already learned that a dollar has fantastic earning potential and that it will work either for you or for the institution to whom you lend it.

Now let's talk about another "fun" game.

Minimum Deposit • Minimum deposit insurance plans, affectionately called "mini-dip" by the salesmen who sell them, are whole life or limited-pay life policies, often "participating," with a very large premium that creates artificially high early cash surrender values. If you have this kind of insurance, it was your money that produced this high cash value. This type of policy is often presented to those in a 40 percent or above tax bracket, usually in the form of impressive computer print-outs that show borrowing out most of the cash values as soon as possible and charging off the interest on their income tax returns. The impression is often given that the IRS is the one actually financing the insurance program. Even if the interest could be deductible in this plan, and there does seem to be some doubt about deducting all of it, especially if the policy was purchased after August 6, 1963, it is not brilliant economics to use after-tax dollars to substitute for insurance dollars that can be bought for pennies, pay a salesman to put those dollars into a savings account, and then pay an insurance company for the privilege of taking them out. No interest at all is better than tax-deductible interest. Only buy "mini-dip" if you have an insurance agent friend whom you want to help prosper and become a member of the Million Dollar Round Table. If your first allegiance is to yourself and the welfare of your family, there is a better way.

• MY SEARCH
FOR INFORMATION

Perhaps it would be well for me to share with you how I have developed such strong convictions about the insurance area of financial planning. Let me go back to the year 1958.

I began to have a gnawing feeling that there was something wrong with my family's life insurance program. (We had bought a policy from a friend some years before while we were still in college, struggling to earn enough money to finish, and had asked him for a policy with the lowest cost.)

I began my search for information by first going to a college library and then to a large public library. To my surprise, information about life insurance was extremely scarce. This was puzzling. Millions of dollars were being spent annually on this commodity, but there was so little information available. I had heard of certain books about the subject, but they all seemed to be "out of print." Laboriously, I began to piece together bits of information in an effort to solve this puzzle of how the various types of insurance policies differed and how they were put together.

Decreasing Term Plus Banking • During this searching period, I awoke early one morning, and like a bolt out of the blue I felt I had solved the insurance mystery. All the policies that were being so aggressively sold by the life insurance community were either pure protection alone or pure protection plus "banking." Whole life, straight life, modified life, 20-pay life, 20-year endowment, executive life, presidential life, and various other golden titles created by the marketing departments of the life insurance companies were actually decreasing term plus a savings account.

I now remembered that the word "term" had come up when we had asked the agent for a low-cost policy. He had recoiled in horror when we asked and said that "term" is only "temporary" insurance, a poor substitute for "permanent" insurance. After all, you don't want to "rent" your insurance; you want to "own" it.

"Permanent" Insurance? • As I began to delve into how our policy was constructed, I began to question how "permanent" our "permanent insurance" really was. According to my understanding of the word "permanent," it is something that doesn't change; yet our insurance was decreasing each time we paid the premium and substituted some of our after-tax hard-earned dollars for a portion of our insurance pro-

tection. The company's risk was decreasing as the burden was shifted to us through "our" increasing savings account.

"Our" Savings Account? • Was it really ours? If it were our savings account, what were its characteristics?

First of all, we found, as you have already seen, that we were using after-tax dollars and substituting them for insurance dollars that we could buy for a few pennies. This did not seem to be brilliant economics. (And here I had a college degree in economics and finance!) Then we noticed from reading the cash surrender value table in the back of the policy that all of our savings the first few years had disappeared. (As I thought back over the explanation the agent had given us about the policy at the time of the sale, I couldn't remember his inserting the word "surrender" in his reference to the cash value. He referred to it as our "building up of cash for the future.")

We also discovered that as we continued to make deposits each year, we were being charged a commission to place money into our "savings account." Once the savings were deposited, we seemed to be losing all their earning power. I knew the agent said we were getting 3 percent on the cash reserve but as we examined the policy, it didn't seem too important what rate was being paid since, if death occurred, the insurance company planned to keep the savings and pay only the face amount of the policy.

We also found that if we wanted to borrow "our" savings, we would have to pay 5½ percent interest to borrow our own money. Really? Our own money? Again we asked, "Is it ours?"

We also found that if my spouse died with the savings there, the unilateral contract signed with the life insurance company specified that they got to keep "our" savings. The savings were part of the face amount, or death benefit of the policy—not an amount in addition to the face amount.

"FUNNY BANKING"

It was then that we asked ourselves this: Suppose we had gone to our banker and said to him, "We want to open a savings account at your bank." And he had said to us, "We're happy to have you, and these are the rules. First, we'll take everything you deposit into the account the first year. After that, we'll charge you to deposit money into your account. If you want to borrow from your savings, we'll charge you 5½ percent to borrow your own money. If you refuse to pay us for the

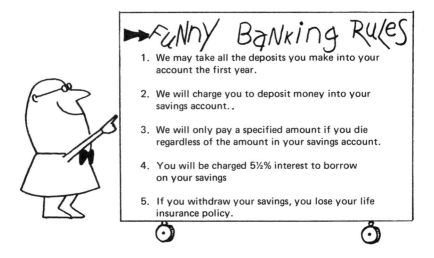

➤ FuNNY BaNking RuleS

1. We may take all the deposits you make into your account the first year.

2. We will charge you to deposit money into your savings account..

3. We will only pay a specified amount if you die regardless of the amount in your savings account.

4. You will be charged 5½% interest to borrow on your savings

5. If you withdraw your savings, you lose your life insurance policy.

privilege of borrowing your own money, and withdraw your savings, you will have to give up your insurance policy." If he had said all of this, would we have opened the savings account?

We then began to analyze our "banking." We examined four major areas: safety, yield, liquidity, and the cost of doing business.

The first thing we examined, as you should, was safety. If your account isn't safe, none of the other characteristics are really all that important. Once you've established that it's safe, you will then want to know what rate of return you are obtaining on your money, because, as you've learned, the rate of return is vitally important to the success of any financial program. After that, you will want to know about liquidity—how readily accessible are your funds? Last, what is the cost of doing business?

Much to my surprise, here is how I tallied the two "banks" with regard to the savings portion of our policy. (See the table on page 277.)

What is your reaction to this comparison? With whom do you feel you should be banking? With the life insurance company? With the bank? We chose the bank.

We had at last discovered that life insurance was for dying and investments were for living; the combining of the two under one insurance policy only built bigger and better life insurance empires. Even though one insurance company is still allowed, in most states, to come into your living room via "living color" television and through national magazines to tell you that you, too, can own a part of a jagged, porous piece of real estate guarding the gateway to the blue Mediterranean, it

With Whom Should You Deposit "Your" Savings?

	Commercial National Bank	"Banking" tally savings with Insurance Company
Safety	Guaranteed by FDIC	Only as safe as the company *
Yield	5–7½%	2½%–3½% on cash reserve (perhaps) **
Liquidity	On demand	Could wait six months and then pay only if they had the money *

Cost of doing business:

To deposit	0	10–55%
To withdraw	0	4½–8%

* Except in states with the Guaranty Association Act. The majority, but not all, of the states have now passed this act. This law guarantees any policy benefits stated in the policy issued by a company doing business in that state, or having domicile in that state. If a company is liquidated and owes more benefits than the liquidation of their assets provides, then all of the other insurance companies are assessed proportionate to their premium income to make up the deficit.
** Many experts agree that the interest return to the policyholder is always 0 percent unless cash surrender value should exceed the face amount.

is not literally true. The state of Florida has now banned this ad, declaring that it is false advertising, and other states have required them to change the wording to "with a piece. . . ."

• BUY WHEN YOU ARE YOUNG

Have you heard, as we had, "Buy your insurance while you are young because it's cheaper" We found that this was not true and that life insurance will cost more each year because it is based on a mortality table. We also found that the more recent the mortality table in use, the better the rates should be, because medical science is helping our population live longer.

Did your agent tell you when he delivered your policy, encased in leather or plastic and embossed in imitation gold, that your policy was sacred and should never ever be changed? Ours did. He said it would cost us dearly if we ever changed.

As I look back now, this is rather ridiculous. This would mean that we had found the most knowledgeable agent, that he had designed the best insurance package, that our needs would never change, and that no new mortality table would ever be used. In many states you can get a 60-day temporary license to sell insurance before even taking an exam. Perhaps your policy was sold to you by one of these. It's just as binding a legal instrument as if he had had 40 years of experience.

Our policy was sold to us by a fellow college student who was working part time to help defray his college expenses.

When we analyzed our policies, we found that changing them was much to our advantage. We had a $25,000 policy, for which we were paying $670.75 per year. It had $5425 of cash surrender value; therefore, our net insurance was $19,575. What was our cost per thousand if we kept this policy?

Face amount	$25,000.00
"Our" savings	5,425.00
Net insurance	$19,575.00
Premium	670.75
Lost earnings on $5,425 @ 5%	271.25
Total cost	$ 942.00

True cost per thousand: $942/19.6 thousand,
48.06 per thousand

Our cost per thousand had increased from $26.83 per thousand, when we took out the policy, to $48.06.

I counted the loss of earning power on our savings because if the savings were in a bank at 5 percent (or in municipal bonds if we were concerned about taxes), the $5425 would have earned us $271.25. We then made the startling discovery that $942.00 would purchase us $180,000 of annual renewable term life insurance.

During that year, if death had occurred, the beneficiaries would have received:

From the bank	$ 5,425
From the insurance co.	180,000
Total	$185,425

Our family's total (death and living) estate had been increased by $160,425 ($185,425 − $25,000) by just repositioning our assets.

How Did It Happen? • How did we ever happen to agree to this original policy? Would we have agreed to it if someone had told us about all the possible kinds of policies? Had we signed a contract without even reading it? We had asked the agent, who was a good friend of ours, for the lowest-cost policy with the maximum coverage. We later discovered he had not intentionally done us a disservice. He had sold us the kind of policy his company told him he should sell. (He was what is called a "captive salesman"—meaning that he could write insurance only for the company he represented.) His general manager had also assured him that this was the best policy for his client, for himself, and for the company. It was the best for him and for the company, but not for us.

It Made a Great Difference • In 1958, when we learned how life insurance policies were put together, we changed all our policies and were able to obtain a larger amount of protection for the same premium and freed our cash value for investments.

On September 29, 1959, my husband was a passenger on the Braniff Electra that crashed near Buffalo, Texas, killing all aboard. My whole world crashed around me.

When everything was settled, I realized that my estate was much larger than it would have been if we had not made changes in our insurance program.

With intelligent investing of these proceeds since that time, I have moved along the road toward financial independence. I'm a financial planner today because I have chosen to dedicate my life to helping as many people as I can become financially independent. I'm a financial planner because I want to be and not out of economic necessity.

I have known how life insurance was packaged and sold since 1958, but it was not until 1971 that I finally had the courage to stand and publicly speak out about this vital subject. What took me so long? I was frankly frightened. I was afraid that if I attacked the institution into which those attending my seminars had been pouring their life blood for years, my investment advice would be questioned. More importantly, I was afraid of the strong and powerful insurance lobby.

Before that time, when those attending the seminar would come in for counseling, as they were entitled to do, I would tell them how life insurance worked and if their program did not fit their needs, I would suggest that they go to their agent and set up the proper program. Many, many times when they went to their agent, he would again sell them the wrong kind of insurance. This happened just once too often.

A couple with five children who had attended one of my seminars came in for counseling. He was a hard-working father, but did not earn a large salary. The mother had no vocational training at all. They wanted to start a $25 a month investment program. After spending a great deal of time on their budget, I asked about their life insurance program and found they had none. I told them that an adequate life insurance program must be their first priority. I then told them exactly what kind to buy and showed them that it could easily be fitted into their budget.

Three months later they called me about another matter and it was then that I learned that an agent had sold them a $10,000 twenty-pay life for the same premium for which he could have sold them $100,000 of pure protection. If that father had died, his family would have been destitute. I was so furious that I swore this would never happen to a client of mine again. That is when I set up our life insurance agency. I truly believe that we do more good in this area to help our clients become financially independent than any other of our programs, especially among our lower-income clients.

•   WILL YOU LOSE
IF YOU CHANGE YOUR POLICIES?

No more than my family did! The belief that you will lose if you change your insurance policies may have scared you away from the common-sense program of pure protection based on need. Your concern should not be how much you will lose by dropping an existing savings policy. This money has already been lost. A large portion of total commissions and other acquisition costs were taken out in the early years of your policy, and this money will never come back to you. Your real question is "How much will I lose in the future by keeping a high-cost, low-protection policy?"

There is nothing sacred about those pieces of paper containing too much fine print glued or stapled together. Life insurance is a commodity like warehouses, pistachio nuts, or rice. You just get more emotional about something that is related to your life. Why should cash value life insurance be considered a sacred cow? Why is it as good today as it was a hundred years ago? Is our economy the same? Is our rate of inflation the same? Can you think of any other product or service that you can purchase today that was as good 100 years ago? Then why cash value life insurance?

Look at it this way. Assume that you are a pilot flying to Miami. On calculating your location, you find that you have overshot Miami and are over the Atlantic Ocean. You also find that you have just enough gas to get back to Miami. If you keep going, you'll run out of fuel and drop into the ocean. If you turn around now, you'll have enough fuel to make it back. Would you bury your error or rationalize it? No. You would change your course and head toward your destination as soon as possible, for every minute wasted could be costly and catastrophic. Successful financial planning is based on the same principle. If you are heading in the wrong direction, alter your course as soon as possible.

Costly Friendship • Not changing a poor policy can be a very expensive error. I remember a young single man, aged 25, who was paying $130 per year for a $5000 whole life insurance policy he did not need. His employer provided in excess of the amount of protection he needed under a company group term insurance policy. I suggested that he might want to consider using this $130 more profitably in the form of a savings plan or investments.

The policy had been sold to him by a good friend whom he felt had his best interest at heart. He did not want to upset his friend and decided to continue the policy. He felt, after all, that he earned an above-average income and was not financially inconvenienced by paying a $130 per year premium. He told me he felt anyone could always use a little extra protection. He reasoned he had $5000 of insurance in case he died, and he would get back $6000 in cash when he was 65, if he lived, and that to him was a pretty good return on $130 per year.

He obviously did not know how to measure what money must do, or he would not have been so complacent.

Here is what $130 per year for 40 years will become (exclusive of taxes) at various rates of return:

$130 per year for 40 years at 15% = $265,973.50

$130 per year for 40 years at 12% = $111,688.20

$130 per year for 40 years at 10% = $ 63,290.50

$130 per year for 40 years at 8% = $ 36,371.40

$130 per year for 40 years at 6% = $ 21,329.10

This particular young man did not need the protection, but had he converted his whole life to level term to age 65, he would have had $80 difference per year ($130 − $50) to invest with these results (exclusive of taxes):

$80 per year for 40 years at 15% = $163,676.00

$80 per year for 40 years at 12% = $ 68,731.20

$80 per year for 40 years at 10% = $ 38,948.00

$80 per year for 40 years at 8% = $ 22,382.40

$80 per year for 40 years at 6% = $ 13,125.60

Remember this in your own planning.

- ## THE $200,000 ESTATE

A minimum estate necessary to maintain a family today should be at least $200,000. At a 6 percent withdrawal, this is only $1000 per month, which is not particularly generous, I'm sure you'll agree in these times of escalating living costs.

If you are a young family man, just beginning your journey down the road toward financial independence, your accumulated assets will probably be small. For example, let's assume that you have accumulated $20,000. This is your "living estate"—meaning that no one has to die to make these funds available. If you need a $200,000 estate, you are $180,000 short. This will need to be provided by life insurance, which will be your "death estate" until you can substitute a "living estate" for it.

A diagram of your estate would look like Fig. 13–7.

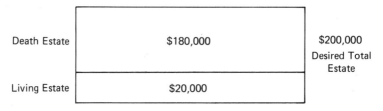

| Death Estate | $180,000 | $200,000 Desired Total Estate |
| Living Estate | $20,000 | |

FIGURE 13–7.

When your "living estate" has grown to $30,000, if your goal is still $200,000, you can reduce your "death estate" to $170,000. You then can keep substituting "living" for "death," "living" for "death," until when you are finished, you'll be self-insured and you and your wife can sit on the veranda and rock together. This is your financial goal—not the acquisition of life insurance policies. Cash or its equivalent is far superior, I'm sure you'll agree, than a collection of life insurance policies.

All life insurance premiums are money down a rat hole unless you die. When you have become self-insured, and have no desire to help your heirs pay estate taxes, stop this waste.

• PROGRAMMING LIFE INSURANCE WITH INVESTMENTS

Let's assume that you are a male, age 35, have saved $20,000, can budget $300 per month to cover your insurance program and your investment program, and desire to have a $200,000 estate. Let's further assume that you use $66 per month to pay the premiums on a $180,000 decreasing term to 65 policy and place your $20,000 and your $234 per month in a "guaranteed" savings account at 5 percent. Your program could be as follows:

| | Death estate | | Living estate | | |
| | Insurance | Lump sum | Monthly | | |
Age	coverage	$20,000	$234/mo.	Total	Total estate
35	$180,000	$20,000	$ 0	$ 20,000	$200,000
45	141,480	32,578	37,094	69,672	211,152
55	84,960	53,066	97,494	150,560	235,520
65	0	86,438	195,886	282,324	282,324

If you obtain a rate of 10 percent on your investment dollars, your results should be as follows:

| | Insurance | Lump sum | Monthly | | |
Age	coverage	$20,000	$234/mo.	Total	Total estate
35	$180,000	$ 20,000	$ 0	$ 20,000	$200,000
45	141,480	51,800	49,224	101,024	242,504
55	84,960	134,600	176,904	311,024	396,464
65	0	349,000	508,080	857,080	857,080

As you can see, if your goal is still only $200,000, at 10 percent you can stop paying insurance premiums before you are 55. You have become self-insured.

• WHICH LIFE INSURANCE COMPANY?

Does it make a difference from which legal reserve life insurance company you buy pure protection? No, it does not. Seek one that offers the best features at the best rates, designed to help you build a living estate. It should offer policies that are renewable and convertible at your option to a variety of their policies, without evidence of insurability, to a ripe old age. This puts you in the driver's seat—and that's where you should be in designing and carrying out your financial plan.

A life insurance company with whose principles I agree states its policy as follows:

1 · We write life insurance policies to protect investors.

2 · We encourage policyholders to continue to accumulate investments outside life insurance policies.

3 · We offer life insurance to the investing public through licensed life insurance agents who are also registered for the sale of investments.

4 · Due to the economic quality of our market and the specialized nature of our representative, we are able to offer life insurance policies at costs considerably lower than ordinarily encountered in the life insurance industry.

5 · We do not write complicated policies nor do we encourage expensive devices. We simply write maximum coverage for a minimum price.

· ## WHICH LIFE
INSURANCE AGENT?

From which agent should you buy your protection? Certainly one of the prerequisites is that he not be a member of a captive sales force —meaning that he can write only for the one company to which he is beholden. He cannot be impartial under these conditions. His company will not let him. Too, his company may not even have a policy that fits your needs, and if it does have one hidden away, his supervisor may severely reprimand him for not selling you the kind that makes him and the company the most profit.

In my opinion, you should plan your life insurance needs with a financial planner who is knowledgeable in investments to help you build a living estate and in life insurance to help you buy the time to build the estate. These two areas of financial planning are inseparable, since you don't know how long your life span will be. Your financial planner should be dually licensed to recommend both investments and life insurance.

Being dually licensed allows the professional to balance your financial program. I should warn you, however, that it does not make him impartial. In fact, some life insurance agents have obtained a securities license as a tool for selling more high-cost, low-protection policies. They maintain that it will not make any difference to them whether you invest in securities or put your investment dollar into your policy. Actually, it makes a whale of a difference in their compensation. If they sell you a whole life policy at a cost of $1000, they may receive as high as

110 percent of that first year's premium (or $1100) over a two-year period, plus some trail commission from the policy in the future. If they sell you "term" and invest the balance for you in a mutual fund, they would receive only a fraction of this amount.

• PAYING MORE WHILE YOU'RE YOUNG

Unfortunately, your family's need for protection is greatest at the time in your life cycle when your income probably has not reached its prime. Despite the fact that your mortality risk is low at that time, most policies are designed so that while you are young you are overcharged at the time your family needs maximum coverage so that you can begin "underpaying" at age 72, when your need for coverage should have diminished or be nonexistent because you have become self-insured.

Figure 13–8 is a diagram of the level premium method. Note how the policy is designed for coverage far beyond life expectancy.

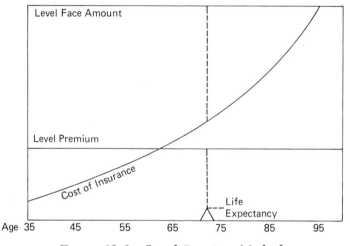

FIGURE 13–8.   Level Premium Method

• "SOMETHING BACK!"

When you buy term insurance on your life, you are doing so because you are concerned about the welfare of your family in the event of your death. You should not be asking, "What am I going to get back?" You know that term is pure protection and pays off only if you die while the policy is in force. You know that your beneficiaries will receive the payoff. You expect nothing in return other than the warm feeling that you have adequate protection for your family.

"Something back" appeals to your selfish instincts—and we all have them—but this is contrary to the purpose of life insurance.

• A GOOD COMPULSORY SAVING PLAN?

Is insurance, in fact, a good compulsory savings plan? The previous analysis of this aspect of "permanent" insurance should indicate that you are much wiser to put savings in a bank, Series E government bonds, or preferably in good growth investments. You should save, but save for you and your family's benefit.

• AN INEXPENSIVE WAY TO BORROW MONEY?

Sometimes a couple will proudly point out to me how very bright they have been to have figured out that they can borrow on their policy for 5 or 6 percent instead of from the bank at 8 to 10 percent. If you are doing this, you are paying to borrow your "own" money. If your savings were in a savings account at your bank, you would not have to pay your bank to take your money out. You are also reducing the amount of your life insurance coverage when you borrow against your policy, because the loan is subtracted from the face amount if it is outstanding at the time of your death. Borrowing against your policies serves only to increase your cost and to reduce your coverage. If you are healthy enough to pass a physical, get pure protection. If you are not, by all means consider borrowing the cash value out and putting it to work, preferably in an investment with a tax-sheltered cash flow. Send the insurance company a check for the interest each year and deduct the interest on your income tax return. You should be safe in deducting if the policy was taken out before August 6, 1963.

• LIFE INSURANCE FOR CHILDREN?

I'm amazed at the amount of money spent each year on premiums for life insurance for children.

Let's reexamine the purpose of life insurance. It's purpose is to protect those dependent upon the policyholder in the event that he does not live long enough to build a living estate. If you have a policy on the life of your child, ask yourself, "Who is dependent on my child for a livelihood?" You should never make a practice of protecting your liabilities, but only of protecting your assets. As much as you love your child or children, they are financial liabilities until they are old enough and well enough prepared to leave your nest.

Should you have enough for burial? You can if you want to, but I don't recommend that you do. There are limited dollars in the family budget for life insurance, and every dollar spent on life insurance to cover the children means one dollar taken away from purchasing life insurance on the life of the breadwinner. You may shun such a somber thought, but a child's funeral expenses will be defrayed by the decrease in the cost of caring for the child, while the loss of a wage earner may be a near economic disaster to the family.

If you would feel more comfortable with a bit of insurance on the kids, you can obtain $1000 (called a unit) on each child, regardless of how many children you have, for about $8 per year total (not $8 for each) by adding this coverage as a rider on your policy. You can usually carry five of these units, and some companies offer 10 or more. For example, five units would cost $40 and you would have $5000 insurance on each child. You can usually carry this coverage on each child until he is 25 years of age. At that time he has the privilege of obtaining five times the coverage carried without evidence of insurability. In other words, when each child reaches 25, he would have the privilege of carrying $25,000 of coverage, in our example, without having to take a physical to prove his insurability, and at the rate of his attained age, based on the current mortality table.

• COLLEGE
POLICIES

I've seen many endowment policies taken out at the time of a child's birth for the purpose of providing the expenses for four years of college, which did not even cover the cost of the first semester. It makes me sad every time I see a billboard portraying a beaming youth with a mortarboard jauntily atop his head, proclaiming that his college endowment policy brought him to this happy occasion.

Although you certainly want to plan for your children's education, a college endowment policy is not an effective way to accomplish this worthwhile goal. Planning for this expense is covered in a later chapter.

• DOUBLE AND TRIPLE
INDEMNITIES

The question often arises about the amount of accidental death insurance a young family should carry. In our financial planning we do not count accidental dealth policies when calculating the family's need for protection. Even though most young fathers are convinced that if they die, that's the way they'll go, it's not too likely—that's why the rates are low. It's more likely that they'll die from a heart attack while mowing their lawns. It doesn't really matter how you die; you are just as dead—and the family's needs are just as real. Buy sufficient life insurance to cover full needs and don't worry about how you may die.

• REPLACEMENT—BENEFIT
OR BLASPHEMY?

As more and more people have become better informed about the potential earning power of their money and also more aware of inflation's devastation to its purchasing power, they have been searching for more productive ways to put their dollars to work. In an attempt to slow this tide of change, some companies have waged very successful campaigns to get regulations passed to require that agents complete and submit lengthy, detailed, and difficult replacement forms if they recommend the replacement of any cash value policy, regardless of which mortality table it was written on.

Replacement forms in some states have become so tedious and time consuming that many a conscientous financial planner has left his clients' present insurance program alone, even when it was grossly inadequate and unnecessarily expensive, rather than spend the many hours required to complete these forms. At the end of this chapter is a completed form taken from an actual case. See if you can calculate the owner's cost per thousand for his present coverage.

The purpose of most replacement forms is to preserve existing cash value insurance policies. Unfortunately, no "full disclosure" forms were required when you first started your life insurance program, and none were required when you bought additional insurance. Also, no replacement forms are usually required if the agent replaces a pure term insurance with a cash value policy.

Consider, if you will for a moment, the viability of the concept that any other financial decision made in this dynamic world in which we live should never be changed. Is it logical that the only exception is a cash surrender value life insurance policy? Yet there are companies that teach their agents that cash surrender value policies are sacred.

You should have complete information about term policies and other policies that are term plus savings. We now have a "truth in lending law." A "truth in insurance law" was proposed by the late Senator Philip Hart, but he died before seeing his proposal enacted.

• TWISTING

Some cash value salesmen refer to a financial planner who recommends term insurance as a "termite," or, if the financial planner has replaced one of their policies, they may call him a "twister." This implies that all who recommend changing your insurance program are "twisters." This is not true. A cash value salesman *or* a term insurance salesman is said to be "twisting" if he uses misrepresentation or an incomplete comparison to induce a replacement to the detriment of the policyholder. If he provides an honest and complete explanation and reduces his cost per thousand, he is not a "twister."

Some insurance companies, when they receive a notice that one of their life policies is going to be replaced, send a dire warning letter and pamphlet to the policyholder, warning him of the serious mistake he is about to make. Often they include an old article from the 1961 publication of the *Changing Times Magazine*.

I wrote to this magazine and asked if they had changed their thinking and if they realized how their article was being used. Mr. Jerome Velbaum, Senior Editor, in a letter to me dated July 16, 1976, stated, "The article which you were given dates back to 1961, when conditions were quite different. I have enclosed a copy of a more recent article on the same subject." The article he enclosed from the August, 1974 issue was titled "Trade One Life Insurance Policy For Another?" with a subtitle, "Sometimes switching makes sense, but don't be talked into it until you've examined all the angles." If you get a 1961 reprint, you may want to suggest that there is a later reprint.

Should You Replace? • Your answer is probably "yes," if you are healthy enough to pass a physical and if you have any one of four things in your policies:

1 • You have more than one policy. There is an extra policy fee paid in addition, or it is already built in, each year for each policy that goes to administration, not for the mortality cost. This fee will average from $10 to $25 per year. If you are carrying six policies and you have a $20 policy fee per policy, you are spending $100 per year unnecessarily that could be used to provide additional insurance coverage.

2 • You have a savings program in your policy. You are probably "saving" with an insurance company under conditions that you would never save with your bank.

3 • Your policies are not on a current mortality table.

4 • It is a "participating" policy.

When Should You Not Replace? • Are there circumstances when you should not replace one or more of your insurance policies? Yes, and here are some of the reasons:

1 • You are uninsurable.

2 • You cannot lower your cost per thousand by obtaining a new policy.

3 • You are planning to commit suicide within the next two years.

4 • You are planning to give false information on your new insurance application. If you do, there will be a two-year contestability period that could result in your heirs receiving only the amount of coverage those premiums would have purchased had you told the truth.

5 • If any of the nonforfeiture provisions of your present policies are important to your current financial planning. These provisions may include paid-up additions and extended-term provisions. Extended term provides that if you quit paying premiums the company uses the cash surrender values in the

policies to extend the period of your coverage. For example, let's say that your cash value was enough to buy you term coverage for 10 years. You chose this option and died in the eleventh year. Your family would receive nothing. If you died the second year, they would only receive the extended term amount and the insurance company would keep the nine years of prepaid insurance premiums. There may be income options and annuity options in your present policies. Examine them. Determine if your financial planner can provide you with better alternatives.

6 • If you bought your policies from a friend and you feel you would lose him as a friend if you replace them, and if a friendship based on *his* economic benefit is more important to you than the economic future of your family.

7 • You cannot withstand the pressure that may be brought to bear on you by your present insurance company or their agent when you attempt to replace.

• THOSE MARVELOUS MONEY MACHINES

Statistics for just one year showed that one well-known U.S. insurance company had a net investment income of $1,332,086,856. (Yes, investment income! You see, their net policy reserves were $22 billion.) They received premium income of $3,694,135,298. Their claims for the year were $310 million. This would make a difference between receipts and claims of $4.716 billion for the year.

An excellent article on this subject appeared in the September 1, 1974, issue of *Forbes* entitled "Those Marvelous Money Machines!" and states:

> While other businesses produce products, the insurance industry produces money, capital. The industry is a wonderful money machine. At a time when presidents of successful companies spend their sleepless hours wondering where to get capital, insurance company bosses worry only about where to invest it. That's a high-class worry.
>
> The numbers are not easy to come by, but FORBES has made some sensible estimates. We figure the industry took in about $91 billion in premiums last year [1973] and earned about $22 billion from investments and other income. Against this it paid out maybe $79 billion in benefits, operating expenses and taxes. The remaining $34 billion or so was added to the industry's capital base—either as plowed-back profits

or as additional reserves. By the year's end the industry boasted $336 billion in assets—against, for comparison, 26.3 billion for the whole U.S. steel industry.*

The life insurance business can be very profitable. You should ask, "For whom?"

Possible profits become very evident when you recognize that the insurance companies have sizable sums to invest, sometimes at rates up to 13 percent. In recent years they have also demanded and received as much as one-half interest in the real estate developments they finance. These funds are available because their policyholders have been enticed to "invest" through them.

Most policies show the company paying 2½ to 4 percent interest on cash reserves. If you leave this cash value with them, I don't see that it makes a great deal of difference. Yes, I know their earnings are supposed to allow them to charge you less for your coverage now and to let you underpay after age 72, but somehow this possibility doesn't seem too attractive to me.

• THE WIDOWS STUDY

The Life Insurance Agency Management Association and the Life Underwriter Training Council conducted a survey. The widows interviewed were all less than 65 years of age and their husbands were still in their earning years at the time of their deaths.

These were some of their findings:

1 • They found that 52 percent of the widows received under $5000 in life insurance proceeds. This is less than half a year's income for most families. (The government classifies a family of four with an income of less than $5500 per year as being below the poverty level.)

2 • In many cases the insurance money received was less than the final expenses connected with her husband's death. Fifty-two percent stated that the medical expenses amounted to $2000 or more.

3 • After paying final expenses averaging $3900, the average widow ended up with about $8000 cash.

* Reprinted by permission of *Forbes Magazine* from the September 1, 1974 issue.

• SELECTED QUOTES FROM OTHER AUTHORITIES

Consumer News, in its February 1973 edition, reporting on the congressional hearing on life insurance company abuses, chaired by the late Senator Philip Hart, chairman of the Senate Antitrust and Monopoly Subcommittee, in February of 1973, states in issue number 72, dated Februrary 26, 1973,

> History's first Congressional investigation into life insurance brought a succession of witnesses last week charging the industry with deceptive selling techniques on such a massive scale that even many agents themselves are unaware of what they are doing to American consumers.

I recommend this issue to you. (It can be purchased by writing to *Consumer Newsweek*, 813 National Press Building, Washington, D.C. 20004.)

At this same Congressional hearing the highly respected Professor Joseph Belth, of Indiana University, called our life insurance industry a "national scandal."

In this hearing, Ralph Nader, the fire-breathing crusader, said, and I quote,

> For almost seventy years, the life insurance industry has been a smug sacred cow, feeding the public a steady line of sacred bull.

Some findings of Mr. Nader's research were

> Life insurance tragically fails to protect sufficiently its ultimate consumers —the widows and children—from the financial risk of premature death of the breadwinner by duping husbands into buying too much of the wrong kind of insurance (or too little of the right kind) at excessive prices. Because there is little or no meaningful and communicated price competition, the high expenses of the life insurance industry—virtually all borne by the consumer—are a national disgrace. . . .

> Cash value policies, which represented 72% of the $731 billion of ordinary life insurance in force in 1970, are a consumer fraud, not because they are inherently valueless, but because purchasers are denied systematic and useful information about alternative plans available.

Unfortunately, Senator Hart died before any changes could be enacted.

• HOW TO ANALYZE
YOUR POLICIES

Let's discuss how to take the first step in analyzing your own policies. First, you'll need to get them out of the safety deposit box or wherever you have them stored. Now read them. I'll bet you never have, even though you've been pouring some of your life blood into them.

After you have finished, look on the front of the policy. There you will find the date the policy was acquired. That's its birthdate. Take today's date, less the policy's birthdate, and this gives you the age of the policy. For example, if you acquired your policy in December 1967, and it is now December 1977, it is 10 years old. Look toward the back of the policy, if you have the "cash value" variety. Go down to the tenth year of the nonforfeiture section. Go across and you will find a "cash surrender" or "loan value." This amount will be for either the face amount or per thousand. It will state one or the other at the top of the chart. For example, if it's a $10,000 policy and your cash value table shows $350 opposite 10 years, and the table shows "per $1000," you would have a cash value of $3500.

To give you a better picture of your policy, you'll find worksheets at the end of this chapter. Worksheet I can be helpful for listing your policies. Worksheet II can be used to obtain a visual picture of them, and Worksheet III will help in computing your present cost per thousand.

How Much Life Insurance? • How do you calculate the amount of life insurance you should carry? First, take your present monthly salary. Let's assume that it is $2000. Multiply this amount by 70 or 75 percent, using 75 percent if you have three or more children. This is about what your family would need to maintain them at their present standard of living if you were not here to provide for them. At 70 percent, $1400 would be needed. Let's assume that your family would be eligible for maximum social security. Your wife may receive around $530 per month until your children reach 18. Thus, $1400 less $530 = $870. How much capital is required to provide $870 per month at 6 percent? Just multiply by 200 (this tells you how much capital is required at 6 percent to produce $870 per month). This gives you $174,000. Let's assume that you have accumulated $20,000 exclusive of home furnishings and non-liquid investments. Subtract this from the $174,000, leaving $154,000 of capital needed.

Calculate the amount you need using this method, adding other appropriate expenses that must be met, such as college costs, etc. Determine if the premiums for this amount can be fitted into your family's budget. If it can, fine. If it cannot, you must reduce the coverage to the amount you can afford and still live today.

An excellent financial planner I know uses a simpler method. Whatever your annual salary is, he just adds a zero to determine the coverage you'll need. He gives no credit for any "living" assets you have acquired. For example, if you earn $24,000 per year, he recommends $240,000. If inflation continues, as it appears it will, and if all our old established methods of investing keep changing, I think his method has merit.

• LIFE INSURANCE, A VERY PERSONAL MATTER

Your life insurance program should be designed to fit your needs at this particular time. Your needs will change from year to year, so your policies should be constantly reviewed. They are not sacred instruments.

Your need for protection may be less, the same, or more each year. Is there a new mortality table now available? If so, you will want to apply for a new policy probably at a lower rate. When you have the new policy safely secured (not before), then consider what should be done with your old policies. Policies can be changed, and riders can be dropped. Work with a creative financial planner to keep your insurance program finely tuned to your changing needs. A good insurance program should not be expensive, if properly designed, and should be well within your family's budget.

Let me reemphasize—life insurance is a necessary umbrella until you've had time to accumulate a living estate. It should be purchased with these ten points in mind:

1 • Determine your life insurance needs as if you were going to die today.

2 • Life insurance is based on a mortality table; therefore, it should cost you more each year, because you are more apt to die.

3 • Every time there is a new mortality table, apply for a new policy. If you pass the physical and are granted a new policy at a lower rate, redeem or cancel the old one. A life insurance policy is no more sacred than a homeowner's policy.

4 • The purpose of life insurance is to protect those dependent upon you in the event that you do not live long enough to accumulate a living estate. Your goal is to become self-insured by age 65 or sooner. You've either made it by then, or you'll

probably never make it financially. (Yes, I know Col. Sanders did!) Life insurance is to protect an economic potential. After 65 your economic potential has greatly diminished. Yes, I also am aware that insurance proceeds can be used to pay estate taxes. If your heirs are in that enviable position, hurrah for you! Here we are speaking of bread on the table in the event that you are not here to provide for it. We can obtain pure protection to age 100, and that should take care of most situations, even including federal estate taxes.

5 • Life insurance is for dying. Investments are for living. Never ever combine the two.

6 • All life insurance is pure protection (term), or pure protection plus "banking." There is no other kind.

7 • Do not "bank" with an insurance company under conditions that you would not accept with your bank.

8 • Be sure that your policies are renewable and convertible without evidence of insurability. You should also consider waiver of premium.

9 • Normally never have more than one policy. (Plus your group and unconverted GI term policy.)

10 • Don't buy a participating policy.

My wish for you is that you'll live a long and happy life and that all the life insurance premiums you'll ever pay will be pure waste!

Application

1 • Complete Worksheet I. Circle in the left-hand column every policy after the first one. Then circle each cash surrender value in (2) and each time you have a policy that is not on the 1958 CSO mortality table. Then circle every time you show "a dividend." This will give you a rough idea of the places you can start lowering your cost per thousand. How many circles did you make?

2 • Complete Worksheet II. You can obtain all this information from Worksheet I. Is this a picture of decreasing insurance and increasing savings?

3 • Complete Worksheet III. What is your present cost per thousand?

4 • What is the available cost per thousand at your age?

5 • What action do you need to take?

Worksheet I
My Life Insurance & Annuity Worksheet
(Use separate sheet for Term, Term Riders & Family Plan Riders)

NAME _____

BIRTHDATE _____ AGE _____

DATE _____

Company	Type Policy	Mor-tality table	(1) Face amt. Basic policy	(2) Cash value	(3) Rate to borrow	(4) Actual ins	(5) Annual premium	(6) Last year's refund (divi-dend)	(7) Net premium	(8) Lost earnings @ ___% on cash value	(9) Total cost	(10) Cost per thousand
TOTALS												

Example:

Company	Type Policy	Mor-tality table	(1) Face amt. Basic policy	(2) Cash value	(3) Rate to borrow	(4) Actual ins	(5) Annual premium	(6) Last year's refund (divi-dend)	(7) Net premium	(8) Lost earnings @ ___% on cash value	(9) Total cost	(10) Cost per thousand
Blessed Assurance Company	Whole Life	1941 CSO	$10,000	$4,000	5½%	$6000	$245	$40	$205	$240	$445	$74.16
						$(1) - (2)$				$(2) \times 6\%$	$(7) + (8)$	$(9) \div (4)$ ($445÷6)

Worksheet II

A Picture of My Present Life Insurance Program

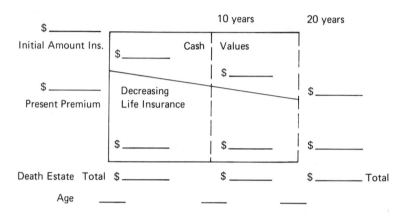

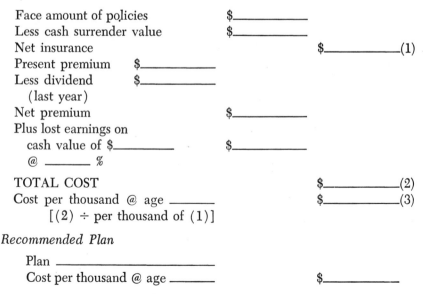

Worksheet III

My age: _____

My Life Insurance Cost Worksheet

Present Plan

Face amount of policies	$_____
Less cash surrender value	$_____
Net insurance	$_____(1)
Present premium $_____	
Less dividend $_____	
(last year)	
Net premium	$_____
Plus lost earnings on	
cash value of $_____	$_____
@ _____ %	
TOTAL COST	$_____(2)
Cost per thousand @ age _____	$_____(3)
[(2) ÷ per thousand of (1)]	

Recommended Plan

Plan _____	
Cost per thousand @ age _____	$_____

Worksheet IV

Replacement Cost Index Worksheet *

Present Program:

    (1) Face amount $_____

    (2) Less cash surrender value $_____

    (3) Net insurance $_____

    (4) Present Premium $_____

    (5) Less cash value increase

             for the year $_____

    (6) Plus lost earnings on $_____

           @ ____ %   (2) $_____

    (7) Less current dividend $_____

    (8) Total cost $_____

    (9) Replacement cost per thousand $_____

           @ ____ age [(8) ÷ no. of thousand in (3)]

Recommended Program:

    Plan _____

    Cost per thousand @ age ____ $_____

* If you are calculating replacement cost use IV. If you want to calculate your cost if you continue to hold your present policies use Worksheet III.

COMPARISON STATEMENT

NAME OF APPLICANT			STREET	CITY	STATE	ZIP CODE
John W. Doe						

NAME OF INSURED IF OTHER THAN APPLICANT	DATE OF BIRTH OF INSURED

1. COMPARATIVE INFORMATION	†Existing Life Insurance	†Existing Life Insurance	†Existing Life Insurance	Total Existing Life Insurance	Proposed Life Insurance
Policy Number					XXXXXXXXXXXX
Insurance Company					
Amount of Basic Insurance					
Currently	$ 15,000	$ 15,000	$ 16,000	$ 46,000	$ 46,000
10 Years Hence	$ 15,000	$ 15,000	$ 16,000	$ 46,000	$ 46,000
20 Years Hence	$ 15,000	$ 15,000	$ 16,000	$ 46,000	$ Ren & conv
At age 65	$ 15,000	$ 15,000	$ 16,000	$ 46,000	$ at client opt
Basic Plan of Insurance	Adj W.L.	Adj W.L.	Adj W.L.	Adj W.L.	10-yr deposit
Present Amount of Term Rider(s)	$	$	$	$	$ level term
Issue Age	30	30	34	Various	51
Issue Date	4-25-56	4-25-56	6-1-60	Various	XXXXXXXXXXXX

Premium For:	Premium	Payable To Age	Age Cov. Ceases	Premium	Payable To Age	Age Cov. Ceases	Premium	Payable To Age	Age Cov. Ceases	Premium	Payable To Age	Age Cov. Ceases	Premium	Payable To Age	Age Cov. Ceases
Basic Policy	$316.20	Life		$316.20	Life		$384.00	Life		$1,016.40	Life		$649.40	'88 at	
*Accidental Death Benefit	$			$			$			$			$	cl opt	
*Waiver of Premium Benefit	$			$			$			$			$	Ren &	
*Disability Income Benefit	$			$			$			$			$	conv	
Family Income or Increased Protection Rider	$			$			$			$			$		
Option to Purchase Additional Insurance	$			$			$			$			$		
Other Benefits (Explain)	$			$			$			$			$		
Total Current Premium	$316.20			$316.20			$384.00			$1,016.40			$649.40	(1	
Frequency of Premium Payment	Annual			Annual			Annual			Annual			Annual		
Tabular Cash Values:															
At Present	$ 5,145			$ 5,145			$ 4,832			$ 15,122 (2			$ 0		
1 Year Hence	$ 5,415			$ 5,415			$ 5,136			$ 15,966			$ 0		
5 Years Hence	$ 6,489			$ 6,489			$ 6,352			$ 19,330			$ 0		
10 Years Hence	$ 7,800			$ 7,800			$ 7,850			$ 23,450			$ 1,610 (2		
At age (Highest age shown in Cash Value Table of existing policy) Age 65	$ 8,820			$ 8,820			$ 8,976			$ 26,616			$ 0 (3		
Cash Value of any existing Dividend Additions or Accumulations (if available from applicant)	$			$			$			$			$		
Amount of any Loan Now Outstanding	$			$			$			$			$		
Amount of Annual Loan Interest	$ 5%			$ 5%			$ 5%			$ 5%			$		
Date Contestable Period Expires	Expired			Expired			Expired			Expired			1980		
Date Suicide Clause Expires	Expired			Expired			Expired			Expired			1980		
Dividends**															
Is Policy Participating?	Yes			Yes			Yes			Yes			No		
Annual Dividend (current scale)															
1 Year Hence	$ 196			$ 196			$ 207			$ 599			$		
2 Years Hence	$ 204			$ 204			$ 217			$ 625			$		
5 Years Hence	$ 236			$ 236			$ 257			$ 729			$		
10 Years Hence	$ 276			$ 276			$ 304			$ 856			$		
Total 10 Years	$ 2,405			$ 2,405			$ 2,595			$ 7,405			$		

(1 Excluding premium deposit of: $621.00 -- Maturity Value is: $1,610

(2 Plus value of investments of $14,501 ($15,122 - $621) plus value of annual premium savings at end of 10 years.

(3 Above at end of 14 years.

*If Premium for Benefits: (A) is not separable from basic policy premium, insert "Included in Basic Policy Premium," or (B) is an aggregate premium, show the aggregate premium.

**Dividends are based on the 19 _77_ dividend scale. The dividends shown are not to be construed as guarantees or estimates of dividends to be paid in the future. Dividends depend on mortality experience, investment, investment earnings and other factors, and are determined each year in the sole discretion of the Company's board of directors.

The agent is responsible for furnishing required dividend information. It is recommended that he obtain this for the policy being replaced from the Company issuing the original insurance. As an alternative, however, he may show dividends on closest comparable policy, amount, age and duration from current statistical manuals. (Interpolating where necessary). It is to be recognized that dividend information under this alternative method, with respect to existing insurance is not likely to be as accurate as dividend information obtained directly from the Company issuing the original insurance.

Source of dividend information used: ___Diamond Life, Flitcraft & Life Rates___

†If more than one existing life insurance policy is to be affected by a transaction included within the definition of a replacement contained in the Regulation, (1) the existing life insurance column of a separate signed Comparison Statement form must be completed for each such policy providing the information required by the form with respect to existing policies, and (II) a separate signed Comparison Statement form must be completed for the proposed policy. The latter form must summarize, to the extent possible, the information concerning the existing policies set forth on the separate forms, and must include the information required in Sections 2 through 5 of the Comparison Statement:

2. Advantages of Continuing the Existing Life Insurance:
    1) Suicide clause expired. 2) Contestable clause expired. 3) Evidence of insurability has been established. 4) First year acquisition costs have been paid.
3. Advantages of the Proposed Replacement of the Existing Life Insurance:

    1) Increase current coverage. 2) Lower unit cost. 3) Purchase of "pure" protection.

4. Additional information:
    (A) The Existing Life Insurance Cannot fulfill Your Intended Objectives for the Following Reason(s):

    1) Basic premiums are excessive for amount of insurance provided. 2) New investment aims and goals cannot be met with existing insurance coverage.
    (B) Under the Proposal, the Existing Insurance Policy Will be Treated as Follows:

    As insured directs.
5. The Primary Reason for the Proposed Replacement of the Existing Life Insurance by New Insurance is as Follows:

    To lower today's cost per thousand.

_____   _____
        (DATE)   (SIGNATURE OF AGENT)

                                 _____
                                        (ADDRESS)

I hereby acknowledge that I received the above "Comparison Statement" and the "Notice to Applicants Regarding Replacement of Life Insurance" before I signed the application for the proposed new insurance.

_____   _____
        (DATE)   (SIGNATURE OF APPLICANT)

14

Investing in Energy

In previous chapters we have studied the investment potential of securities and real estate. In this chapter we will consider the potential of investing in energy. Energy is a broad category, and not all areas will be viable considerations for you if your investment funds are limited.

- ## BACKGROUND OF THE ENERGY CRISIS

In 1974 the average man on the street came face to face with the fact that energy was not a magical manna that dropped from heaven and ran into his electric light switch and into the tank of his automobile. With the Arab oil embargo he discovered that he could no longer drive into the corner gas station; say, "Fill'er up"; receive a sheet of green trading stamps (double on Tuesdays) plus a drinking glass with the insignia of his local football team; and be merrily on his way in a few minutes.

The "energy crisis" did not just suddenly arrive on the scene, although it may have appeared to from listening to and reading the news media. In 1967, I interviewed Michael T. Halbouty, a highly respected independent oil producer, on my CBS affiliate television program,

"Successful Texans." He warned then, as he had been doing since 1960, of the impending energy crisis if steps were not taken to allow a reasonable return on capital invested in the oil industry. At that time he was making warning speeches across the nation, and he has continued to do so. Two years later, I interviewed J. Hugh Liedtke, Chairman of the Board of Pennzoil. He also warned of the problems that were imminent if proper action was not taken. He quoted extensively from comprehensive government studies on the subject.

I also interviewed George Mitchell, Chairman of the Board and President of Mitchell Energy and Development. He gave the same warning and continues to do so.

He and others pointed out over and over again that the flow of new oil could not possibly meet the new and increasing demands.

The need to encourage production seemed obvious to those who were in production, but the opposite view was taken by those who controlled the legislation to fulfill the need.

The Federal Power Commission continued to hold down the price of natural gas to the $.10 to $.16 per cubic foot price to which they had arbitrarily rolled it back, despite the continuous pleas of the oilmen. The Commission took the pose of the three little monkeys, put their hands over their eyes, and said, "Hear no evil, see no evil, speak no evil," and all these bad, bad predictions will "fade away." Of course, the big bad wolf, called energy shortage, did not fade away.

The attitudes of the eastern congressmen also aggravated the picture as they took the attitude, "How dare you talk of raising the price of the natural gas used to bake the bread for the dear families residing in my state?" And then they added, "And don't you muss our scenic coast lines with refineries either; keep them down in Texas and Louisiana where they belong."

They also insisted that the federal government allow massive amounts of foreign oil to be imported into the United States at prices so low that domestic producers could not compete.

At this time a shortage of risk capital to be used to drill oil wells also occurred.

In the 1950s the corporate tax rate was 60 percent to 70 percent, and the individual rate could go as high as 90 percent. At these confiscatory levels there was a tremendous incentive to search for ways of turning tax liabilities into potential capital assets. Oil drilling programs fit this possibility because of the 100 percent write-off potential of intangible drilling costs. Large amounts of risk capital, therefore, were made available.

But in the 1960s, the maximum corporate tax level was reduced to around 48 percent and the individual's to the 50 percent to 70 percent level. This greatly reduced the tax incentive.

All of these factors combined to reduce the profitability of searching for oil and gas reserves.

The number of independent oil operators dwindled from 35,000 to 5000 and the number of rig operators from 3500 to around 900.

As the supply of oil and gas was decreasing, the demand was increasing. A collision course was already in the making when the Arabian bloc discovered our great vulnerability and decided that their best bargaining tool against Israel was the U.S.'s dependence on their oil.

• TURNING LEMONS INTO LEMONADE

If the Arabian embargo had come just two years earlier, the United States could have absorbed the consequent cutbacks fairly easily and would not have become disturbed enough to do anything about its impending future shortage. If, on the other hand, the situation had developed two or three years later, it would have been catastrophic. It was a blessing that it happened late enough to make us aware of the problem facing us and early enough for us to take corrective steps if our regulatory agencies squarely face reality.

There is no question in my mind that the government's ostrichlike policy created the "energy crisis of 1973–74." But instead of wasting our energies condemning their actions, let's examine ways that you might benefit from this situation by viewing it as an "Energy Opportunity" rather than an "Energy Crisis."

How can you best avail yourself of these opportunities? There are three areas that you should consider: investing in energy-related securities, investing in oil- and gas-producing wells, and investing in oil and gas exploration.

• ENERGY STOCKS

I believe that we may be beginning a new Sputnik-like era. Our reaction to the Sputnik shock in 1957 caused a big boom in technical equipment. Fortunes were made in semiconductors. Looking ahead, President Nixon set 1980, unrealistically perhaps, as the target year for energy self-sufficiency. Oilmen tell me it will be nearer to 1985 and will be even further away if more constructive steps are not taken. This will take massive capital expenditures. But that should not discourage us. A nation that can put a man on the moon can surely solve her energy

problems, especially in view of the fact that we are blessed with an abundance of two great energy sources, coal and uranium, in addition to oil and gas. With the proper investment incentives other natural sources such as hydrogen, thermal energy, solar energy, and wind generating power also offer great potential. Unfortunately the government to date has floundered and instead of providing investment incentives has enacted punitive laws that discourage research and development.

There is a trend toward more electrification and toward nuclear reactors as a source of power. It looks as if the trend will continue. It appears that nuclear power makes one of the cheapest, as well as the best, uses of resources. Some of the processes involved in nuclear power have not yet hit the large scale. The fabrication of nuclear fuels is a tiny industry, but an industry that has the potential of tremendous savings from mass production.

The U.S. has enough uranium for the production of significant supplies of nuclear energy. Companies like Kerr-McGee and Anaconda are top producers. A large number of the oil companies are entering the field. Uranium may some day overshadow oil as a source of energy. Another energy source is the manufacture of crude oil from coal. This should be no more expensive than importing oil. We still have untapped sources of hydroelectricity.

The industries that will benefit from the new push to be self-sufficient in energy will offer a vast range of investment opportunities. Study each carefully, and pick the leader in the industries you choose.

I believe that the "energy crisis" has set up one of those rare investment opportunities that comes along maybe only once every ten years.

You should use the same basic criteria that we've outlined earlier in the selection of your energy stocks. Some of the older, more heavily capitalized companies should fit the income category if this is your financial objective. The smaller, more aggressive companies, which may have more venturesome drilling programs, may fit the growth and speculative categories.

Many companies will broaden their base and engage in exploration, production, refining, and distribution. They may even go into the manufacture of products that use petrocarbons as their base.

You should consider not only these companies, but also those who build offshore drilling rigs and those who build refineries. Oil without refineries is of no use. We faced a refinery bottleneck long before the Middle East embargo.

Management skills, company's assets, and consumer demand are vital areas for study, whether you are selecting an oil company or a company in a related field.

• ENERGY PRODUCTION

We have been examining investing in oil and gas and other energy through the stock market. This is a legitimate consideration for your investment dollars. But let's look at other ways. One way that I feel is worthy of your consideration is participation in energy through investing in oil and gas income limited partnerships.

To compare investing in energy through stocks with investing through partnerships, let's look at the characteristics of each. First, let's look at the numbers, using our largest oil company, Exxon. Here are the figures for 1972.

EXXON

1972 Figures per Share

22.39	Earnings before depreciation and taxes
4.72	Depletion and depreciation
17.67	Pretax earnings
10.83	Corp. taxes (including minority interest expenses and excise taxes)
6.84	After-tax earnings
3.80	Dividend (taxable to the shareholder, thus double taxation)
3.04	Retained earnings (corp. decides how they will be used)

As you can see, if you owned a share of Exxon, only $6.84 of cash flow was left after taxes; $3.80 of this was paid out to you as a dividend, on which you probably paid federal income taxes, therefore suffering double taxation; and $3.04 was retained by the company. The company did not ask you whether you would like to have these funds reinvested. This was decided for you by the board of directors. You do hope, however, that these funds will be used to find more oil and gas, which should increase the profitability of the company and eventually be reflected in the price of the stock.

Exxon is a corporation; therefore, as an investor, your liability is limited to the amount of your investment. If you have invested $10,000, that is all you can lose, even if their stock were to become nonexistent. It is also readily saleable, since it is listed on the New York Stock Exchange. Its value may fluctuate, but it is a liquid investment.

Is there a way that you can obtain the same limited liability while avoiding some of the double taxation, get the benefits of the depreciation and depletion allowance, and avoid the worry of market fluctuation by giving up the privilege of being able to see a daily quote in the paper and for the minimal sacrifice of accepting some limited liquidity?

Yes, there is, through the investment medium of oil and gas income limited partnerships.

• OIL AND GAS
INCOME LIMITED PARTNERSHIPS

In making any investment decision you should attempt to find a vehicle that will supply a product that everyone wants, that everyone needs, and that is in short supply. There is no such thing as an ideal investment, but oil and gas income limited partnerships fit a number of the criteria.

Oil and gas drilling programs have been offered to high-tax-bracket investors for many years, but it has only been in recent years that you have had the opportunity to invest in production without the drilling risks, through a product designed for the smaller, lower-tax-bracket investor.

The concept of owning oil and natural gas reserves is more than 100 years old, but before the advent of oil and gas income limited partnership, ownership in production was limited almost entirely to oil companies, wealthy individuals, and institutional investors.

These partnerships are based on a simple concept, with a series of limited partnerships acquiring existing, producing oil and gas properties for the income that they generate. The production from these wells is sold and the income flows back to you, the limited partner, and to the managing general partner. They offer good income potential, an opportunity for appreciation to stay abreast of inflation and some tax relief.

As in real estate limited partnerships, you, the limited partner, have limited your liability to the amount of your investment. The general partner has unlimited liability, and the expertise. He is to secure the proper producing properties and to operate them on a profitable basis. For doing so, the general partner usually shares 15 percent of the costs and the revenues.

Despite the oil business' reputation for riskiness, in my opinion a well-managed oil income program has less risk than most stock investments. This is true because oil income programs are not particularly subject to market fluctuations. The value of an oil income program depends upon the value of its reserves and the level of income that it produces.

When an oil company drills a discovery well, it will normally drill additional development wells since the oil or gas reservoir usually cannot be fully drained by only one well. Drilling of these development wells can take several years.

After sufficient time has passed, oil reservoirs have enough production history and reservoir data so that reasonably accurate estimates of reserves can be made. Once those estimates are ascertainable, producing properties can be evaluated within an acceptable margin for error. It is at that stage that oil income programs become buyers of producing properties.

In these income limited partnerships, the major portion of the oil and gas proceeds flow directly to you—you receive the depletion and depreciation allowance that shelters part, and sometimes all, of your cash flow and you pay taxes only once on the remainder.

Cash Flow Investment Options • Some programs offer three options for the disposition of your quarterly distributions.

The first option is to reinvest all of your quarterly distributions into subsequent partnerships. This gives you the opportunity to increase your capital base if your objective is asset growth rather than current income.

A second option is to receive a portion of your distributions quarterly or monthly in cash and to reinvest the balance into future partnerships. This is designed to provide you with a way to use a portion of your income while maintaining your capital base. The objective of the partnership is a 10 to 12 percent true yield with cash flow in excess of this amount. If they can achieve this objective, you should be able to take this amount of withdrawal without depleting your investment base.

A third option that you may elect if you need maximum current cash flow is to receive all your distributions in cash quarterly. Each distribution would contain a portion of original capital as well as income earned on the capital.

Past Performance • How would you have fared if you had invested in one of the early offerings in October 1970, and were appraising your results on December 31, 1976?

Hypothetical Investment of $10,000 in an Oil & Gas Income Program

Option I–: All distributions reinvested:

Distributions reinvested	$20,657
Repurchase price	$59,566

Option II–Accepting 12 percent withdrawal:

Distributions in cash	$ 7,200
Distributions reinvested	$ 9,911
Total	$17,111
Repurchase price	$48,227

Option III–All distributions in cash:

Distributions in cash	$14,734
Repurchase price	$38,168

Another program that we have used had hoped for a 13–14 percent cash flow (including depreciation and depletion) with 40 percent of the income tax sheltered, and a 5.3-year payout. This means that the program's specialists hoped to have your $10,000 back through cash flow by then. This is called *restored liquidity.* They also hoped that you would have recovered your $10,000 in quarterly checks (they did not offer the reinvestment option) and would continue to pay out a cash flow for 10 to 15 years more. The results through the first quarter of 1977 were as shown in Table 14–1 with a large percentage of the cash flow tax sheltered.

At the end of the second quarter of 1975, you could have had $9444 of your investment restored with $556 to go. By the first quarter of 1977 you would have received $31,784.00 and reserve estimates were $31,381.00.

What Should You Expect Today? • Should you expect to do this well if you were to invest in an oil and gas income limited partnership today? I really don't know. I do know that the 1970 and 1971 timing was exceptionally good, and that these were and still are excellent management teams. They did, however, reap the advantages of greatly accelerated oil prices, for which they cannot claim credit. I truly hope that oil prices won't accelerate as rapidly in the future; however, it appears to me that there will still be significant price increases.

Table 14–1.

	$10,000 investment quarterly distributions	Accumulative distributions
1971	44.00	44.00
	400.00	444.00
	400.00	844.00
	650.00	1,494.00
1972	400.00	1,894.00
	400.00	2,294.00
	400.00	2,694.00
	800.00	3,494.00
1973	450.00	3,944.00
	500.00	4,444.00
	500.00	4,944.00
	800.00	5,744.00
1974	1600.00	7,344.00
	2100.00	9,444.00
	1930.00	11,374.00
	1840.00	13,214.00
1975	1920.00	15,134.00
	1890.00	17,024.00
	2350.00	19,374.00
	2340.00	21,714.00
1976	2290.00	24,004.00
	1890.00	25,894.00
	1840.00	27,734.00
	1920.00	29,654.00
1977	2130.00	31,784.00

Another investor, who made a $10,000 investment in another oil and gas limited partnership managed by still another oil company in 1973, received back a year later over $16,000. Amoco bought one of the fields in the fund. If you decide that this investment fits your needs, I hope you will be as fortunate.

Leveraged and Nonleveraged Programs • Oil income programs can be of two types: leveraged and nonleveraged. Leveraged oil income programs use bank production loans to finance a portion of the purchase price.

In the first example above leverage was used; it works something like this: For every $1 that you invest, about $.80 remains after start-up costs for doing the research on production and general expenses (it's actually running about $.84). This $.80 is supplemented by borrowing of up to $.80 to provide total purchasing power of about $1.60 for each gross dollar invested. The bank loans allow the general partner to purchase larger reserves from which to obtain cash flow. The loans are usually paid back to the banks in the first five years, approximately half of the cash flow being used. For a well-managed program this should not reduce cash flow unnecessarily, and you could have the potential for an increase in cash flow after the bank borrowings are repaid. This type of financing can produce favorable results. We all know that our country runs on energy. We also should be aware that the energy business runs on money. Several companies have done a superb job of combining the two.

Restored Liquidity • Restored liquidity is a difficult concept to understand. This means how much of your original investment has been "restored" to you—in other words, how long did it take for you to get your money back? For example, if you had invested $10,000 in the October, 1970 program discussed above, your restored liquidity was as shown in Table 14-2.

Table 14-2. $10,000 Investment

Year	Annual cash flow	Cumulative cash flow	Restored liquidity
2nd	$1920	1,920	19.2%
3rd	1610	3,530	35.3
4th	1400	4,930	49.3
5th	3630	8,560	85.6
6th	3480	12,040	120.3

Perhaps you did not need current income, chose not to reinvest in the next program, and could not think of anything more constructive to do with your checks than put your quarterly distributions back into a savings account. If you did, by the middle of the sixth year you would have put all of your funds back into your savings account, where it would be drawing interest, and you would still be receiving a cash flow from your oil and gas program. You now have the potential for two incomes from the same original $10,000.

Compare this restored liquidity with an investment of $10,000 in a corporate bond paying 8 percent. It would have taken you 12½ years to receive interest checks totaling $10,000. Always keep indelibly pressed on your mind the time-use of money.

Buying Reserves • How does the general partner determine how much to pay for oil and gas properties? First of all, if his financial objective is to provide you with a yield of 12 percent, he must discount the amount that he will pay for the oil in excess of 12 percent for each year that they must wait to get the oil out of the ground, send it to market, and send you your quarterly check.

Discounting is nothing more than compounding in reverse. When you learned the "Rule of 72" earlier, you learned that money that is invested and compounded at 12 percent per year will double every six years. Conversely, if we wish to see our money compound at 12 percent per year, we would pay only half today what we would expect to realize in six years. With this in mind, we would only be willing to pay $.50 for a dollar of net revenue to be realized in six years. If a dollar of revenue would not be realized for twelve years we would only be willing to pay $.25 today for that future dollar of revenue. If the dollar of revenue is not to be realized for 18 years, we would only pay $.12½ today for that future dollar of revenue. With this formula we would only be willing to pay $.87½ for $3 of future revenue, that would be realized, $1 each in the sixth, twelfth and eighteenth years.

In diagram form this would look something like Table 14–3.

For Your Added Protection • For your added protection, the discounting does not stop here and the general partner, who is acquiring the production on your behalf, then begins what is called "haircutting," or applying a risk factor. He does this because he knows that engineering of reserves is more of a scientific art than an exact science, so he wants to build in protection by haircutting the 87½ cents.

With this discounting of future net reserves and haircutting the resulting figures they provide a substantial degree of protection to an investor acquiring producing oil and gas properties.

The actual risks hinge on two elements: (1) Is the engineering accurate? (2) Will the energy be sold for the prices anticipated? However, it would seem that the error in either of these areas would have to be extremely large in order for an investor not to realize a return of his capital over the partnership's life. Therefore, if you are considering this as a viable investment, to me the real risk is not so much if you will get your money back, but rather if the profitability will be as large as anticipated.

Table 14–3. Purchase Price per $1

Years before recovery	Amount would pay	Reserves
1		
2		
3		
4		
5		
6	$.50	$1.00
7		
8		
9		
10		
11		
12	.25	1.00
13		
14		
15		
16		
17		
18	.12½	1.00
	.87½	for $3.00

Companies offering oil and gas income programs attempt to minimize errors in engineering by using several different experts to estimate reserves. If multiple evaluations arrive at comparable results, then the risk of surprises should be minimized.

First, they look at the history of the wells they are considering for purchase for the program. If this looks promising, their in-house engineering staff does an in-depth study. If it still looks good, they submit it to one or more independent engineering firms for study and calculation of reserves. Once they, too, feel that the properties are attractive, the general partner submits the properties for study to the oil and gas department of the bank that will be doing the matching financing, if leverage is to be used. If all of these agree, then an offer is made at a price that they feel will allow them to fulfill their financial objective for their investors.

All of these studies do not guarantee that errors of judgment cannot be made, but I do know from discussing this matter with independent oil consultants that they make very conservative estimates for banks and then discount these estimates sometimes as much as 30 percent.

Partnerships usually diversify into a number of acquisitions with 50 to 250 wells in each partnership.

In analyzing the risks you may be taking in any investment, always look at potential supply and demand. From all the projections I have so diligently studied, I am convinced that demand should exceed supply, which in turn should be translated into higher oil and gas prices over the next ten- to fifteen-year period.

Depreciation and Depletion • Depreciation in an oil and gas program is similar to that which you obtain in a real estate investment. The depreciation schedule for each piece of equipment depends on its expected life.

Depletion allowances are unique to natural resources and have been allowed because the resource is being depleted; therefore, a portion is considered to be a return of capital.

As you are probably aware, percentage (statutory) depletion has constantly been under attack by Congress for several years. With the Tax Reduction Act of 1975, percentage depletion is no longer allowed for those buying already producing oil and gas properties. However, they are allowed cost depletion.

If Congress continues to chip away further at percentage depletion alllowance, then you should anticipate paying more for gas at the pumps.

Since the oil and gas income funds now use cost depletion instead of statutory or percentage depletion, their tax shelter benefits should not be greatly affected. Cost depletion works similarly to a depreciation schedule.

Depletion is one of the reasons for the high cash flow usually received from an income program. After the funds placed in the program are invested in properties, the company may begin to send checks at the rate of 12 to 16 percent on the original investment. However, you should realize that a portion of this money is a return of your own capital.

It is important to distinguish between return of capital and return on capital. Both are represented in the distributions sent to limited partners. Obviously, if a program returns only 20 percent per year for five years and then stops, it would not be a good investment.

A good rule of thumb is that a successful oil and gas income program should return at least double the original investment over the life of the partnership. Some of our earlier programs, as you have seen, should do far better than this.

Some oil and gas limited partnerships are sold in units, with each unit $50, $500, or $1000, while others will accept any amount above their minimum. In most states the minimum investment per partnership is $2500. Companies offer a new partnership every month or every quarter, and some states require that the minimum be invested in each new one. Other states let you add as you go along once you've met the original minimum per offering. The wells in each partnership are selected for a broad blend of payouts. Some wells should have a high cash flow and deplete more rapidly. Others should deplete over a much longer period of time. The operators continuously work to increase production. The reason for this is that in some programs, management's compensation and interest in the program parallels that of the limited partnership investor. As they increase productivity for you they increase their own revenues.

• TAX-SHELTERED
CASH FLOW

The goal of any investment program is to obtain a good cash flow, tax sheltered with appreciation potential. To date, tax-sheltered cash flow has been a delight to many owners of previous income programs. They must realize, though, that the IRS never truly forgives a tax. The limited partners are reducing their tax basis, and will have a capital gains tax on selling, if the sales price is above the cost basis that is left. My philosophy is to take the tax-sheltered cash flow now. In the meantime, you'll have the time-use of your money, and we will surely be able to think of a way to avoid paying the tax again, or at least reduce it when and if that time should come.

• MINIMUM
REPURCHASE PRICE

Some programs offer you the guarantee that if within ten years after you invested in one of their partnerships your total distributions plus your repurchase price does not equal 100 percent of your investment, they will add an amount necessary to reach that minimum repurchase price.

Doubling Your Pleasure • Let's think big for a moment and thinking big is a powerful impetus for success. Let's assume that you have $100,000 and are in the 40 percent tax bracket. (If you don't have $100,000, but only $10,000, just drop the last digit in these calculations.) Let's invest the $100,000 in a single-premium deferred annuity. This is where the interest compounds without tax until it is withdrawn. Let's further assume that this annuity is paying 7.5 percent. To be conservative, let's assume that interest rates will drop (*The Kiplinger Letter* predicts the opposite) to 6 percent for the next four years and down to 4 percent for the next 20 years. Let's also assume that you borrow 90 percent of the investment you've made at a rate of 6 percent per year and that the annuity company keeps paying you 4 percent on the funds borrowed, and their regular rate on the 10 percent left in. Now let's look at the value of your annuity plus the value of your $90,000 loan after paying $5400 interest per year and the taxes due in your 40 percent bracket, with the $90,000 invested at interest rates of 7 percent, at 7.5 percent, and at 8 percent. (See Table 14–4.) These results are before taxes. I recommend instead investing these funds where the cash flow from the investments is at least partially or entirely tax sheltered. This provides you with a tax deduction for the interest paid the annuity company on one side and a tax-sheltered cash flow on the other.

Now let's further assume that you were fortunate enough to have placed these borrowed funds into an oil and gas partnership in 1970, which had obtained the results in Table 14–5 and from which you had withdrawn $5400 to pay your interest on your loan against your single-premium deferred annuity. Results: $344,035 oil and gas plus $28,437 annuity = $372,472.

If you were to invest today, would you have comparable results? Probably not, for there have been significant price increases in oil and gas in the past. However, looking at the various alternatives for your money, it is one you may want to consider for some of your after-tax dollars. Again, let me caution you that this is the past. There is no way that you or I can predict the future.

Disadvantages of Oil and Gas Income Programs • There are two disadvantages to oil income programs of which you should be aware. These are investment lag time and liquidity.

Oil income programs ordinarily raise all of their money before they identify the properties that they intend to buy. After the partnership is organized, funds are usually invested in Treasury bills or certificates of deposit. The program manager then looks for suitable purchases. He may be able to find high-quality properties immediately, but we have found that it may take as long as a year. During that year you do not have oil income; however, you do receive interest on your funds.

A more important disadvantage of some oil income programs is their limited liquidity, since there is no ready market for limited partnership interests.

In the programs we prefer, the general partner is contractually

Table 14-4. A Hypothetical One-time Investment of $100,000 in an SPDA; Borrowing $90,000 for Subsequent Investment Purposes

Year	Annuity net C.V. beginning of year	Annuity amount earned	Annuity year end net C.V.	Annuity interest paid	Combined year-end value of a $90,000 loan compounding at selected rates after paying $5400 interest per year and the taxes due in your 40% bracket		
					7.00%	7.50%	8.00%
1	$ 6,000	$4,050	$10,050	$(5,400)	$100,590	$100,860	$101,130
2	$10,050	$4,203	$14,253	$(5,400)	$105,356	$105,909	$106,465
3	$14,253	$4,455	$18,708	$(5,400)	$110,397	$111,249	$112,106
4	$18,708	$4,722	$23,431	$(5,400)	$115,731	$116,896	$118,072
5	$23,431	$5,006	$28,437	$(5,400)	$121,373	$122,868	$124,380
6	$28,437	$4,737	$33,174	$(5,400)	$126,774	$128,615	$130,483
7	$33.174	$4,927	$38,101	$(5,400)	$132,392	$134,596	$136,841
8	$38,101	$5,124	$43,225	$(5,400)	$138,236	$140,823	$143,465
9	$43,225	$5,329	$48,554	$(5,400)	$144,316	$147,304	$150,365
10	$48,554	$5,542	$54,096	$(5,400)	$150,640	$154,050	$157,554
11	$54,096	$5,764	$59,860	$(5,400)	$157,219	$161,071	$165,044
12	$59,860	$5,994	$65,854	$(5,400)	$164,062	$168,380	$172,847
13	$65,854	$6,234	$72,089	$(5,400)	$171,181	$175,988	$180,977
14	$72,089	$6,484	$78,572	$(5,400)	$178,586	$183,907	$189,447
15	$78,572	$6,743	$85,315	$(5,400)	$186,290	$192,150	$198,272

The assumptions used to determine the above results were as follows:
Annuity Interest Earned Each Year

First Year	7.50%
2–5 Years	6.00%
Thereafter	4.00%

Annuity Interest Earned on Loan Each Year   4.00%
Interest Charged on Annuity Loan Each Year   6.00%
Your Taxable Income Will be Between $22,000 and $26,000

Flexibility. The contract owner may from time to time as explained in the Transfer Between Accounts section of the prospectus invest the cash value into a group of investment companies' funds without charge and at some later date, if desirable, switch back again to a fixed guaranteed rate.

obligated to repurchase the value of your investment after the partnership's inception, subject to its financial ability to do so. You should always view your investment as a long-term one, but of course you never know when you might need to convert your investment into cash.

After the acquisitions are made, the general partner may give you a cash selling price each year. You may choose to cash in your units or continue to retain them. We find that our clients usually choose to retain

Table 14–5. Hypothetical Results of a One-Time Investment of $90,000 in an Oil and Gas Program Taking $5400 of Annual Cash Flow

Year	Beginning year cash sales price	Cumulative cash flow received	Cash flow reinvested	Year-end cash sales price
1971	$ 72,000	$ 5,400	$12,923	$ 81,522
1972	$ 81,522	$10,800	$11,692	$ 91,099
1973	$ 91,099	$16,200	$11,156	$226,320
1974	$226,320	$21,600	$34,539	$280,023
1975	$280,023	$27,000	$38,185	$344,035

These assumptions do not take into consideration a tax deduction earned in 1970 of $18,180 and subsequent year taxable income of 1971; $3534; 1972; $3546; 1973; $2052; 1974; $18,200; 1975; $1453.

them, since they do not know of another investment that has offered them a comparable cash flow, tax shelter, and potential for appreciation.

In summary, if you desire a relatively low-risk investment in energy, give serious thought to oil and gas programs for your "hard" after-tax dollars.

These programs have made it possible for investors to join together and combine their resources in order to acquire a diversified portfolio of producing oil and gas properties that are managed professionally. Typically, the programs are designed for the generation of immediate income, but may, through reinvestment of distributable cash flow, offer an excellent opportunity for asset accumulation.

"Hard" and "Soft" Dollars • Above I used the term, "hard dollars." I consider that there are two kinds of dollars: "hard" and "soft." "Hard" dollars are the ones that you have left after you have sent to Washington that portion of your income that the IRS requires. "Soft" dollars are the dollars that you are going to lose to taxes if you don't take some constructive steps to prevent their journey to Washington. These are your before-tax dollars.

If you have "soft" dollars, meaning some of those dollars above $44,000 taxable income when a joint return is filed, or $32,000 on a single return, another way you should consider investing in energy is through oil and gas drilling programs.

If your taxable income is below these figures, you may want to skip to the application at the end of this chapter. If you want to get a preview of the possible tax incentives with which you may want to be familar when you cross into the 50 percent tax bracket, do read on. As inflation continues its destructive path, more and more of our citizens will move across that line. Inflation is "taxation without representation" —and that provoked a little tea party in Boston once upon a time. With inflation our taxes increase even without Congress increasing the percentage tax schedule.

• OIL AND GAS DRILLING
LIMITED PARTNERSHIPS

Historically, oil drilling programs have raised far more money than income programs. In recent years, public and private drilling programs have attracted approximately $1 billion per year, whereas the newer income programs have attracted much less. However, the amount of capital attracted to this investment greatly increased in the mid-1970s as the stock market held less and less appeal and as energy prices soared.

You may be asking, "Aren't drilling programs high risk?". The answer is "Yes, they are!" Searching for oil does involve considerable risk. However, paying taxes is risky, too. (Your chances of getting those tax dollars back are quite slim.) The oil programs attempt to reduce your risk by drilling a large number of holes spaced over wide geographic areas on which a large amount of geological study has been done.

Should you invest in a drilling program? It all depends on your tax bracket, the form of your income, and your temperament. The question was much easier to answer before the passage of the Tax Reform Act of 1976 and its many provisions to reduce incentives for investing.

Feature of the 1976 Tax Reform Act • I always endeavor to make any of my explanations as simple as I possible can. My philosophy is that the height of sophistication is simplicity. However, and it's a big however, there is no way that I have found to make the so-called Tax Reform Act of 1976 simple. It should have been called the Tax Revenue Act, for increasing revenues was its purpose. It is composed of over 1500 pages of legal jargon that touches every facet of our personal and business life. Even summaries of the Act and its major features contain hundreds of pages, and litigation of this ponderous law will probably take years.

Provisions that are applicable to the oil and gas industry are listed below. If you have a corporation, the provisions may vary when applied.

- The deduction for losses incurred in oil and gas operations by taxpayers other than regular corporations is limited to the amount "at risk."

- Intangible drilling costs (IDCs) on productive wells is a tax preference item for taxpayers other than regular corporations.

- The minimum tax rate on preference is increased to 15 percent from 10 percent.

- The minimum tax is applicable to total tax preferences less the greater of $10,000, or one-half of the taxpayer's regular tax liability for the year.

- IDC incurred and deducted after December 13, 1975, in excess of allowable amortization, must be recaptured as ordinary income on sale or other disposition of the property.

- All tax preference items, including IDC on productive wells, reduce earned income subject to the 50 percent maximum tax rate.

- Rules concerning utilization of the foreign tax credit on oil and gas income have been changed. (Refer to your CPA or a tax guide.)

- Technical changes have been made with respect to classification of retail operations and transfer of proven oil and gas properties.

- An overall "at risk" limitation on the deduction by a partner of the individual share of partnership loss is included.

- Retroactive allocation of income or loss to a partner for the portion of the taxable year before entry into the partnership is prohibited.

- Specific rules for treatment of partnership organization and syndication costs are provided.

The Three Most Important Considerations • The items that will probably be of greatest significance to you are

1 • Losses are limited to the amount "at risk" (what you can lose if the venture fails completely).

2 • IDCs on productive wells are now preference items.

3 • Earned income is reduced, shifting a larger portion to higher-bracket unearned status, which raises the total tax payment.

If you are an "average" investor, say in the 50 percent tax bracket, the overall effect is surprisingly small, perhaps less than $100 more tax during the year as a result of participating with a $10,000 contribution as illustrated below.

At Risk Limitation • Partnership tax provisions have allowed you, the limited partners (usually the arrangement in oil and gas programs), to share in nonrecourse debt (taxpayer has no personal liability, lender can rely only on the pledged property for recovery) for purposes of "leveraging" deductions beyond the amount that is at risk.

Heretofore, some promoters of tax shelters used this method to create and market investments on the basis of tax economics rather than on the merits of the program, or the reputation of its manager.

Under the new law, deductions claimed by all taxpayers other than regular corporations, in certain specified industries including oil and gas, cannot exceed the actual amount at risk by the taxpayer. This eliminates using nonrecourse financing to generate deductions on or applicable to the property subject to the debt.

This places a stronger burden than ever before on the economics rather than the tax advantages of tax-sheltered investments. The economics of oil and gas can withstand this burden.

IDC on Productive Wells • Intangible drilling costs incurred on productive wells by a taxpayer other than a regular corporation, in 1976 and subsequent years, is a tax preference item subject to the 15 percent minimum tax rate. The amount of the preference item is the actual IDC incurred on a productive well in excess of the amount deductible if the IDC were capitalized and either claimed as cost depletion or amortized over a period of 120 months from first production. This computation must be made on a well-by-well basis.

This provision does reduce the tax benefits of IDC deductions, but does not eliminate them. Only IDC on productive wells is affected, so a taxpayer still receives the full benefit of the IDC deduction on nonproductive wells, and the productive well may generate large amounts of income or gain, relative to the amount invested.

Yes, it's true that under the new law only IDC dry holes can be charged off in the year they are drilled. If the well is completed as a producing well, it must be capitalized according to this formula. (Yes, we do have an energy shortage! You then might ask why production is being penalized. Never make the mistake of thinking that tax laws are logical. Just learn them, apply them, and when they change, change your strategy. Flexibility is the key for financial survival.)

Actually, since we invested with the hopes of finding production, we should not be displeased with a lot of preference items, since it will mean that we have completed a number of successful wells.

Effect on Earned Income • Prior to the 1976 Act, 50 percent rate earned income was reduced by the greater of: average excess of five-years preferences or current-year preferences over $30,000. Now earned income is reduced dollar for dollar by all tax preference items. This provision may or may not be a significant deterrent to your investing in tax shelters if you have large amounts of earned income.

• HOW TRA '76 MAY AFFECT YOU

Let's assume that you are a professional and your income is mostly what is called earned income, meaning salary, wages, or commissions received for services you rendered. Let's further assume that you are married, file a joint return, and have taxable income of $85,000, of which $75,000 is earned and $10,000 unearned income. (You saved some money, invested it, and it earned $10,000.) What would be the effect on your tax liability if you invested $10,000 in a drilling program and had no other tax preference items?

Let's further assume that the drilling is completed in the year that you made your investment and that you are credited with $7500 worth of IDCs, which include $6000 dry-hole IDC and $1500 producing-well IDC. See Table 14–6.

The first year you would have invested $10,000 but saved $4,278 in taxes for a net investment of $5722 of your money and $4278 of Uncle Sam's.

Tax Aspects of Disposing of Your Property • Using the same assumptions, let's assume that you sold your production after four years in the program for $20,000. See Table 14–7.

In this example, where you found production, your investment earned a net after-tax profit of $9129 on your $10,000 investment, or an average annual yield of 23 percent.

I must again emphasize that drilling programs are inherently high risk with also high potential for gains. You must ask yourself if you are emotionally suited to risking $5722 for the potential of getting back $10,000, $20,000, or more or nothing if each hole drilled is a duster.

Table 14–6.   Example of $10,000 Investment—First Year

	Without investment	With investment
Taxable income		
Earned	$75,000	$75,000
Unearned	10,000	10,000
Total	85,000	85,000
IDC deduction	–	–7,500
Net taxable income	$85,000	$77,500
Components of taxable income		
Earned income	$75,000	$73,575 *
Unearned income	10,000	3,925 †
Total	$85,000	$77,500
Tax computation		
Earned income		
First $52,000	$18,060	$18,060
Excess over $52,000 @ 50%	11,500	10,788
Unearned income		
$64,000–$76,000 @ 55%	550	1,334
Above $76,000 @ 58%	5,220	870
Total tax	$35,330	$31,052
Tax savings due to investment		$ 4,278

* Tax preference = IDC on producing well ($1500) less amortization for first year
($1500/120 × 6) = $1425
   Earned income =$75,000 – $1,425 = $73,575
† Unearned income = $2500 + 1425 $ 3,925.

Table 14–7.

	Without investment	With investment
Cash received		
Ordinary income ($85,000 × 4)	$340,000	$340,000
Sale of property	–	$ 20,000
	$340,000	$360,000
Cash disbursed		
Federal income tax	$141,320	$142,191
Cash invested	–	$ 10,000
	$141,320	$152,191
Net cash after tax	$198,680	$207,809
Net cash generated by investment in program	–	$ 9,129

• REDUCING
RISKS

Drilling limited partnerships use various ways of distributing their drilling dollars in an attempt to reduce risks.

Some divide each program's capital into three parts. One-third goes into development wells, where they feel the odds on finding reserves are 1:2, with the value of the reserve ranging from 5:1 to 20:1 and return on risk on invested dollars ranging from 1:1 to 2:1. Another third is invested in controlled wildcats, where they feel the odds on finding reserves are 1:4, value of reserves 5:1 to 30:1, and return on risk on invested dollars 1:1 to 3:1. The last third is invested in wildcats, with odds on finding reserves moving up to 1:15, value of reserves 5:1 to 50:1, and return on risk on invested dollars 1:1 to 5:1.

If all their odds worked perfectly, they would drill a minimum of 21 wells and find 3 producers and 18 dry holes. However, it would have been worth the risk they took, for the 3 producers should return to them one to three times their investment.

As you can see from the above, it should greatly enhance your potential if each drilling program in which you invest has sufficient capital to drill a large number of wells. Drilling for oil and gas takes skillful geologic research, but your chances are greatly increased as you increase the number of wells drilled.

Structure of a Drilling Program • There are many ways to structure a program with regard to who bears the cost, who receives the tax advantages, and who receives the income.

In the program described above, the general partner trades the limited partners (which would be you if you chose this medium) all of the tax advantages and 60 percent of the revenues for a free look at the bottom of the hole.

Let's use an example of a successful well drilled at a cost to the partnership of $100,000. The limited partner would provide $60,000, deduct all the intangible drilling costs, and receive 60 percent of all revenues. The general partner would bear all the tangible costs of $40,000 that are capitalized over the life of the assets and receive 40 percent of all the revenues.

Many oil and gas managements offer four to five drilling programs per year. Others will offer larger but fewer programs.

In no sooner than 18 months to $2\frac{1}{2}$ years after the initial investment has been made in a drilling program, the company has had time to complete a cycle that consists of the following: (1) drilling the wells in each prospect, (2) arranging financing for any subsequent drilling, (3) carrying out subsequent drilling, (4) being evaluated and (5) perhaps offering to exchange for stock or cash a buy-out at a stated amount. Some programs exchange for stock that did not previously exist; hence there is no way of establishing a true market value for it. If this course is used, no taxable gain is made at the time of exchange. Another way is for the limited partners to be offered registered stock in exchange for partnership interests. When this is done, a capital gains tax is realized, and you would have a tax liability. When the latter course is followed, the price is determined by the average of the bid and asked prices of the stock for two months previous to the exchange. There is no question of true value of the stock for which it is exchanged, while in the case of new stock this can certainly be a factor. In the past, this has been a very definite shortcoming with too ambitious pricing on the new stock.

You must usually decide within a specified period of time whether to make the exchange for stock. If you do not, you will continue to receive the oil income, but you may not have an opportunity to exchange at a later date.

A third choice may be offered and that is for the general partner to buy your production for cash. The value will be based on the evaluation placed on the reserves by an independent geological engineering firm and discounted back to give credit for the earning power of money.

Your choice will probably be dependent on your income needs at the particular time and your tax considerations.

The program described above is only one of the ways a drilling program can be structured by a sponsor. There are six different ways commonly in use.

Let's first look at the one described above, and then look at five other ways:

Tangible–Intangible Sharing • For income tax purposes, the IRS refers to two basic types of costs in connection with drilling for oil and gas. These are tangible costs and intangible costs. Tangible costs are expenditures for items that can be salvaged. The intangibles, the nonsalvageable costs, may be deducted as described above. In the tangible–intangible sharing, the general partner bears the tangible expenses, and the limited partners bear the intangible expenses.

Working Interests • In this structuring, the general partner shares in the operating expenses and net profits of the producing wells. This formula may or may not entail investment by the general partner. If the general partner pays no part of further costs, it is called a "carried working interest."

Net Profits Interests • This formula entails no expenses on the part of the general partner. The investor pays all drilling costs and bears all expenses of operating the wells. The general partner receives a stated percentage of net profits.

Carried Interests • In this case, the investor carries the general partner, usually to the casing point, at which time the general partner is permitted to buy into the partnership at the original price.

Disproportionate Sharing • This is a common feature. The investor bears one-third of the total cost of a program and in return receives one-fourth of any profits.

Overriding Royalty Interest • Under this formula the investor pays the cost of drilling and completing wells, and the sponsor receives a percentage of gross revenues. Generally speaking, I prefer programs in which the general partner bears some portion of the risk along with the limited partners. It seems more equitable and also tends to make the general partner more careful in his expenditure of partnership capital.

If You Have Capital Gains • If you have sizable gains and earned income in the year that you are contemplating investing in a drilling program, be sure to have your CPA run the numbers for you. Instead of investing 50¢ dollars, you could be investing 70¢ dollars under the TRA of 1976 with all its preference item provisions.

Corporations • Corporations did not bear the brunt of TRA 1976, so if you have a profitable corporation you may want to consider a drilling program for the corporation. The corporate tax rate presently is 20 percent on the first $25,000 of taxable income, 22 percent on the next $25,000, and 48 percent on taxable income over $50,000. See Table 14–8.

Out-of-pocket cost to the corporation from a $50,000 investment is $28,400.

Do your tax planning early. This gives you an opportunity to look over the many viable possibilities. If you are considering drilling programs, it also gives the companies time to do the drilling before year end and give you possibly a larger write-off that year. It also gives you the additional benefit of having your annual investment deductible in advance against your estimated quarterly tax liability. I usually recommend investing smaller amounts in several partnerships rather than a large amount in one. This allows you to spread your risk over a larger number of wells.

Table 14–8.

	Without investment	With investment
Taxable income	$100,000	$100,000
Deductions from $50,000	–	$ 45,000
Revised taxable income	$100,000	$ 55,000
Federal tax		
First $25,000 @ 20%	$ 5,000	$ 5,000
Second $25,000 @ 22%	$ 5,500	$ 5,500
Remaining $50,000 @ 48%	$ 24,000	$ 2,400
Taxes	$ 34,500	$ 12,900

Depletion Allowance • If production is found in your drilling program, then another possible tax advantage occurs that we call depletion allowance. In addition to the write-off of a portion of your intangible drilling costs, presently the first 22 percent of the gross income each year from oil and gas is tax sheltered due to the depletion allowance.

Depletion allowance has been given over the years because the asset is being depleted. This same principle is also applied to other areas. However, Congress seems to get emotional when it is applied to oil and gas, and has reduced the allowance for oil and gas so that by 1984 percentage depletion will be 15 percent vs. the current 22 percent.

Although the Tax Reduction Act of 1975 virtually eliminated percentage depletion for major oil companies and other large oil producers, an important exemption was created for small producers which enables most investors in public drilling programs to retain this significant tax benefit. The so-called "small producer exemption" allows the continuation of percentage depletion on a specified quantity of average daily production of crude oil and natural gas. For 1977, this quantity is set at 1600 barrels of crude oil and gas equivalent per day and then gradually declines each year until it reaches 1000 barrels per day for 1980 and thereafter. The small producer exemption is separately applied to each limited partner; therefore, an investor would personally require annual oil and gas revenue in excess of several million dollars before losing the exemption.

Transfers of public drilling programs between members of the same family, or among certain other related parties do not affect the percentage depletion benefit. This is very important from a financial planning point of view. However, there are circumstances under which you as an investor might possibly lose part or all of your percentage depletion. The small producer exemption does not apply, for example, to a transferee who obtains an interest in a proven oil or gas property through a transfer made after December 31, 1974 if it was not made between certain related parties. In addition, if you are engaged in refining crude oil, have an interest in foreign production, are involved in the retail sale of oil and gas products, or have a percentage depletion deduction that exceeds 65 percent of your adjusted taxable income, the depletion benefits are reduced or eliminated. You should consult your own tax advisor to determine the extent, if any, of the application of these limitations to your situation.

You should also be aware that a portion of percentage depletion is now a tax preference subject to the 15 percent minimum tax and will also reduce the benefits available under the 50 percent maximum tax rate on earned income.

Upside Potential • The industry is too young to have developed meaningful statistics as to what your chances are of getting your money back.

On the upside what can you hope for? The best drilling program I know of is one that discovered a major gas field in California in 1962. With a $58,000 investment in the program it is estimated that by 1983, the return will be roughly $3 million, based on old oil prices—a 51 to 1 return. Obviously, the possibility of your being so lucky is remote.

Importance of Management • As in any business venture, management is the single most important consideration. Determine before you invest if the general partner has substantial assets, a good reputation in the industry, and an excellent performance record.

You will find drilling program management difficult to evaluate, because future performance cannot be directly related to past success. Management's drilling success ratio does not lend itself to making a judgment regarding profitability potential. A company that drills successful wells 90 percent of the time, for example, may not have any profitable wells; but a company with a 10 percent record of drilling success can be profitable.

I try to avoid both high and low success ratios. (Not that I consider this very scientific, but it has been effective.) A balanced drilling program that consistently achieves a success ratio of 85 percent to 95 percent may be concentrating on low-risk/low-return prospects. On the other hand, if the company has a low success ratio, it may indicate that they are drilling too many high-risk prospects or that they are not successful oil finders.

Even this approach does not lend itself to accurate selectivity. The majority of drilling programs now in existence were started since 1968.

This means that few of the programs have been in operation long enough for you to judge their success. Drilling programs take time before all prospects have been developed and transportation channels worked out, to permit production of the reserves discovered.

Too, the Securities and Exchange Commission requirements for publishing reserve estimates for past programs in prospectuses are extremely hard to comply with. Cash pay-out tables can often be very misleading, especially if the program is a nonassessable one that relies heavily on bank borrowings to finance their development work. This could mean that a large portion of the initial revenues have been used to repay loans; therefore, the investor has not yet realized much of his potential return.

Should You Invest in Exploration? • Not everyone should invest in drilling programs. You should look at your personal finances very critically before reaching a decision. Factors you should consider are

1 • *Do you have a stable high-level income taxed in the 50 percent or above tax bracket?* I would recommend that you should anticipate this high income for at least three years.

    The reason I recommend that you should have a high income for at least three years is the fact that even good program managements will have bad years. You should plan to diversify your drilling program investments over several years with the same company. Consistent investment with the same company increases your chances of overall success.

2 • *Do you have substantial assets?* You should not consider investing unless you have assets of $50,000 plus a 50 percent tax bracket or, in the absence of the latter, a net worth of over $300,000. You should also probably have equity in a home, adequate life and medical insurance, and cash reserves.

3 • *Are you temperamentally suited to investing in exploration?* That is, are you willing to assume the risks involved, and do you have the patience to wait for the exploration to be done? If you should draw a blank in your drilling program, will it cause you to lose sleep? You should invest in anticipation of gains, but you must be prepared to accept losses.

Drilling programs are relatively illiquid, and if you are forced to sell your interest in a hurry, you may have to do so at a substantial discount.

You should anticipate being locked in for a period of time sufficient to allow the completion and development of most of the drilling prospects. Otherwise, until drilling is completed, the program's value cannot be accurately determined.

Before investing in any tax shelter, discuss the matter with your CPA, but do find one who has tax savings for you as his chief concern, not just tax tallying.

I have a doctor client in a very high tax bracket who has needed some tax-sheltered investments every year I've had him for a client. Whenever I would suggest a particular shelter to him, he would ask that I submit it to his CPA, which I was happy to do. Unfortunately, his CPA was an uncreative soul who could tell him to the penny how much taxes he owed at the end of the year, but he could not imagine taking any "risks" to prevent paying taxes. So the CPA always turned down each proposal. Finally, I told the doctor, "By saying 'no' to all my proposals, your CPA will never be wrong, but he'll never be right either." The doctor admitted that this was true and joined with me in investing in the oil and gas drilling program that discovered a gas field in Louisiana.

Investing in oil and gas exploration is attractive today because the demand has drastically outstripped supply. Oil and gas account for three-fourths of all the energy we consume, and the demand is growing at an unprecedented rate, both here and in foreign countries. It is estimated that on a worldwide basis, there will be more oil consumed during the decade of the 1970s than has been consumed during the entire previous 115 years since petroleum was discovered.

An intelligent approach to financial planning cannot ignore the potential rewards of investing in energy.

Application

1 • Should some of your "hard" dollars be invested in oil and gas income-producing programs?

2 • What dollar amount should you invest this year?

3 • Should you invest in energy stocks? If so, which four offer the greatest potential for price appreciation?

Stock	Market Price	Yield	Price/Earning Ratio
1. _____	$_____	_____%	_____
2. _____	_____	_____	_____
3. _____	_____	_____	_____
4. _____	_____	_____	_____

4 • If you have some income that will be taxed at 50 percent or above, how much of it should be invested in drilling programs? Determine this by early consultation with your CPA. You may do some preliminary figures by using this tentative worksheet. Under TRA 1976, I have not been able to design a worksheet that seems to fit all of my clients.

Drilling Program Worksheet

	Without investment	With investment
Taxable income		
Earned	$_____	$_____
Unearned	$_____	$_____
Total	$_____	$_____
IDC deduction (est.)	$_____	$_____
Net taxable income	$_____	$_____
Components of taxable income		
Earned income (est.)	$_____	$_____
Unearned income (est.)	$_____	$_____
Total	$_____	$_____
Tax computation		
Earned income		
First $52,000	$_____	$_____
Excess over $25,000 @ 50%	$_____	$_____
_____ @ 55%	$_____	$_____
Above_____ @ _____	$_____	$_____
Total tax	$_____	$_____
Tax savings due to investment		$_____

15

How to Become a Millionaire

It is only fair to tell you that I've never helped anyone become wealthy overnight. I've never helped someone with $10,000 turn it quickly into a million. The only people I've ever helped make a million dollars in a relatively brief period of time are those who brought me a million dollars to invest. Before you become too impressed, remember that it takes only an average return of 10 percent compounded to double your money in 7.2 years. At 12 percent it takes 6 years, and at 15 percent, 4.8 years.

I remember calling the office of Percy Foreman, the nationally known and brilliant criminal lawyer. I was calling to invite him to be my guest on my weekly television program, "Successful Texans."

When I asked to speak to him, the receptionist blurted out "He's in jail." After chuckling over this literal response, I left word for him to call me when he "got out of jail." Later that afternoon he called, and I invited him to be my guest. He accepted my invitation; and just as I was about to say my goodbye, he said, "Aren't you that lady stockbroker? Can you make me rich?" I answered, "Mr. Foreman, I understand you are already rich; but I believe I can make you richer."

Let's assume that you do not have the elusive million with which to start your high adventure. Is it still possible for you to become a millionaire? The answer is probably Yes, if you have the discipline to save, the inclination to study, and a life span of sufficient length.

First, let me say that there are more desirable goals in life than becoming a millionaire. But if this is your desire, there are some very practical ways to approach your objective. To reach any goal, the first step is to divide it into its component parts so that it can be approached one step at a time.

• COMPONENT PARTS
OF A MILLION DOLLARS

What are the component parts of a million dollars? It's $1000 multiplied by 1000, isn't it? Trying to reach a million dollars in your lifetime may not be all that difficult to do.

How do you obtain the first $1000? The most obvious beginning is to save from current income. If you save slightly under $20 per week, you should have your $1000 in a year. Or if you do not want to wait until you have saved the $1000, you can start investing as you earn on a weekly or monthly basis from your current income. Another possibility is to borrow the $1000 from the bank at the beginning and pay the bank back on a monthly basis. This could give you a head start toward your goal.

Therefore, the first requirement for reaching your goal is the ability to set aside the relatively small amount of $20 per week.

• MONEY,
YIELD, TIME

The second requirement is to obtain a high return produced by adherence to aggressive but sound investment practices. These can be readily learned if your desire is strong enough.

Third, a life span of sufficient length.

So you see, the two most important things are time and yield. If you set your sights on a million dollars, you must keep these two factors in mind. Time is something over which you have very little control. But yield is different. I personally feel that anyone of good intelligence has the potential of earning a high return on his investment, and high returns are absolute musts if you ever expect to become a millionaire. When we speak of "yield," we ordinarily think of income (dividends or interest) as an annual return on the sum invested, expressed in the form of a percentage. For instance, if you receive $5 at the end of a year on a $100 investment, your yield is 5 percent. However, we shall broaden this definition for the purpose of this chapter and use "yield" to describe any distribution, plus any growth in market value. For example, if $100 grows to $318 in 10 years, we would say its "yield" is 12 percent.

One thing I think you must be fully aware of is the magic that comes from compounding the rate of return. This means that you are never to treat any income, capital appreciation, or equity buildup as spendable during the period you are building toward your million-dollar goal, but only as returns that are to be reinvested to increase your accumulation. In other words, don't eat your children. Let them produce more children, and before long you'll have a whole army of dollars working for you.

Forward March!

For the purpose of our calculations, any taxes that you must pay on your investments are deemed as having come from another source.

One of the most important things you must remember is how important the rate of return you receive on your investment is to your compounding. For instance, if you can put to work $1000 each year and average a compound rate of 10 percent per annum, you will be able to reach your goal in 48.7 years. However, if you can increase this compound rate to 20 percent per annum, you can reach your goal in 29.2 years. So you see, it does make a great deal of difference what return you obtain on your money.

• DIVERSIFICATION—BASED ON DEMAND/SUPPLY

Risk in investing can be reduced by following some basic investment principles. As you have already become aware, one of the most important principles is diversification—spreading your risks.

After you've made that important decision, what investment media do you use? You stand back and determine where the demand is greater than the supply. You learned that in Basic Economics 101, something you must never forget: the law of supply and demand. Regardless of how diligently governments and economists have tried over the years, they have never been able to repeal it for any length of time. Russia has tried it and failed, as is evidenced by the millionaires now appearing on the scene in Communist Poland; England has attempted it and brought a once proud empire of plenty to its knees, and our own Congress continues to attempt to repeal this universal law. Their action has caused shortages and disruptions in energy, beef, housing, etc.

In making your determination of where the demand is greater than the supply, be an alert reader of the daily metropolitan newspaper; also read such papers and publications as *The Wall Street Journal, Time, Business Week, U. S. News and World Report, Fortune, Forbes,* and *Money Magazine.* Also begin to study the St. Louis Federal Reserve Board reports. You'll begin to develop an awareness of demands and shortages.

• AVOID THE BLUE CHIP SYNDROME

There are those who have the mistaken idea that all one has to do to make money in the stock market is to buy "blue chips" and throw them in the drawer and forget about them. In my opinion, this can be riskier than buying more aggressive stocks and watching them like a hawk. The "blue chips" of today may become the "red chips" or "white chips" or "buffalo chips" of tomorrow. We live in a dynamic, throbbing, changing economy.

Just think back a few years. What car did the "man of distinction" drive? A Packard. I would have had difficulty convincing my father that only a few years later the manufacturers of the Packard automobile would be out of business. At the same time, what was the chief family home entertainment medium before television? It was radio, wasn't it? And who was the chief manufacturer of that half-egg-shaped wooden box in every home? Atwater-Kent. As you know, the Atwater-Kent Company no longer exists. You live in a world of constant change, and you must always be alert and ahead of this change if you want to become a millionaire through your investment know-how. You must sharpen your talents to predict trends before they happen, and move out before the trend has run its course.

If the money supply is being greatly restrained in our country, as you've already learned, you will want to develop a more conservative approach to the stock market. As the supply is even more diminished, move into money market funds so that you will have adequate liquidity to go back into the market as the money supply is accelerated and also to enjoy the higher yield that money will attract during this period of short supply.

• DOLLAR-COST-AVERAGING

As discussed previously, dollar-cost-averaging is another approach. Timing can be difficult. Dollar-cost-averaging in large and small amounts can be done by anyone who has a regular amount to invest over a period of years. Using this plan, you invest the same amount of money in the same security at the same interval. This will always buy you more shares at a low cost than a high cost and give you an average cost for your securities. If the market eventually goes up (so far, it always has), you should increase your capital.

• CAPITAL
SHORTAGE

Shortage of capital probably will give you more opportunities for the triple-net leases we discussed in our chapter on investing in real estate. When money is tight, it is difficult for even major corporations to float bond issues at good rates, so they may sell their buildings and then lease them back. This gives them working capital and can also provide them with tax advantages. Triple-net leases of buildings of major corporations to me represent a safer investment than corporate bonds; in addition, they offer the investor some tax shelter and the opportunity for equity buildup and appreciation. Any court in the land will evict for nonpayment of rent, but not for nonpayment of interest on bonds.

• HOUSING
SHORTAGE

Another investment potential occurs when housing is in short supply. Again, as we found in our real estate chapter, this can provide investment potential. For example, if you read that the average family income of the nation is $13,800 and the average home is $53,800, then you know that a large number of families cannot qualify for a home loan even if they were to be granted interest-free mortgages. So their only alternative is a garden-type apartment or trailer home. Often, if they want to live in the most desirable part of town, and have access to a swimming pool and tennis court, they have no other alternative than to rent a garden-type apartment.

• ENERGY

Another area is the shortage of energy that we have already described in the chapter on energy. Here is a product that everyone wants and everyone needs that is in short supply. If you have the product to supply this need, this should indicate a good investment potential.

The list goes on. Suffice it to say that your role is to develop the sense of being able to unemotionally stand back from your money and the investment scene and determine the various areas where the demand exceeds the supply, and move your funds into those areas, so long as it appears that that situation will continue.

You can never rest on your laurels. We live in a dynamic world— that's why this book is entitled *The New Money Dynamics*—the world of money changes every day. That is what I love about my profession, financial planning. Every day is a new day! I must meet it with intelligence, energy, gusto, and enthusiasm, if I am going to help my clients and myself have our money in the right places at the right times.

• HISTORIC
RETURNS

What skillfully selected investments have offered compound growth rates in excess of 15 percent in the past? This is no guarantee of what may occur in the future, but should shed some light on areas for you to explore. Those you will want to study are

1 • Carefully managed family businesses.

2 • Well-located real estate: raw land, croplands, ranches, commercial income properties, using leverage. For every $1 you invest consider borrowing another $3 to put with it through long-term mortgages.

3 • Quality growth common stocks. The combined annual return from dividends and capital appreciation on common stocks in Standard and Poor's Industrial Stock Average has been over 15 percent for a number of periods. Stocks in some industry groups with proper timing have done even better.

4 • Some growth mutual funds.

5 • Some oil and gas income programs.

6 • Investment-quality diamonds and precious jewels.

7 • Antique furniture and art objects.

8 • Paintings and sculpture of gifted artists.

9 • Rare stamps and coins.

Be alert, pick a specialty that especially appeals to you, be imaginative, and see if you can turn it into a healthy profit.

• REACHING A MILLION DOLLARS

Let's assume that you are 25 years of age, have saved $1000, can save $50 per month, can maintain an average of 15 percent performance on your investments, and can pay income taxes from another source. Your progress report should then look something like this:

Age 25	$1000 + $50 per month
25	$ 1,000
30	8,663
35	18,054
40	40,967
45	87,052
50	179,745
55	466,185
60	741,183
65	1,495,435

If you are 30 years of age and fortunate enough to be able to make a lump-sum investment of $10,000, and can obtain an average return of 15 percent compounded annually, without adding new money to your investment, but reinvesting all distributions, your progress report should look something like this over a 35-year period:

Age 30	$10,000
35	20,113
40	40,456
45	81,371
50	163,670
55	329,190
60	662,120
65	1,331,800

• WORKING DOLLARS
ARE A NECESSITY

Remember, we are not talking about "guarantees." All we are doing here is obtaining a visual picture of what compounding accomplishes over a period of years if you are able to maintain a 15 percent average.

We do not know what our future economy will be. Of one thing we can be certain, however—you will never reach the million dollars with this amount of savings using "guaranteed" dollars. If you hope to reach your goal of becoming a millionaire, you must save and let your money grow. Investing your money in well-managed American companies, real estate, and natural resources will not guarantee growth of capital, but it certainly provides the opportunity for your money to work as hard for you as you had to work to get it. The working dollar is an absolute necessity if your goal is to become a millionaire.

Figure 15–1 shows how money compounds in a curve, not a straight line.

• SITTING
TIGHT

Do not be tempted to rationalize that market conditions are unsettled now so you should postpone starting your investment program. When has the outlook been so obvious that you knew exactly what course to follow? If you take this attitude, you might as well dig a hole and bury your money. There is risk in any investment at any time. There is also a risk in a liquid position because of the steady erosion of fixed dollars due to inflation.

I'm indebted to *Brevits* for the graphic illustration in Figure 15–2, printed with their approval. As the illustration shows, there are always good reasons for investment inactivity and our "sitting tight" friend was expert in discovering them. In so doing he missed an entire lifetime of opportunities.

• THE COMMON DENOMINATOR
OF SUCCESS

During my 9 years as moderator of a television show, and my 17 years as a financial planner, I've searched for the common denominator of success. In my search one particular characteristic seems to run through each life. That characteristic is that the successful person has formed the habit of doing things that failures do not like to do.

Perhaps you feel that you have certain dislikes that are peculiar

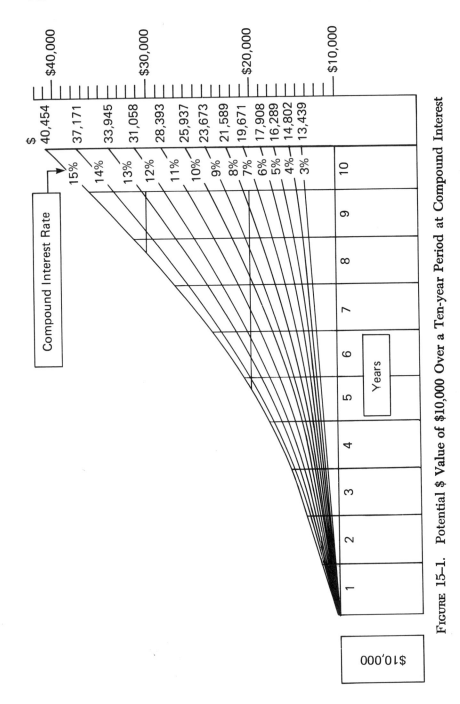

FIGURE 15-1. Potential $ Value of $10,000 Over a Ten-year Period at Compound Interest

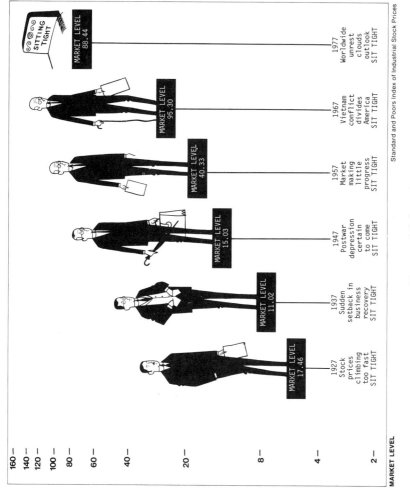

MARKET LEVEL

160 —
140 —
120 —
100 —
80 —
60 —
40 —
20 —
8 —
4 —
2 —

1927
Stock
prices
climbing
too fast
SIT TIGHT

MARKET LEVEL
17.46

1937
Sudden
setback in
business
recovery
SIT TIGHT

MARKET LEVEL
11.02

1947
Postwar
depression
certain
to come
SIT TIGHT

MARKET LEVEL
15.03

1957
Market
making
little
progress
SIT TIGHT

MARKET LEVEL
40.33

1967
Vietnam
conflict
divides
America
SIT TIGHT

MARKET LEVEL
95.30

1977
Worldwide
unrest
clouds
outlook
SIT TIGHT

MARKET LEVEL
88.44

SITTING TIGHT

Standard and Poors Index of Industrial Stock Prices

FIGURE 15-2.

to you, and that successful people don't have these dislikes but like to do the very things that you don't like to do. This isn't true. They don't like to do them any more than you do. These successful people are doing these very things they don't like to do in order to accomplish the things they want to accomplish. Successful people are motivated by the desire for pleasing results. Failures search for pleasing experiences and are satisfied with results that can be obtained by doing things they like to do.

Let's assume that your purpose is to become a millionaire—that your purpose is strong enough to make you form the habit of doing things you don't like to do in order to attain this goal.

To have maximum creativity, your body needs to have pure air, wholesome food, and creative thoughts. When you get home from work, do you grab a can of beer, light up a cigar, and sit in front of the tube to watch a wrestling match or the solving of one of the three to four murders that occur on television each night? Or do you jog, ride a bicycle, or walk a distance; eat a light nutritious dinner, sans large amounts of carbohydrate, sugar, salt, caffein, and saturated fats, but high in proteins, vitamins, and minerals; and then study *Barrons, The Wall Street Journal,* and *Business Week?* The successful investor does these things not because he wants to, but because he must to accomplish his goal.

You must, too, if you desire to become knowledgeable. Then you must learn to act upon that knowledge. Failures avoid decision making. Successful people know they must act. They have no other choice if they want to reach their goal.

Time plus money plus American free enterprise may make you a millionaire. If it does, fine. If it makes you financially independent, that will be a major accomplishment of which you can be justly proud.

Application

1 · What metropolitan newspaper will you subscribe to immediately?

2 · What current affairs magazines?
   (1)
   (2)

3 · What business publications?
   (1)
   (2)

4 · What period each week will you faithfully set aside to read and study financial publications?

5 · What uninterrupted one-hour period will you set aside each week to contemplate where demand is greater than supply in our country?
   Day of week
   Time of day

6 · What two-hour period will you spend driving around your city or a city nearby to observe building and land developments?
   Week of the month

7 · What day each year will you take a financial inventory to see your progress dollarwise?
   Month
   Date

8 · What self-improvement course will you take or motivational tapes will you order to stimulate your thinking and improve your mental attitude?
   When?

16
Avoiding the One-Way Trip to Washington

Learning to keep your hard-earned dollars from taking a one-way trip to Washington may become an all-consuming passion with you as it has with many of our citizens as inflation continues to escalate, pushing your tax bills higher and higher.

This is understandable when you consider that if you were in the 30 percent tax bracket last year, you did not start working for yourself until well into the month of April. If you were "blessed" with a 50 percent tax bracket, you quit working for the government after the middle of the year. I do say "blessed" because it is a blessing to live in a country where you can earn a high income. Of course, you would feel twice as "blessed" if you could keep more of it.

Tax avoidance is using your intelligence. Tax evasion is illegal, and the consequences are unpleasant. It is essential to observe the line of demarcation between the two. How much you can earn is not as important as how much you are allowed to keep. That is what adds to your net worth and buys your daily groceries. If there are legitimate ways of lowering your tax bite, it behooves you to find out what they are and to take advantage of them.

Congress periodically has enacted laws to encourage the shift of funds from taxable sectors of our economy to areas of public need or good by creating tax-free, tax-sheltered, or tax-deferred investments.

There are those who delight in referring to these incentives as loopholes, inferring that Congress was not intelligent enough to design a proper tax bill. They fail to recognize that without the incentives of a potential gain, no funds would be risked in areas when money is much needed for the welfare of our citizens.

Judge Learned Hand, the famous New York State jurist said:

> Anyone may so arrange his affairs that his taxes shall be as low as possible: He is not bound to choose that pattern which best pays the treasury Everyone does it, rich and poor alike, and all do right; for nobody owes any public duty to pay more than the law demands.

Senator Harrison of Mississippi, former Chairman of the Senate Finance Committee, expressed the matter in this way: "There's nothing that says a man has to take a toll bridge across a river when there is a free bridge nearby."

Unfortunately, over the years our tax laws have become so complicated that it takes a great deal of study to avail ourselves of some of their benefits. Jerome Kurtz, a Philadelphia lawyer at the time, and now a Director of Internal Revenue, has told Congress, "The existing estate and gift tax system could well be characterized as a government levy on poor advice."

So that you will not suffer any more than is absolutely necessary from the government levy, I will point out a few of the ways you may legitimately use to turn some of your tax liabilities to potential net worth.

But before I do, let's determine your tax bracket. I find that most people do not know their bracket. They assume, for instance, that if they earn $50,000 and do not pay $25,000 in taxes, they are not in the 50 percent tax bracket. Your bracket refers to the amount you will lose to taxes for each additional taxable dollar you add. For example, if you are filing a joint return and have taxable income of $44,000, your federal income tax would be $14,060, your bracket would be 50 percent, and you will lose one-half of any dollar you receive until you reach $52,000; then you begin at the 53 percent level.

To determine your tax bracket refer to Table 16–1.

Let's now make a decision among tax-free, tax sheltered, and tax-deferred.

Tax-free means that you will never pay a tax on the income received. Tax sheltered and tax-deferred mean you will pay a tax at a later date, and, it is to be hoped, at a lower rate than if you were taxed

Table 16–1. Income Tax Tables

Taxable income	Table I Separate return		Table II Joint return		Table III Unmarried Individual		Table IV Head of Household	
	Tax on Col. 1	% on Excess	Tax on Col. 1	% on Excess	Tax on Col. 1	% on Excess	Tax on Col. 1	% on Excess
$	$	14	$	14	$	14	$	14
500	70	15	70	14	70	15	70	14
1,000	145	16	140	15	145	16	140	16
1,500	225	17	215	15	225	17	220	16
2,000	310	19	290	16	310	19	300	18
3,000	500	19	450	17	500	19	480	18
4,000	690	22	620	19	690	21	660	19
6,000	1,130	25	1,000	19	1,110	24	1,040	22
8,000	1,630	28	1,380	22	1,590	25	1,480	23
10,000	2,190	32	1,820	22	2,090	27	1,940	25
12,000	2,830	36	2,260	25	2,630	29	2,440	27
14,000	3,550	39	2,760	25	3,210	31	2,980	28
16,000	4,330	42	3,260	28	3,830	34	3,540	31
18,000	5,170	45	3,820	28	4,510	36	4,160	32
20,000	6,070	48	4,380	32	5,230	38	4,800	35
22,000	7,030	50	5,020	32	5,990	40	5,500	36
24,000	8,030	50	5,660	36	6,790	40	6,220	38
26,000	9,030	53	6,380	36	7,590	45	6,980	41
28,000	10,090	53	7,100	39	8,490	45	7,800	42
32,000	12,210	55	8,660	42	10,290	50	9,480	45
36,000	14,410	55	10,340	45	12,290	50	11,280	48
38,000	15,510	58	11,240	45	13,290	55	12,240	51
40,000	16,670	58	12,140	48	14,390	55	13,260	52
44,000	18,990	60	14,060	50	16,590	60	15,340	55
50,000	22,590	62	17,060	50	20,190	62	18,640	56
52,000	23,830	62	18,060	53	21,430	62	19,760	58
60,000	28,790	64	22,300	53	26,390	64	24,400	58
64,000	31,350	64	24,420	55	28,950	64	26,720	59
70,000	35,190	66	27,720	55	32,790	66	30,260	61
76,000	39,150	66	31,020	58	36,750	66	33,920	62
80,000	41,790	68	33,340	58	39,390	68	36,400	63
88,000	47,230	68	37,980	60	44,830	68	41,440	64
90,000	48,590	69	39,180	60	46,190	69	42,720	64
100,000	55,490	70	45,180	62	53,090	70	49,120	66
120,000	69,490	70	57,580	64	67,090	70	62,320	67

Table 16–1. (*Continued*)

Taxable income	Table I Separate return		Table II Joint return		Table III Unmarried Individual		Table IV Head of Household	
	Tax on Col. 1	*% on Excess*	*Tax on Col. 1*	*% on Excess*	*Tax on Col. 1*	*% on Excess*	*Tax on Col. 1*	*% on Excess*
140,000	83,490	70	70,380	66	81,090	70	75,720	68
160,000	97,490	70	83,580	68	95,090	70	89,320	69
180,000	111,490	70	97,180	69	109,090	70	103,120	70
200,000	125,490	70	110,980	70	123,090	70	117,120	70

EXPLANATION OF TAX TABLES

"*Separate return*" table applies to separate returns of married persons and to returns of estates and trusts.

"*Joint return*" table applies to joint reutrns of married persons and returns of qualified surviving widow or widower.

"*Unmarried individual*" table applies to returns of single persons except for qualified surviving widows or widowers and heads of households.

Note: Special tax tables issued for persons with *taxable* income of up to $20,000, *even if deductions are itemized.*

now. Tax shelter usually occurs when the income is classified as a return of principal, thereby reducing your cost basis on the asset that is producing the income. When the asset is sold at a later date, the difference between your remaining cost and your sale price will usually be taxed on a capital gains basis. Tax-deferred means that the taxes are not paid as the income is accrued, but are to be paid at a later date. In a tax-exempt and a tax-sheltered investment there is current income. There is no current income with a tax-deferred investment.

• TAX-FREE
INCOME

Tax-exempt bonds are commonly known as municipal bonds because these securities are issued by local governments, public authorities, and special agencies to finance various needs of the people in their communities. Such services as water and sewer systems, bridges, airports, and schools have been financed in this manner.

Their tax-exempt status comes from a Supreme Court decision that created reciprocal immunity from taxation between the federal and local government. By this ruling, the interest on municipal bonds is exempt from taxation by the federal government, and the converse is true for federal government securities.

If your state has a state income tax, there may be an added ad-. vantage to buying municipal bonds issued in your state, for such bonds are usually exempt from state taxes as well.

Most municipal bonds are issued in serial form, meaning that a portion matures in fixed amounts at regular intervals ranging from 1 year to 50 years. As a result of this feature there is a vast supply of bonds available maturing in virtually any year you may choose.

Tax exemption can provide you with more spendable income. For example, if you are in the 40 percent tax bracket (you probably should not consider municipals if you are not), only 60 percent of your pretax income is available after taxes. An 8 percent taxable yield provides an after-tax return of only 4.8 percent. Therefore, a tax-free municipal providing a return in excess of 4.8 percent would provide more spendable income.

There has been talk from time to time about Congress eliminating the tax-exempt privilege inherent in municipal bonds. This speculation has existed for some time, and each attack has been unsuccessful. If such a change should be legislated, it should not have an effect on those bonds issued prior to the legislation, and their scarcity could easily enhance their value. Before the onerous Tax Reform Act of 1976 we always assumed that the government would not change the rules after the game had been played. Now retroactive legislation has become a reality and a future threat. However, federal taxation of state and municipal bonds does require an amendment to the Constitution ratified by two-thirds of the states. Heavily indebted states are not likely to look favorably on such an amendment.

Another important feature of municipal bonds is their relative safety. Next to U.S. government bonds, municipal bonds have been the safest of all securities. The New York City fiscal debacle has placed a cloud on bonds of cities that do not practice prudent financial policies. Puerto Rican bonds also have received lower ratings in recent years.

I have been amazed at the surge of interest in municipal bonds since all the publicity about The Big Apple and its fiscal problems. Even the proverbial "little ole lady in tennis shoes" is asking for them. This seems to have been caused by several things:

1 • Many people were not aware of the existence of tax-free bonds before this publicity.

2 • This interest in municipals occurred at a time when the stock market had not been a rewarding place to have money, chiefly because of the tight money policies of the Federal Reserve.

3 • These policies pushed the market down and interest rates up on corporate bonds, attracting funds from the market and into fixed-dollar guaranteed investments.

4 • Since the return from these corporate bonds was fully taxable, the next step was to look for tax relief.

5 • Then along came the Tax Reform Act of 1976, making it possible to have managed municipal bond funds with monthly distributions, systematic additions, and reinvestments. A large number of mutual fund distributors then formed municipal bond funds and began active advertising campaigns in our daily newspapers. Since that time the interest of the lay public has been very great.

If you are selecting your own bond portfolio, it will be essential for you to learn something about quality ratings. If you are letting the professionals select them through municipal bond funds or trusts, a knowledge of ratings will still be helpful as you study their portfolios. Moody's Investor Service and Standard and Poor each rate municipal bond obligations according to relative investment qualities.

Here are the rating systems used by each service for the most prominent categories:

Moody's	Standard and Poor's
Aaa	AAA
Aa	AA
A	A
Baa	BBB
Ba	BB
B	B

Using the Standard and Poor's notation system, the following rough definitions can be given to the more prominent categories for corporate bonds, with similar logic applying to municipal bonds:

AAA • Prime or highest-grade obligations, possessing the ultimate degree of protection as to principal and interest.

  AA • High-grade obligations, differing from AAA issues only in small degree.

    A • Upper-medium grade with considerable investment strength, but not entirely free from adverse effects of changes in economic and trade conditions.

BBB • Medium-grade category bonds on the borderline between definitely sound obligations and those in which the speculative element begins to predominate. These bonds have adequate asset coverage and normally are protected by satisfactory earnings. This is the lowest category that qualifies for commercial bank investment.

  BB • Lower-medium grade, possessing only minor investment characteristics.

    B • Speculative, with payment of interest not assured under difficult economic conditions.

Types of Municipal Bonds • Municipal bonds fall into three main categories:

Full faith and credit bonds of a state or political subdivision of the state have the full taxing power of the issuing local government available to pay both the principal and the interest.

Special tax bonds have a designated tax (gasoline, liquor, cigarettes) specifically pledged to pay the interest and principal.

Revenue bonds are backed by the earnings generated in a particular facility and do not have the taxing power of a local government upon which to draw. Many of these bonds are of a very high quality and are often rated equal to or higher than some bonds backed by taxes.

There are also a limited number of hybrid bonds that are paid from both taxes and revenues. Industrial revenue bonds have also appeared in recent years. These bonds generally are secured by a corporation that has entered into a lease agreement with a community. The bond issuer is normally a public authority that issues the bonds under its municipal title but receives annual installments from the corporation that is using the facility sufficient to pay the principal and interest on the bonds.

Municipal Bond Trust Funds • If tax-free income fits your financial plans, yet you do not have the expertise to select, the time to supervise, or sufficient funds to diversify, you should consider investing in a municipal bond trust fund. There are some excellent funds offered regularly. They are usually sold in units of $1000, plus accrued interest to settlement date. Most of them contain a well-selected diversified portfolio of municipal bonds selected from the top four categories. They provide a tax-exempt yield between 6 and 7 percent, which they will pay to you on a monthly basis. The funds are closed-end and self-liquidating, and usually do not carry a management fee (because they are not managed), though a nominal sales charge of around 3½ percent is charged when they are purchased. Although the sponsors are usually not required to do so, they do make a secondary market in the trusts, thereby giving you liquidity if you should so desire.

Municipal Bond Funds • As mentioned, the Tax Reform Act of 1976 made possible the offering of municipal bond funds. These are managed funds that allow additions of smaller amounts of money, a check-a-month, and the various other conveniences of a regular mutual fund, such as redemption at net asset value, reinvestment of distributions, etc. The municipal bond trust places bonds in a portfolio where they remain until maturity. The bond fund has a professional management that buys and sells bonds in an attempt to maximize yield and safety.

Should You Invest in Municipal Bonds? • When I am asked that question, my answer is, "It depends on what you are going to do with the money if you do not." If you are planning to put it into a savings account at 6 percent or a corporate bond at 8 percent, and you are in a 39 percent bracket, you obviously would receive more keepable income from municipal bonds. As you will note from the tax equivalent table (Table 16–2), you would have to receive an income of 9.84 percent to equate a 6 percent tax-exempt income. If you are in a 55 percent bracket, you would need to receive a 13.33 percent yield to be equivalent to 6 percent tax exempt.

Tax-free vs. Taxable Income • Table 16–2 gives the approximate yields that taxable securities must earn in various income brackets to produce after-tax yields equal to those on tax-free bonds yielding from 5 percent to 6.9 percent.

The table is computed on the theory that your highest bracket tax

Table 16–2. Yields from Taxable Securities to Equal Savings from Tax-free Bonds (Taxable Income in Thousands)

Joint Return	$8 to $12	$12 to $16	$16 to $20	$20 to $24	$24 to $28	$28 to $32	$32 to $36	$36 to $40	$40 to $44	$44 to $52	$52 to $64	$64 to $76	$76 to $88	$88 to $100	$100 to $120	$120 to $140	$140 to $160
% Bracket	22	25	28	32	36	39	42	45	48	50	53	55	58	60	62	64	66
5.00%	6.41	6.67	6.94	7.35	7.81	8.20	8.62	9.09	9.62	10.00	10.64	11.11	11.90	12.50	13.16	13.89	14.71
5.10	6.54	6.80	7.08	7.50	7.97	8.36	8.79	9.27	9.81	10.20	10.85	11.33	12.14	12.75	13.42	14.17	15.00
5.20	6.67	6.93	7.22	7.65	8.13	8.52	8.97	9.45	10.00	10.40	11.06	11.56	12.38	13.00	13.68	14.44	15.29
5.30	6.79	7.07	7.36	7.79	8.28	8.69	9.14	9.64	10.19	10.60	11.28	11.78	12.62	13.25	13.95	14.72	15.59
5.40	6.92	7.20	7.50	7.94	8.44	8.85	9.31	9.82	10.38	10.80	11.49	12.00	12.86	13.50	14.21	15.00	15.88
5.50	7.05	7.33	7.64	8.09	8.59	9.02	9.48	10.00	10.58	11.00	11.70	12.22	13.10	13.75	14.47	15.28	16.18
5.60	7.18	7.47	7.78	8.24	8.75	9.18	9.66	10.18	10.77	11.20	11.91	12.44	13.33	14.00	14.74	15.56	16.47
5.70	7.31	7.60	7.92	8.38	8.91	9.34	9.83	10.36	10.96	11.40	12.13	12.67	13.57	14.25	15.00	15.83	16.76
5.80	7.44	7.73	8.06	8.53	9.06	9.51	10.00	10.55	11.15	11.60	12.34	12.89	13.81	14.50	15.26	16.11	17.06
5.90	7.56	7.87	8.19	8.68	9.22	9.67	10.17	10.73	11.35	11.80	12.55	13.11	14.05	14.75	15.53	16.39	17.35
6.00	7.69	8.00	8.33	8.82	9.38	9.84	10.34	10.91	11.54	12.00	12.77	13.33	14.29	15.00	15.79	16.67	17.65
6.10	7.82	8.13	8.47	8.97	9.53	10.00	10.52	11.09	11.73	12.20	12.98	13.56	14.52	15.25	16.05	16.94	17.94
6.20	7.95	8.27	8.61	9.12	9.69	10.16	10.69	11.27	11.92	12.40	13.19	13.78	14.76	15.50	16.32	17.22	18.24
6.30	8.08	8.40	8.75	9.26	9.84	10.33	10.86	11.45	12.12	12.60	13.40	14.00	15.00	15.75	16.58	17.50	18.53
6.40	8.21	8.53	8.89	9.41	10.00	10.49	11.03	11.64	12.31	12.80	13.62	14.22	15.24	16.00	16.84	17.78	18.82
6.50	8.33	8.67	9.03	9.56	10.16	10.66	11.21	11.82	12.50	13.00	13.83	14.44	15.48	16.25	17.11	18.06	19.12
6.60	8.46	8.80	9.17	9.71	10.31	10.82	11.38	12.00	12.69	13.20	14.04	14.67	15.71	16.50	17.37	18.33	19.41
6.70	8.59	8.93	9.31	9.85	10.47	10.98	11.55	12.18	12.88	13.40	14.26	14.89	15.95	16.75	17.63	18.61	19.71
6.80	8.72	9.07	9.44	10.00	10.63	11.15	11.72	12.36	13.08	13.60	14.47	15.11	16.19	17.00	17.89	18.89	20.00
6.90	8.85	9.20	9.58	10.15	10.78	11.31	11.90	12.55	13.27	13.80	14.68	15.33	16.43	17.25	18.16	19.17	20.29

Tax Exempt Yield

rate is applicable to the entire amount of any increase or decrease in your taxable income resulting from a switch from taxable to tax-free securities, or vice versa.

When you are considering tax-exempt income, you should also include your first $200 of dividends from American corporations if you are filing a joint return, or $100 on a single reutrn. If you are not receiving at least these amounts in dividends, you are missing some tax-free income.

• TAX-DEFERRED INCOME

Tax-deferred income is income that is accrued to your account, but you do not currently receive it nor is it currently taxed. For example, if you invest $10,000 in a single-premium deferred annuity that is earning 7 percent, at the end of a year your account will be $10,700. Until you withdraw the $700 no tax is due, and it compounds tax sheltered.

If you want some of your funds guaranteed and do not want the income from these funds to be taxed currently, you may want to consider a single-premium deferred annuity. It offers:

1 • Guaranteed principal.

2 • Interest guarantees.

3 • Tax deferral.

4 • Special tax treatment at retirement if annuitized.

5 • Tax-free exchange from one custodian to another.

Some charge an acquisition fee with no charge for early withdrawals. Others do not charge an acquisition fee, but if you withdraw more than 6 percent in any one year during the first 5 years they charge a percentage on the amount. Table 16–3 gives the after-tax results you would have received in a 30 percent and in a 50 percent bracket if you had placed $10,000 in a savings and loan at 6 percent interest, as compared with having placed $10,000 in a single-premium deferred annuity at 7 percent with interest accumulating without current taxes. (It will however, be taxed on withdrawal at your then current rate.)

Another illustration that may be of interest to you is tabulated in Table 16-4. You could have placed $20,000 in a single-premium deferred annuity, let it compound at 7 percent for 10 years, and then started withdrawing $2000 per year for 10 years. This $2000 per year is not taxed, because it is a part of the original $20,000 after-tax dollars you invested. At the end of this second ten years, after you have withdrawn $20,000, you would still have $49,761. Any additional withdrawal would be taxable.

Table 16–3.

No. of Years	$10,000 savings & loan accounts at 6% interest (interest taxed as accrued)		$10,000 in a single-premium deferred annuity (interest accumlates without current tax)
	50% tax Bracket	30% tax bracket	@7%
5	$11,593	$12,284	$ 14,026
10	13,439	15,090	19,672
15	15,580	18,536	27,590
20	18,061	22,770	38,697
25	20,938	27,970	54,274
30	24,273	34,358	76,123
35	28,139	42,206	106,766
40	32,620	51,845	149,745

Table 16–4. Illustration of an Assumed $20,000 Single-premium Deferred Annuity Investment @ 7% Interest for 20 Years

End of Year	Value at end of yr	Withdrawal at end of year	Net amount
1	21,400		
2	22,898		
3	24,501		
4	26,216		
5	28,051		
6	30,015		
7	32,116		
8	34,364		
9	36,769		
10	39,343		
11	42,097	2,000	40,097
12	42,904	2,000	40,904
13	43,767	2,000	41,767
14	44,691	2,000	42,691
15	45,679	2,000	43,679
16	46,737	2,000	44,737
17	47,868	2,000	45,868
18	49,079	2,000	47,079
19	50,375	2,000	48,375
20	51,761	2,000	49,761

• TAX-SHELTERED
INVESTMENTS

An investment to be sound must be a good investment first and a tax shelter second. However, I find many that are potentially good investments only with the tax shelter. Before making any investment that attracts you because of its tax-sheltered features, consult with your certified public accountant, who should be thoroughly familiar with your tax situation. If he is not or does not become so, change to one who is knowledgeable and creative.

Always remember that tax shelters involve risk and are usually difficult to sell in a hurry. Funds committed to this type of investment should not be a part of your emergency reserves. You should also be willing to wait for results. The sponsors must have time to put your money to work. Your waiting period for tangible results will probably be at least six months and could be two years or longer.

In chapter 14 on energy I discussed the tax advantage of investing in oil and gas income limited partnerships and oil and gas drilling programs. These can play a vital role in your program to save taxes, and deserve your conscientious study. There are others with economic and social merit that you should also consider.

• CABLE
TELEVISION

Cable television offers attractive potential if the program is structured properly and has top-quality management. While cable television is a relatively new and small industry, it has exhibited a consistent growth profile and a remarkable record of stability, and it may offer you a unique opportunity for investing.

Traditional cable systems are built in towns that do not have good television reception due to mountainous terrain or long distances from TV stations. A cable system receives TV signals by using a tall tower and distributes the signal throughout the town on a coaxial cable. Subscribers are charged a monthly fee for the service. After a cable system is built in a community, the maintenance and operating expenses are very low in relation to income. The business is generally very predictable and operates much like a utility company.

The capital required to construct or purchase a cable system is substantial, but the investor can leverage his equity investment by utilizing an institutional lender specializing in making first-lien mortgage loans on good cable systems. The collateral on this loan is the cable system itself, and in many cases the personal guarantee of the investor is also required.

The tax shelter is created primarily by the depreciation of the system, the interest on loans, the investment tax credit earned on purchasing the system, and, in the case of a new system, actual operating losses in the first year or two.

A high-quality cable television limited partnership may offer you an investment period of two or three years with an equivalent tax write-off of 200 percent during that period, and with an additional two or three years of tax write-off with no additional investments.

In this same limited partnership, you may look forward to a cash flow starting in the second or third year and continuing throughout the life of the partnership. A total cash return of 200 percent or 250 percent may occur over an eight- to ten-year partnership, in addition to the tax advantages.

One other substantial advantage in these investments is that normal inflation can be expected to also inflate the market value of the cable system, therefore offering a potential hedge against inflation, if and when you and the other limited partners choose to sell the system.

•   CATTLE-FEEDING
PROGRAMS

Cattle-feeding program tax objectives can be summarized in two words: "tax deferral" (postponing a tax liability until a later, more convenient time, or, usually, buying time to figure out a way to avoid the tax altogether). There's no write-off or depreciation on the cattle, but feed costs, interest, and management fees are deductible as they are consumed. Because of the "capital at risk" limitations in the Tax Reform Act of 1976, your deduction will generally be limited to 100 percent or less.

The typical cattle-feeding operation is basically conducted in the following manner. Buyers for the lots purchase calves weighing between 400 and 600 pounds. These feeder calves are purchased and placed in feedlot pens of 100 to 200 animals. The feedlot operators feed them a scientifically designed diet in order to maximize their weight gain at the lowest possible cost. In about four to six months, they reach a level referred to as "finished"; they weigh between 900 and 1100 pounds. Finished cattle are sold quickly at prevailing market prices, since additional feed costs make it uneconomical to hold them after they reach their optimum weight.

The price that the general partner must pay to obtain feeder calves, the cost of feed, and the price of finished fat cattle fluctuates with supply and demand. An investment in only a single feeding program, therefore, generates for you a significant profit or a significant loss. This will depend on timing of purchases and sales. Price changes are the major cattle-feeding risk. However, in recent years many cattle feeders have employed the use of commodity futures hedging their cattle to lessen the impact of rapid price declines.

When the cattle are sold the following year, your net profit, if any, after loan repayment, sponsor's compensation, and operations expenses, is taxed as ordinary income. This allows you to shift taxable income from one year to the next, giving you the flexibility of deferring the tax into a more favorable year. Most of the programs currently being offered are designed to carry over several years in order to allow more flexibility in your tax planning. Almost all cattle-feeding programs employ borrowed funds. If you are a limited partner, your funds are used for the equity purchase of young feeder cattle. The general partner then borrows additional funds to finance a portion of the cattle purchases, plus the cost of feed to be fed during the period.

If you feel that cattle feeding fits your tax picture, let me recommend that you diversify. Pick out a sponsor with a good success record and plan to make a small investment in each of his programs for a period of time, depending on your tax picture. This should help to smooth out the peaks and valleys you are likely to encounter, but does not assure a profit. Cattle feeding is a high-risk investment, as those who were feeding in 1974 discovered.

• CAPITAL GAINS ON STOCK TRANSACTIONS

Capital gains, for the most part, unless you receive a large amount in one year, are half tax-free.

What is a capital gain? It is any asset that you have held for a year and sold at a profit. For example, let's assume that you bought 100 shares of a stock for $50 a share or $5000, and three years later sold it for $100 a share, or $10,000. You would realize a $5000 capital gain. Our tax laws allow you to divide this amount in half, put $2500 in your pocket without taxes, and pay on the other $2500 at your regular tax bracket.

If you are in a 50 percent bracket or above, your maximum tax is 25 percent of the gain, unless you have received extraordinarily high income and capital gains in that year. (With the passage of the Tax Reform Act of 1976, 50 percent of the amount by which net long-term capital gains exceed net short-term capital losses became what is called a tax preference item when minimum tax is figured, so that your tax may now be greater if your capital gain is in excess of $50,000.)

• PROFIT-SHARING AND PENSION PLANS

If you work for a corporation with a profit-sharing and/or pension plan, you may also be avoiding the one-way trip to Washington, at least for the present. Your company's contribution, and yours, and the compounding return it produces are tax sheltered. When you retire, money that was allocated to service prior to December 31, 1974, will come to you as capital gains, and that contributed since that date will be taxed as ordinary income.

There are several ways to reduce the tax bite at that time. First, since you'll be retired, you may be in a lower tax bracket. Second, you can income average over a 10-year period of time. Third, most retirement programs permit you to draw income in several optional ways—in one lump sum, or by conversion into an annuity. In my opinion, your best option may be to accept a lump-sum distribution and then roll it over into what is called an *individual retirement account rollover*. I'll discuss this in detail later.

If you are the president of your own small corporation, you may want to consider setting up a profit-sharing and/or pension plan. It allows you to get before-tax dollars into a retirement program and lets them compound tax-free. Since you are no doubt calling the shots, you can have a skilled specialist design a plan that will give you the maximum benefit both now and when you retire, while keeping within the IRS guidelines.

Technically, profit-sharing and pension plans are designed to attract and hold good employees, which they do if employees are kept adequately informed. However, since your pay is probably higher than most of your employees', the greatest advantage will usually accrue to you. An even greater advantage may accrue to you if you are older than your employees and set up a defined benefit pension plan.

Qualified pension and profit-sharing plans are undoubtedly the most attractive of all corporate fringe benefits. Specific details are beyond the scope of this book. Suffice it to say that more and more Americans will be receiving retirement benefits, and these benefits will become a more significant percentage of the average person's accumulated wealth. The impact this will have can be better seen when we realize that total pension/profit-sharing assets now have a value of over $200 billion.

There are many variations of qualified pension and/or profit-sharing plans that can be tailored to the individual employer. However, the basic concept is simple.

1 • The employer contributes dollars in a special account, taking a current tax deduction.

2 • The employee is not taxed at the time of contribution, and assets are allowed to grow without taxation until retirement.

3 • Death benefits paid to a named beneficiary or intervivos trust are estate-tax free, if the beneficiary chooses to accept distributions over three-year installments.

4 • Taxes on lump-sum distributions can be postponed and probably reduced by an IRA rollover (covered below).

• COMPOUNDING WITH TAX SHELTER

In both pension and profit-sharing plans the income from the investments made under the plans is permitted to compound tax sheltered.

Let's look at the difference this can make to *you* if your employer contributes $1000 per year and you are in a 35 percent tax bracket.

Without tax shelter	With tax shelter
5 yrs. $ 3,560	$ 5,751
10 yrs. $ 8,006	$13,817
15 yrs. $13,560	$25,130
20 yrs. $20,499	$40,996

If your company had invested in the Seminar Fund $1000 each year for 43 years for your benefit, you could retire very comfortably. Table 16–5 is a summary of past results for 43 years; the total amounts to the princely sum of $706,622. (During the next 43 years, as in the past 43 years, there will probably be periods of escalating stock prices, as well as periods of severe market corrections.)

Since this is a book on investments, I shall not detail the requirements, tax status, advantages, or disadvantages of various types of pension plans versus profit-sharing plans, or combinations of both.

Investing Retirement Funds • However, since this is a book on investments, I would like to call your attention to a study made by the highly respected A. S. Hansen, Inc., Actuaries and Consultants, and published in their report titled, "Investment Performance Survey, 1966–1975." One of the areas the study included was a composite of the performance of 204 banks, 39 life insurance companies, and 73 growth and income mutual funds. If you are acting in a fiduciary capacity, making investment decisions regarding your pension plan, I recommend that you obtain a copy of this report and carefully study the findings.

Table 16–5. $1000 Annual Investment in the Seminar Fund for 43 Years (1937–1976)

DATE	INITIAL INVESTMENT	OFFERING PRICE	SALES CHARGE INCLUDED	SHARES PURCHASED	NET ASSET VALUE PER SHARE	INITIAL NET ASSET VALUE
1/ 1/37	$1,000.00	$6.54	8.50%	152.905	$5.987	$915

| | | COST OF SHARES | | | | VALUE OF SHARES | | | | | |
DATE	CUM INV'M'T	ANNUAL INCOME DIVS	CUM INCOME DIVS	TOTAL INV'M'T COST	ANNUAL CAP GAIN DISTRIB'N	FROM INV'M'T	FROM CAP GAINS REINV'D	SUB-TOTAL	FROM DIVS REINV'D	TOTAL VALUE	SHARES HELD
12/31/37	1,000	30	30	1,030	8	536	4	540	23	563	160
12/31/38	2,000	13	42	2,042	78	1,746	97	1,843	44	1,887	447
12/31/39	3,000	62	104	3,104	74	2,540	180	2,720	105	2,825	701
12/31/40	4,000	134	238	4,238	56	3,191	224	3,415	235	3,650	981
12/31/41	5,000	239	477	5,477	12	3,587	208	3,795	435	4,230	1,302
12/31/42	6,000	277	753	6,753	48	4,946	282	5,228	779	6,007	1,683
12/31/43	7,000	297	1,050	8,050	98	7,445	458	7,903	1,287	9,190	2,027
12/31/44	8,000	363	1,413	9,413	434	9,633	974	10,607	1,857	12,464	2,386
12/31/45	9,000	364	1,777	10,777	1,260	13,113	2,488	15,601	2,702	18,303	2,819
12/31/46	10,000	571	2,348	12,348	1,239	12,428	3,414	15,842	2,930	18,772	3,265
12/31/47	11,000	837	3,185	14,185	915	12,299	4,053	16,352	3,525	19,877	3,754
12/31/48	12,000	959	4,144	16,144	646	12,281	4,410	16,691	4,188	20,879	4,247
12/31/49	13,000	994	5,138	18,138	823	13,324	5,277	18,601	5,260	23,861	4,810
12/31/50	14,000	1,222	6,359	20,359	873	15,830	6,749	22,579	7,121	29,700	5,390
12/31/51	15,000	1,356	7,716	22,716	1,544	18,155	8,868	27,023	9,079	36,102	6,052
12/31/52	16,000	1,451	9,166	25,166	1,821	19,718	10,998	30,716	10,847	41,563	6,747
12/31/53	17,000	1,684	10,850	27,850	1,137	19,384	11,445	30,829	11,865	42,694	7,386
12/31/54	18,000	1,798	12,648	30,648	3,135	29,290	11,689	48,979	19,146	68,125	8,178
12/31/55	19,000	2,229	14,877	33,877	5,991	34,204	28,482	62,686	23,944	86,630	9,196
12/31/56	20,000	2,466	17,342	37,342	6,964	35,196	35,433	70,629	26,379	97,008	10,287
12/31/57	21,000	2,765	20,107	41,107	5,329	29,059	33,591	62,650	23,674	86,324	11,388
12/31/58	22,000	2,938	23,046	45,046	4,365	40,665	50,250	90,915	35,438	126,353	12,303
12/31/59	23,000	3,172	26,218	49,218	9,546	43,334	61,975	105,309	40,075	145,384	13,599
12/31/60	24,000	3,706	29,924	53,924	8,239	42,558	68,122	110,680	42,307	152,987	14,896
12/31/61	25,000	3,841	33,764	58,764	9,821	49,625	87,667	137,292	52,195	189,487	16,181
12/31/62	26,000	4,201	37,966	63,966	7,409	41,000	77,658	118,658	46,579	165,237	17,411

Table 16–5. (Continued)

DATE	COST OF SHARES				ANNUAL CAP GAIN DISTRIB'N	VALUE OF SHARES					SHARES HELD
	CUM INV'M'T	ANNUAL INCOME DIVS	CUM INCOME DIVS	TOTAL INV'M'T COST		FROM INV'M'T	FROM CAP GAINS REINV'D	SUB-TOTAL	FROM DIVS REINV'D	TOTAL VALUE	
12/31/63	27,000	4,457	42,422	69,422	8,414	48,199	97,878	146,077	58,155	204,232	18,736
12/31/64	28,000	4,983	47,406	75,406	13,663	52,683	118,645	171,328	67,234	238,562	20,424
12/31/65	29,000	5,660	53,066	82,066	18,279	52,513	157,120	219,633	84,426	304,059	22,340
12/31/66	30,000	7,273	60,339	90,339	23,392	58,030	165,704	223,734	84,302	308,036	24,761
12/31/67	31,000	8,634	68,973	99,973	18,805	70,673	217,856	288,529	109,761	398,290	26,730
12/31/68	32,000	10,667	79,640	111,640	16,882	78,043	258,012	336,055	130,952	467,007	28,774
12/31/69	33,000	11,960	91,601	124,601	28,258	64,314	235,448	299,762	118,232	417,994	31,642
12/31/70	34,000	12,929	104,530	138,530	18,395	61,929	241,931	303,860	126,092	429,952	34,313
12/31/71	35,000	13,556	118,086	153,086	9,127	70,234	279,400	349,634	154,678	504,312	36,048
12/31/72	36,000	14,226	132,311	168,311	17,302	77,933	323,399	401,332	184,052	585,384	38,235
12/31/73	37,000	15,886	148,197	185,197	12,912	61,801	266,627	328,428	159,333	487,761	40,680
12/31/74	38,000	24,906	173,104	211,104	0	48,482	205,919	254,401	146,636	401,037	43,308
12/31/75	39,000	23,824	196,928	235,928	3,117	63,610	267,981	331,591	212,676	544,267	45,698
12/31/76	40,000	22,258	219,186	259,186	10,79	79,667	341,619	421,286	285,336	706,622	48,102
				TOTAL	271,213						

A distillation of this information, as I interpret it, is as follows: The Standard and Poor average outperformed the Dow in all but one of the periods in the study and was equal once. The growth and income mutual funds outperformed the Standard and Poor in six of the 10 periods studied, and was equal once. The mutual funds outperformed the bank management in each of the 10-year periods. They also outperformed the insurance companies in all of the periods studied. The banks outperformed the Standard and Poor in one of the periods, and the insurance companies did not perform as well as the Standard and Poor in any of the periods studied.

Table 16–6 is a composite of that study.

At one time common stocks—even those of the largest and best-managed companies with long dividend records—were rarely purchased by fiduciaries, who often favored all-bond portfolios. But inflation has changed that. Today a fiduciary portfolio without common stocks is unusual.

The figures below illustrate the dramatic shift into common stocks by private pension funds. The portion of assets held in stocks rose from just under 43 percent in 1960 to 63 percent by mid-1976. Stocks now account for $108 billion of private pension fund assets, nearly two-thirds of the total and steadily climbing.

Private Pension Fund Portfolio Composition

	December 31			June 30
	1960	1965	1970	1976
Assets (in billions)	$38.148	$73.647	$110.617	$170.919
Portions in stocks	43%	55%	61%	63%
Portion in bonds	41%	31%	27%	23%

Source: Flow of Funds Accounts, Federal Reserve System.

One compelling reason that pension funds have increased their stock holdings is inflation. Fiduciaries realize that in these inflationary times investing for current income alone is not enough; they need to increase their capital as well as the income stream it produces.

Over the past 25 years, stock prices—despite periodic declines—have more than maintained the purchasing power of the prudent investor's dollar. This is documented in Figs. 16–1 and 16–2. Since 1952, the cost of living has doubled, while common stock prices, as measured by the Dow Jones Average of 30 Industrial Stocks, have more than tripled. An investment in the unmanaged Dow Jones Average 25 years ago would have produced, in capital appreciation with dividends reinvested, an average annual return of 9.8 percent through December 31, 1976.

Table 16–6. Compound Annual Rates of Return

Number of years	1	2	3	4	5	6	7	8	9	10
Dates	1967	1967–68	1967–69	1967–70	1967–71	1967–72	1967–73	1967–74	1967–75	1967–76
S&P better than Dow	X	X	X	X	X	X	X	X	X	—
Funds better than S&P	X	X	X		X			X	—	X
Funds better than bank	X	X	X	X	X	X	X	X	X	X
Funds better than ins. co.	X	X	X	X	X	X	X	X	X	X
Bank better than S&P			X							
Ins. co. better than S&P	———————————————————— NONE ————————————————————									

Study includes 204 banks, 39 life insurance companies, 73 growth and income mutual funds.

Purchasing Power of the U.S. Dollar, 1951–1976

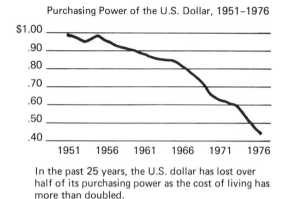

In the past 25 years, the U.S. dollar has lost over half of its purchasing power as the cost of living has more than doubled.

FIGURE 16–1.   Purchasing Power of the U.S. Dollar, 1951–1976

Common Stock Prices, 1951–1976

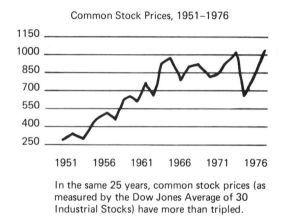

In the same 25 years, common stock prices (as measured by the Dow Jones Average of 30 Industrial Stocks) have more than tripled.

FIGURE 16–2.   Common Stock Prices, 1951–1976

Let's assume that you have managed your pension fund well, or that those in charge have done so, and it's time for you to retire. Let's look at some choices you will need to consider.

• INDIVIDUAL RETIREMENT
ACCOUNT ROLLOVER

First of all, consult with a competent financial planner. Together calculate the advantages and disadvantages of taking your pension benefits in a lump sum and paying the taxes due in that year, taking a 10-year averaging formula, or rolling over the funds into what is called an individual retirement account rollover. Under the ERISA legislation there is a small section that may be of great benefit to you. It allows you to choose, within 60 days of the time of receipt of your benefits, to pay the taxes or rollover the proceeds and pay the taxes at a later date.

This section of the law was chiefly designed to give portability of accrued pension benefits to those who were moving from one company to another. Let's say that an engineer wants to move from one large company with a pension plan in which he has a vested interest (meaning that he can take it with him) to another firm. Under the new law he can move his funds into a rollover account, not pay any current taxes, which he would have had to do formerly on all the company's contributions, and there the funds can compound without tax. Later, if he desires, and it is agreeable to his new company, he can again roll it over into their pension plan, or if he prefers, he can just leave it in the account where he had originally rolled it.

However, it is interesting to note that the people who are making the greatest use of this rollover provision are retirees who are rolling their pension proceeds into a rollover account that meets IRS custodian guidelines. (To qualify they must have been participants in the retirement plan for five years.)

Let's say that after carefully weighing your alternatives, you choose to rollover. You will avoid current taxation on your lump-sum distribution.

You must now leave the funds there until you are 59½ years of age (in the event that you have taken early retirement) and you must start withdrawing at 70½. When withdrawals are made the amount withdrawn is taxed as ordinary income.

You must rollover the company's total contribution in kind. For example, if you receive both stock and cash you must roll it over as received. After it is rolled over, the custodian can then sell the stock if this is desired. You are not allowed to rollover your contribution. You wouldn't want to, anyway, because those were after-tax dollars you contributed and for that reason are not taxed when you withdraw them.

An Actual Case Study • A couple who had attended my three-session financial planning seminar in Foley's Almeda store auditorium requested an appointment, as every attendee is entitled to do. When we sat down for our two-hour uninterrupted personal session in my office, I discovered that he had taken early retirement, had received his distribution 50 days previously, and they were faced with a $14,056 tax bill on a $88,201 distribution. I quickly ordered out the computer printout shown in Table 16–7, giving the past results if the funds were not rolled over and if they

Table 16–7. Without IRA Rollover

$88,201 distribution
$14,056 taxes due
$74,145 Balance Invested in The Seminar Fund
9% withdrawal for first 11 years

January 1, 1944 - December 31, 1954
Self-Liquidating for the next 21 years
January 1, 1955 - January 1, 1976

DATE	INITIAL INVESTMENT	OFFERING PRICE	SALES CHARGE INCLUDED	SHARES PURCHASED	NET ASSET VALUE PER SHARE	INITIAL NET ASSET VALUE
1/ 1/44	$74,145.00	$4.75	4.50%	15,609.470	$4.532	$70,742

SYSTEMATIC WITHDRAWAL PLAN
DIVIDENDS AND CAPITAL GAINS REINVESTED
MONTHLY WITHDRAWALS OF $556.09 (9.0% ANNUALLY) BEGINNING 1/31/44

| | ==========AMOUNTS WITHDRAWN========== | | | | | ====VALUE OF REMAINING SHARES==== | | | |
DATE	FROM INCOME DIVS	FROM PRINCIPAL	ANNUAL TOTAL	CUM TOTAL	ANNUAL CAP GAIN DISTRIB'N	REMAINING ORIGINAL SHARES	CAP GAIN SHARES	TOTAL VALUE	SHARES HELD
12/31/44	1,920	4,753	6,673	6,673	2,536	76,330	2,609	78,939	15,116
12/31/45	1,640	5,033	6,673	13,346	6,235	89,410	9,567	98,977	15,245
12/31/46	2,243	4,430	6,673	20,019	5,407	75,400	13,751	89,151	15,509
12/31/47	2,869	3,804	6,673	26,692	3,446	65,696	16,086	81,782	15,448
12/31/48	2,854	3,819	6,673	33,365	2,108	57,444	17,047	74,491	15,152
12/31/49	2,556	4,117	6,673	40,038	2,311	53,652	19,522	73,174	14,752
12/31/50	2,715	3,958	6,673	46,711	2,134	55,373	23,854	79,227	14,378
12/31/51	2,668	4,005	6,673	53,384	3,327	55,971	29,189	85,160	14,276
12/31/52	2,550	4,123	6,673	60,057	3,514	53,577	33,694	87,271	14,167
12/31/53	2,637	4,036	6,673	66,730	1,956	46,278	33,551	79,829	13,811
12/31/54	2,526	4,148	6,673	73,403	4,844	61,744	53,290	115,034	13,809
TOTALS	27,178	46,225	73,403		37,818				

NOTE: 20.0% SUBTRACTED FROM DIVIDENDS AND 10.0% SUBTRACTED FROM CAPITAL GAIN DISTRIBUTIONS AS PAID TO REFLECT LIABILITY FOR FEDERAL INCOME TAXES.

Table 16–7. (Continued)

DATE	INITIAL INVESTMENT	OFFERING PRICE	SALES CHARGE INCLUDED	SHARES PURCHASED	NET ASSET VALUE PER SHARE	INITIAL NET ASSET VALUE
1/ 1/55	$115,034.00	$8.33	0.00%	13,809.600	$8.330	$115,034

SYSTEMATIC WITHDRAWAL PLAN
DIVIDENDS AND CAPITAL GAINS REINVESTED
MONTHLY WITHDRAWALS BEGINNING 1/31/55 BASED ON A 21-YEAR SELF-LIQUIDATING PROGRAM DESIGNED TO EXHAUST PRINCIPAL

	=======AMOUNTS WITHDRAWN=======					====VALUE OF REMAINING SHARES====			
DATE	FROM INCOME DIVS	FROM PRINCIPAL	ANNUAL TOTAL	CUM TOTAL	ANNUAL CAP GAIN DISTRIB'N	REMAINING ORIGINAL SHARES	CAP GAIN SHARES	TOTAL VALUE	SHARES HELD
12/31/55	2,875	3,313	6,188	6,188	8,659	126,629	8,995	135,624	14,397
12/31/56	2,958	4,240	7,198	13,386	9,286	122,702	18,229	140,931	14,945
12/31/57	3,060	4,083	7,164	20,550	6,642	95,234	21,012	116,246	15,335
12/31/58	3,035	4,692	7,727	28,277	5,028	123,528	33,939	157,467	15,332
12/31/59	3,034	6,923	9,956	38,233	10,188	121,668	45,649	167,317	15,651
12/31/60	3,265	6,917	10,182	48,415	8,273	109,723	52,479	162,202	15,793
12/31/61	3,110	9,242	12,352	60,767	8,904	115,628	68,904	184,532	15,758
12/31/62	3,113	8,187	11,300	72,067	6,286	85,837	61,439	147,276	15,519
12/31/63	3,015	9,746	12,761	84,828	6,304	88,472	77,080	165,552	15,188
12/31/64	3,055	12,318	15,373	100,201	9,260	82,725	91,923	174,648	14,952
12/31/65	3,116	14,800	17,916	118,117	11,159	80,791	118,649	199,440	14,653
12/31/66	3,563	16,289	19,852	137,969	13,120	58,249	120,820	179,069	14,394
12/31/67	3,739	20,086	23,825	161,794	9,038	49,174	154,042	203,216	13,638
12/31/68	3,992	22,827	26,819	188,613	7,572	28,944	177,080	206,024	12,694
12/31/69	3,615	23,521	27,336	215,949	10,930	1,893	153,972	155,865	11,798
12/31/70	3,483	20,319	23,802	239,751	5,988	0	131,831	131,831	10,521
12/31/71	2,957	25,919	28,876	268,627	2,044	0	122,503	122,503	8,756
12/31/72	2,386	30,509	32,895	301,522	2,899	0	105,567	105,567	6,895
12/31/73	1,862	28,842	30,704	332,226	1,447	0	58,008	58,008	4,838
12/31/74	1,582	24,489	26,071	358,297	0	0	23,515	23,515	2,539
12/31/75	414	29,620	30,034	388,331	14		0	0	0
TOTALS	61,451	326,880	386,331		143,040				

NOTE: 20.0% SUBTRACTED FROM DIVIDENDS AND 10.0% SUBTRACTED FROM CAPITAL GAIN DISTRIBUTIONS AS PAID TO REFLECT LIABILITY FOR FEDERAL INCOME TAXES.

were, using The Seminar Fund. I had the computer show a 9 percent withdrawal for eleven years, and, beginning in the twelfth year, use a 21-year self-liquidating program designed to exhaust the principal over their combined expected lifetimes. I had the program done this way even though they did not need to start withdrawal immediately. It was the only fair way to compare the two alternatives, because they planned to hold their Exxon stock if they did not choose to rollover.

In reality they had other funds that I recommended they use first if they decided to rollover so that their rolled-over funds could continue to compound tax sheltered.

In the first printout in Table 16–7 we have assumed that they did not rollover and paid the tax of $14,056, leaving a net of $74,154 to invest in The Seminar Fund. From the 9 percent monthly withdrawals of $556.09 we have deducted 20 percent in taxes on all dividends and 10 percent on capital gains.

As you can see, at the end of eleven years their after-tax distributions were $73,403, and the remaining value was $115,034. The twelfth year begins a 21-year liquidation. During the 32-year period $388,331 after taxes would have been withdrawn.

Table 16–7 is their computer printout. You should have your financial planner obtain a similar one for you using your data.

Now let's turn and look at the past results, and I emphasize past, that would have resulted from rolling over their pension distribution. See Table 16–8. As you will note, they had $88,201 to roll over, because they did not owe the $14,056 in taxes that year. Again 9 percent is withdrawn, or $661.51 per month, for eleven years. From these distributions shown under "Annual Total" has been subtracted 20 percent for federal income taxes. By the end of the eleventh year $69,854 after taxes had been withdrawn and the balance, shown under the column "Total Value," of $167,258 was still in the account. Again we started a 21-year self-liquidating program designed to exhaust principal. As you will note from the totals, $520,789 was withdrawn. (Incidentally, you are not limited to withdrawing just the annual amount shown. If you think your ball of twine is about to unwind, you can make larger withdrawals.)

It may be of great interest to you to note that in the period studied, you would have had $132,458 more distributions ($520,789 − $388,331) by rolling over than if you had not rolled over. In this couple's case it could make an even larger difference because we anticipate their leaving their funds there to compound tax sheltered for several years before making any withdrawals. I also recommend that you postpone withdrawals as long as you comfortably can do so.

Table 16–8. With IRA Rollover

$88,201 Invested in The Seminar Fund

9% withdrawal for 11 years

Self-Liquidating for the next 21 years

January 1, 1955 through January 1, 1976

DATE					NET ASSET VALUE PER SHARE	INITIAL NET ASSET VALUE
1/ 1/44	$88,201.00	$4.75	4.50%	18,565.630	$4.532	$84,153

SYSTEMATIC WITHDRAWAL PLAN
DIVIDENDS AND CAPITAL GAINS REINVESTED
MONTHLY WITHDRAWALS OF $661.51 (9.0% ANNUALLY) BEGINNING 1/31/44

DATE	FROM INCOME DIVS	FROM PRINCIPAL	ANNUAL TOTAL	CUM TOTAL	ANNUAL CAP GAIN DISTRIB'N	REMAINING ORIGINAL SHARES	CAP GAIN SHARES	TOTAL VALUE	SHARES HELD
	====AMOUNTS WITHDRAWN====					====VALUE OF REMAINING SHARES====			
12/31/44	2,864	5,074	6,350	6,350	3,367	91,396	3,464	94,860	18,165
12/31/45	2,471	5,467	6,350	12,701	8,365	107,664	12,790	120,454	18,554
12/31/46	3,425	3,513	6,350	19,051	7,346	91,560	18,498	110,058	19,147
12/31/47	4,451	3,487	6,350	25,402	4,766	80,893	21,769	102,662	19,392
12/31/48	4,506	3,432	6,350	31,752	2,969	71,941	23,185	95,126	19,350
12/31/49	4,112	3,826	6,350	38,102	3,319	68,577	26,728	95,305	19,214
12/31/50	4,459	3,479	6,350	44,453	3,126	72,437	32,869	105,306	19,111
12/31/51	4,469	3,469	6,350	50,803	4,980	75,002	40,618	115,620	19,383
12/31/52	4,363	3,575	6,350	57,154	5,375	73,777	47,378	121,155	19,667
12/31/53	4,621	3,317	6,350	63,504	3,064	65,961	47,488	113,449	19,627
12/31/54	4,527	3,411	6,350	69,854	7,764	90,907	76,351	167,258	20,078
TOTALS	44,267	43,051	69,854		54,442				

NOTE: 20.0% SUBTRACTED FROM TOTAL AMOUNTS WITHDRAWN TO REFLECT LIABILITY FOR FEDERAL INCOME TAXES.

Table 16-8. (*Continued*)

DATE	INITIAL INVESTMENT	OFFERING PRICE	SALES CHARGE INCLUDED	SHARES PURCHASED	NET ASSET VALUE PER SHARE	INITIAL NET ASSET VALUE
1/ 1/55	$167,258.00	$8.33	0.00%	20,078.990	$8.330	$167,258

SYSTEMATIC WITHDRAWAL PLAN
DIVIDENDS AND CAPITAL GAINS REINVESTED

MONTHLY WITHDRAWALS BEGINNING 1/31/55 BASED ON A 21-YEAR SELF-LIQUIDATING PROGRAM DESIGNED TO EXHAUST PRINCIPAL

	===========AMOUNTS WITHDRAWN===========					====VALUE OF REMAINING SHARES====			
DATE	FROM INCOME DIVS	FROM PRINCIPAL	ANNUAL TOTAL	CUM TOTAL	ANNUAL CAP GAIN DISTRIB'N	REMAINING ORIGINAL SHARES	CAP GAIN SHARES	TOTAL VALUE	SHARES HELD
12/31/55	5,248	3,797	7,236	7,236	14,050	185,168	14,592	199,760	21,205
12/31/56	5,462	5,180	8,514	15,750	15,259	180,421	29,767	210,188	22,289
12/31/57	5,762	4,972	8,587	24,337	11,050	140,959	34,508	175,467	23,148
12/31/58	5,744	5,975	9,376	33,713	8,466	183,947	55,963	239,910	23,360
12/31/59	5,796	9,447	12,194	45,907	17,312	182,044	75,792	257,836	24,119
12/31/60	6,320	9,472	12,633	58,541	14,201	165,071	87,615	252,686	24,604
12/31/61	6,076	13,249	15,461	74,002	15,462	174,631	115,644	290,275	24,788
12/31/62	6,146	11,712	14,286	88,288	11,005	130,332	103,523	233,855	24,642
12/31/63	6,001	14,332	16,266	104,554	11,161	134,828	130,432	265,260	24,335
12/31/64	6,134	18,581	19,772	124,326	16,541	126,264	156,428	282,692	24,203
12/31/65	6,324	22,786	23,288	147,614	20,138	123,137	203,093	326,230	23,969
12/31/66	7,324	25,342	26,133	173,748	23,910	88,313	208,183	296,496	23,834
12/31/67	7,762	31,838	31,680	205,428	16,683	73,127	266,570	339,697	22,798
12/31/68	8,387	36,714	36,081	241,509	14,064	40,049	307,617	347,666	21,421
12/31/69	8,103	38,361	37,171	278,679	20,493	0	266,168	266,168	20,148
12/31/70	7,475	33,447	32,737	311,417	11,362	0	227,621	227,621	18,166
12/31/71	6,395	43,606	40,001	351,418	3,937	0	213,107	213,107	15,232
12/31/72	5,198	52,185	45,907	397,324	5,625	0	185,164	185,164	12,094
12/31/73	4,091	49,925	43,213	440,537	2,832	0	102,684	102,684	8,564
12/31/74	3,513	42,802	37,052	477,588	0	0	42,129	42,129	4,549
12/31/75	929	53,073	43,201	520,789	27	0	0	0	0
TOTALS	124,190	526,796	520,789		253,578				

NOTE: 20.0% SUBTRACTED FROM TOTAL AMOUNTS WITHDRAWN TO REFLECT LIABILITY FOR FEDERAL INCOME TAXES.

It is very difficult for the "without rollover" account to ever make up the $14,056 deficiency caused by the taxes.

Table 16–8 is the "with rollover" computer printout.

• COMPANY TERMINATION OF RETIREMENT PROGRAMS

Perhaps you are not retiring, but your company decides to terminate its retirement plan and makes a lump-sum distribution to you. (This has occurred at an alarming rate since the passage of the punitive ERISA bill.) Under this type of rollover the requirements are exactly the same as above, with one exception. That exception is that you do not have to have five years of plan participation at the time you receive your lump-sum distribution. However, all of the other requirements must be met. Rollovers as a result of such decisions also may later be transferred into a new employer's retirement plan, if the employer's plan permits and is similar to the one from which the distribution was originally made.

Finally, there is the rollover that results if you move your IRA contribution from one IRA program to another. This type of rollover may be done only once every three years. However, you do not have to rollover all of your assets, nor do you have to have been a participant for five years, but you must carry out the rollover within the 60-day period. Here is where a mutual fund IRA plan that offers a family of funds may prove additionally advantageous. With a family of funds, you can exchange one fund for another (i.e., move from growth of capital to income and safety of principal, or other available combinations) under the same plan as often as you wish and never violate the three-year rule. Why? Because you are not moving to a new program. Insurance company and savings bank plans generally don't offer this advantage.

• WHAT ABOUT ESTATE TAXES?

If your IRA plan permits you to name a beneficiary (other than your estate), your IRA account can also be saved from federal estate tax. However, in order for the total value of your IRA account not to be included in your estate for tax purposes, one important step must be taken. That step is that the beneficiary must receive distribution from your IRA program in installments spread evenly over a period of at least 36 months. Mutual funds as well as annuities offer distribution arrangements that enable you to take advantage of this estate tax savings.

• NONQUALIFIED DEFERRED COMPENSATION PLANS

A nonqualified deferred compensation plan is a commitment by an employer to pay an employee a predetermined amount of money for a specified period of years upon his retirement or termination of employment.

Let's assume that you are a highly paid executive. You could choose to have your income reduced and have the amount of the reduction become the substance of a deferred compensation plan. You could also have additional amounts deferred in lieu of a salary increase. This would allow you to reduce your current income tax and have an investment compounding under a tax shelter.

When you reach retirement, you would begin to pay income taxes on your withdrawals. At that time you will no doubt be eligible for additional tax exemptions as a retiree, and you will probably be in a lower tax bracket.

The nonqualified plan can be installed without prior approval of the IRS. The rules for adoption and maintenance are few, and the plan can be discriminatory. You may have a deferred plan in addition to a qualified profit-sharing or pension plan.

Your corporation, however, cannot deduct its contributions from its federal income tax. As your taxes on this money come due, then the corporation begins to enjoy a corresponding tax deduction.

Deferred compensation is now a personal service income under the maximum tax law of 50 percent tax, and neither you nor the corporation has to pay the social security tax. Nor does the corporation have to pay federal unemployment tax. Deferred compensation does not reduce the Social Security benefits you are entitled to receive.

• SELF-EMPLOYED, NOT INCORPORATED

If you are self-employed and not incorporated, you should consider a Keogh Plan, a tax-sheltered retirement plan established by Congress in 1962. I have covered this in detail in Chapter 17 entitled, "Are You Self-employed?" The Keogh Plan allows you to contribute 15 percent of your earned income from self-employment to your own retirement plan, up to a maximum of $7500, and to deduct this contribution as an expense of doing business. Also, all earnings compound tax-deferred.

• TAX-SHELTERED ANNUITIES FOR EMPLOYEES OF NONPROFIT INSTITUTIONS

If you work for a nonprofit institution such as a school, city, or hospital, you may also qualify for a tax-deferred retirement plan.

Let's assume that you are a school teacher. You may request that the school reduce your salary up to 16⅔ percent and have the funds placed into a qualified annuity program through a life insurance company. You thereby avoid paying current taxes on the amount of the reduction. You may also reduce your income sufficiently to reduce the taxes on the remainder.

There are two types of annuities: (1) the fixed and (2) the variable. Many of the older fixed annuities still pay a very low rate of return—many under 3 percent annually. Even with tax shelter that is not progress at our present rate of inflation.

The Consumer Price Index of the Bureau of Labor and the University of Chicago Center for Research project an average rate of inflation through the year 2000 of 6.2 percent. Whether one considers inflation a destructive force, real or pseudo-prosperity, or merely a normal way of life, one must recognize that it will forever be a part of the nation's economic environment.

Despite the foregoing, many people still feel that conservative investment requires a "riskless" savings device such as a fixed annuity, and that any nonguaranteed equity investment is automatically speculative. This attitude is dedicated to the proposition that the long-range economy will be deflationary rather than inflationary, and that the world's economy will stand still awaiting one's retirement.

History, however, has proved beyond any doubt that basing one's financial security on fixed-guaranteed savings vehicles is the ultimate in absurd speculation. In recent years a few progressive insurance companies have been offering fixed annuities in the 7 to 8 percent range and are also allowing you to move from a fixed to variable position for only a small transfer fee.

Variable Annuities • Another choice you may make is to use a variable annuity. I have examined a large number and find the performance of many of them discouraging. They are usually middle-of-the-road, which may or may not fit your needs. You may be relatively young and interested in growth, but your money may be pooled with a person who is about ready to retire and whose objective is income. Do considerable study of the pros and cons of establishing a tax-sheltered annuity. If you do decide to use one, spend considerable time and effort selecting the best one possible.

• INDIVIDUAL RETIREMENT ACCOUNTS

With the signing of the Employee Benefit Security Act of 1974, if you are not covered by any retirement plan other than Social Security, you may now set up one for yourself, tax deductible.

You may create an Individual Retirement Account, commonly referred to as an "IRA." You may invest as much as 15 percent of your pay into IRA, up to $1500 a year, and take a tax deduction for that amount. If both you and your spouse receive taxable compensation and both are not covered by a retirement plan, you may each establish your own IRA. Together you may contribute up to $3000 annually ($1500 × 2). However, your individual deductible contribution may not exceed 15 percent of your compensation for that year. For example, if Mary and John Smith earn $8000 and $15,000, respectively, Mary can contribute up to $1200 and John $1500 to their individual IRA plans. This results in a total federal tax deduction on their joint 1040 return of $2700.

The Non-working Spouse • In cases where one spouse works and contributes to an IRA but the other spouse receives no employment (or self-employment) compensation, an even larger tax-deductible contribution than $1500 is possible. The law now permits a working spouse to establish a similar IRA account for the nonworking spouse. However, certain requirements must be met. First, separate accounts must be established for each spouse. Second, the total yearly contribution to both accounts can not exceed the lesser of 15 percent of the compensation of the working spouse or $1750. The total contribution must be equally divided between the two accounts if you want the full tax deduction.

Time For Making The Contribution • At present, the IRS will permit tax-deductible IRA contributions to be made if such action is taken within 45 days *after the end* of your taxable year. The taxable year for most of us ends on December 31. Therefore, a deductible IRA contribution can be made up to the following February 14. Equally important is the fact that you can also establish your IRA during that 45-day period and still get the full deduction for the prior year. You may take the deduction even if you take only the "standard" deduction rather than itemizing when you file your income tax return.

You may invest your funds in one of these three ways:

1 •   You may buy a special annuity that will not begin to pay off until age 59½.

2 •   You may invest in a special type of U.S. Treasury bond.

3 •   You may place the funds in a trust or custodial account to be invested and held by a bank or other approved institution.

An excellent way to accomplish the last alternative would be to select a well-managed mutual fund. Most funds provide IRA plans that enable low-cost administration and automatic reinvestment. This method can make available the possible advantage of dollar-cost-averaging, as explained in the chapter, "Is There an Infallible Way to Invest?"

I must warn you that I have never found a way to move a client out of the special U.S. Treasury bond into another IRA investment. From all the interpretations I have been able to find, funds placed there must be left until you are 59½ years of age. If you don't want your IRA investment decisions written in stone, you may want to avoid this choice.

Your annual earnings on your investment will compound tax sheltered. When you withdraw your funds at age 59½ or later, the amounts withdrawn are fully taxable as income, though perhaps your tax bracket may be lower than when you were working, or there may be a more advantageous income-averaging plan available by then. You should also be aware that there are tax penalties if you withdraw your funds before age 59½, or if you withdraw insufficient amounts after you are age 70½.

The Family Installment Sale •   You may own stocks or other assets that have greatly appreciated in value. These may no longer fit your financial objective of more income, or you may desire to lower your risks through better diversification. However, if you sell the asset, you will incur capital gains taxes. This leaves you with that locked-in feeling. Is there a way to postpone a portion of the taxes, obtain diversification, increase your income, and possibly decrease future inheritance taxes?

Yes, there is through the use of an installment sale.

To illustrate the possible advantages of this approach, let's consider the options open to you.

First, you can hold onto your present investments. By taking no action you remain locked in. To avoid capital gains taxes, you would have to keep these investments for the rest of your life. Also, any additional appreciation will further increase the value of your estate for federal tax purposes, as well as your potential capital gains tax.

Second, you can sell your investment for cash and reinvest the proceeds. This creates an immediate capital gains tax on which taxes must be paid. Assume that you have a cost basis of $20,000 on assets that now have a value of $100,000. Upon sale you realize an $80,000 capital gain that will be taxable.

Third, you can make an installment sale. Under this plan you would sell your asset to a buyer at its full market value. The buyer would give you an interest-bearing installment note. In this way you incur capital gains liability only as you actually receive payments from this note. The provisions of the note establish the amount of money you will receive at specified intervals and the period of years over which the periodic payments will be made.

Advantage to the Seller • There can be advantages to you, the seller, and to the buyer. Let's examine some of them, and for the purpose of our discussion let's assume that the buyer is your son.

First, you can unlock your gains and spread your tax liability over a period of years, possibly putting you into a lower tax bracket. Second, you can increase your income over the term of the note. Third, the payments you receive are mostly taxable as capital gains. Fourth, as the note is repaid and the payments spent, the value of your estate decreases for federal estate tax purposes. Any growth in assets you have sold now belongs to the buyer and will not be reflected in your estate. Fifth, it protects your estate against possible increases in estate taxes on the future appreciation of your investments.

Advantages to the Buyer • The installment sale allows your son to become the owner of substantial assets, without making any large and immediate cash outlay. He can now sell his newly acquired stocks or other assets without the payment of substantial income gift or estate taxes and put the proceeds into a more appropriate investment. He may also receive an annual tax deduction for the interest he is paying on the note. In the meantime, all future growth belongs to him.

How To Fund the Installment Sale • One of the best ways, in my opinion, to provide the necessary funds for the monthly payments your son will need to make to you is for him to invest the proceeds from the sale of the assets in shares of a high-quality, middle-of-the-road mutual fund and begin a systematic withdrawal program. In this way the investment would be diversified in a quality cross section of stocks and bonds and be professionally managed, and the custodian bank would send a monthly check to you.

The proper legal instruments to accomplish an installment sale should be prepared by your attorney and should be coordinated with the advice of your CPA. Remind them that the note should be carried at interest. The interest may be stated or unstated. If stated (which I recommend), it must be at least 4 percent per year. In the event the interest stated is less than 4 percent, or if no interest is stated at all, Uncle Sam will impute a 5 percent interest rate.

A summary of the advantages of the installment sale are

1 • Avoids some of the cost of probate (balance of the note is in the estate).

2 • Saves on the costs of federal estate taxes (since only the balance of the note is in the estate).

3 • Saves on state inheritance taxes (since only the balance of the note is in the estate).

4 • Spreads the long-term capital gains tax over a number of years.

5 • Eliminates or drastically reduces the preference tax.

6 • The transfer is not a gift.

7 • There is no future appreciation to increase estate valuation.

Private Annuity • Another tool that may fit your financial objective is the private annuity. This type of an annuity involves the transfer of your property to a transferee—an individual, a partnership, or a corporation—in exchange for an unsecured promise to make periodic payments to you in fixed amounts for a designated period of time. In most cases, this will be for your lifetime.

The assets you may use for this are real property, stocks, bonds, mutual funds, limited partnerships, and so forth.

The advantage to you in using this method is that it can usually increase your cash flow from your assets without substantially increasing your income tax liability. Capital gains taxation will be spread over the life of your agreement. This should serve to reduce and probably eliminate any minimum preference tax that otherwise might accrue on the sale of your assets.

Since these assets are generally not includable for estate tax purposes, there could be a savings on estate taxes in the event of your premature death. The private annuity can be partially taxable under the estate under certain conditions which your attorney can detail for you. This transaction does not have to show a gain as in the case of an installment sale.

There are some disadvantages to the private annuity. If you should die prior to completion of the agreement, your son would have a low basis in the property. If your son holds the property for more than a year the gain is subject to treatment as a long-term capital gain. If you live longer than the life expectancy table indicates, the payments may be greater than the original value, but the tax savings and appreciation could more than make up for this. Also, there is no tax deduction accruing to your son for interest paid to you. Too, another disadvantage is the provision that you are unable to secure the annuity payments by collateralizing through a trust or by mortgage.

The installment sale and private annuity can be funded in various ways. Some that you should consider are oil and gas income-limited partnerships, mutual funds, real estate limited partnerships, tax-free bonds, and quality stocks with generous dividends.

In summary, the advantages of the private annuity are

1 · Avoids all the costs of probate.

2 · Saves on federal estate taxes in premature death and after the transferor's mortality.

3 · Saves on state inheritance taxes.

4 · Spreads the long-term capital gains tax over a number of years.

5 · Eliminates or reduces the preference tax.

6 · The transfer can be a gift or not a gift.

7 · There is no future appreciation to increase estate valuation.

The Living Trust · The proper use of the living trust (also referred to as the revocable or the intervivos trust) can reduce the cost of passing your assets to your heirs.

With the living trust a pour-over will should be drawn to cover all assets you have not registered to the trust. You should have the trust drawn in the state you reside.

Your trust can be written so as to pass your assets as you would do in a will. Some states will allow you to be your own trustee. Some require co-trustees. You may also use a bank or corporate trustee. All of the assets you want to place in the trust should be listed. As changes are made the list should be changed.

The trust can offer the following benefits:

1 · The cost of probate and administration fees saved because the trust assets are not probated through the courts.

2 · The prolonged probate time can be saved as the assets can be passed immediately. All creditors must be paid, and the federal estate taxes and the state taxes can be put into an escrow account with the trustee liable.

3 · The problem of incapacity is lessened. Generally, under the will method the individual has no document while he is alive, and, should incapacity occur, the court must be petitioned to declare him incapacitated in order to sell any property. The document can state that three doctors can declare the individual incapacitated and the co-trustees or successor trustee assume trustee role.

4 · The trust can afford privacy in death as to the amount of the assets held in the estate, since it does not go through the probate court. No listing of assets is required, which usually ends up in the local papers.

5 · A trust can keep the estate under family control. Since assets such as stock, property, or closely held corporations or businesses are not under court control, these can be sold to raise cash for costs and fees and for state and federal estate taxes.

6 · The savings of federal and state inheritance and estate taxes may be achieved by splitting the assets between husband and wife into two trusts.

First $100,000—marital gift tax-free
Second $100,000—fully taxable (can use unified gift credits)
Over $200,000—50 percent taxable, 50 percent marital gift tax-free.

There are some assets that you should avoid placing in the living trust. Some of these are cars, jewelry, furs, and furnishings. You also should not place in the trust professional corporation stock, since most states require that the stockholder be of the same profession as the original stockholder.

Also, you cannot place in the trust tax option corporations and subchapter "S" corporations, since a trust cannot be the owner of such stock, as it would terminate the election.

The transfer of assets into a living trust is not of taxable consequence. (Gift taxes can occur when assets are placed into short-term or irrevocable trusts.)

• SUMMARY

If you are in the 50 percent tax bracket or realize a large capital gain in a particular year, you should consider investing in properly structured oil and gas drilling programs, mining, real estate with high tax deductions, cattle feeding and breeding programs, cable television, record companies, research and development, etc.

These can be in the form of registered limited partnerships, joint ventures, or private placements exempt from registration. You may want to restrict yourself to limited partnerships registered with the SEC unless you or your respected advisor has considerable sophistication in the particular field under consideration and have personal knowledge of the joint venture and private placements.

Effective June 10, 1974, the SEC issued a "Notice of Adoption of Rule 146 Under the Securities Act of 1933—Transactions By an Issuer Deemed Not to Involve Any Public Offering." This ruling exempted certain offerings with less than 35 investors. The burden of determining who is eligible to qualify as an investor was shifted to the financial planner selling the partnership.

My interpretation of the rule boils down simply to this: To be eligible to make the investment in an exempt partnership, you must be rich and smart, or be rich and have a smart friend (technically called the "offeree representative").

With the increased scarcity of venture capital, Rule 146 may prove to be very essential to the maintenance of the capitalistic system in the United States.

If your tax bracket is below 50 percent, you should consider such investments as oil and gas income-limited partnerships and real estate income-limited partnerships with smaller or no tax deductions on your original investment, but with the opportunity for tax-sheltered cash flow from the investment.

In all of these you should look for a capable management team with an excellent past record. You should not try to make a killing on any one of your investments. Keep in mind that your goal is to take ordinary income and convert it into long-term capital gains within certain guidelines under the Tax Reform Act of 1976, or to delay the income to a lower tax year. Remember that income from shelters is not usually earned income, which receives the more favorable 50 percent maximum tax consideration. It is "other income," which may be taxed up to 70 percent.

If you invest in tax shelters, do so as early in the year as possible. Drilling rigs are usually less expensive, and drilling prospects may offer greater profit potential. Cattle and feed may be lower-priced. Your interest deductions on real estate construction are prorated on the basis of the number of days that year you have been an investor. At the end of the year, everyone is looking for shelters, and the competition is fierce. Pressure to save your tax dollars may cause you to invest without proper investigation.

The operation, taxation, and investment characteristics of the various tax shelters vary greatly; however, most of them have certain aspects in common: They are complex, involve risk, and are illiquid. But then the alternative involves considerable risk, too—that of paying taxes. The expected rate of return on paying taxes is zero, and the risk is 100 percent. If you can improve those odds, do consider avoiding sending your hard-earned dollars on their one-way trip to Washington.

Application

1 • What do you project will be your taxable income this year?

2 • What tax bracket will you be in?

3 • Do you have a knowledgeable and caring financial planner?

4 • Do you have a creative and competent CPA?

5 • If your answer to the two above questions is no, what constructive efforts are you going to make to obtain:
   A financial planner
   A CPA?

6 • Should you invest in municipal bonds? Read again the chapters on real estate and energy. Are the income programs available there better alternatives?

7 • Should you consider single-premium deferred annuities?

8 • Do you have a retirement program?

9 • If not, what constructive steps will you take today to start one?

10 • What is the dollar amount that you project will be available at your retirement?

11 • Will this be sufficient for your and your dependents' needs at our present rate of inflation?

12 • If not, what plan of action will you now begin?

13 • Should you talk to your financial planner and attorney about a living trust?
   An installment sale?

14 • What constructive steps will you take this year to reduce your taxes?
   a.
   b.
   c.

17

Are You Self-Employed?

• **MR. KEOGH**

Are you self-employed as a professional person, a proprietor, or a partner of an unincorporated business? If so, you probably work longer hours than your friend who works for a corporation, but you probably enjoy your freedom and independence. However, when you sit down at the beginning of each year to assess your financial progress and begin to make plans for the new year, you may become painfully aware that the tax bite left you with very little to invest for the golden years of retirement.

At that time you may look with envy at your friend who works for a corporation with a pension and/or profit-sharing plan or who has incorporated his business and set up such a plan. Contributions have been made for his benefit in a retirement plan with "before-tax" dollars, while you, if you are in a 30 percent tax bracket, had to earn $1.42 to have $1.00 left to set aside to invest for your retirement, and if that $1.00 produced income, you also lost 30 percent of that amount to taxes.

Congressman Keogh felt this was an inequitable arrangement, so in 1962, he was successful in getting Congress to enact the Self-Employed Individuals Tax Retirement Act, HR-10. With the passage of this legislation and later amendments, it became possible for you, if you are self-employed, to establish a Keogh Plan for your retirement.

• YOUR CONTRIBUTIONS

The plan allows you as a self-employed individual to set aside 15 percent of your earned income (after expenses and before income taxes) or $7500, whichever is the smaller of the two. These contributions are fully deductible, and all earnings accumulate over the years tax-sheltered.

If you have employees, you must also include all full-time employees who have been in your employ for three years. A full-time employee is defined as one who works for you at least 1000 hours per year (but may drop below this number without elimination).

If you have had your self-employed status less than three years and are setting up a plan for yourself, you must also do the same for each employee who has worked for you the same period of time. Here is a rule that may help you to answer questions you may have with regard to contributions you must also make for employees: "You must do for your employees what you are doing for yourself, if all conditions are the same."

The amount you must contribute for them must be the same percentage you contribute for yourself, with certain variations.

HR-10 Calculations • As an example: if your earned income from self-employment is $25,000 for the year, if you have been in business two years, if you have an employee who has worked for you for those two years, and if you pay him $6000 per year, you must include him. Your Keogh contributions would be

$$\$25,000 \times 15\% = \$3750 \text{ contribution for yourself}$$

$$\$ 6,000 \times 15\% = \frac{\$ \ 900}{\$4650} \text{ contribution for your employee}$$

In a 36 percent bracket Uncle Sam contributes $1674 of the $4650, and you contribute $2976, making it possible for you to invest $3750 for your benefit at a cost to you of $2076.

The Higher Your Income, the Greater Your Advantage • If, however, you are netting $50,000 annually, and have one employee whom you pay $6000, you may contribute $7500 on your behalf, and you must contribute 15 percent of the employee's income, or $900. Your net gains would be as follows:

Contribution for your Keogh	$7500
Contribution for employee	900
Total contribution deductible	8400
Your tax deduction ($8400 × 50%) =	$4200
Tax savings	4200
Investment you make for yourself	7500
Net gain in year contribution made	3300

If your income is above $100,000, you will not be permitted to count more than $100,000 of earnings in figuring the amount you may set aside. Therefore, you would use a set-aside factor of 7½ percent to invest the maximum of $7500. To meet the nondiscrimination rules, you must also contribute 7½ percent of your employees' pay, or $450 for an employee who earns $6000.

Do You Have a Large Payroll? • Not all self-employed persons, of course, can benefit equally from the law. Take the case of Dr. Williams, age 35, who has a taxable income of $22,000 and an eligible payroll of $12,000.

The law allows Dr. Williams to invest $3300, or 15 percent of his income. His tax saving on this amount would be $1056 in a 32 percent tax bracket. But he must also contribute 15 percent of his payroll, or $1800. This, of course, is classified as a business expense and gives him a further tax savings of $576. By adding the $1056 to the $576, we have a total tax saving of $1632. That means that the cost of the Keogh Plan to Dr. Williams is $168 a year ($1800 less $1632).

Remember, though, that's not the end of the story because of the tax-free accumulation feature. Over the years this could overshadow the small annual cost, since no taxes are payable until retirement, and the plan could also create considerable good will.

If Dr. Williams did not want to contribute to his employees' retirement program, he could set up his own individual retirement account (covered more fully in the chapter "Avoiding the One-way Trip to Washington") and set aside $1500 tax-deductible. The same provision was made for those who do not qualify for Keogh or are not under a qualified pension or profit-sharing plan. The amount of $1750 can now be set aside and deducted by a married cople if $875 is registered in the nonworking spouse's name and $875 in the working spouse's name.

Voluntary Contributions • If you have at least one participant in your plan who is not a greater than 10 percent owner (owner-employee), you may also make a $2500 voluntary contribution (or 10 percent, whichever is the smaller). This must be made with after-tax dollars, but, again, the dividends and capital gains compound tax-sheltered during the time that they are in the plan.

Your employees must also have the same privilege and may also make voluntary contributions up to 10 percent of their salary.

The principal in this account may be withdrawn without penalty. If you are in this position and have children whom you plan to send to college, this may be a good way to accumulate funds for this purpose. For example, let's assume that you have placed $2500 per year into your voluntary account. In ten years it's college time. You may withdraw the $25,000, leaving the earnings to continue compounding tax-free.

If you are an employer and have too many employees to make a maximum tax-deductible contribution economically feasible, you could make a 1 percent deductible contribution and a 10 percent voluntary contribution. Under this arrangement you would be required to contribute only 1 percent for each of your eligible employees. Then you could make your 10 percent voluntary contribution and have all the earnings from it tax-sheltered.

• INVESTING YOUR RETIREMENT FUNDS

Once you have decided to adopt the Keogh Plan, you are then faced with a decision as to how to invest your contributions. The law permits alternatives: annuities, face amount certificates, life insurance, a special series of government bonds, an investment portfolio administered under a bank trusteeship, or under a trusteeship not administered by a bank but acceptable to the IRS, and approved mutual fund prototype plans. Of these, in my opinion, none compares with the mutual fund plans from the standpoint of flexibility, convenience and potential for growth. They also publish their past performance records, which may be of help to you in programming possible future benefits (with no guarantee, of course).

Another plan that you may also consider is one administered under a trusteeship. This plan allows you to place a wide variety of investments in the plan, such as registered oil and gas income limited partnerships and registered real estate limited partnerships.

You may move from one investment to the other without tax consequences under that trusteeship. This gives you the flexibility needed for this dynamic world that we live in. Avoid like the plague the special government bond.

You do have some limitations on moving from one fiduciary to another. You may move once every three years. For example, if you opened an account with a savings and loan, and later wanted to move it to a mutual fund, you may do so without waiting, but if you decide to move again you must wait three years. Three-year wait periods must occur for all your following moves.

If you have chosen the mutual fund route, you may want to consider investing monthly as you earn. This gives you the possible benefits of dollar-cost-averaging. For example, if you are contributing $3600 to the plan, you might invest $300 per month.

You may also consider a lump-sum investment at the beginning of the year, so that your dividends and capital gains, if any, can be compounding throughout the year. Market conditions each year will determine which approach would have been best.

I find that most of my clients wait until we call to remind them that it's time to make their yearly Keogh contributions. We do this at the end of November.

If you have not established a Keogh Plan, you must do so and make your contribution before the end of your fiscal year. If you have already established your plan, you must make your contribution some time before you pay your federal income taxes.

•   UNDERSTANDING
YOUR BENEFITS

In my opinion, if you are self-employed, do not have too many employees, and do not have a Keogh plan, you just do not understand the situation. (An exception might be if you are in a 50 percent tax bracket or above and are willing to use these dollars in over 100 percent tax-deductible investments.)

First, it allows you to invest at a discount. Uncle Sam is paying part of the cost of your retirement program. (At least, he is not taking this amount away from you, so you can have some to set aside.)

Second, the earnings compound tax-sheltered. We are so accustomed to paying taxes that we've forgotten what tax shelter can mean. You may begin withdrawing retirement benefits at $59\frac{1}{2}$ years of age and must begin withdrawals at $70\frac{1}{2}$.

Some self-employed professionals will not set up a Keogh Plan because they can't withdraw these funds until they are $59\frac{1}{2}$ years of age without some penalties. It is usually a blessing that the funds cannot be withdrawn or pledged at the bank for collateral. You would be amazed at the number of professionals who arrive at what was supposed to be their golden years and find themselves scrimping to eke out an existence that is not so golden.

The Magic of Tax-sheltered Compounding • When you add to the benefit of tax shelter the phenomenon of compounding, you have double forces working for you.

Let's assume that you can afford to set aside $7500 per year and do so for 20 years. (If your contribution is less, just adjust by what percentage $7500 is of the amount you can invest.)

If you contribute $7500 per year from age 45 to age 65, you will have contributed $150,000. (Remember, these are before-tax dollars.) If you average 6 percent on your funds, this sum will grow to $292,443. If you move up to 10 percent, this amount will grow to $472,512. If you do as well as our Seminar Fund did over the 20-year period December 31, 1957 to December 31, 1976, your funds would have grown to $429,248.

These funds are "tax-sheltered" instead of "tax-free" because at retirement you will have several choices as to how you will receive your benefits, and your tax will vary accordingly. These conditions seem to be changing so rapidly that it's difficult to give you any estimates about what will be your tax status in the future. However, after retirement, you may be in a lower tax bracket. Also, there is presently an income-averaging formula that the IRS allows. Even if the funds were taxed as ordinary income, which can usually be avoided, just the privilege of compounding without taxes for 20 years will make a tremendous difference in your results.

It Does Make a Difference • Here is an example using the Seminar Fund with and without Keogh:

A. Without tax-sheltered benefits (assumed 35 percent tax bracket)

B. With tax-sheltered benefits.

Tables 17–1 and 17–2 cover the 20-year period from December 31, 1957, through December 31, 1976, and now here comes my disclaimer. "Results shown should not be considered as a representation of the dividend income or capital gain or loss that may be realized from an investment made in the fund today. A program of the type illustrated does not insure a profit or protect against depreciation in declining markets." I might add that this 20-year period contained one of the worst declining markets.

The illustrations assume an investment in the Seminar Fund by a self-employed individual in a 35 percent bracket who invests $7500 each year. If you do not use some tax planning, your tax bracket will be 50 percent and the advantage of Keogh even greater.

Table 17-1. Illustration of a 20-year Assumed Retirement Program—Without Tax Shelter

DATE	INITIAL INVESTMENT	OFFERING PRICE	SALES CHARGE INCLUDED	NET ASSET VALUE PER SHARE	SHARES PURCHASED	INITIAL NET ASSET VALUE
1/ 1/57	$4,875.00	$10.31	8.50%	$9.430	472.842	$4,459

ANNUAL INVESTMENTS OF $4,875.00 -- SAME DAY AS INITIAL INVESTMENT
DIVIDENDS AND CAPITAL GAINS REINVESTED

CUMULATIVE VOLUME DISCOUNT REFLECTED WHERE APPLICABLE IN THIS ILLUSTRATION

	=====COST OF SHARES=====					=====VALUE OF SHARES=====					
DATE	CUM INV'M'T	ANNUAL INCOME DIVS	CUM INCOME DIVS	TOTAL INV'M'T COST	ANNUAL CAP GAIN DISTRIB'N	FROM INV'M'T	FROM CAP GAINS REINV'D	SUB-TOTAL	FROM DIVS REINV'D	TOTAL VALUE	SHARES HELD
12/31/57	4,875	81	81	4,956	199	3,584	190	3,774	73	3,847	507
12/31/58	9,750	181	262	10,012	341	10,903	628	11,531	305	11,836	1,152
12/31/59	14,625	263	525	15,150	1,004	16,043	1,671	17,714	583	18,297	1,711
12/31/60	19,500	372	898	20,398	1,054	19,744	2,704	22,448	942	23,390	2,277
12/31/61	24,375	451	1,349	25,724	1,463	27,736	4,572	32,308	1,538	33,846	2,890
12/31/62	29,250	547	1,895	31,145	1,230	26,190	4,802	30,992	1,804	32,796	3,455
12/31/63	34,125	648	2,544	36,669	1,551	35,342	7,117	42,459	2,749	45,208	4,147
12/31/64	39,000	784	3,327	42,327	2,723	42,862	10,369	53,231	3,719	56,950	4,875
12/31/65	43,875	941	4,269	48,144	3,855	55,370	16,062	71,432	5,345	76,777	5,641
12/31/66	48,750	1,250	5,519	54,269	5,126	54,866	19,521	74,387	6,112	80,499	6,470
12/31/67	53,625	1,538	7,057	60,682	4,250	71,290	27,763	99,053	8,886	107,939	7,244
12/31/68	58,500	1,937	8,994	67,494	3,929	82,776	35,062	117,838	11,750	129,588	7,984
12/31/69	63,375	2,204	11,198	74,573	6,690	71,203	34,561	105,764	11,709	117,473	8,892
12/31/70	68,250	2,427	13,625	81,875	4,426	72,000	37,258	109,258	13,723	122,981	9,814
12/31/71	73,125	2,601	16,226	89,351	2,215	85,643	43,852	129,495	17,988	147,483	10,542
12/31/72	78,000	2,775	19,001	97,001	4,271	98,871	52,342	151,213	22,569	173,782	11,350
12/31/73	82,875	3,130	22,132	105,007	3,218	81,114	44,321	125,435	20,668	146,103	12,185
12/31/74	87,750	4,964	27,096	114,846	0	66,279	34,230	100,509	20,660	121,169	13,085
12/31/75	92,625	4,821	31,917	124,542	798	91,295	44,828	136,123	31,445	167,568	14,069
12/31/76	97,500	4,551	36,468	133,968	2,790	118,408	58,156	176,564	43,491	220,055	14,979
TOTAL					51,134						

NOTE: 35.0% SUBTRACTED FROM DIVIDENDS AND 17.5% SUBTRACTED FROM CAPITAL GAIN DISTRIBUTIONS AS PAID TO REFLECT LIABILITY FOR FEDERAL INCOME TAXES.

Table 17–2. Illustration of a 20-year Assumed Retirement Program—With Tax Shelter

DATE	INITIAL INVESTMENT	OFFERING PRICE	SALES CHARGE INCLUDED	SHARES PURCHASED	NET ASSET VALUE PER SHARE	INITIAL NET ASSET VALUE
1/ 1/57	$7,500.00	$10.31	8.50%	727.449	$9.430	$6,860

ANNUAL INVESTMENTS OF $7,500.00 -- SAME DAY AS INITIAL INVESTMENT
DIVIDENDS AND CAPITAL GAINS REINVESTED

CUMULATIVE VOLUME DISCOUNT REFLECTED WHERE APPLICABLE IN THIS ILLUSTRATION

	========COST OF SHARES========					========VALUE OF SHARES========					
DATE	CUM INV'M'T	ANNUAL INCOME DIVS	CUM INCOME DIVS	TOTAL INV'M'T COST	ANNUAL CAP GAIN DISTRIB'N	FROM INV'M'T	FROM CAP GAINS REINV'D	SUB-TOTAL	FROM DIVS REINV'D	TOTAL VALUE	SHARES HELD
12/31/57	7,500	194	194	7,694	373	5,514	358	5,872	173	6,045	797
12/31/58	15,000	435	628	15,628	646	16,773	1,186	17,959	732	18,691	1,819
12/31/59	22,500	641	1,270	23,770	1,930	24,795	3,189	27,984	1,406	29,390	2,749
12/31/60	30,000	923	2,192	32,192	2,052	30,594	5,201	35,795	2,299	38,094	3,709
12/31/61	37,500	1,126	3,318	40,818	2,880	42,920	8,860	51,780	3,781	55,561	4,744
12/31/62	45,000	1,384	4,702	49,702	2,440	40,588	9,358	49,946	4,474	54,420	5,734
12/31/63	52,500	1,651	6,353	58,853	3,118	54,843	13,965	68,808	6,863	75,671	6,942
12/31/64	60,000	2,012	8,365	68,365	5,515	66,445	20,520	86,965	9,340	96,305	8,245
12/31/65	67,500	2,447	10,812	78,312	7,902	85,861	32,068	117,929	13,512	131,441	9,657
12/31/66	75,000	3,307	14,119	89,119	10,635	85,096	39,355	124,451	15,594	140,045	11,257
12/31/67	82,500	4,115	18,234	100,734	8,963	110,594	56,376	166,970	22,866	189,836	12,740
12/31/68	90,000	5,265	23,499	113,499	8,333	128,349	71,630	199,979	30,531	230,510	14,202
12/31/69	97,500	6,076	29,575	127,075	14,356	110,356	71,229	181,585	30,767	212,352	16,075
12/31/70	105,000	6,776	36,351	141,351	9,641	111,540	77,312	188,852	36,493	225,345	17,984
12/31/71	112,500	7,317	43,668	156,168	4,926	132,620	91,329	223,949	48,244	272,193	19,456
12/31/72	120,000	7,869	51,537	171,537	9,571	153,135	109,702	262,837	60,971	323,808	21,150
12/31/73	127,500	8,971	60,508	188,008	7,292	125,655	93,456	219,111	56,329	275,440	22,972
12/31/74	135,000	14,409	74,917	209,917	0	102,692	72,177	174,869	57,146	232,015	25,055
12/31/75	142,500	14,179	89,096	231,596	1,855	141,384	94,697	236,081	87,828	323,909	27,196
12/31/76	150,000	13,521	102,617	252,617	6,560	183,401	123,535	306,936	122,312	429,248	29,220
TOTAL					108,986						

Example A—Without Tax Shelter • In example A, without tax shelter (Table 17–1), only $4875 is available for investment after taxes; also, 35 percent of the income dividends and 17½ percent of the capital gain distributions received go for taxes each year.

An initial investment of $4875 ($7500 less taxes of $2625) was made on December 31, 1957, and additional investments of $4875 were made annually each December 31. Income dividends were reinvested, and capital gains distributions were taken in additional shares. As you can see from Table 17–1, you would have made original contributions totalling $97,500 and your end results would be $220,055.

Example B—With Tax Shelter • Example B (Table 17–2) is an illustration of an assumed investment program in which the entire $7500 is available for investment. All income dividends and capital gain distributions are reinvested without taxes, since they are free from federal income tax until they are withdrawn from the plan. During this 20 years $150,000 was invested ($97,500 that you contributed, is the same as without Keogh, plus $52,500 that Uncle Sam contributed). Here the end results were $429,248.

Summary

Potential Tax Savings on $7500 per Year for 20 Years

	Example A Without tax shelter	Example B With tax shelter
Total invested over 20 years	97,500	150,000
Income dividends reinvested	36,468	102,617
Total cost (including dividends reinvested)	133,968	252,617
Value of investment on December 31, 1976	220,055 *	429,248 *

* Includes value of shares acquired through capital gain distributions.

The above figures summarize Tables 17–1 and 17–2, which show two assumed investment programs in The Seminar Fund and are based on an assumed tax bracket of 35 percent. Investors in other tax categories would have proportionately larger or smaller savings.

Over the 20-year period during which the program was in effect, Example B would have produced $429,248 (before taxes), or twice the amount produced by Example A (after taxes). Three basic factors accounted for this result:

1 • The investor was able to invest $52,500 more under Example B, because he did not have to use this money to make tax payments.

2 • $102,617 in untaxed dividends were reinvested instead of the $36,468 left after taxes in Example A.

3 • Shares were received for the full capital gain distributions instead of the amount left after taxes in Example A.

The $429,248 produced by Example B, however, would be subject to income taxes when distributed from the retirement plan.

Guaranteed Retirement Income Plus • If guarantees are important to you, you might consider investing your funds in a combination of participating insurance annuity and mutual funds.

Had you invested $1000 per year for the 25½-year period of December 31, 1951 to June 30, 1976, and put $500 each year into the annuity and $500 into the Seminar Fund, you would have invested $13,000 in the annuity and would have had a guaranteed cash value of $20,449 (accumulating at 4 percent). Furthermore, if the annuity company accomplishes the dividend payments they anticipate, adding another 2½ percent, the guaranteed cash value would be $31,434. The other $500 each year would have been invested in the Seminar Fund. Your total investment in that half would again be $13,000 and the value on June 30, 1976 would be $61,308. Your total investment would have been $26,000, and your total value would have been $31,434 on the annuity side and $61,308 on the "plus" side, for a total of $92,742, as seen in Table 17–3.

If you are willing to have only one-third on the guarantee side, you could have placed $333 per year into the participating insurance annuity and $667 into the Seminar Fund. The annuity side would have grown to $20,935 on an $8658 investment, and the "plus" side in the Seminar Fund would have grown to $81,944 on a $17,342 investment for a total of $102,879.

These are the numbers for $1000 per year. If you can invest $7500, just multiply by 7.5. In the above example your total would have been $771,592.50.

If you want all of it guaranteed you could have placed $1000 in just the annuity side, making your investment $26,000 and your net result $62,868. (Some states allow them to show only 4 percent guarantee, which would be $40,898.) If you want to use only the fund side, the results would have been $122,616.

When using the combination annuity and fund, you should make

Table 17–3.

$1,000 per year in a tax-sheltered GRIP Plan

($500 per year in a participating annuity and $500 per year in The Seminar Fund)

PART I of your GRIP Plan
Your participating
insurance annuity

This hypothetical case assumes
a contribution of $1,000 every year on
January 1, $500 of which went into the
annuity. Actually, you may change the
amount of your contribution (within the
legal limits) or interrupt it at any time.

✚ PART II of your GRIP Plan
Your investment
program

Example: The Seminar Fund
These historical figures show what actually
would have happened if you could have used
this fund in a tax-sheltered Plan starting in
1951 through June 30, 1976

▬▬ TOTALS for your GRIP Plan
Your annuity PLUS your
investment program

Now put it all together—
guaranteed cash value plus
projected additional dividends
plus the historical growth of
the fund investment program.

1	2	3	4	5	6	7	8	9
As of the end of year:	Your yearly contribution:	Guaranteed cash value of your annuity is: †	Total projected value (including anticipated additional dividends) is: ††	Year:	Your yearly contribution:	Total value of your Fund shares (if sold at year-end) would have been:	Total of your yearly contributions to date (col. 2 + 6):	Total year-end cash value of your Plan (col. 4 + 7):
1	$ 500	$ 104	$ 107	1951	$ 500	$ 539	$ 1,000	$ 646
2	500	602	617	1952	500	1,118	2,000	1,735
3	500	1,120	1,165	1953	500	1,583	3,000	2,748
4	500	1,659	1,747	1954	500	3,186	4,000	4,933
5	500	2,219	2,366	1955	500	4,569	5,000	6,935
6	500	2,802	3,025	1956	500	5,567	6,000	8,592
7	500	3,408	3,726	1957	500	5,308	7,000	9,034
8	500	4,039	4,473	1958	500	8,347	8,000	12,820
9	500	4,694	5,267	1959	500	10,055	9,000	15,322
10	500	5,376	6,112	1960	500	10,989	10,000	17,101
11	500	6,085	7,041	1961	500	14,089	11,000	21,130
12	500	6,822	8,033	1962	500	12,620	12,000	20,653
13	500	7,589	9,091	1963	500	16,070	13,000	25,161
14	500	8,387	10,221	1964	500	19,221	14,000	29,442
15	500	9,216	11,426	1965	500	24,987	15,000	36,413
16	500	10,079	12,761	1966	500	25,707	16,000	38,469
17	500	10,976	14,188	1967	500	33,740	17,000	47,928
18	500	11,909	15,715	1968	500	40,015	18,000	55,730
19	500	12,880	17,347	1969	500	36,160	19,000	53,507
20	500	13,889	19,091	1970	500	37,591	20,000	56,682
21	500	14,938	21,028	1971	500	44,542	21,000	65,570
22	500	16,030	23,101	1972	500	52,147	22,000	75,248
23	500	17,165	25,320	1973	500	43,775	23,000	69,095
24	500	18,346	27,696	1974	500	36,306	24,000	64,002
25	500	19,573	30,238	1975 to June 30,	500	49,789	25,000	80,027
25½	500	20,449	31,434	1976	500	61,308	26,000	92,742
	Total of your 26 yearly contributions is: $13,000	Remember: amounts in this column are guaranteed.	Amounts in this column include the insurance company's estimate of participating dividends, which are not guaranteed.		Total of your 26 yearly contributions is: $13,000			This projection comes from a combination of guaranteed, projected, and historical amounts. In years to come, the amount could be smaller or larger.

† The guaranteed cash value in column 3 accumulates at 4% per year.

†† The anticipated additional dividends included in column 4 are calculated at 2½% above the
guaranteed cash value. This rate will fluctuate and it could be more or less in future years.

sure that you will be able to continue the plan for several years before
entering one, because higher costs are charged at the beginning on the
annuity portion.

• COMMONLY ASKED QUESTIONS ABOUT KEOGH

Here is a list of the most commonly asked questions about Keogh plans. I have given the answers as I interpret the Keogh provisions. If you have a question not answered here, I suggest you call the IRS. You'll find them most helpful.

1 • *Q: How much can I contribute to a Keogh plan?*
   A: You can contribute up to 15 percent of your earned income with a maximum of $7500.

2 • *Q: Do I save federal taxes by contributing to a Keogh plan?*
   A: Yes, you are allowed to deduct from your pretax earnings the total contribution made on behalf of yourself and your employees during the taxable year.

3 • *Q: Are there other tax benefits for the Keogh plan?*
   A: Yes, all interest and all dividends and capital gains earned by your Keogh plan are accumulated free from current taxation.

4 • *Q: Is a "silent partner" eligible for a Keogh plan?*
   A: No. To be eligible for a Keogh plan your income must be derived from personal services and be considered "earned income." An individual who has merely contributed capital to an enterprise, but not his time, is not considered eligible for Keogh.

5 • *Q: Can I be covered under a corporation or government retirement plan and also have a Keogh plan?*
   A: Yes, if you have earned income from personal services, as well as corporate or government income, you are eligible for a Keogh plan.

6 • *Q: What if my partners refuse to join the Keogh plan—may I have one?*
   A: Yes, as long as the partnership establishes the Keogh plan, each partner who has a greater than 10 percent interest can elect not to participate.

7 • *Q: Do I have to include my employees?*
   A: Yes, but you may exclude all part-timers who work less than 1000 hours per year and employees with less than three years of service (with some exceptions).

8 • *Q: Do I have to contribute 15 percent of my employees' pay?*
   A: No, not necessarily—the "minimum" percentage that you may contribute is determined by what percentage of your

personal income you are contributing to the plan. For instance, if you are earning $50,000 a year and contributing $2500 to a Keogh plan, you are contributing only 5 percent of your pay to the plan, and you may apply that same 5 percent figure to all of your employees.

9 · Q: *Are there other tax advantages for my employees?*
A: Yes, your employees have the same advantage of employees covered by corporate retirement plans. For instance, they are not taxed currently on the plan contribution made in their behalf, and their earnings under the plan compound for them tax free.

10 · Q: *Can I put my wife on the payroll so that she can qualify for Keogh benefits?*
A: Yes, if your wife is now an employee of yours, she'll be covered under the Keogh plan. If she works for you but is not formally recorded as an employee, you may place her on the payroll and she will become qualified for Keogh coverage.

11 · Q: *Can my employees and I make voluntary contributions that are not tax deductible but have the same tax shelter on earnings?*
A: Yes, if your plan covers at least one participant who is not a greater than 10 percent owner (owner-employee), and you permit him to make voluntary contributions, you and your employee can contribute up to 10 percent of compensation. Though you receive no tax deductions for these contributions, the money does compound tax free in the plan. You may withdraw from the plan, at any time, up to the amount you have contributed voluntarily without incurring any tax liability.

12 · Q: *When may I receive distributions from my plan?*
A: Your retirement benefits may not ordinarily be withdrawn from the plan until you reach the age of 59½ years, and you must start withdrawing at age 70½ years. You may select any age within this range as your retirement age. Though you must start withdrawing at 70½, you may still contribute and get your tax deduction on your contribution.

13 · Q: *How are my distributions taxed at retirement?*
A: You are entitled to treat as capital gains that portion of your taxable distribution which reflects your participation in the plan measured by the number of calendar years before 1974. You may elect to apply a ten-year averaging rule to that portion of your lump-sum distribution which reflects your par-

ticipation in the plan for years beginning after 1973, and which is treated as the ordinary income portion of the distribution. If you choose periodic installments or an annuity, payments received over a period of time are taxed in the years received as ordinary income.

14 · *Q: I have a Keogh plan with XYZ Fund. Is it possible to switch my plan to another fund?*
A: Yes, you have two possible choices: (1) Keep your Keogh plan with XYZ Fund and start a new Keogh plan with ABC Fund; (2) Establish a new plan in ABC Fund and have the custodian of your XYZ Fund transfer your total assets to your new plan.

• A SLICE IS BETTER THAN NONE

Just because corporate executives can have a much larger amount than $7500 set aside for their benefit is no reason to pass up the advantages that are offered to you. To pass up the $7500 allowance now is like passing up the enjoyment of eating two slices of German chocolate cake just because your neighbor has a whole cake. If this bugs you too much, look into the pros and cons of incorporating. Many professionals are doing so.

The Professional Corporation · In 1970 the IRS threw in the sponge in its long fight to keep incorporating professionals from being treated as corporations for tax purposes. By 1973, one-third of the physicians in the U.S. had incorporated, and it is estimated that at least half have now incorporated their practices. These can be one-man corporations.

The main advantage that you will have if you are self-employed and incorporated is that you will then be considered an employee as well as an owner. As an employee of a corporation you may then participate in retirement and insurance programs on a tax-deductible basis.

Let's assume that you are earning $50,000 as a physician and have incorporated. A comparison under Keogh and under a professional corporation would be as follows.

As a sole practitioner you may deduct $7500 annually and put it in your Keogh plan.

As a principal of Doctor, Inc., you draw a salary of $50,000 and set up a combined profit-sharing and pension plan. You may now contribute $12,500 (25 percent of $50,000) on a tax-deductible basis to your retirement plan. The corporate retirement plan may also have estate tax benefits if paid out over a period of over 36 months.

As you can see, the corporate plan would allow you to set aside $5000 more than would a Keogh plan.

There are also insurance advantages under the corporate structure. You may also be eligible for substantial life, health, and disability insurance coverages, deductible to the corporation and not taxable as income to you.

Some of the extras you would be entitled to are

1 •   Group life insurance—up to $50,000 tax free. Above that you would pay a nominal tax on term cost of insurance.

2 •   Group health insurance—hospital, surgical, major medical, and dental.

3 •   Disability—you would be eligible for long-term disability for life or up to age 65.

4 •   Key man insurance—the corporation could insure your life as a key employee.

5 •   You also may elect to set up a nonqualified deferred compensation plan and a medical expense reimbursement plan. The plan also permits a $5000 federal-income-tax-free death benefit.

You should weigh carefully the pros and cons of incorporation. Your attorney and certified public accountant should be consulted, and the financial and legal possibilities should be studied thoroughly before you take this step.

Do Get Started   •   While you are studying the pros and cons of incorporation, go ahead and start your Keogh plan. Even if you incorporate later, this money can be left in your Keogh plan to grow. If you skip this year, you can never make it up. When they blow the horn to signal a new year, you've passed up this year's tax savings forever.

Application

1 • Are you eligible for a Keogh Plan?

2 • Can you contribute more than $1500 a year? (If not, an Individual Retirement Account covered in the chapter "Avoiding the One-way Trip to Washington" may be more advantageous.)

3 • Work through the calculations with and without Keogh, using the worksheet.

4 • Investigate the pros and cons of setting up a professional corporation.

KEOGH TAX-SAVINGS WORKSHEET

CONTRIBUTIONS FOR EMPLOYER

	Example	Your Figures
1. Annual Earned Income (Schedule C, Line 21 of Federal Tax Return)	$ 30,000	$
2. Standard Deduction and Personal Exemptions	$ 3,500	$
3. Taxable Income (Form 1040, line 48)	$ 26,500	$
4. Percentage Tax Rate on Top Dollar (See table below)	36 %	%
5. Deductible Keogh Contribution (Up to 15% of Line 1 or $7,500, whichever is less)	$ 4,500	$
6. Tax Savings (Line 5 x Line 4)	$ 1,620	$

CONTRIBUTIONS FOR EMPLOYEE

	Example	Your Figures
7. Eligible Employees' Earnings	$ 8,000	$
8. % Contributions for Employees (Must be same percentage as used by employer in Line 5)	15 %	%
9. Deductible Contribution for Employee	$ 1,200	$
10. Tax Savings (Line 9 x Line 4)	$ 433	$
11. Cost of Employee Contribution (Line 9 less Line 10)	$ 767	$

SUMMARY

	Example	Your Figures
12. Total Keogh Contribution (Line 5 plus Line 9)	$ 5,700	$
13. Net Tax Savings (Line 6 less Line 11)	$ 853	$

INCOME TAX RATES FOR MARRIED COUPLES FILING JOINT RETURN

(1) Taxable Income Is: Over	(2) But Not Over	(3) The tax is:	(4) Plus % of excess over Col. 1	(1) Taxable Income Is: Over	(2) But Not Over	(3) The tax is	(4) Plus % of excess over Col. 1
$ 0	$ 1,000	$ 0	14%	32,000	36,000	8,660	42
1,000	2,000	140	15	36,000	40,000	10,340	45
2,000	3,000	290	16	40,000	44,000	12,140	48
3,000	4,000	450	17	44,000	52,000	14,060	50
4,000	8,000	620	19	52,000	64,000	18,060	53
8,000	12,000	1,380	22	64,000	76,000	24,420	55
12,000	16,000	2,260	25	76,000	88,000	31,020	58
16,000	20,000	3,260	28	88,000	100,000	37,980	60
20,000	24,000	4,380	32	100,000	120,000	45,180	62
24,000	28,000	5,660	36	120,000	140,000	57,580	64
28,000	32,000	7,100	39				

Source: IRS Instructions for preparation of 1974 tax returns. The tax on earned taxable income is limited to a maximum rate of 50%.

18
How to Read a Prospectus

The first rule is—Don't! At least, don't try to read the prospectus from cover to cover as you would a mystery novel. Use the prospectus as you would a handy reference guide. It can be horribly long, confusing, and worthless unless you know beforehand what to look for and who wrote the prospectus.

It is usually very long and contains many things to which you may not be able to relate. The Securities and Exchange Commission has many bright young men (some in training for top corporate or legal jobs) and many dedicated career servants, but the information that it usually requires a company to transmit to potential investors can at times be extremely confusing, with great emphasis on all the negative aspects of the offering and little or no emphasis on the positive aspects.

If a company wants to offer shares to you and the general public, it must submit a "registration statement" to the SEC, together with a copy to each state in which shares are to be sold. Nine-tenths of the information called for by the registration statement constitutes the "prospectus." It contains information required by a checklist compiled by the SEC. There are about 15 different forms, each pertaining to a different kind of company. Each form is designed to cover every conceivable type of information about the company. And each time the checklist is revised it gets longer. This has been going on since 1934. By now, the average prospectus contains about 30 to 50 pages of fine print, which may cause you to miss seeing the forest because of the many mesquite trees. I hope in the not-too-distant future the prospectus can be shortened to no more than ten pages, free of "legalese." As it is now, it usually takes the proverbial Philadelphia lawyer to make heads or tails of all that mass of fine print, and I suspect he often has difficulty with it too.

• **UNDULY
   LONG**

The undue length of the prospectus does serve one very practical purpose, however. Past experience has shown that small enterprises have a much higher mortality rate than do the larger and older ones. It does cost a great deal of money to gather together all the financial data and other information required by the SEC for the prospectus. Small companies are often presented with insurmountable expense hurdles to overcome if they intend to offer their shares publicly. A few have actually gone bankrupt in the attempt. If the SEC wants the company to change the terms of its offering or if it believes the company to be weak, it can delay the offering, require new audits, and increase the burden of expenses. The final draft of the prospectus may, for all intents and purposes, have been edited by SEC examiners to such an extent that it may bear little similarity to the original document presented to them.

The SEC rarely makes any field investigation of a company. Their primary function is to determine that the prospectus contains information required by its rules. Their rules do not relate to merits or fairness of the offering (as do the rules of some states) nor the value of the securities, and the SEC does not check out or investigate the accuracy of the information contained in the prospectus; hence, the disclaimer that appears in bold type on the face of every SEC prospectus:

THESE SECURITIES HAVE NOT BEEN APPROVED OR DISAPPROVED BY THE SECURITIES AND EXCHANGE COMMISSION NOR HAS THE COMMISSION PASSED UPON THE ACCURACY OF THIS PROSPECTUS. ANY REPRESENTATION TO THE CONTRARY IS A CRIMINAL OFFENSE.

This legend must be placed on every prospectus, regardless of the size or quality of the offering, to emphasize the fact that the Commission has not approved or disapproved the securities, and that it is a criminal offense to make a representation to the contrary. The reference "criminal offense" relates to someone's making a representation that the Commission has passed upon the merits of the offering. This applies to any company, whether it be General Motors or a new company offering its stock for sale. Even the most conservative of investment company trusts have this caption in bold, frightening print on the front. As I mentioned earlier I recommended to a prospective woman client a particular mutual fund that has a portfolio of such high quality that every stock in it is taken from the Legal List of the Registry of Wills of the District of Columbia. In keeping with what registered representatives are legally required to do, I gave her the prospectus of the fund with the above in bold print on the front. She called me the next day, absolutely incensed that I dared recommend to her something that the Securities and Exchange Commission had not approved. I explained the reason, but I was never able to really satisfy her, and she did not make the investment. This caption has frightened away a host of people who should have become investors. The SEC no doubt is fully aware of the problems of the length and complicated nature of the prospectus. Their theory is that they require detailed information so that the professionals in the investment community can analyze and interpret it for the less sophisticated investor. Unfortunately, it usually does not work out that way. Many brokers have never even read the prospectuses and, even if they have, are not sufficiently knowledgeable to discuss such diverse areas in real estate as debt financing, gross rent multipliers, equity buildup, etc.; or in oil and gas, such things as depletion, restored liquidity, intangible drilling costs, tax preference items, investment tax credit and depreciation; or in agriculture as crop loan reduction, unamortized loan fees, and prepared cultural costs.

I truly believe in having all my clients completely informed of the nature of the investment they are about to make, the risks involved, and what they may reasonably hope to accomplish if they do decide to invest, but the prospectus as it is presently required can be a serious deterrent. My sincere hope is that the Securities and Exchange Commission will make the simplification of the prospectus their top priority for the near future.

• INVESTOR LOSSES

Most investors' losses occur from factors that never appear in the prospectus. The number one factor is the market system itself. It is a mechanism that favors the large institutional investor over the small investor. The reason is simple. Many small investors tend to buy when everything looks great and common stocks are performing well. They tend to sell when everything looks gloomy. Hence, the tendency for small investors is to buy a stock near its peak price and sell it near its low. It is the large investors who more often do just the opposite. Fortunes were made in common stocks by those investors who bought in 1931 to 1933, not those who bought in 1929. The same story holds true for all the peaks and valleys in share prices since then. Small investors have their best chance by buying into the large investment funds or large individual companies at a time when most people regard them with disfavor and when most people think the country is at an all-time economic or political low. If history repeats itself, they will then participate in their subsequent rise.

• MANAGEMENT IS THE KEY

The other major factor that doesn't appear in the prospectus is the honesty, integrity, and ability of company management. Management is a vital ingredient of success, yet most investors fail to make any independent investigation of the company in which they are investing.

• MAKE A CHECKLIST

It is essential that you go beyond the prospectus in determining whether to buy shares in a new offering. Your "checklist" for determining whether a company is a good investment is short and simple. If your research is competent and your timing is good (which is vastly important), then you may be able to make money on new stock issues by making these determinations, in order of their importance:

1 • Who is really running the business? Find out which persons are actually in day-to-day charge of company affairs. It is usually no more than a handful. Try to determine if the outside directors are "window dressing" or are making a worthwhile contribution to the company by watching over the activities of management. Then independently check out in detail the reputation for honesty, integrity, and ability of those persons who are in charge. You won't find this in the prospectus. But it is worth more than 10 prospectuses. Check on these corporate officers as if they were filling out an employment application. After all, if you buy shares in the company they run, they should be working for *you*. If you find any lack of good character, don't invest.

2 • Are shares owned by management? If they don't own any, why should you? If they own a bunch, you should make a serious study of the company. Be careful about "dilution." If management owns a lot of shares, that's great. But did they pay 20¢ two years ago for shares they are offering to you for $20? If so, this usually is picked up in the prospectus under a separate paragraph headed "Dilution." It will give you the details.

3 • Look at the *size* of the company. This appears in the balance sheet. The smaller the size, usually the more risk involved. For every large company that fails, a hundred small ones go under. You will find the size of the company in the balance sheet. If there are less than seven figures in assets, the company has a high risk. Of course, if you are looking for a long shot that could pay off handsomely, such a company might be for you. Otherwise, pass.

4 • Look at the *debt* of the company. This is also in the balance sheet. If shareholder equity is less than 30 percent of total assets, watch out!

5 • Age. Time often cures all. The first five years are the biggest risk. Over 10 is usually over the hump.

6 • Management take. Compare management compensation with other, similar companies. Often, as may be the case with your auto repairman, the best job is also the least expensive job. Think in terms of percentage of company income. The presi-

dent of General Motors can be paid an enormous sum (which he is) without hurting the percentage. But when a small company pays an enormous sum, then doublecheck who runs the business and the number of shares they own.

7 · Preferred stock and debentures. The safest policy is to put your money in a company with little or no "senior" securities. This is just another form of debt. Take senior securities into account when figuring debt risk.

8 · Earnings. Why does this come last? Because management will think of every accounting possibility to show high earnings during a stock offering. Go back over the past five years and see what the trend has been.

THE "RED HERRING"

Most brokers mail to prospective investors a preliminary or "red herring" prospectus in advance of a company's offering. This prospectus is used to solicit preliminary orders called "indications of interest." The "red herring" prospectus has not been finally reviewed by the SEC. Use the "red herring" to do your homework on the kind of people who are running the business and how many shares they own. On the basis of your preliminary investigation you may decide to place a preliminary "order." You are under no obligation to place the actual purchase order even after you have received the final prospectus unless you decide to do so. Don't send in your check until you have reviewed the final prospectus carefully as to each of the above eight points.

A Great Need · It has not been my intent to be unduly critical of the Securities and Exchange Commission. They do an admirable job with dedicated and limited personnel. I am, however, keenly aware of the great need for a simpler, more understandable prospectus that the person who has not had the benefit of legal training can read and grasp in order to make an informed investment decision.

There are indications that this may occur in time. In a speech given by SEC Chairman Ray Garrett and reported in the October 23, 1975 issue of *The Wall Street Journal*, he was quoted under the caption "Prospectus Parodies" as having said:

"We all know the somber, liturgical disclaimers" that appear in corporate prospectuses, says Ray Garrett. "There can be no assurance that a heavier-than-air machine can be made to fly, or that if it can, anyone will want to buy one, or if someone wants to buy one, he will be willing to pay enough to make production profitable."

"Or suppose General Eisenhower's D-Day order had to be filed with the SEC," says Mr. Garrett, "The officers who planned this assault, including myself, have never before planned anything like this. In fact, I have never commanded any troops in combat. The airborne and other methods being employed have never before been tried by our Army. The weather forecast is only slightly favorable and such forecasts have a high degree of unreliability. Therefore, there is no assurance that any of you will reach Normandy alive, or, if you do, that you can secure the beach."

Go to a financial planner and obtain a prospectus and then answer the questions in the application.

Application

1 · What industry is involved?

2 · Is this an ascending industry?

3 · What products or services are produced?

4 · What is the demand/supply situation today regarding these products or services?

5 · How many years experience does the chief executive officer have in this field?

6 · How many shares are owned by management?

What is their compensation?

	Shares owned	Compensation
President	_____	$_____
Vice President	_____	$_____
Secretary	_____	$_____
Treasurer	_____	$_____

7 · Total net worth of the company?

8 · What is the debt/equity ratio of the company?

9 · What other alternative investments can you find that offer as much potential for the same or less risk?

10 · Is it feasible to make an on-the-spot investigation of the company and their facilities?

19

Planning for Your Children's Education

If your son or daughter asked you for $14,000 to $30,000 for college expenses, would you be able to make the college of his or her choice a reality instead of a dream? Costs for a year of college today begin in the neighborhood of $5100. Future costs are unknown; however, if the present trend of escalation continues, this cost could run as high as $9600 per year by 1993.

- ### BASIC COSTS

Here's a graphic projection if costs continue to increase as they have in recent years.

Using these projected cost figures, let's assume that you have two children. One will start to college in 1987 and the second in 1990. Their college cost picture might look something like this.

	Child No. 1	Child No. 2
1987	$ 7,800	
1988	8,100	
1989	8,400	
1990	8,700	$ 8,700
1991		9,000
1992		9,300
1993		9,600
	$33,000	$36,600
		$33,000
		$69,600

• COLLEGE FINANCING FORMULA

Let's now change our basic formula to read: Time plus money plus American companies equals opportunity for a college education.

Often I'm counseling a couple that has stated that their financial goal is to provide the funds to send their children to college. After I have outlined a plan, one of them will ask, "Is it 'guaranteed'?"—meaning every hour of every day.

Of course, it's not "guaranteed" on a daily basis. Their goal is to have the necessary college funds in 10 to 15 years. They may not be able to afford a "guaranteed" investment.

For example, let's assume that they can save $150 a month toward building a college fund to educate their two children. One will be going to college in ten years and the other in 14 years.

• THE GUARANTEED ROUTE vs. THE UNGUARANTEED

At 5 percent compounded annually $150 a month in 10 years will be $23,778. In 14 years it's $37,044. This brings them up short for Child No. 1, to say nothing of Child No. 2.

At 12 percent, on the other hand, $150 per month would be $35,370 in 10 years and $65,304 in 14 years. You may be concerned with the fact that if child No. 1 is taking from the kitty, funds will not be there to compound. This is true. However, Child No. 1 does not need the total amount of $33,000 the day he enters the vine-covered portals. He just needs the funds for one semester, which allows the remainder to grow until it is needed.

A plan that I have used successfully to accomplish this objective has been a check-a-month withdrawal from a fund similar to the Seminar Fund. While the student has been taking out funds, American industry has been putting funds back in.

Don't worry about the short-term fluctuations of the market. If you want to have enough money in the college fund using the "guaranteed" route, you will have to increase your savings to such a huge amount that you will have to drastically reduce your present standard of living. The "guaranteed" dollar in many cases becomes an academic discussion rather than a workable plan.

• DON'T FIGHT
THE BATTLE ALONE

Don't try to fight the battle for college funds alone. Give American industry a chance to help. You may find that American industry will contribute more to your child's educational funds than you do, if you'll give it a chance through proper investing.

On March 21, 1965, I was interviewed by Patricia Shelton, who was then a reporter in the women's department of *The Houston Chronicle*. She is now a well-known syndicated fashion writer. Her question to me in her interview was how to go about financing a college education. At that time we estimated that if parents had a child who would be entering college in 10 years, they would need to save $5400 at $45 per month. If they had 15 years, they would need to save $3600 at $20 per month. (See how important time is to the accomplishment of any financial objective?)

This would not be sufficient if they used the guaranteed route, but we found that it should be if they had used a specific local mutual fund. We arrived at these figures by working backward using the bank's computer. We wanted to be able to withdraw $3000 a year or $250 per month each month for four years. Working backward, we found that if the account had $9565 in it at registration time and $250 a month had been drawn out each month for four years, a total of $12,000 would have been withdrawn and there would have been $440 left.

Again, here is an example to encourage you not to fight the battle alone, but to let American industry help you. In this case American industry had contributed $7040, and the parents had contributed $5400 (at $45 per month). These parents had placed their money in a position to let American industry pay more of their child's college costs than they had contributed.

College costs have skyrocketed since this article was published,

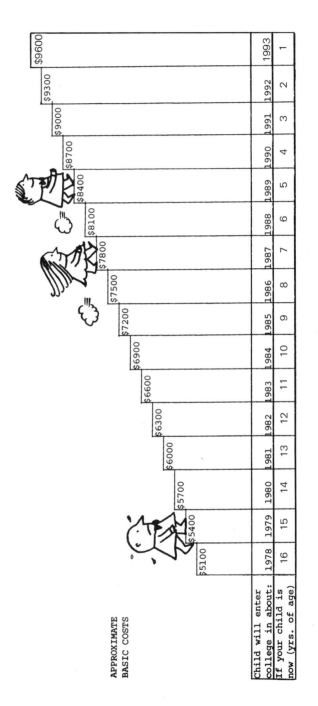

FIGURE 19-1. Anticipated College Annual Costs

APPROXIMATE BASIC COSTS	$5100	$5400	$5700	$6000	$6300	$6600	$6900	$7200	$7500	$7800	$8100	$8400	$8700	$9000	$9300	$9600
Child will enter college in about:	1978	1979	1980	1981	1982	1983	1984	1985	1986	1987	1988	1989	1990	1991	1992	1993
If your child is now (yrs. of age)	16	15	14	13	12	11	10	9	8	7	6	5	4	3	2	1

and stock market performance has been erratic; however, it seem evident that American industry can provide a very helpful hand to you if you are a parent desiring to send your child to college.

Figure 19-1 shows anticipated college costs.

• UNIFORM GIFTS
TO MINORS

If you are in a fairly high tax bracket, you should consider setting up custodial accounts for each child and registering the stock in this manner:

John E. Jones, Custodian for
John E. Jones, Jr., under the
_____ Uniform Gifts to
(State)
Minors Act.

This should allow most of the dividends and capital gains to compound tax-free. You should use your child's Social Security number for the account. You will still be able to claim the child as a deduction if you supply over 50 percent of his support. I should caution that you may not use any of these funds for things that you are legally obligated to provide for your child—items such as food and clothing. But you can use the funds for college education.

If your estate is large you may want to name as custodian someone other than yourself. In the event of your death, the value of the account could be considered a part of your estate for estate tax purposes if you are the custodian.

• DON'T
PROCRASTINATE

Time plus money—both are essential to combine with American free enterprise. The sooner you start, the easier it will be to reach your goal. By starting five years earlier, you can usually reduce the amount you must invest by one-half. A college education can add a new dimension to a life. If you have children, help them to reach their maximum potential.

Application

College Worksheet

Name of child	Years before college	Amount needed *	Amount saved	Amount can save per month	Estimated results †	Deficiencies
1.						
2.						
3.						
4.						
Totals						

* Use Fig. 19–1 for estimates.
† Choose compound rate of return and calculate by using tables in Chapter 1.

If you have a deficit, can you increase the amount you can save per month?

If not, can you increase your "yield"?

Immediate action you plan to take:

1. _____
2. _____
3. _____
4. _____

20

Financial Planning Is Like Navigation

Financial planning is like navigation. If you know where you are and where you want to go, navigation isn't such a great problem. It's when you don't know the two points that it's difficult.

To find out where you are, take an in-depth financial inventory. Table 20–1 is the personal planning data sheet that I hand out at the first session of my three-session financial planning seminars.

I encourage each person in attendance to complete and return it to me before our consultation. This allows me sufficient time to map out tentative recommendations. If they do not return it or bring it with them, we complete one together. Without this information, I'm flying blind. If they do not choose to give me this information, we usually do not accept them as clients. It would be as if they had gone to their family doctor in pain and refused to tell him where the pain was located.

Here is your personal planning data sheet. Please stop now and complete it.

Table 20–1.   Personal Planning Data Sheet

Name		Date

Address

Telephone: Home		Office

Marital Status   Age   Do you have a current will?

MY FINANCIAL RESOURCES

I.   *Loaned dollars*

     A.   Checking account $_____

     B.   Savings at bank $_____

         Certificates of deposit * $_____

     C.   Savings and loan $_____

         Certificates of deposit * $_____

     D.   Government bonds

         and instruments * $_____

     E.   Corporate bonds * $_____

     F.   Municipal bonds * $_____

     G.   Credit union $_____

     H.   Mortgages receivable $_____

     I.   Loans receivable $_____

     J.   Cash value of insurance policies

         (Worksheet follows) $_____

            TOTAL LOANED DOLLARS $_____(1)

Present Life Insurance and Annuities
(Worksheet to Compute Item J)

Com-pany	Type	Mortal-ity table	Face amount	Cash value	Net in-surance†	Annual premium
___	___	___	___	___	___	___
___	___	___	___	___	___	___
___	___	___	___	___	___	___
___	___	___	___	___	___	___
___	___	___	___	___	___	___
___	___	___	___	___	___	___
___	___	___	___	___	___	___
___	___	___	___	___	___	___
TOTAL:			___	___	___	___

* List with a description on separate page, giving amount, rate, and maturity date.
† Face amount less cash value = net insurance.

II.   *Working dollars*

    A. *Stocks*

No. of shares	Name of company	Date of purchase	Cost	Market value
			$_____	$_____
			$_____	

                 TOTAL MARKET VALUE $_____(2)

    B. *Real estate*

       Equity in home (market value
          less mortgage) $_____

       Other real estate
          (net after mortgage):

                              $_____

       Limited partnerships:

                              $_____
                              $_____
                              $_____
                              $_____
                              $_____

                 TOTAL REAL ESTATE $_____(3)

    C. *Other investments*

       Limited partnerships:

                              $_____
                              $_____

       Commodities:

                              $_____

       Silver and gold:

                              $_____

Art objects and antiques:

_____ $_____

Other (specify):

_____ $_____

TOTAL	$_____(4)
TOTAL WORKING DOLLARS	
(2, 3, and 4)	$_____(5)
TOTAL LOANED AND WORKING	
DOLLARS (1 and 5)	$_____

D. Loans outstanding (other than mortgages above) $_____

MY FINANCIAL OBJECTIVE

(Please number in order of importance)

_____ Income now

_____ Income at retirement

_____ Maximum tax advantage

_____ Educate children

_____ Travel

Present annual income $_____

Taxable income last year $_____

Amount I could save per month $_____

My tax bracket _____%

How many years before retirement? _____ yr

Desired monthly income at retirement $_____

SOURCES OF MONTHLY RETIREMENT INCOME:

Social Security $_____

Pensions $_____

Other $_____

TOTAL	$_____
ADDITIONAL INCOME NEEDED	
PER MONTH	$_____

If education of child is objective:

Name of child	Years before college	Estimated cost
_____	_____	$_____
_____	_____	$_____
_____	_____	$_____
_____	_____	$_____
_____	_____	$_____
TOTAL COST		$_____
AMOUNT SET ASIDE		$_____
ADDITIONAL NEEDED		$_____

• YOUR
WILL

You will note that I ask if you have a will. This is a very important part of your financial planning.

In reality, you have or will have a will. It will be the one that you have written to fit your own wishes or the one that the state writes for you after your death. However, the state's will most likely will not bear any resemblance to the way you would have written it, had you done so during your lifetime.

I urge you to obtain a properly drawn will prepared by a competent lawyer in the state where you are living.

I won't go into details about all the will should contain. However, let me make this one suggestion as to what you should not do. Do not, for example, will so many shares of XYZ company to your daughter Sally, nor your credit union account to your son Johnny. If you do, every time you change your investments, which you may need to do often, you'll need to change your will. Plan for the disbursement of your assets by percentages. If you have four children and want your estate to be equally divided among them, specify in your will that 25 percent of your assets should go to each.

If you want a portion to go to charity, reduce these percentages so as to have some left for this purpose.

In making these suggestions, I'm not trying to practice law. A competent lawyer in the state in which you reside should prepare your will. I'm a financial planner, and I should and will stick to recommending financial plans that can fulfill your needs. How I've often wished that lawyers would do likewise and stick to their profession and let me practice mine.

The temptation to give financial advice seems at times to be just too great for some of them. Often her lawyer is the only strong man in the life of a widow at a time when she is very lonely and insecure. She naturally turns to him for advice. Unfortunately, many times lawyers take the easy way out and tell her to just put her funds where they will be "safe," meaning a savings account. Here the ravages of inflation can destroy the only value the money has—purchasing power.

Many a large law firm has very strong ties with a particular bank in its city. The firm secures clients for the bank's trust department by drawing up the will in such a way that the bank becomes the trustee. This may be a good arrangement if the heirs have a spendthrift nature and little or no knowledge of money management. It may be a very poor arrangement otherwise. Many bank trust departments are understaffed. They may also be forced by regulations to choose investments based on what will please the bank examiners rather than what might be the most advantageous to the beneficiaries.

• LOANED
DOLLARS

We have already listed many of the ways that you can loan money. I've covered these in detail in the chapter entitled "Lending Your Dollars" and will not repeat them here.

All of these ways of "lending" money offer you a reasonably good guarantee of return of principal and a stated rate of return, with the exception of the cash value of life insurance policies. Technically, as you have seen, it belongs to the insurance company. You can obtain that portion designated as cash surrender value by borrowing it from them, and paying interest to do so, or surrendering your protection. If it is left with the insurance company and death occurs, the beneficiary receives only the face amount of the policy, regardless of how much you have "saved" using this method.

Included in the data sheet is a worksheet for the calculation of your cash surrender value. As you will remember, this is done by looking at the date of issue of the policy and subtracting that date from today's date. That gives the age of your policy. Look toward the back of the policy and find the nonforfeiture table, which will be either for the face amount or per $1000. For example, let's assume that you have a $10,000 whole life policy that you've had for 10 years, and the cash surrender value is per $1000. You look down the table to 10 years and go across the chart to the cash value column, where it states a value of $365. You multiply the $365 × 10, which is $3650. On your data sheet then write the name of the insurance company, type of policy, face amount of $10,000, cash value of $3650, and net insurance of $6350. Do this for each policy and then total them.

The net insurance is the face amount less the cash surrender value. The annual premium is next. List and then total.

At this point take time to calculate your present cost per thousand for life insurance protection.

This can be done very simply in this manner:

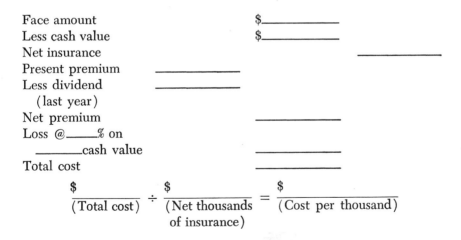

Assuming a loss of earnings at 6 percent and a premium of $200 per annum on the above policy, you would calculate your total cost by multiplying $3650 times 6 percent ($219) and then add this total to the $200 ($419).

$$\$419 \div 6.4 = \$65.47 \text{ per thousand}$$

Your cost per thousand has increased from $20 to $65.47. It should be increasing because you are older and every year you live you are that more apt to die. All the "funny banking" in the world will not repeal a mortality table.

• HOW MUCH
IN CASH RESERVES?

As you make a total of your "loaned dollars" you may be asking, "How much should I keep in cash reserve?"

As I mentioned earlier, when I first started giving investment seminars, I suggested three months' expenses in cash reserve.

Now I suggest that my clients leave as much money idle as it takes to give them peace of mind, for peace of mind is a good investment.

I don't seem to have peace of mind with any of my money idle, with the exception of a checking account. You may not have any peace of mind without a lot in a "guaranteed" savings account where you can give it a comforting pat every now and then.

If you need cash and have your funds invested in good stocks, mutual funds, oil and gas income limited partnerships, and commercial income real estate limited partnerships, you can sell the first two any time you desire. However, it may not be the right time in the market, or you may not want to destroy this goose that is laying the golden eggs. If not you can take your stock certificates to the bank and use them for collateral for a loan.

You can rent a lot of time for a reasonable amount of rent (interest) and deduct the rent on your income tax. Therefore, I don't feel I need to keep money idle working for someone else while waiting for an emergency. I have cash any time I need it.

• WORKING OR
"OWNED" DOLLARS

The four main categories in this area are stocks, real estate through individual ownership or through limited partnerships, energy, and other commodities through the same form.

Stocks • Under "stocks" you should list your common stocks, preferred stocks, convertible bonds, and any warrants or rights you may own. List the number of shares, the cost basis, date of purchase, and today's market value.

Knowing your cost basis is very important in doing good financial planning for two reasons. First of all, you need to unemotionally take a good hard look at your performance in the market. For example, let's say that you purchased 100 shares of XYZ Corporation five years ago for $10 per share. Today's market value is $14\frac{5}{8}$. Your average gain per year has been 8 percent compounded. If the stock pays a significant dividend that you are reinvesting, add this to your return after adjusting for your tax loss.

Is 8 percent gain per year within your investment results guideline? If you have calculated that you must have a result of 12 percent a year to reach your goal and your investments are not reaching this objective, you will need to consider making some changes in your investment program.

Another important reason for knowing your cost basis is that you need to know how much capital gains would be realized if you were to sell at a profit or capital loss if selling at a loss. You need to weigh how much you will have to gain from another investment to overcome the tax loss if you are selling at a profit, to come out ahead. On the other hand, if you have a loss, you may need to know how much you could save on your income taxes by establishing the loss.

Many have difficulty figuring cost basis. This is because of poor record keeping or because they become confused by stock splits. It only takes a small amount of time to keep good records if done as the transactions are made. In the back of this book I have a stock record sheet that you may want to consider using. I like to use this sheet in a looseleaf notebook, and then pull and file the sheets after the stock has been sold. Both the buy and sell confirmations that you receive from your broker should be kept in your permanent files.

Figuring the effect of stock splits and dividends is not difficult if done as they are made. Let's look at an example. You purchased 100 shares of XYZ Corp. at $50 per share, or $5000, in 1970. You received a stock dividend of 2 percent or two shares in 1971, and a two for one stock split in 1972, which gives you a total of 204 shares. You have added no new money. Your cost basis is still $5000. Your cost basis per share, however, has changed. You now have 204 shares. Your original 100 plus 2 = 102 × 2 = 204 shares. You paid $5000, and you have 204 shares, so your new cost basis per share is $24.51. If you should sell 50 shares, your cost basis would be 50 × $24.51 or $1225.50, and the cost basis for your remaining shares would be $3774.50.

Real Estate • Real estate can also be a good variable dollar investment. First, list your home (its current market value less the mortgage). Then list your equity in other real estate holdings. Others: limited partnerships in oil and gas, commodity accounts, silver bullion and coins, gold jewelry, art works, antiques bought as investments, rare stamps, etc. Now total your assets and subtract any liabilities. This should give you your net worth.

• YOUR FINANCIAL OBJECTIVES

The last section of the personal planning data sheet is designed to help you determine your financial objectives. Number these in the order of their priority to you.

_____ Income now
_____ Income at retirement
_____ Maximum tax advantage
_____ Educate children
_____ Travel

• HOW MUCH CAN YOU SAVE?

"Present annual income" is followed by "Taxable income last year." Look on last year's tax return for this figure. The next is "Amount I could save per month." Sit down with your family and determine how much you can comfortably save each month—not too comfortably, or you won't save anything. However, don't set the amount too high, but establish an amount you can actually save. If you set it too high, you may become discouraged, abandon the plan, and fail to reach your goal of financial independence.

• YOUR TAX BRACKET

Your tax bracket is a very important item, for it should influence your selection of investments. If you are in the lower brackets, you can afford to invest for income that is taxable. The higher your bracket, the more you should consider tax-sheltered investments.

• IF RETIREMENT IS YOUR OBJECTIVE

Determine when you plan to retire and map your plan accordingly. Sometimes I'll be counseling a couple age 50 who solemnly tell me that they plan to retire at age 55. When I look at their assets, I realize that there is just no way. They are not being realistic. Regardless of how much they may "want to" retire in five years, they will not be able to do so with only the income from the assets they have accumulated.

Desired Monthly Income • Decide what you feel would be an adequate or desired monthly income and adjust for inflation. Use no less than 3½ percent for an inflation factor. You would probably be safer using the 6.2 percent compounded for the next 25 years projected by the University of Chicago and the Bureau of Census.

Sources of Monthly Income

Social Security • I had planned to include in the back of the book a table for your use in making this calculation; however, the amount seems to be changing so rapidly that it is impossible to keep it current. I suggest that you call your local Social Security office and request this information. You may want to consider whether you think there will be any funds in the Social Security Account by the time you retire.

Pension • If your company has a pension and/or profit-sharing plan, find out how much your pension will be and what has been credited to your profit-sharing account. Also find out how much is vested (meaning how much you could take with you if you should leave).

Be sure to read about the possible tax advantages of an IRA rollover in the chapter entitled "Avoiding the One-Way Trip to Washington" before you choose your distribution of your pension benefits.

• COLLEGE FINANCING NEEDS

The chapter on college education will be helpful in calculating how much you are going to need for college expenses.

• HOW DID
YOU DO?

You've now completed your personal planning data sheet. You have, haven't you?

How did you do? How many years have you worked? How much have you earned? How much have you saved? How many years before retirement? What do you plan to do about your financial situation beginning today? Write down specific steps that you are going to take to reach your goal. Have a family council and plan your attack.

Financial planning should be a joint endeavor if a couple is involved

and a family matter if there are children. When it comes to financial planning, I find that love is not so much looking into each other's eyes as looking in the same direction. If both have the financial vision, the chances for attaining their financial goal are vastly improved.

• FINANCIAL
ADVICE

For advice on a legal question, go to a competent lawyer; for advice on taxes, go to a CPA; for advice on banking, go to a banker—but don't expect good money management advice from any of them. Yes, I did intend to include the banker. Many bankers are trained to be money changers, money counters, and money lenders, but few are trained to be money managers. I say this even though I am an Advisory Director of a national bank.

Seek out a financial planner who has an excellent reputation and in whom you truly have confidence. Then follow his advice. Don't make the mistake of going from person to person asking their opinions. This will only serve to confuse you, causing you to make poor decisions. You'll always find those eager to give free advice about your money. Often the more readily they give advice, the more miserable the job they have done with their own money.

Your financial planner should be experienced in investments, life insurance, tax shelters, and estate planning, and have a close working relationship with a creative CPA and a competent attorney.

All of these areas must be skillfully meshed together in the complex money arena you will find yourself in today.

Application

1 • Complete the Financial Data Sheet.

2 • How many dollars do you have idle?

3 • Should you have more idle?

4 • Do you feel that these dollars are safe?
(Safety means that you will be returned the same amount of purchasing power at a point of time in the future that you have today.)

5 • Should you have more dollars working for you?

6 • In what areas today is demand greater than supply?

7 • Do these areas lend themselves to convenient and prudent investing?

8 • Which are best for you?

9 • What yield are you averaging on your fixed-dollar investments ?

Fixed Dollar	Yield
_____	_____
_____	_____
_____	_____

10 • What rate of return are you averaging on your working dollars?

Investment	Rate of Return
_____	_____
_____	_____
_____	_____
_____	_____

11 • What date each year have you set aside to update your analysis and consider alternative courses?

21
To Win the Money Game

My dear investor, it is now time to summarize my years of observations of why so many are failing to win the money game and what you must do to become a winner.

• WHY SO MANY FAIL

Lack of a Well-defined Goal • The greatest cause for failure is the lack of a well-defined goal and a step-by-step plan to accomplish that goal. I have never interviewed anyone who has said to me, "I plan to fail." Unfortunately, I have visited with many who were well down the road to failure because they had "failed to plan."

Lack of Self-discipline • Another cause of failure is lack of self-discipline. The secret of financial independence is not brilliance or luck, but the discipline to save a part of all you earn and to put it to work in shares of American industry, real estate, natural resources, and collectibles.

Procrastination • Procrastination is a deadly enemy to success. Time is a tremendous asset. If you have a sufficient amount of time, you do not need as large an amount of money to combine with American industry or the other major areas of investing. Do not waste this precious commodity —a commodity that is distributed to each of us equally.

Procrastination always stands in the shadows, awaiting his opportunity to spoil your chance for success. You will probably go through life as a failure if you wait for the "time to be right" to start doing something worthwhile. Do not wait; the time will never be "just right" to start your journey down the road to financial independence. Remember our illustration of "Mr. Sitting Tight."

Lack of Persistence • Don't be a good "starter" and a poor "finisher," as is true with so many. Each year we must close our reservations early for our January financial planning seminars because we cannot seat all those who want to come. Many years we have had to hold duplicate sessions of our three-session seminars to accommodate those who wanted to attend. It's obvious that many have made good New Year's resolutions to "get organized" and do something about their finances. We can usually accommodate those wanting to attend the fall sessions.

If you experience a temporary setback, do not give up at the first sign of defeat. I've often observed this in a monthly investment program. If the market goes up after they start their program, they'll happily put in their investment each month, but if it goes down, they'll abandon the program, regardless of how I've tried to explain that dollar-cost-averaging results can benefit from stock market fluctuations. There is no substitute for persistence. If you make persistence your watchword, you'll discover that "old man failure" will finally become weary of you and make his exit. Failure cannot cope with persistence.

Lack of Ability To Make a Decision • I have found over and over again that men who succeed reach decisions promptly and change them, if at all, very slowly. I have found that men who fail reach decisions, if at all, very slowly and change them frequently and quickly. Procrastination and indecision are twins. Pluck this grim pair out of your life before they bind you to the treadmill of financial failure.

Making a Decision is a Privilege • No one can make your decisions for you. You will find that free advice about your money is always available. It's usually those who lean back and give you the most "positive" advice whose finances are bordering on catastrophe. They are often wrong, but never in doubt.

There are times when I have counseled a couple who have attended all three sessions of our investment seminar and thus have listened to me for at least 4½ hours. They have asked for an appointment, and I have spent two hours with them in an uninterrupted personal conference. When it comes time to apply this information to their own personal finances, they will say, "This sounds fine, but let us go home and think it over." On the surface this sounds like a prudent, sensible thing to do, doesn't it? However, I find that it usually is not. They already have all the information they need. They will not be "thinking it over" after they leave. Dozens of other matters will require their attention. They are trying to avoid making a decision, not realizing that no decision is a decision. They are deciding that where their money is now is the best place for it to be—for that is the result brought about by their lack of action.

Overcaution • The person who takes no chances generally must take whatever is left over after others have finished choosing. Overcaution is as bad, if not worse, than lack of caution. Both should be avoided. Life will always contain the elements of chance. Not to win is not a sin. But not to try is a tragedy.

If you've never missed when investing, you've not been in there trying or you've been holding your losers far too long for maximum profits. Play the money game well, but never safely.

Avoid a life of no hits, no runs, no errors!

Prejudice • We all have prejudices, but we should continually work to rid ourselves of them. In counseling, I sometimes encounter a couple who seem to be saying to me, "Please don't confuse us with facts." They do not want to know the truth. The truth will not make them free, regardless of how carefully or intelligently it may be presented to them.

Lack of Concentrated Efforts • To become a good investor you must seriously apply your intelligence, use your ability to acquire knowledge, and give your attention to details and timing. If you cannot, will not, or do not have the ability to do these things successfully for yourself, do not take a distorted ego trip, by not admitting that someone may be able to do something better than you can do it, but put the professionals to work for you.

Desiring Something for Nothing • If I were to distill all the wisdom I've ever learned into nine words, they would be: "There is no such thing as a free lunch." To summarize what I have said earlier, there may be two drives where this is evident: One is the gambling instinct, which has driven many to failure in the market. Investing, properly approached with constant supervision, may be one of the safest long-term things that can be done with money. Speculation, on the other hand, can be the riskiest.

This desire for a "free lunch" is often seen in the opposite manner by those who will leave their funds in a savings institution because they refuse to pay a brokerage commission to get their funds invested. What did it cost to leave $10,000 in a savings institution instead of investing it in the Seminar Fund for the past 43 years? It cost $724.18 per month, $8690 per year, or a total of $373,670. The "cost" would have initially been $750 to $850. The "pay" would have been $383,670, making the true cost $373,670. This obsession with what something "costs" rather than what it "pays" may also lead them into investing in a lower-performance mutual fund that does not charge a commission rather than in a better performing one that does. (There are some that do not charge that perform well, but do not entitle you to the services of a financial planner.) The money that they often "save" is very costly. In making an investment decision the important factor is not what it "costs." You do not care what it costs, but you are truly concerned with what it pays.

Lack of Enthusiasm • I do believe I can forgive almost any shortcoming other than lack of enthusiasm. It is essential in the acquisition of money. Enthusiasm is contagious; if you have it in sufficient quantities, others will welcome you into their group. You will be more in touch with the needs and thinking of the people around you, and you can profit from the investment opportunities that will become obvious to you.

Guessing Instead of Thinking • Information is available about almost any subject you need. Don't let indifference or plain laziness keep you from acquiring the facts essential to making good judgments. Acquire the major points of information you need—you'll never have "all" the information. If you wait that long, you'll probably make your decision too late for maximum profit. I find that most decisions are made too late rather than too soon. We all have a tendency to have a good laugh when someone says, "Do something, even if it's wrong." I have found that there is usually more merit in this than is apparent on first blush. As Emerson said, "Do the thing and you will have the power."

Lack of Capital • Build up your nest egg, and do it while you are young. Don't spend the nest egg but use it for collateral to leverage for a larger egg and then a larger one. Remember again, money gives you options. Your banker will usually welcome you with open arms, if you have collateral to back your bankable idea.

Being Overinfluenced by the Opinions of Others • I have observed that those who fail to accumulate sufficient amounts of money are easily influenced by the opinions of other people. Opinions are cheap. You will find them everywhere. There are always those who are just waiting to foist their opinions on anyone who will accept them. If you let others overinfluence you when you are reaching decisions about your money, you will not succeed.

•   WHY SOME
SUCCEED

The Plan • Success in money management is not a will-o'-the wisp that comes to some and not to others because of fate, chance, or luck. If you've held this idea in the past, do get rid of it now. Success in money management can be predicted, but you must have a plan and follow that plan.

If you give a blueprint to a skillful builder, do you think that it will be a matter of chance, or luck, that he will complete the structure

successfully? Of course not. He merely begins at the beginning and follows the plan step by step to its completion.

This book is your blueprint for success. If you follow it, financial independence can be yours.

Attitude • There is a "magic" word you must place not only in your vocabulary but also in the very fiber of your being if you are to be successful in money or any other area of life. That magic word is ATTITUDE!

Everything in life operates on the law of cause and effect. You must produce the causes—the rewards will take care of themselves. Good attitude—good results. Fair attitude—fair results. Bad attitude—bad results.

There are five affirmations that I repeat each evening before I go to bed and often before arising in the morning. I learned them in an Omega Seminar of the Institute for Executive Research. They have had a positive effect on my attitude, and I recommend them to you. They are:

1 • I like myself unconditionally. I have love.
2 • I never devalue myself through destructive self-criticism.
3 • I have unconditional warm regard for all persons at all times.
4 • I am easily able to relax at any time, and every day through every affirmation I grow healthier, in both mind and body.
5 • I am completely self-determined, and allow others the same right.

You will shape your own financial life by the attitudes that you hold each day. If you have a poor attitude toward learning about money management, you will not learn very much until you change your attitude. If you have an attitude of failure, you are beat before you start.

Sometimes a prospective client will say, "If I invest, the market will go down. I've never made any money in the market." Until he can change his attitude, he probably will not become a successful investor. Optimists make money. Pessimists rarely do.

If your present attitude is not a winning one, don't let that discourage you. The brilliant William James of Harvard University put it this way: "The greatest discovery of my generation is that human beings can alter their lives by altering their attitude of mind."

You see, this is an area over which you have control. You have control over what's going to happen to your money and to you.

Look around you. Study successful people. How privileged I have been over these past eight years to visit with at least one successful man or woman each week on my television program, "Successful Texans." They go sailing through life from one success to another, and when they occasionally fail at something, they shrug it off and head right out again. These people take the attitude toward themselves that they can accomplish what they set out to accomplish. Because of this, they achieve some remarkable things and are called successful, brilliant, lucky, and so on.

Luck • I personally do not believe in luck. Luck is when preparedness and opportunity get together. If you are prepared, you become lucky. A close friend of mine, who is a well-known and respected business consultant, studied a particular company and bought shares of stock while it was still in its infancy. These shares have now grown tremendously in value and have made him a very wealthy man. There are those who would scoff and say, "I should be so lucky." It wasn't just luck. He was prepared. When he and his wife were first married, they had scrimped and saved and lived in a modest apartment. They even sold their car and rode the bus to work so they could save a nest egg. It was this nest egg, which they had so painfully saved, that was used to make their "lucky" investment.

Had they not prepared, they would not have had the means by which to avail themselves of all this "luck." Remember our example of the wood burning stove. You must put in the wood before you can warm yourself.

Expectations • The successful people with whom I have visited seem to find their accomplishments not too difficult and many times surprisingly easy, simply because it seems so few are really trying—so few really believe in themselves.

I have found throughout life that successful people come in all shapes and sizes. They have widely different backgrounds, intelligence, and education. But I have found the one thing they have in common is that they expect more good out of life than bad and that they expect to succeed more often than fail—and they do!

Money • Rid yourself of an old myth, if such has been plaguing you, that money is not important. It is important, vitally important! It is just as important as the food it buys, the shelter it provides, the doctor bills it pays, and the education it helps to procure. Money is important to you as you live in a civilized society. To split hairs and say that it is not as important as other things is just arguing for the sake of the exercise. Nothing will take the place of money in areas in which money works.

"What is money?" Money is the harvest of your production. The amount of money you will receive will always be in direct ratio to the need for what you do, your ability to do it, and the difficulty of replacing you.

I'm amazed at the number of people who tell me that they want money but don't want to take the time and trouble to qualify for it. Until they qualify for it, there's no way they can earn it.

All you need is a plan—a road map—and the courage to arrive at your destination, knowing in advance that there will be problems and setbacks, but knowing also that nothing can stand in the way of your completing your plan if it is backed by persistence and determination.

Keep money in its proper place. It is a servant, nothing more. It is a tool with which you can live better and see more of the world around you. Money is necessary in your modern life. But you need only so much of it to live comfortably, securely, and well. Too much emphasis on money can reverse your whole picture and make you the servant and your money your master.

You do want to have money and the things it can buy, but you also must check up continually to make sure that you haven't lost the things that money cannot buy.

My dear investor, the world can be your oyster. Approach it with enthusiasm, intelligence, and gusto. The ultimate in satisfaction can be yours!

Glossary of Investing

ACCRUED INTEREST • Interest accrued on a bond since the last interest payment was made. The buyer of the bond pays the market price plus accrued interest.

ACCUMULATION PLAN • A plan for the systematic accumulation of mutual fund shares through periodic investments and reinvestments of income dividends and capital gains distributions.

AGENT • One who acts for another. The broker/dealer acts as an agent when he buys or sells for the account of someone other than himself.

AMORTIZATION • Accounting for expenses or charges as applicable rather than as paid. Includes such practices as depreciation, depletion, write-off of intangibles, prepaid expenses, and deferred charges.

ANNUAL REPORT • The formal financial statement issued yearly by a corporation. The annual report shows assets, liabilities, earnings, how the company stood at the close of the business year, how it fared profit-wise during the year, and other information of interest to shareowners.

432

ARBITRAGE • Dealing in differences. Example: buying on one exchange while simultaneously selling short on another at a higher price.

ASKED PRICE • The price asked for a security offered for sale. Quoted, bid, and asked prices are wholesale prices for interdealer trading and do not represent prices to the public.

ASSET • On a balance sheet, that which is owned or receivable.

AUCTION MARKET • A term applied to dealings on a securities exchange where a two-way auction is continuously in effect.

AUTHORIZED STOCK • The total number of shares of stock authorized by a company's shareholders to be issued.

AVERAGES • Various ways of measuring the trend of stocks listed on exchanges. Formulas—some very elaborate—have been devised to compensate for stock splits and stock dividends and thus give continuity to the average. In the case of the Dow-Jones Industrial Average, the prices of the 30 stocks are totaled and then divided by a figure that is intended to compensate for past stock splits and stock dividends and that is changed from time to time.

BALANCE SHEET • A condensed financial statement showing the nature and amount of a company's assets, liabilities, and capital on a given date. In dollar amounts the balance sheet shows what the company owned, what it owed, and the ownership interest in the company of its stockholders.

BALANCED FUND • A mutual fund that is required to keep a specified percentage of its total assets invested in senior securities.

BEAR • Someone who believes the stock market will decline.

BEAR MARKET • A declining stock market.

BEARER BOND • A bond that does not have the owner's name registered on the books of the issuing company and that is payable to the holder.

BID AND ASKED • Often referred to as a quotation or quote. The bid is the highest price anyone has declared that he wants to pay for a security at a given time; the asked is the lowest price anyone will take at the same time.

BIG BOARD • A popular term for the New York Stock Exchange, Inc.

BLOCK • A large holding or transaction of stock, popularly considered to be 10,000 shares or more.

BLUE CHIP • A company known nationally for the quality and wide acceptance of its products or services, and for its ability to make money and pay dividends.

BLUE SKY LAWS • A popular name for laws various states have enacted to protect the public against securities frauds. The term is believed to have originated when a judge ruled that a particular stock had about the same value as a patch of blue sky.

BOND • Basically an IOU or promissory note of a corporation, usually issued in multiples of $1000. A bond is evidence of a debt on which the issuing company usually promises to pay the bondholders a specified amount of interest for a specified length of time and to repay the loan on the expiration date. In every case a bond represents debt—its holder is a creditor of the corporation and not a part owner, as is the shareholder.

BOND FUND • A mutual fund invested completely in bonds.

BOOK VALUE • An accounting term. Book value of a stock is determined from a company's records by adding all assets and then deducting all debts and other liabilities, plus the liquidation price of any preferred issues. The sum arrived at is divided by the number of common shares outstanding, and the result is book value per common share. Book value of the assets of a company or a security may have little or no significant relationship to market value.

BROKER • An agent who handles the public's orders to buy and sell securities, commodities, or other property. For this service a commission is charged.

BULL • One who believes the stock market will rise.

BULL MARKET • An advancing stock market.

BUSINESS CYCLE • The long-term boom-recession cycle that has been characteristic of business conditions not only nationally, but on a worldwide basis.

CALL • An option to buy a specified number of shares of a certain security at a definite price within a specified period of time.

CALLABLE • A bond issue, all or part of which may be redeemed by the issuing corporation under definite conditions before maturity.

The term also applies to preferred shares, which may be redeemed by the issuing corporation.

CAPITAL GAIN OR CAPITAL LOSS • Profit or loss from the sale of a capital asset. A capital gain, under current federal income tax laws, may be either short term (six months or less) or long term (more than six months). A short-term capital gain is taxed at the reporting individual's full income tax rate. A long-term capital gain is subject to a lower tax.

CAPITAL MARKET • The market that deals in long-term securities issues of both debt and equity.

CAPITAL SHARES • When referred to a dual- or leveraged-type closed-end investment company, those shares to which all gains or losses accrue and which have no claim on dividends.

CAPITAL STOCK • All shares representing ownership of a business, including preferred and common.

CAPITALIZATION • Total amount of the various securities issued by a corporation. Capitalization may include bonds, debentures, preferred and common stock, and surplus.

CERTIFICATE • The actual piece of paper that is evidence of ownership of stock in a corporation. Loss of a certificate may cause, at least, a great deal of inconvenience; at worst, financial loss.

CLOSED-END INVESTMENT COMPANY • An investment company which issues a fixed number of shares and which does not redeem them. It may also issue senior securities and/or warrants.

COLLATERAL • Securities or other property pledged by a borrower to secure repayment of a loan.

COMMISSION • The broker's basic fee for purchasing or selling securities or property as an agent.

COMMON STOCK • Securities that represent an ownership interest in a corporation. If the company has also issued preferred stock, both common and preferred have ownership rights. Claims of both common and preferred stockholders are junior to claims of bondholders or other creditors of the company. Common stockholders assume the greater risk, but generally they exercise the greater control and may gain the greater reward in the form of dividends and capital appreciation.

COMMON STOCK FUND • A mutual fund that has a stated policy of investing all of its assets in common stocks. The term is also applied to funds which normally invest only in common stocks though not restricted to them by charter.

CONFIRMATION • A written description of the terms of a transaction in securities supplied by a broker/dealer to his customer or to another broker/dealer.

CONGLOMERATE • A corporation that has diversified its operations, usually by acquiring enterprises in widely varied industries.

CONSTRUCTIVE RECEIPT • A doctrine of the Internal Revenue Service that requires the reporting of income (including capital gains) in the year in which it could have been received had the taxpayer so wished. Thus, dividends of a mutual fund automatically reinvested are taxable in the year in which reinvested on the basis that the taxpayer could have received them by check and then reinvested them or not at his option.

CONVERTIBLE • A bond, debenture, or preferred share that may be exchanged by the owner for common stock or another security, usually of the same company, in accordance with the terms of the issue.

CORPORATE BOND • An evidence of indebtedness issued by a corporation, as distinct from the U.S. government or a municipality.

CORPORATION • An organization chartered by a state government. When the term is used without qualification, it generally refers to an organization carrying on a business for profit. However, there are nonprofit corporations and municipalities, which differ from the corporation organized for profit in that they do not issue stock.

COUPON BOND • Bond with interest coupons attached. The coupons are clipped as they come due and are presented by the holder for payment of interest.

CUMULATIVE PREFERRED • A stock having a provision that if one or more dividends are omitted, the omitted dividends must be paid before dividends may be paid on the company's common stock.

CUMULATIVE VOTING • A type of shareholder voting in which the number of shares held is multiplied by the number of directors to be elected to determine the number of votes a shareholder may cast. He may cast these votes all for one director or may allocate them in any way he sees fit.

CURRENT ASSETS · Those assets of a company that are reasonably expected to be realized in cash, or sold, or consumed during the normal operating cycle of the business.

CURRENT LIABILITIES · Money owed and payable by a company, usually within one year.

CUSTODIAN · The corporation, usually a bank, charged with the safe-keeping of an investment company's portfolio securities.

DEALER · An individual or firm in the securities business acting as a principal rather than as an agent. Typically, a dealer buys for his own account and sells to a customer from his own inventory. The dealer's profit or loss is the difference between the price he pays and the price he receives for the same security. The dealer's confirmation must disclose to his customer that he has acted as principal. The same individual or firm may function, at different times, as either a broker or dealer.

DEBENTURE · A promissory note backed by the general credit of a company and usually not secured by a mortgage or lien on any specific property.

DEPLETION · Natural resources, such as metals, oils and gas, and timber that conceivably can be reduced to zero over the years, present a special problem in capital management. Depletion is an accounting practice consisting of charges against earnings based upon the amount of the asset taken out of the total reserves in the period for which accounting is made. A bookkeeping entry, it does not represent any cash outlay, nor are any funds earmarked for the purpose.

DEPRECIATION · Normally, charges against earnings to write off the cost, less salvage value, of an asset over its estimated useful life. It is a bookkeeping entry and does not reprsent any cash outlay, nor are any funds earmarked for the purpose.

DIRECTOR · Person elected by shareholders to establish company policies. The directors elect the president, vice president, and all other operating officers. Directors decide, among other matters, if and when dividends shall be paid.

DISCOUNT · The amount by which a preferred stock or bond may sell below its par value.

DISCRETIONARY ACCOUNT · An account in which the customer gives the broker or someone else discretion, which may be complete or within specific limits, as to the purchase and sale of securities or commodities, including selection, timing, amount and priee to be paid or received.

DIVERSIFICATION • Spreading investments among different companies in different fields. Another type of diversification is also offered by the securities of many individual companies because of the wide range of their activities.

DIVERSIFIED INVESTMENT COMPANY • An investment company which, under the Investment Company Act of 1940, must invest 75 percent of its total assets so that not more than 5 percent of total assets is invested in the securities of any one issuer. Also, the company may not own more than 10 percent of the voting securities of any one issuer.

DIVIDEND • The payment designated by the board of directors to be distributed pro rata among the shares outstanding. On preferred shares, it is generally a fixed amount. On common shares, the dividend varies with the fortunes of the company and the amount of cash on hand, and it may be omitted if business is poor or the directors determine to withhold earnings to invest in plant and equipment. Sometimes a company will pay a dividend out of past earnings even if it is not currently operating at a profit.

DIVIDEND REINVESTMENT PLAN • A mutual fund share account in which dividends are automatically reinvested in additional shares. With this type of account, capital gains distributions are also automatically reinvested. Dividends (but not capital gains) may be invested at offering price (i.e., with a sales charge), but are more commonly reinvested at asset value.

DOLLAR-COST-AVERAGING • A system of buying securities at regular intervals with a fixed-dollar amount. Under this system the investor buys by the dollars' worth rather than by the number of shares. If each investment is of the same number of dollars, payments buy more when the price is low and fewer when it rises. Thus temporary downswings in price benefit the investor if he continues periodic purchases in both good times and bad, and the price at which the shares are sold is more than their average cost.

DOUBLE TAXATION • The federal government taxes corporate profits once as corporate income; any part of the remaining profits distributed as dividends to stockholders may be taxed again as income to the recipient stockholder.

Dow Jones Average • Widely quoted stock averages computed regularly. They include an industrial stock average, a rail average, a utility average, and a combination of the three.

Dow Theory • A theory of market analysis based upon the performance of the Dow-Jones industrial and transportation stock price averages. The theory says that the market is in a basic upward trend if one of these averages advances above a previous important high, accompanied or followed by a similar advance in the other. When the averages both dip below previous important lows, this is regarded as confirmation of a basic downward trend. The theory does not attempt to predict how long either trend will continue, although it is widely misinterpreted as a method of forecasting future action.

Dual Fund • A closed-end investment company with two classes of shares—income and capital-outstanding. Also designated as a "leveraged fund."

Equity • The ownership interest of common and preferred stockholders in a company. Also refers to excess of value of securities over the debit balance in a margin account.

Ex-dividend • A synonym for "without dividend." The buyer of a stock selling ex-dividend does not receive the recently declared dividend. Every dividend is payable on a fixed date to all shareholders recorded on the books of the company as of a previous date of record. For example, a dividend may be declared as payable to holders of record on the books of the company on a given Friday. Since five business days are allowed for delivery of stock in a "regular way" transaction on the stock exchange, the exchange would declare the stock "ex-dividend" as of the opening of the market on the preceding Monday. That means anyone who bought it on and after Monday would not be entitled to that dividend. When stocks go ex-dividend, the stock tables include the symbol "x" following the name.

Ex-rights • Without the rights. Corporations raising additional money may do so by offering their stockholders the right to subscribe to new or additional stock, usually at a discount from the prevailing market price. The buyer of a stock selling ex-rights is not entitled to the rights.

Extra • The short-form of "extra dividend." A dividend in the form of stock or cash in addition to the regular or usual dividend the company has been paying.

FACE VALUE • The value of a bond that appears on the face of the bond, unless the value is otherwise specified by the issuing company. Face value is ordinarily the amount the issuing company promises to pay at maturity. Face value is not an indication of market value. Sometimes referred to as par value.

FIDUCIARY • One who acts for another in financial matters.

FLOOR • The huge trading area where stocks and bonds are bought and sold.

FLOOR BROKER • A member of the stock exchange who executes orders on the floor of the exchange to buy or sell any listed securities.

FULLY MANAGED FUND • A mutual fund with an investment policy that gives its management complete flexibility as to the types of investments made and the proportions of each. Management is restricted only to the extent that federal or blue sky laws require.

GILT-EDGED • High-grade bond issued by a company that has demonstrated its ability to earn a comfortable profit over a period of years and pay its bondholders their interest without interruption.

GOOD DELIVERY • Certain basic qualifications must be met before a security sold on the exchange may be delivered. The security must be in proper form to comply with the contract of sale and to transfer title to the purchaser.

GOOD 'TIL CANCELLED ORDER (GTC) OR OPEN ORDER • An order to buy or sell that remains in effect until it is either executed or cancelled.

GOVERNMENT BONDS • Obligations of the U.S. government, regarded as the highest grade issues in existence.

GROWTH FUND • One whose rate of growth over a period of time is considerably greater than that of business generally. An average rate of 10 percent per year is used by some analysts as definitive.

GROWTH STOCK • Stock of a company with a record of growth in earnings at a relatively rapid rate.

HOLDING COMPANY • A corporation that owns the securities of another, in most cases with voting control.

INCOME FUND • A mutual fund with a primary objective of current income.

INDENTURE • A written agreement under which bonds and debentures are issued, setting forth maturity date, interest rate, and other terms.

INSTITUTION • An organization holding substantial investing assets, often for others. Includes banks, insurance companies, investment companies, and pension funds.

INTEREST • Payments a borrower pays a lender for the use of his money. A corporation pays interest on its bonds to its bondholders.

INVESTMENT • The use of money for the purpose of making more money, to gain income or increase capital or both.

INVESTMENT BANKER • Also known as an underwriter. He is the middleman between the corporation issuing new securities and the public. The usual practice is for one or more investment bankers to buy outright from a corporation a new issue of stocks or bonds. The group forms a syndicate to sell the securities to individuals and institutions. Investment bankers also distribute very large blocks of stocks or bonds (perhaps held by an estate).

INVESTMENT COMPANY • A company or trust that uses its capital to invest in other companies. There are two principal types: the closed-end and the open-end, or mutual fund. Shares in closed-end investment companies are readily transferable in the open market and are bought and sold like other shares. Capitalization of these companies remains the same unless action is taken to change, which is seldom. Open-end funds sell their own new shares to investors, stand ready to buy back their old shares, and are not listed. Open-end funds are so called because their capitalization is not fixed; they issue more shares as people want them.

INVESTMENT COMPANY ACT OF 1940 • An act passed by the Congress for the specific purpose of empowering the SEC to regulate investment companies.

INVESTMENT COUNSEL • One whose principal business consists of acting as investment adviser, and a substantial part of his business consists of rendering investment supervisory services.

INVESTOR • An individual whose principal concerns in the purchase of a security are regular dividend income, safety of the original investment, and, if possible, capital appreciation.

ISSUE • Any of a company's securities, or the act of distributing such securities. Upon the death of a joint tenant, his interest passes, not to his heirs, but to his co-owner.

Legal List • A list of investments selected by various states in which certain institutions and fiduciaries, such as insurance companies and banks, may invest. Legal lists are often restricted to high-quality securities meeting certain specifications.

Leverage • The effect on the per-share earnings of the common stock of a company when large sums must be paid for bond interest or preferred stock dividends, or both, before the common stock is entitled to share in earnings. Leverage may be advantageous for the common stock when earnings are good but may work against the common stock when earnings decline. Leverage also refers to mortgage funds used in real estate and oil limited partnerships financing.

Liabilities • All the claims against a corporation. Liabilities include accounts and wages and salaries payable, dividends declared payable, accrued taxes payable, fixed or long-term liabilities such as mortgage bonds, debentures, and bank loans.

Lien • A claim against property that has been pledged or mortgaged to secure the performance of an obligation. A bond may be secured by a lien against specified property of a company.

Limited Order • An order to buy or sell a stated amount of a security at a specified price, or at a better price.

Liquidating Value • When referred to the shares of an open-end investment company, the value at redemption. Usually the net asset value.

Liquidation • The process of converting securities or other property into cash. The dissolution of a company, with cash remaining after sale of its assets and payment of all indebtedness being distributed to the shareholders.

Liquidity • The ability of the market in a particular security to absorb a reasonable amount of buying or selling at reasonable price changes. Liquidity is one of the most important characteristics of a good market.

Listed Stock • The stock of a company that is traded on a securities exchange.

Locked In • An investor is said to be locked in when he has a profit on a security he owns, but does not sell because his profit would immediately become subject to the capital gains tax.

MANAGEMENT • The board of directors, elected by the stockholders, and the officers of the corporation, appointed by the board of directors.

MANAGEMENT FEE • The fee paid to the investment manager of a mutual fund. It is usually about one-half of one percent of average net assets annually. Not to be confused with the "sales charge," which is the one-time commission paid at the time of purchase as a part of the offering price.

MANIPULATION • An illegal operation. Buying or selling a security for the purpose of creating false or misleading appearance of active trading or for the purpose of raising or depressing the price to induce purchase or sale by others.

MARGIN • The amount paid by the customer when he uses his broker's credit to buy a security.

MARGIN CALL • A demand upon a customer to put up money or securities with the broker. The call is made when a purchase is made; also if a customer's equity in a margin account declines below a minimum standard set by the exchange or by the firm.

MARKET ORDER • An order to buy or sell a stated amount of a security at the most advantageous price obtainable.

MARKET PRICE • In the case of a security, market price is usually considered the last reported price at which the stock or bond sold.

MATURITY • The date on which a loan or a bond or a debenture comes due and is to be paid off.

MEMBER FIRM • A securities brokerage firm organized as a partnership or corporation and owning at least one seat on the exchange.

MORTGAGE BOND • A bond secured by a mortgage on a property. The value of the property may or may not equal the value of the so-called mortgage bonds issued against it.

MUNICIPAL BOND • A bond issued by a state or a political subdivision, such as county, city, town, or village. The term also designates bonds issued by state agencies and authorities. In general, interest paid on municipal bonds is exempt from federal income taxes and from state and local income taxes within the state of issue.

MUTUAL FUND • An open-end investment company that continuously offers new shares to the public in addition to redeeming shares on demand as required by law. While in common use, the term "mutual fund" has no meaning in law.

NASD · The National Association of Securities Dealers, Inc. An association of brokers and dealers in the over-the-counter securities business. The Association has the power to expel members who have been declared guilty of unethical practices. NASD is dedicated to, among other objectives, "adopt, administer and enforce rules of fair practice and rules to prevent fraudulent and manipulative acts and practices, and in general to promote just and equitable principles of trade for the protection of investors."

NASDAQ · An automated information network that provides brokers and dealers with price quotations on securities traded over the counter. NASDAQ is an acronym for National Association of Securities Dealers Automated Quotations.

NEGOTIABLE · Refers to a security, title to which is transferable by delivery.

NET ASSET VALUE · A term usually used in connection with investment companies, meaning net asset value per share. It is common practice for an investment company to compute its assets daily by totaling the market value of all securities owned. All liabilities are deducted, and the balance is divided by the number of shares outstanding. The resulting figure is the net asset value per share.

NET CHANGE · The change in the price of a security from the closing price on one day to the closing price on the following day on which the stock is traded. The net change is ordinarily the last figure on the stock price list. The mark $+2\frac{1}{8}$ means up $2.125 a share from the last sale on the previous day the stock traded.

NEW ISSUE · A stock or bond sold by a corporation for the first time. Proceeds may be issued to retire outstanding securities of the company, for new plant or equipment, or for additional working capital.

NONCUMULATIVE · A preferred stock on which unpaid dividends do not accrue. Omitted dividends are, as a rule, gone forever.

NYSE COMMON STOCK INDEX · A composite index covering price movements of all common stocks listed on the "Big Board." It is based on the close of the market December 31, 1965, as 50.00 and is weighted according to the number of shares listed for each issue. The index is computed continuously and printed on the ticker tape each half hour. Point changes in the index are converted to dollars and cents to provide a meaningful measure of changes in the average price of listed stocks.

ODD LOT • An amount of stock less than the established 100-share unit or 10-share unit of trading: from 1 to 99 shares for the great majority of issues, 1 to 9 for so-called inactive stocks. Odd-lot prices are geared to the auction market. On an odd-lot market order, the odd-lot dealer's price is based on the first round-lot transaction that occurs on the floor following receipt at the trading post of the odd-lot order. The differential between the odd-lot price and the "effective" round-lot price is 12½ cents a share. For example: You decide to buy 20 shares of ABC common at the market. Your order is transmitted by your commission broker to the representative of an odd-lot dealer at the post where ABC is traded. A few minutes later there is a 100-share transaction in ABC at $10 a share. The odd-lot price at which your order is immediately filled by the odd-lot dealer is $10.125 a share. If you had sold 20 shares of ABC, you would have received $9.875 a share.

OFFER • The price at which a person is ready to sell. Opposed to bid, the price at which one is ready to buy.

OPEN ACCOUNT • When referred to a mutual fund, a type of account in which the investor may add or withdraw shares at any time. In such an account, dividends may be paid in cash or reinvested at the account holder's option.

OPEN-END INVESTMENT COMPANY • By definition under the 1940 act, an investment company that has outstanding redeemable shares. Also, the term is generally applied to those investment companies which continuously offer new shares to the public and stand ready at any time to redeem their outstanding shares.

OPTION • A right to buy or sell specific securities or properties at a specified price within a specified time.

OVERBOUGHT • An opinion as to price levels. May refer to a security that has had a sharp rise or to the market as a whole after a period of vigorous buying which, it may be argued, has left prices "too high."

OVERSOLD • An opinion, the reverse of overbought. A single security or a market that, it is believed, has declined to an unreasonable level.

OVER-THE-COUNTER • A market for securities made up of securities dealers who may or may not be members of a securities exchange. Over-the-counter is mainly a market made over the telephone. Thousands of companies have insufficient shares outstanding, stockholders, or earnings to warrant application for listing on an exchange. Securities of these companies are traded in the over-the-counter market between dealers who act either as principals or as brokers for customers.

PAPER PROFIT • An unrealized profit on a security still held. Paper profits become realized profits only when the security is sold.

PAR • In the case of a common share, par means a dollar amount assigned to the share by the company's charter. Par value may also be used to compute the dollar amount of the common shares on the balance sheet. Par value has little significance so far as market value of common stock is concerned.

PENNY STOCKS • Low-priced issues, often highly speculative, selling at less than $1 a share. Frequently used as a term of disparagement, although a few penny stocks have developed into investment-caliber issues.

POINT • In the case of shares of stock, a point means $1. If ABC shares rise three points, each share has risen $3. In the case of bonds, a point means $10, since a bond is quoted as a percentage of $1000. A bond that rises three points gains 3 percent of $1000, or $30 in value. An advance from 87 to 90 would mean an advance in dollar value from $870 to $900 for each $1000 bond. In the case of market averages, the word point means merely that and no more. If, for example, the Dow-Jones Industrial Average rises from 870.25 to 871.25, it has risen a point. A point in this average, however, is not equivalent to $1.

PORTFOLIO • Holdings of securities by an individual or institution. A portfolio may contain bonds, preferred stocks, and common stocks of various types of enterprises.

PREFERRED STOCK • A class of stock with a claim on the company's earnings before payment may be made on the common stock and usually entitled to priority over common stock if the company liquidates. Usually entitled to dividends at a specified rate, when declared by the board of directors and before payment of a dividend on the common stock, depending upon the terms of the issue.

PREMIUM • The amount by which a preferred stock or bond may sell above its par value. In the case of a new issue of bonds or stocks, premium is the amount the market price rises over the original selling price.

PRICE-EARNINGS RATIO • The price of a share of stock divided by earnings per share for a 12-month period. For example, a stock selling for $100 a share and earning $5 a share is said to be selling at a price–earnings ratio of 20 to 1.

PRIMARY DISTRIBUTION • Also called primary offering. The original sale of a company's securities.

PRINCIPAL • The person for whom a broker executes an order, or a dealer buying or selling for his own account. The term "principal" may also refer to a person's capital or to the face amount of a bond.

PROFIT-TAKING • Selling stock that has appreciated in value since purchase to realize the profit that has been made possible. The term is often used to explain a downturn in the market following a period of rising prices.

PROSPECTUS • The document that offers a new issue of securities to the public. It is required under the Securities Act of 1933.

PROXY • Written authorization given by a shareholder to someone else to represent him and vote his shares at a shareholders' meeting.

PROXY STATEMENT • Information required by the SEC to be given stockholders as a prerequisite to solicitation of proxies for a security subject to the requirements of Securities Exchange Act.

PRUDENT MAN RULE • An investment standard. In some states, the law requires that a fiduciary, such as a trustee, may invest the fund's money only in a list of securities designated by the state— the so-called legal list. In other states, the trustee may invest in a security if it is one that a prudent man of discretion and intelligence, who is seeking a reasonable income and preservation of capital, would buy.

PUT • An option to sell a specified number of shares at a definite price within a specified period of time. The opposite of a call.

QUOTATION • Often shortened to "quote." The highest bid to buy and the lowest offer to sell a security in a given market at a given time. If you ask your broker for a "quote" on a stock, he may come back with something like "45¼ to 45½". This means that $45.25 is the highest price any buyer wanted to pay at the time the quote was given on the floor of the exchange and that $45.50 was the lowest price any seller would take at the same time.

RALLY • A brisk rise following a decline in the general price level of the market, or in an individual stock.

RECORD DATE • The date on which you must be registered as a shareholder on the stock book of a company to receive a declared dividend or, among other things, to vote on company affairs.

RED HERRING • A preliminary prospectus used to obtain indications of interest from prospective buyers of a new issue.

REDEMPTION PRICE • The price at which a bond may be redeemed before maturity, at the option of the issuing company. Redemption value also applies to the price the company must pay to call in certain types of preferred stock.

REIT • Real estate investment trust, an organization similar to an investment company in some respects but concentrating its holdings in real estate investments. The yield is generally liberal, since REITs are requested to distribute as much as 90 percent of their income.

REDEMPTION PRICE • The price at which an open-end investment company redeems its shares. It is usually the net asset value per share—it fluctuates with the value of the company's investment portfolio.

REGISTERED BOND • A bond that is registered on the books of the issuing company in the name of the owner. It can be transferred only when endorsed by the registered owner.

REGISTERED REPRESENTATIVE • A registered representative is a full-time employee who has met the requirements of an exchange as to background and knowledge of the securities business. Also known as an account exchange or customer's broker.

REGISTRAR • Usually a trust company or bank charged with the responsibility of preventing the issuance of more stock than authorized by a company.

REGISTRATION • Before a public offering may be made of new securities by a company, or of outstanding securities by controlling stockholders—through the mails or in interstate commerce—the securities must be registered under the Securities Act of 1933. Registration statement is filed with the SEC by the issuer. It must disclose pertinent information relating to the company's operations, securities, management, and purpose of the public offering. On security offerings involving less than $300,000, less information is required.

Before a security may be admitted to dealings on a national securities exchange, it must be registered under the Securities Exchange Act of 1934. The application for registration must be filed. with the exchange and the SEC by the company issuing the securities. It must disclose pertinent information relating to the company's operations, securities, and management.

REGULATION T • The federal regulation governing the amount of credit that may be advanced by brokers and dealers to customers for the purchase of securities.

REGULATION U • The federal regulation governing the amount of credit that may be advanced by a bank to its customers for the purchase of listed stocks.

RETURN • Another term for "yield."

RIGHTS • When a company wants to raise more funds by issuing additional securities, it may give its stockholders the opportunity, ahead of others, to buy the new securities in proportion to the number of shares each owns. The piece of paper evidencing this privilege is called a right. Because the additional stock is usually offered to stockholders below the current market price, rights ordinarily have a market value of their own and are actively traded. In most cases they must be exercised within a relatively short period. Failure to exercise or sell rights may result in actual loss to the holder.

ROUND LOT • A unit of trading or a multiple thereof. On most exchanges the unit of trading is generally 100 shares in stocks and $1000 par value in the case of bonds. In some inactive stocks, the unit of trading is 10 shares.

SEAT • A traditional figure of speech for a membership on an exchange. Price and admission requirements vary.

SEC • Securities and Exchange Commission, established by Congress to help protect investors. The SEC administers the Securities Act of 1933, the Securities Exchange Act of 1934, the Trust Indenture Act, the Investment Company Act, the Investment Advisers Act, and the Public Utility Holding Company Act.

SECONDARY DISTRIBUTION • Also known as a secondary offering. The redistribution of a block of stock some time after it has been sold by the issuing company. The sale is handled off the exchange by a securities firm or group of firms, and the shares are usually offered at a fixed price that is related to the current market price of the stock. Usually the block is a large one, such as might be involved in the settlement of an estate. The security may be listed or unlisted.

SINKING FUND · Money regularly set aside by a company to redeem its bonds, debentures, or preferred stock from time to time as specified in the indenture or charter.

SPECIAL OFFERING · Occasionally a large block of stock becomes available for sale that, due to its size and the market in that particular issue, calls for special handling. A notice is printed on the ticker tape announcing that the stock will be offered for sale on the floor of the exchange at a fixed price. Member firms may buy this stock for customers directly from the seller's broker during trading hours. The price is usually based on the last transaction in the regular auction market. If there are more buyers than stock, allotments are made. Only the seller pays a commission on a special offering.

SPECIALIST · A member of an exchange who has two functions: First, to maintain an orderly market, insofar as reasonably practicable, in the stocks in which he is registered as a specialist. The exchange expects the specialist to buy or sell for his own account, to a reasonable degree, when there is a temporary disparity between supply and demand. The specialist also acts as a broker's broker. When a commission broker on the exchange floor receives a limit order, say, to buy at $50 a stock then selling at $60, he cannot wait at the post where the stock is traded to see if the price reaches the specified level. So he leaves the order with the specialist, who will try to execute it in the market if and when the stock declines to the specified price. At all times the specialist must put his customers' interests above his own.

SPECULATOR · One who is willing to assume a relatively large risk in the hope of gain. His principal concern is to increase his capital rather than his dividend income. The speculator may buy and sell the same day or speculate in an enterprise he does not expect to be profitable for years.

SPLIT · The division of the outstanding shares of a corporation into a larger number of shares. A 3-for-1 split by a company with 1 million shares outstanding results in 3 million shares outstanding. Each holder of 100 shares before the 3-to-1 split would have 300 shares, although his proportionate equity in the company would remain the same; 100 parts of 1 million are the equivalent of 300 parts of 3 million.

SPREAD • The difference between the bid price and the offering price. Also, the combination of a put and a call "points away" from the market.

STATEMENT OF POLICY • The SEC's statement of its own position as to those things considered "materially misleading" in the offer of shares of open-end investment companies.

STOCK • Ownership shares of a corporation.

STOCK CERTIFICATE • A certificate that provides physical evidence of stock ownership.

STOCK EXCHANGE • An organization registered under the Securities Exchange Act of 1934 with physical facilities for the buying and selling of securities in a two-way auction.

STOCK DIVIDEND • A dividend paid in securities rather than cash. The dividend may be additional shares of the issuing company or shares of another company (usually a subsidiary) held by the company.

STOCK POWER • An assignment and power of substitution separate from a stock certificate authorizing transfer of the stock on the books of the corporation.

STOCKHOLDER OF RECORD • A stockholder whose name is registered on the books of the issuing corporation.

STOP ORDER • An order to buy at a price above or to sell below the current market. Stop buy orders are generally used to limit loss or protect unrealized profits on a short sale. Stop sell orders are generally used to protect unrealized profits or limit loss on a holding.

STREET NAME • Securities held in the name of a broker instead of his customer's name are said to be carried in a "street name." This occurs when the securities have been bought on margin or when the customer wishes the security to be held by the broker.

SUITABILITY RULE • The rule of fair practice that requires a member to have reasonable grounds for believing that a recommendation to a customer is suitable on the basis of his financial objectives and abilities.

TENANTS IN COMMON • A form of registration of property, frequently used with securities. An undivided estate in property whereupon the death of the owner, the undivided estate becomes the property of his heirs or divisees and not of his surviving co-owner.

TENANTS BY THE ENTIRETY • A form of registration of property, usually real estate.

TIPS • Supposedly "inside" information on corporation affairs.

TRADER • One who buys and sells for his own account for short-term profit.

TRANSFER • This term may refer to two different operations. For one, the delivery of a stock certificate from the seller's broker to the buyer's broker and legal change of ownership, normally accomplished within a few days. For another, to record the change of ownership on the books of the corporation by the transfer agent. When the purchaser's name is recorded on the books of the company, dividends, notices of meetings, proxies, financial reports, and all pertinent literature sent by the issuer to its securities holders are mailed directly to the new owner.

TRANSFER AGENT • A transfer agent keeps a record of the name of each registered shareowner, his or her address, and the number of shares owned, and sees that certificates presented to his office for transfer are properly cancelled and new certificates issued in the name of the transferee.

TREASURY BILL • Short-term U.S. government paper with no stated interest rate. It is sold at a discount in competitive bidding and has a maturity of 90 days or less.

TREASURY BOND • U.S. government bonds issued in $1000 units with maturities of five years or longer. They are traded on the market like other bonds.

TREASURY NOTE • U.S. government paper, not legally restricted as to interest rates, with maturities of from one to five years.

TREASURY STOCK • Stock issued by a company but later reacquired. It may be held in the company's treasury indefinitely, reissued to the public, or retired. Treasury stock receives no dividends and has no vote while held by the company.

UNDERWRITER'S FEE • In the sale of mutual fund shares, the difference between the total sales charge and the underwriter's reallowance to the dealer.

UNLISTED • A security not listed on a stock exchange.

VOTING RIGHT • The stockholder's right to vote his stock in the affairs of his company. Most common shares have one vote each. Preferred stock usually has the right to vote when preferred dividends are in default for a specified period. The right to vote may be delegated by the stockholder to another person.

WARRANT • A certificate giving the holder the right to purchase securities at a stipulated price within a specified time limit or perpetually. Sometimes a warrant is offered with securities as an inducement to buy.

WHEN ISSUED • A short form of "when, as, and if issued." The term indicates a conditional transaction in a security authorized for issuance but not as yet actually issued. All "when issued" transactions are on an "if" basis, to be settled if and when the actual security is issued and the exchange or National Association of Securities Dealers rules that the transactions are to be settled.

WITHDRAWAL PLAN • A mutual fund plan that permits monthly or quarterly withdrawal of specified dollar amounts, usually involving the invasion of principal. Alternately, a plan may permit varying withdrawals based on the liquidation of a fixed number of shares monthly or quarterly.

WORKING CONTROL • Theoretically, ownership of 51 percent of a company's voting stock is necessary to exercise control. In practice— and this is particularly true in the case of a large corporation —effective control sometimes can be exerted through ownership, individually or by a group acting in concert, of less than 50 percent.

YIELD • Also known as "return." The dividends or interest paid by a company expressed as a percentage of the current price. A stock with a current market value of $20 a share that has paid $1 in dividends in the preceding 12 months is said to return 5 percent ($1.00/$20.00). The current return on a bond is figured the same way.

STOCKS

Company _____

Date Bought	No. of Shares	Price Per Share	Total Cost	Date Sold	No. of Shares	Price Per Share		Total Net Proceeds		

DIVIDEND RECORD

Company _____

Date Dividend Paid	Number of Shares	Rate per Share	Total Amount of Dividend

Index